W0246600

Parde *Ke* Peechhey

ILA ARUN

Parde *Ke* Peechhey

An Autobiography

AS TOLD TO **ANJULA BEDI**

EBURY
PRESS

An imprint of Penguin Random House

EBURY PRESS

Ebury Press is an imprint of the Penguin Random House group of companies whose addresses can be found at global.penguinrandomhouse.com

Published by Penguin Random House India Pvt. Ltd
4th Floor, Capital Tower 1, MG Road,
Gurugram 122 002, Haryana, India

First published in Ebury Press by Penguin Random House India 2024

Copyright © Ila Arun 2024

All images are from the author's personal collection

All rights reserved

10 9 8 7 6 5 4 3 2 1

The views and opinions expressed in this book are the author's own and the facts are as reported by her which have been verified to the extent possible, and the publishers are not in any way liable for the same.

Please note that no part of this book may be used or reproduced in any manner for the purpose of training artificial intelligence technologies or systems.

ISBN 9780143469759

Typeset in Sabon by MAP Systems, Bengaluru, India
Printed at Thomson Press India Ltd, New Delhi

This book is sold subject to the condition that it shall not, by way of trade or otherwise, be lent, resold, hired out, or otherwise circulated without the publisher's prior consent in any form of binding or cover other than that in which it is published and without a similar condition including this condition being imposed on the subsequent purchaser.

www.penguin.co.in

Applause

My mother, Bhagwati Pandey, wrote her first children's book, Sunhere Baalon Waali Rajkumari *and dedicated it in her handwriting to her grandchildren. In Norwegian playwright and theatre director Henrik Ibsen's last words 'On the contrary', I am dedicating my first book to my granddaughters' great-grandmother, who taught me my first words, and the art of expressing oneself and of storytelling. I call her the headmistress of my* 'Masti Ki Paathshaala'.

Cue Sheet

Foreword

UMAID BHAWAN PALACE
JODHPUR - 342 006
RAJASTHAN

23rd July 2024

Dear Kaji,

Heartfelt congratulations on the release of your autobiography!

This remarkable milestone is a testament to your courage, determination and the extraordinary journey that has brought you to this moment. It's inspiring to see how you have shaped your narrative by mentioning about your ancestors in your chapter "Origins". Interwoven with the rich and vibrant histories of Kannauj and Jodhpur, this adds profound depth and color to your life's story that will not only enlighten readers but also bring a sense of pride and admiration for these places.

Your autobiography is more than just a book; it's a legacy, a beacon of inspiration for those who seek to understand the power of music, theatre, heritage, and identity. May your book reach countless readers, touching their hearts and inspiring them to reach great heights while keeping the roots alive. May your journey as an author continue to be as enriching and fulfilling as your musical journey.

Wishing you all the best and immense success,

Yours sincerely,

Warm greetings,

GAJ SINGH
MAHARAJA OF JODHPUR

Smt. Ila Arun
401, Paradise Apts, 7th Road,
Santa Cruz East,
Mumbai – 400 055
Email: msilaarun@gmail.com
TEL : PALACE : 0291 - 2510101 - 8,   OFFICE : 2511118, 2511199   e-mail : office@maharajajodhpur.com

Curtain-Raiser

As I walked into a room at the National School of Drama (NSD), where I was doing a short-term course, a gentleman from the group gathered there said to me out of the blue in Bengali, '*Ma, tum stage par hi akhri saans lega* (Ma, you will breathe your last onstage).' I did not know then that this was the renowned director, Ritwik Ghatak. Being a newcomer, I was a little taken aback and embarrassed too. At that time, I did not consider this a blessing, but over the years, I recall his words with fondness and give thanks to his amazing intuition.

For most of us actors, waiting in the wings, behind the curtain, is the most exhilarating part of our lives. The world is obliterated, and we are one with our roles and the words we have been rehearsing for months. Then the curtain goes up, and we are on display—to do or die. But others too live behind curtains—a curtain that never really exposes them and that perhaps is the actor's role; to draw the curtain aside and bring the shortcomings and faults of society centre stage.

My theatre journey was still undecided. Though I was convinced that this was the path I longed to follow, I recalled my mother's words that all these creative activities were just like a pinch of salt in one's life and that they could not be the be-all and end-all of one's existence.

I had just completed a short-term course at the NSD, and when I was leaving, Ebrahim Alkazi, the godfather to most actors and directors of the time, advised me to join the three-year diploma course and also the repertory after my graduation. I hesitatingly told him my family would not allow that and in response his words were: 'All right then. Just go and sit at home and produce seven daughters like your mother did!' I was stunned beyond words. But I took that up as a challenge. And years later, when I had my own theatre group,

Surnai Theatre and Folk Arts Foundation, I met Alkazi Sahib at an art exhibition in Mumbai. I went up to him and said, 'Sir, I have only one daughter, but I have given birth to a theatre group and ten plays!' He gave me his quizzical smile and nodded his head.

Another great influence in my theatre journey was Jennifer Kapoor, who gave me the opportunity to perform at the newly opened Prithvi Theatre. That is when my theatre group, Surnai, was born, on 11 June 1982, with its first performance, *A Musical Sandstorm*. I had called folk artistes from Rajasthan. It was a grand affair. This was during the Mumbai monsoons. As we were getting ready for the opening, the heavens opened up. There was torrential rain and suddenly there was a power failure, and we were enveloped in darkness. There was panic backstage. The audience was waiting. What were we to do? My theatre group was being aborted before it was born! Then Jennifer came backstage and said, 'You are all folk artistes, used to performing in villages and rural areas. Why should a power failure deter you? The show must go on!' And so it did. With lanterns and candles at Prithvi! And since then, the show has been going on, despite plenty of obstacles and difficulties, despite the lack of funds and performing platforms, and of course, actors' tantrums. But despite all odds, we recently proudly celebrated our forty-second year.

Is this why I am writing this book? Is it a volume of an ordinary life, turned into something never imagined? A memoir for myself and my friends that includes part of their lives, intertwined with mine? My stream of consciousness spills out. 'All the world's a stage' is a clichéd aphorism but very appropriate in my world. Someone has said, '*Zindagi guzar rahi hai kirdar nibhaate nibhaate, main kaun hoon, yeh sawal aaj bhi hai.*' (Life passes us by as we fulfil several roles/yet the question remains unanswered/Who am I?)

Who was I? Which *kirdar*, or part, was I going to enact? Doesn't everyone play some character in real life too? We all wear a *mukhota*, a mask, and we must take off that mask and look at ourselves, no matter what role we play in our lives. Perhaps this is what I am trying to do—take off a mask to look at myself.

When I first contemplated writing a book on my life and experiences, I received several suggestions for the title. Most friends thought the obvious title should be *Choli Ke Peechhey*, a title that would tickle the imagination of the readers and be the USP of the book. I was also carried away by the idea. But as days went by and the book took shape, I realized that the popularity I had garnered from that song was short-lived; it was for just a couple of years of my life as compared to my real journey, the miles and miles I had covered from adolescence to adulthood. One day, as I tried to get my ten thousand steps by walking on the terrace, there was a sudden revelation. There could be no other title but *Parde Ke Peechhey*. I called up my friend Anjula and her excited response was 'This is it, Ila!' So here it is, my life told through my association with the performing arts, theatre, music and film, from the time the seed was planted in my mind, to the present. *Parde Ke Peechhey*. Could this also be my answer to *'Choli Ke Peechhey'*?

I had embarked on a journey without knowing where I was going. As I rode on my father's peon Raghunath's bicycle to school, with him singing Marwari songs in his loud, rustic voice, I was like Shakespeare's 'whining schoolboy . . . creeping like snail unwillingly to school', for no other reason but the fact that his singing drew attention and embarrassed me. It strikes me now that he was also a player on the stage of my life—Shakespeare's seven stages. His notes and untrained voice perhaps were my first introduction to music, which was soon to be my raison d'être.

The house in Purohitji-Ka-Bagh was our first stage and each one of us had their exits and their entrances, playing our part in this large family. The director was always our mother, Bhagwati Pandey, who had never been trained in direction but seemed to have a flair and intuition for it. Our characters were defined by her, though like any good director, she gave us a certain amount of leeway to mould ourselves. To this day, I still count her among the foremost directors I have worked with, imbibing her creativity, her love of words and her curiosity for new frontiers.

School, college and NSD—these were my later performing spaces. Folk music and dance had become a part of my life by then. And after all these years, I give silent thanks to Raghunath for initiating me into something that went beyond language and culture. With the opening of Ravindra Manch and the existence of many local actors who had passed out of NSD, Jaipur was burgeoning as the centre of Hindi theatre. One could exclaim with Wordsworth that 'Bliss was in that dawn to be alive' for actors and writers.

I realized that theatre is a medium that plays upon speech and words. It is communicative and interactive. Even Ramakrishna Paramahansa has said that theatre is a medium of mass communication.

Words flow out in a soliloquy as you examine your inner self. There are monologues and dialogues while the face communicates a wealth of emotions. It is life recreating itself in front of an audience. My book is the story of my life, dramatic incidents from my childhood to show business, a flowing of thoughts and ideas, from backstage to front stage, stages of creation and performance.

As the words streamed out onstage, my love of the spoken word grew, and I was drawn to writing and adapting. And more epithets were added to my name: singer, dancer, actor and now writer.

I sit on my favourite sofa, a sofa that I think can write more than half my story, walk the short distance on the tiny terrace of my building, every morning photographing a swarm of parrots that sit on the wires in front of me. I sometimes wonder if they, like me, are also reminiscing about their nomadic life. Is that why I am writing this book? For my love of words and stories? As a Chinese proverb goes: 'The palest ink is better than the best memory.' And I will follow my passion till the 'last scene of all that ends this strange, eventful history', hoping that Ritwik Ghatak's prophecy comes true.

Chapter 1

Origins: The Voices of My Ancestors

'Monsoon,' said the salesman at the gift shop at Mehrangarh Fort in Jodhpur, Rajasthan. 'A fragrance from Kannauj [a city in Uttar Pradesh], given this name by His Highness.' I held the bottle to my nose, took a whiff, and was immediately transported to the season of romance, to the fragrance of freshly soaked *mitti*, or earth, the sheer ecstasy of feeling the rain on one's face, the joyous chirping of birds fluttering their wings in pools of water, the fading away of the desert heat.

Kannauj—the fragrance also stirred memories of tales my mother used to tell us, of how our origins were in Kannauj, that we were Kanyakubja Brahmins, from the group of the Pancha Gauda Brahmins. She would proudly proclaim that in the old days, our community was involved solely in the research of the Vedas and other ancient texts and that we did not, like 'lesser' Brahmins, perform pujas for benefactors or take *dakshina*, or alms.

Of course, like most children, we would brush aside her extolling the virtues of the community and equally proudly retort that as far as we knew, we were Rajasthanis!

I was born in Jodhpur, the capital of the Marwar region, in House No. 532, Sardarpura. Rajasthan was my home, and I grew up imbibing Marwari traditions, its music, its folk forms and its customs. Basically, I think we were embarrassed being associated with that community because we believed that Kannaujia Brahmins were very conservative. And because we didn't want to be circumscribed by any caste or creed, we were always apprehensive of being labelled as

1

a particular caste or group. The only connection we were conscious of was that one of my aunts, Sonkali, was from Kannauj.

Much later, when I, along with Amitabh Bachchan and Aamir Khan, was shooting in Jodhpur for *Thugs of Hindostan* (2018), we stayed at Ajit Bhawan, a palace that has been converted into a heritage hotel. I remembered that this palace was built by my father's elder brother, Har Narayan Pandey, who was a civil engineer from the prestigious College of Civil Engineering, University of Roorkee. It was a free day for me and suddenly, as I walked on the lawns of the hotel, I had a strong urge to visit my childhood home, the house where I was born. The producers were kind enough to let me have a car at my disposal and I set off with two of my staff members who always accompany me on shoots: Tulsi, my hairdresser, and Firoze, my make-up man. I was excited to share my memories with them. The house, 532 Sardarpura, has long been demolished and I think a mall is coming up in its place. But strangely enough, there before me, in solitary splendour, stood just that one room, that familiar room where all of us seven sisters were born. The hammer of demolition had paused just for that moment, when I could

Tauji Har Narayan Pandey outside 532 Sardarpura

come and bid my home a tearful farewell. I turned my back on the room, carrying lost moments of childhood with me and crossed the road to the park where we all played as children. It was in a dilapidated condition, neglected and unkempt, another memory trod upon by time. It still had the board with the name inscribed on it: 'Baby Park'. The lock on the gate didn't deter me; I was a baby once more! I was chasing memories and would at least relive some of them once again. Jumping over the low wall, with Tulsi and Firoze looking on incredulously, I climbed up the broken steps of the slide and slid down memory lane.

There is a Chinese proverb that says: 'To forget one's ancestors is to be a brook without a source, a tree without a root.' I did not want to be that brook or that tree, so I was glad this trip led me to connect with my heritage, and my roots.

Now that I had started retracing my steps into the past, I decided to visit Mandore, the first capital of Marwar. As children, we would go there on picnics, since the garden there was very beautiful and it was just 9 km out of Jodhpur. It was dotted with cenotaphs of the erstwhile rulers and their *ranis*, and the thought came to me that my old house, which I had just left behind, was also a cenotaph for all those who had passed away. Tracing the steps of the Rathores of Jodhpur, we went up the steep climb to Mehrangarh Fort, founded as a new capital by Rao Jodha, since Mandore was vulnerable to attacks by enemy armies. Legend has it that the foundation of this fort, which was built in 1459, was laid by a sage called Karni Mata, who belonged to the Charan community, and was thus believed to be impregnable.

Unbeknown to us, there are chance encounters and trips we undertake in our lives that change our view of events and people. The visit to Mehrangarh was one such encounter with my past. And it was associated with that perfume, *mitti* from Kannauj, shown to me by the salesman. An *attar* from Kannauj at Mehrangarh, what was the connection? But besides that, there had been many references to Kannauj in connection with the history of Mehrangarh Fort which set my mind on another journey, the connection of Jodhpur with Kannauj. In these days of ancestry.com, where they entice you to discover your ancestors' incredible journeys, I also decided to do a little detective work. 'Discover the town where your great-grandfather grew up' and with that your ancestors become more than a name. Somehow, we never thought of asking our parents and grandparents about our journey to this point. There was an Uttar Pradesh (UP) connection since my mother was from Fatehpur Chaurasi in Unnao district and my father from Kakupur, in Kanpur.

We were all familiar with the romance of the Rajput Prithviraj Chauhan with Princess Sanyogita, daughter of Jaichand of Kannauj. But after the visit to Mehrangarh, it was as if all my ancestors were surrounding me, and I started recalling some of the details. In our

Jodhpur house, we had seen many bottles made of camel skin and were told that these contained perfumes. I remembered that the perfumes were brought by my aunt's relatives from Kannauj. One of the relatives was Chhedda Lal, whom we called 'Mama' since he was Taiji's brother. He would bring perfumes packed in these containers. It showed that the royal family of Jodhpur still called for perfumes from their original home, Kannauj.

Although it is not known when *attar* started being manufactured in Kannauj, the seventh-century biography *Harshacharita* (The deeds of Harsha), written by Emperor Harsha's court poet, Banabhatta, contains references to the use of agarwood oil for *attar*. It is also believed that the manufacturing of *attar* attained great heights during the Mughal period. What is fascinating about Kannauj's *attar*-making industry is that despite the passage of time, it still follows the traditional method, a highly labour-intensive and time-consuming hydrodistillation process called *deg bhapka*.

I also recollected stories told to me by my aunts and my older sister, of our ancestors carrying mail from Kannauj to Jodhpur on camels. One of them I remember was known as Matadin. He, I presume, was a postman who carried mail for those Kannaujias who had settled in Jodhpur. I wondered why so many post-office employees were Kanyakubja Brahmins. I have seen many postmaster generals with last names such as Pande, Shukla, Bajpeyi and Trivedi even outside UP. Since they were well-educated, the Kanyakubjs took up professions that required reading skills, like postmasters and announcers on radio or in the media. Wherever there was the need for good spoken Hindi, the Kanyakubjs were always present. My father's sister's husband, my *phupaji*, was also a postmaster.

The Rathore clan's shift to Marwar from Kannauj came about through Rao Siyaji who, on a pilgrimage to Dwarka, stopped at a town called Pali. The local Brahmin community asked him to settle there and become their chief to protect them from raiders. In his chronicle, *Marwar Ra Pargana Ri Vigat*, the royal bard, Nainsi, too noted that the Rathores originated from Kannauj before migrating to Marwar. The Rathores gained full power in Marwar and Jodhpur after wresting it from the Islamic rulers of Delhi. From this point onwards, Marwar was ruled by the Rathores. The first fully independent king of Jodhpur, Jodha, reconquered Mandore from the

Sisodias of Mewar before he founded the city of Jodhpur. The city is named after him and forms the capital of the Rathore state. After their move from Mandore to the impressive fort of Mehrangarh in 1459, it was the fort of Mehrangarh that dominated the territory held by the Rathores of Marwar.

But of course, in India, legend is always more acceptable, more believable than history! And every story has several colourful versions. The origin of the name Kannauj is one such fascinating story. Legend has it that Lord Brahma had a son called Kush, who had four sons: Kushabh, Kushnabh, Ashrutrajas and Vasu. Kushnabh formed his own empire and named it Madhya Desh. He had a hundred very beautiful daughters through his dalliance with an *apsara*, or celestial being, called Ghritachee. Vaayu, the god of wind, was attracted by the beauty of these fair ladies and wanted to marry them. These maidens rejected his proposal, saying that their husbands would be chosen by their father. The gods of Hindu mythology are only human and share human traits like anger and violence. Vaayu was mortified and laid a curse on these hundred beautiful virgins, turning them into hunchbacks—*kubja*, in Hindi. One of the rajas of Kushnabh's empire, Raja Brahm Dutt, of Kampilya, associated in the Mahabharata as Panchaal, the birthplace of Draupadi, consented to marry all the 100 hunchbacked princesses. And the minute Brahm Dutt touched the girls, their hunchbacks disappeared and they regained their renowned beauty. *A hundred daughters!* I thought to myself. Did the Kannaujiyas have a proclivity to produce daughters? If an *apsara* could produce 100 daughters, my mother at eight was in close competition in modern times. This story relates the ancient name of Kannauj, Kanyakubj, to the 100 *kanyas*, or maidens, who were *kubjis*. This area was later known as Kanyakubja Pradesh and the descendants of Brahm Dutt and the daughters of Kushnabh were later known as Kanyakubja Brahmins. This finds reference in Valmiki's Ramayana too. Kushnabh's great-grandson, King Vishwaratha, became the renowned sage Vishwamitra, the first of the twenty-four sages who deciphered the Gayatri Mantra.

'When grandmothers speak, the earth will be healed,' believe the Hopi Native Americans. I wish I had let my grandmother speak and recount stories of the past. But now, through some pages of history, some words on Google, I have at least garnered knowledge that has made me proud of my heritage. I had connections with Raja Brahm Dutt and through him, with Draupadi! I could count Sage Vishwamitra among my ancestors, the sage who also had connections with Rajasthan since he came to Pushkara to perform his *yagnas*, or ritual fire sacrifices. I was one up with my friends and acquaintances. It did not matter that I went to a government school, with a monthly fee of five rupees, or less, it was still the Maharaja's School, then Maharani's College, which faced Maharaja's College, synonymous with royalty! Kannauj and Rajasthan, I had found the connection!

Kannauj was visited by famous travellers from around the world. The Chinese monk Fa-Hsien was one of them. During his travels in India when he visited Kannauj, he remarked, 'This country is very productive and the people are flourishing and happy beyond compare.' Another Chinese pilgrim, Hiuen Tsang, visited Kannauj in 643 CE. While others called it Kanyakubja, he referred to it as Kusumapura, the city of flowers. Perhaps the name carried the prophecy for the future perfume capital of India. Was it a coincidence too that my daughter Ishitta's name, according to her horoscope, was Kusum Kumari Bajpai? Since she was born during the month of *shraadh,* when we pay tribute to our forefathers, perhaps the ancestors we were remembering that day were blessing her from the ancient capital of Kusumpura . . .

My traveller of course was Matadin, the *dakia*, riding on a camel. It must have been through his travels and stories that my father's family moved to Marwar. It was my father's uncle, Jisaji, who first moved to Jodhpur, presumably in search of work. He was a writer and perhaps was in the same job as Matadin, in the postal service. My paternal grandfather, Banarasi Das Pandey, who was from Kakupur, was not so well-educated, though he had educated both his sons, my uncle Har Narayan Pandey and my father Indra Narayan Pandey. My Tauji was an engineer, and my father had passed his LLB exams. My grandfather was happy when his cousin Jisa suggested that he would take his two sons with him to Jodhpur, a city with better job prospects.

My mother's advent into Marwar was an unbelievable story, which I have learnt only recently. Perhaps we did not give her the time of day, or she was embarrassed to mention this incident to us. We will never know. But it was during an interview with a foreign student who was staying in our Jaipur house as a paying guest that she let her guard down. As I mentioned earlier, she grew up in the tiny village of Fatehpur Chaurasi, a name I found fascinating enough to use as a backdrop for one of my plays. Bhagwati grew up in a family of conservative Kanyakubja Brahmins. Her father, Baldev Prasad, was an enlightened farmer, who though not well-educated himself, had started a middle school for girls. He was also a member of the Congress Party and had taken part in the freedom movement. Bhagwati herself was a voracious reader and a very creative writer. When the time came for her marriage, there was a proposal from a widower with two children. He had a coveted *sarkari naukari*, a government job, that of a clerk in an office, which was a plus point. But to the feisty Bhagwati, the word 'clerk' was anathema since it was suggestive of a boring record keeper! Not having the courage to say no to her parents, she was so miserable that she tried to make herself sick by bathing in ice-cold water in winter. She did fall sick with pneumonia, and her brother, who was like a father to them, wondered why a girl who was going to be married looked like death warmed up. She then wrote a three-page letter to her brother. She had great faith in her writing skills. Her brother was moved to tears on reading the letter and told her that her words were so powerful that he had decided to call off her engagement. This brought down the wrath of their parents, who could not understand the reason why he was paying heed to his sister's request. Bhagwati herself said that the whole community came down on her, accusing her of being shameless and inconsiderate. In those days, a girl opposing her family's wishes with regard to her *rishta*, or alliance, was unheard of.

I must say, her brother was pretty liberal for his time and did not force his sister to marry against her wishes. The usual threat in families used to be someone dramatically proclaiming 'Over my dead body!' The engagement was over, but what next? My mother again followed the forbidden path. She spoke to the *maalin*, the gardener's wife, telling her of her decision, and when the *maalin*'s sister, who was visiting, offered to carry a proposal for a young man in her village, my mother told her to do so. She asked the woman to talk to her father first. The young man, Indra Narayan Pandey, belonged to Kakupur but had settled down in Jodhpur. For the young Bhagwati, though he was also a widower, he seemed like the husband she had been looking for. According to the *maalin*'s sister, he was good-looking, educated and from the same community as them. The match was made and Bhagwati, daughter of Baldev Prasad of Fatehpur Chaurasi, put her footprint on the sands of Jodhpur as Bhagwati Pandey.

The house in Fatehpur Chaurasi has been demolished in 2022. It was a 100-year-old house, with a hundred memories and millions of stories. No amount of persuasion from any of us could convince the cousin who lived there to spare some part of it. My last visit to this house, *nani-ka-ghar*, was as a five-year-old, travelling in a bullock-cart, through mud paths with swaying wheat stalks on either side. It remained a blurry memory in my mind till one day, one of the directors I had worked with, Pankaj Shukla, surprised me with a delightful picture of this house on Kisan Channel. I was a judge on a reality show, *Maati Ke Lal*, presented by the channel, and the director thought it would be a good idea to connect the judges with their past, especially if there was a rural connection. Surprisingly, he happened to be from the same district as my mother's village,

and as I watched the film, lo and behold, there was my *nani*'s house, just as I had imagined it, flitting past in the film. Of course, my tears flowed unashamedly. When my brother Prasoon heard of this, he decided to visit the house to try to save it from being demolished. As he walked into the *rasoi*, the kitchen, he could hear the clattering of *pateelas* and *kadais* (pots and pans) and could smell the aromas of my *nani*'s and her five daughters' cooking. *Nani-ka-ghar*, the words have a wonderful ring to them. I wished that time could stand still and that the house would resound once again with voices from the past.

Malti Mausi standing at the door outside the house in Fatehpur Chaurasi

On a lighter note, being a theatre person and a writer, I would like to reiterate what the playwright George Bernard Shaw has said, 'If you cannot get rid of the family skeleton, you may as well make it dance!' So, my skeletons, ancient and recent, have been let loose and I hope they will dance with me on stage and off it, as I write, write, write . . .

Chapter 2

Birthday: The Blue Diary

February 18, my date of birth according to the blue diary, my mother's diary, which I discovered after she passed away. All the previous dates of my birthdays had been crossed out!

I have several vivid memories of my childhood, which I don't think I can ever forget, but one that stands out is an argument I had with my mother about my date of birth. It lingers in my memory as a special conversation that carried on till the end of her life. And now I had the blue diary in my hand and a date crossed out.

With my mother Bhagwati Pandey

My father, whom we called Kakaji, would often get up at 4.30 in the morning. He liked to have his morning tea in bed. My mother would make tea and bring it to his bed. Then they would have their tea together, talking and gossiping, the one intimate moment they shared before the bevy of children woke up. My father loved poetry and had a sonorous voice. He would start singing early in the morning. Of course, this poetry session disturbed our sleep, and we would grumble, cover our ears and turn over to try and go back to sleep. I always liked to have my share of this early-morning tea made by my mother. Not that I ever made tea for the two of them, but from my bed I would call out, '*Amma, chai pakai kya*?' (Amma, have you made tea?) My father, with a burst of laughter, would start singing a song for me: '*Lillo padi bichonae/ Poochhe, Amma, chai pakai kya.* (Lying in bed, Lillo calls out/ Mother, have you cooked the tea?) Perhaps *pakana* was an Urdu word. We usually say, '*Chai banayi kya*?' I somehow found the name Lillo very unfashionable. Now when I see Karisma being called Lolo and Kareena, Bebo, I wonder whether I should have remained Lillo. My father would often lie in bed and sing: *Bhadon ki andherii raat thi/ rohini nakshtra tha . . .* It was a dark night in the monsoons/the constellation Rohini was aligned with the stars. He had written these lines on the birthday of Lord Krishna, a day we celebrate as Janmashtami. This would set my mind thinking, that even our god Krishna had a birthday. So, Krishna had been born too! That is why we celebrate Janmashtami and Ram's birthday on Rama Navami. Everyone had a birthday. So why was it that my mother did not remember the birth date of her sixth child?

The world now knows my birthday as 15 March, but my mother would often say, 'Ila, I can say with certainty that 15 March is not your birthday.' I would retort, 'Then do you mean that I have made up this date?' This was always followed by the same explanation that when school admissions were taking place, my father was out of town and had deputed his friend Mishrilal Jain to get us admitted into school. She would say, 'So he must have entered this date in the form.' Horrified, I would say, 'Are you saying that even my father does not know when I was born?' This argument between us carried on all through her life. 'So, am I not a March child, Mummy?' I would ask. She would say, 'No, that is not the case. You were born in the month of Phagun, but it was not March. Magh had come and gone, the cold had decreased because I remember, we had a Punjabi neighbour in Jodhpur whose mother would send us some *pakwans*, or dishes, for Baisakhi, which she distributed to all the neighbours. Now Baisakhi is on 13th April, so I know that you were born by then.' And I had to be satisfied with that explanation.

As I have mentioned earlier, I was born at 532 Sardarpura, 9th B. Road, Jodhpur. My Tauji, Baaji, had constructed several quarters for refugees from Pakistan, mostly Sindhis. But who was this Punjabi neighbour my mother always referred to, I don't remember. For years, I quarrelled with my mother about my date of birth, but she would often just pass it off as a joke. Sometimes she would say, 'Remember you were my sixth offspring and a girl at that. My mental turmoil was worse than my physical discomfort. There was no sonography, those days to detect the sex of a child. Everything was *rambharose*, in God's hands. There had already been five girls born before you, and three after.' I would say, 'So why did you give birth to girls only? You needn't have.' Eight daughters! Either Devaki had them or my mother! This would embarrass my mother. 'Have some shame,' she would say. 'In those days, you did not have a choice. There was the question of carrying on the family name. Tauji had no children and neither did your father's cousin who lived with us, so the responsibility to carry on the family name fell on your father!' My father, as I have mentioned earlier, was one of two brothers. We lived together in a joint family. My mother called my father's elder brother Daiji and we called him Baaji. With them lived their cousin, Shambhu Ratan Pandey, called Papaji by us, who didn't have any children either. It was his father Jisa, who had brought my father and his brother to live with him in Jodhpur and provided them with an education. Because of this obligation, my eldest sister, Hemlata, known as Binno at home, was given in adoption to this Papaji.

Now I can understand why there was this yearning for a son. There was the obligation to continue one's family name, one's *vansh*. My mother would say that on the one hand, she was fearful of her sisters-in-laws' digs, and then seeing our father's downcast face, each time she went into labour, she would be nervous to begin with. '*Pehle hi ghabra jati thi* (I would get scared at the outset),' she would say. 'But how come you remember the birth dates of my sisters? There seems to be no problem with your remembering the dates of the sisters older than me and you also know the birthdays of those after me, so what happened to your senses in my case? *Mati kyon maari gayi thi*, why did you lose your mind just then? Did I not have any importance in your life? My entire being, my life is connected to the date I was born. If I was not born, or my date of birth is wrong, then my whole existence is wrong, a lie.' I would not let her get the better of me in this fight. I would enjoy her discomfort.

'*Arre bhai*, now I remember . . . once your birthday and the festival of Holi were celebrated on the same day, 15 March. That day I remembered the *tithi* (a lunar day) and it happened to be 15 March. Holi and 15 March. And I just accepted that 15 March was your birthday! According to the Hindu calendar, that *tithi* is your date of birth.' Again, I would provoke her, 'So please at least tell me now, Mother, what was the *tithi* that day according to the Hindu calendar?' She would say that I should stop harassing her. 'I don't remember it all. I remembered it that one day and you have hung on my words. Now you have started celebrating that day, so keep it up.' She would carry on to tell me that no one ever celebrated a daughter's birthday; sons' birthdays were celebrated with sweets like *gulgulas* and *kheer*. 'Then you could have made *gulgulas* for us too so that our hearts would also bubble up with some feelings.' She would laugh, '*Wah wah! Kya tukbandi hai, gulgule aur bulbule*—What a wonderful rhyme—*gulgule* and *bulbule* (bubbles).' *Gulgulas* are made of flour kneaded in *gur* (jaggery) and then deep-fried. It was a celebratory offering and there is no doubt that they are delicious. 'But then why does my passport have 5 March?' Again, she would protest 'No, no, that is quite out of the question. March it definitely was not.' I would say, 'Then did I make up this date on my passport?' The whole story of Mishrilal Jain's faux pas would be repeated. 'Your father was out on tour and maybe Mishrilal Jain . . .' 'Then why did he ask you if he had to write it according to his own wishes?' I told her that till today, HSBC Bank sends me flowers on 5 March. Who is responsible for this? Her comment was quite natural: 'So, why should that make you unhappy? Look, Ila, girls in those days were shy; these days, girls have thrown modesty out of the window. Things were kept under wraps and not discussed openly. Do you know when I named my daughters, my sisters-in-law taunted me saying, "Yes, she is educated, of course she will name her daughters. Who are we?"'

I believe my grandmother had named me Leela. My mother told me that she was not happy about it. For her, the association with that name was with the Satyanarayan puja every full moon day. 'I would listen to the stories about Kalavati and Leelawati, and Leelawati's life was miserable. Life was unfair to her. At that time, I was reading a book by a Bengali writer that had a woman named

Ila, Ila which means the earth. You don't ever thank me for that, that I gave you a beautiful Bengali name.' I exclaimed, '*Kya baat hai, Ma, kya baat hai!*' (How wonderful, Ma, wonderful indeed!)— as if this name has given me a lot. This myth was also in jeopardy when I started looking for my origins. Somewhere I read that Ila was the daughter of Vaivasvata Manu but had to live the life of both a male and a female. According to the Shrimad Bhagavata Purana, Ila is the goddess of speech, and the mother and the father of the Chandravanshis, or the Lunar Dynasty. She was both mother and father because she was able to transition between genders, a trait she was bestowed with because of her father's desire for a son. So unknowingly, my mother's *naam karan,* or naming ceremony, for me could have been a manifestation of the same desire. Fortunately, I discovered this story long after she was gone, or I would have had another issue to call her out on.

'Forget about me, your father never had the courage to display any affection for his children in the presence of his parents and elders. They would always say sarcastically, "Are we all dead that you have to fondle your children?" In fact, once your grandfather even slapped your father over this issue, and that was after he had become the father of five or six girls. I watched this, *khoon ki ghoont peekar rah gayi thi* (swallowed my anger) but did not have the courage to open my mouth. These were family *sanskars,* values.' 'Oh my God, was my grandfather such a monster?' She would ask me to be quiet. 'See, that is why I never tell you anything. You bear grudges. *Arre bhai* he was sick and irritable, but one thing was sure, he loved your Kaka very much. Even in his last days, he would call out "Babu, Babu".' That was my father's pet name. Not a bitter word against her father-in-law. I found it unbelievable that despite all this she herself did not bear any grudges.

Well, these stories and arguments continued, but I did not give up asking. My mother was my father's second wife. The first wife, Kamala, had died in an accident; she slipped and fell into a sunken well, in the centre of the *aangan,* the courtyard, and drowned. They had not even had their *gauna,* a ritual after the wedding ceremony, when the bride formally enters her husband's home after she reaches puberty. My father, who had gone back to Jodhpur, was in a state of shock when he came to know of the unfortunate accident. These stories smack of untruth; you imagine that either someone pushed her in or she had died by suicide. But this was the truth, verified by my mother, who said that she had once almost slipped into that well herself. But these stories are now in the past, almost seventy to eighty years ago. Anyhow, I kept at it. Kamala's story gave me a new lead. 'Amma, are you sure I am not Kamala's daughter?' 'Go on,' said my mother, 'if you were Kamala's daughter, you would have been older than Binno.' Binno, as mentioned earlier, was my parents' first child, who was given for adoption to my father's first cousin, Shambhu Ratan and his wife Shanti Devi. We were eight sisters, but my fourth sister, Shobhna, took ill and died at the age of one and a half. I have heard that she was the prettiest of us all. If she had survived, it would have been such fun. Our home would have been no less than a girls' hostel! As it is, our house was always full of conversation and laughter, quarrels and teasing. We didn't need any outsiders for entertainment. Out of the eight girls born to my parents, two lived away from the family fold, Binno and Deepa.

My sister Deepa's adoption was almost like a film story. She was adopted by my Tauji, Har Narayan Pandey. Perhaps she was given away since there was only a difference of eleven months between me and her. So, when she fell ill as a child, my Taiji was the one who looked after her very lovingly. When Deepa was about a year old, my father was transferred to Jaipur in the co-operative office. We were going away from the joint family fold, leaving Taiji and Tauji for the first time. My mother and all of us sisters were travelling in the third-class compartment. My Tau and Tai were very sad that all the children were leaving. Tauji stretched out his arms and said, 'Will you come to me, Deepalia (Deepa)? Will you stay with us?' And before anyone could stop her, she had gone out of the compartment window, which in those days didn't have any bars, and was in Tauji's arms. The guard blew the whistle, and the train pulled out of the station, leaving our sister Deepa behind. My father was not with us and somehow no one thought of pulling the alarm chain. My mother must have been in a state of shock, not knowing what to do. From then on, Deepa was *their* daughter and was brought up by them. And she always had this complaint against my parents that she was left alone in Jodhpur, without the benefit of growing up with her siblings.

The three powerful women of my family at Jodhpur. Ammi,
my Taiji Jiya-Amma in the middle and my mother on her left

I did not realize that my entire family was involved in trying to
confirm my date of birth. I was really surprised when one day my
sister Binnoji, who was living in Bhopal at that time, called me up
saying, 'I have finally found out your date of birth!' '*Kya*? How?'
I said. She went on to unravel the mystery. 'Mummy has probably
forgotten about this. When you were born, I had three very close
friends in school. Two sisters, Shanno and Manno, and another
girl called Beatrice. This time when I went back to Jodhpur, I asked
Beatrice if she knew where Shanno and Manno were. Beatrice asked
me why I wanted to know about them, after all these years. I said,
"I remember once Shanno and Manno had distributed sweets in
school saying that they had a new arrival . . . a baby sister. So, I had
shyly told them that I also had a new sister born that day. So, I want
to find out from Shanno and Manno what the date was." Beatrice
said she would try to find out about the sisters' whereabouts.
And today, there was a call from Beatrice telling me that she had
talked to Shanno and Manno and they have confirmed the date as
25 February!' I leapt up and called my mother in Jaipur. 'I have found
out my date of birth.' She asked what date that was. '25 February'
was my reply. 'Wrong! Who has told you this?' she asked. I told her
about the cold chain: that Binno had asked Beatrice and Beatrice
had called the two sisters. My mother laughed. 'Have I given birth

to you or have Shanno–Manno? Perhaps that is according to the English calendar, but definitely not according to the *tithi*. Look, I do remember that Magh had gone, winter had still not set in, the cool breeze of Phagun had started cooling the land . . . it was the month of Chait-Baisakh because I remember our Punjabi neighbour used to celebrate Baisakhi—' 'You remember all this, but not my birth date?' I cut in. 'Go on now, don't trouble me. If I don't remember, then I don't! What can you do about it? Yes, it was February but not the 25th, that I can say with conviction. Perhaps it was Magh Purnima because Taiji's puja was still on.' 'Oh Mother, is that why they named me Leelavati? Yes, it must have been *purnima*. Try and remember the date.'

'Ila, please stop harassing me. This was not the date. I will try and remember, but it was definitely not the 25th. I remember that on the 25th your father had gone to Lucknow on work. And my sister, Chaubey, had sent some *jhablas* [garment that is worn over a baby's top] for you.' I could not believe this. 'You remember the date of Kaka's tour, but not the date when I was born. You wanted a son; you have no love for me!'

'Look, Ila, the moment a child is born, it is yours for life. If I didn't love you, I could have thrown you off the balcony!' She would laugh heartily. 'You should understand. You have done BA in psychology, don't talk like an ignorant child. In those days, sons were given preference since they carried on the family name. Daughters, in any case, change their last names when they get married. I was a Bajpai, Kaka's family name was Pandey, so naturally our children have taken his family name, Pandey. Both your brothers carry the family name, Pandey, but you are no more a Pandey. They will be the ones to carry on Kakaji's name. And then it will be Prasoon's son, Ayushman. He will carry the torch of the Pandeys.' I told her that it was because of these ideas of hers that my sister, Rama, still kept her maiden name, Rama Pandey, even after marrying Najam Saqib! Tripti was even better. She was steadfast in her decision to retain her single status. 'You don't remember my date of birth, that is why I shall name Ishitta's son Benarsidas Indra Narayan Pandey Kakupuri Kannaujia Ghanekar! What will you say to that?' She could not stop laughing. 'You are a drama queen,' she said.

One day, my mother called me and asked, 'Does it really bother you that I don't remember the exact date of your birth?'

'No, Mother, I do it as I love to pull your leg!' She would always wish me on 15 March. Sometimes she would send me some money, sometimes a kurta or churidar from Anokhi, a piece of jewellery from Amrapalli. Often, she would give me Rs 500, saying, 'I am giving you this. You put in a little more money and get yourself a kurta from Anokhi.' I would teasingly say, 'That is great! But why should I have to add more money to it?' I would always berate her saying, 'I know you love your sons more, especially Piyush; he is your *aankhon ka tara,* the light of your eyes.' She would deny that vehemently but very gently try to convince me saying, 'People say all five fingers cannot be the same, but I say, try and poke a thorn into all five, they bleed in the same way. When a *maali* plants flowers in his garden, each flower is dearer than life for him. But it is true that your brother Piyush was born after a long wait. The second one. Well, I had given up all hope, but he was God's gift.' Tears would well up in her eyes. She would say, 'What have I done so special for your brothers that I did not do for you?' I reminded her that the girls studied in Maharaja's Multipurpose High School, where you didn't have to pay a penny, while the two boys went to an English-medium school, St Xavier's. I also told her that our school admissions were done by Mishrilalji, who got our dates all wrong. 'So much so that you do not remember my date of birth. How can I forget that Piyush and Prasoon's birthdays were celebrated with a party on the terrace. My father's friend Singhi Sahib ordered *kabuli* (biryani) for the party and they were gifted bicycles.'

'Spare me,' she would say. 'The bicycles were gifted by Rakshpal Chacha, not us. And it was Uma who got the boys admitted into St Xavier's since all her friends' brothers went to St Xavier's. She was the one who had Tripti's hair styled into a bob, don't you remember? By the hairdresser, Sartar. All those smocking frocks were ordered by Uma too. I wasn't aware of any of those trends. But how do you still remember all these childhood happenings? Guddie [my youngest sister, Tripti] complains that I did not make her a doctor, but I think that because Piyush was born after so many years, the sibling rivalry continues. What can I do? Deepa also complains that she was not happy, that we left her alone in Jodhpur. I tell her that because she lived with Tauji, she could become a doctor. She has so much money, their own yacht. Did we have the capacity to send her to medical school? She was sent to the Post Graduate Institute of Medicine, Chandigarh, by your uncle. Her complaint is that she wanted to live with her sisters, that she was not interested in becoming a doctor. Perhaps I should have left Guddie with Daiji, she would have been a doctor then.' Sometimes fed up with our leg-pulling and arguments, she would say, 'It would have been better if I had been childless for seven lives, rather than have children like you!' But it was true that each one of her children was very dear to her. Considering her financial condition, she did whatever she could for each of us. Festivals were celebrated with gusto, new clothes, new shoes, new ribbons, *mehndi* on the festival of Gudiyan along with bangles. Our house was like a *mela*, a *jhamela, a* noisy birdcage, a *dhobi ghat*. It had the sounds and chatter of a *sabzi mandi*, a vegetable market; on the dining table it was a political *chaupal,* a stadium. But I never let go. Come March and I would start needling my mother. 'Mother, it is March, now do you remember when I was born?' 'Go on I will never tell you.'

From October 2010, my mother's health started deteriorating when she was diagnosed with dengue. I was in Jodhpur for a programme on 18 November when I got the news. I had decided that after the programme I would go to Jaipur to see her. We were staying at Ajit Niwas. That evening, the Maharani asked us to come over for a visit. As we sat in the drawing room, facing me was a girl who was smiling at me. She said she knew my older sister, Hemlata. I inquired how, and she said, 'I am Shanno–Manno's sister.' 'Wait . . . if you are their sister, then we share the same birth date, 25 February.' Then I went on to recount the story of how Beatrice had verified this. She said, 'Yes, I am that sister, but I was not born on 25 February. It was on the 20th.' So slowly, we seemed to be coming closer to that date in February. I thought of probing my mother's memory again when I saw her. I felt we should conclude this argument. Mother was in the hospital, on a ventilator. I was going to tell her about the new date, but I kept quiet. Somehow, I didn't have the heart to pull her leg this time. I remember when I walked into the ICU, this lady, with tubes and respirators around her, beckoned me. As I bent down, she ran a finger over the dark rings under my eyes saying, 'Why don't you use cucumbers for this?' And her next question was, 'How far has the story of *Pavitra Rishta* reached?' Her favourite serial, which she never missed.

My mother left us for her heavenly abode on 31 December 2010. I spent six days with her at the hospital. It was around Christmas. I had decorated the ICU cabin with bunting and Christmas decorations. On her passing away, among her papers, we found the blue diary in which she used to record many things. Surprisingly, the diary contained the birthdays of several people, their wedding anniversaries as well as their phone numbers. Each of them received either a card or a phone call on these special occasions. Perhaps she learnt this art of remembering birthdays from Ranjan Kapur's wife, Jimi. I saw that the diary contained the birth dates of all her children and grandchildren. There, in front of my name, 15 March had been crossed out and there was another entry—18 February. Finally, she had arrived at that date! She must have spent days agonizing over whether to change the date or not. How did she suddenly hit upon the correct date? If she had been alive, perhaps she would have wished me on 18 February, accepting the fact that my controversial and debatable birth date, which she was never able to remember, was written down in her diary. She must have spent a long time searching for it in various contexts. It hurts me that I didn't know she had taken this so seriously. During her illness, before she was admitted to the hospital, she must have consulted the Hindu calendar, calculated the *tithi* and the date, trying to jog her memory before finally sealing it at 18 February.

When the song *'Choli Ke Peechhey'* became a huge hit, my mother came to my flat on the night of 14 March. From early the next morning, the doorbell rang continuously and every half hour a huge bouquet of flowers would arrive at my doorstep. She had never seen so many flowers before. 'What is the occasion, Ila? You have suddenly become so papular?' She would always use the American accent for two words: 'papular' and 'lats of love'! 'One thing I have to grant you, Ila, you have made a name for yourself. When people ask me whether I am Ila Arun's mother, my heart swells with pride. Often, I use your name to get things done. Please *jaldi jaldi karo*, hurry up, I am Ila Arun's mother. You won't believe it, the work indeed gets done in no time!' Then she would smile her usual whimsical smile and say, 'Don't worry! I don't always do that, only when something needs to be done urgently.' I would also smile and say, 'No, Mother, please use this name if it helps you. It has never been of any use to me!' She wondered what would happen with the fifty bouquets I received. 'If this was Jaipur, I would have got Nandu (our household help) to open up a shop outside our gate. The money I made from the sale of these beautiful flowers would be spent on buying some vitamins. As it is, all the prizes you have received in the past, all those cups are lying around the house. I always say, a tea set would have been better! Or money, which would have been useful.' Much later, when she visited me again on 14 March, she seemed to be waiting for something. When she couldn't contain herself, she finally said, 'It is already 9 o'clock, Ila, and there has been no sound of the doorbell.' I asked her why she was waiting for the doorbell. 'Why should the doorbell ring? Are you expecting someone?' She replied, 'Why, won't your bouquets arrive?' Then two small bouquets did arrive, from Tips, the music company, one from Ramesh Taurani and one from Kumar Taurani. 'But these are very small bouquets, Ila.' I replied, 'These are formal symbols of reality. They increase and decrease with the worth of your work and time.' My mother frowned. '*Kya*, don't you have work now? Are you happy?' 'Mummy, don't worry, a person is always happy doing freelance work. *Parwah ille*! (Tamil for don't worry).' When two more bouquets arrived, my mother put on her spectacles and read the note attached to each. One was from Juhi Chawla, the actress, and the other from Sudesh Bhosale, the playback singer. 'Oh, these came even when I was here two years ago? So, these are relationships of the heart, not merely a formality,' she said. 'Yes, they always remember me on 15 March.' She said 'They seem to be nice people. When you meet Juhi Chawla, tell her I like her as an actress. And Sudesh Bhosale is the person who does playback singing for Dada Moni, or Amitabh Bachchan, right?' I was surprised. 'Mummy how do you know all this?' She laughed and said, 'Don't forget I am your mother!'

One person who would always visit me on 15 March was Pinchoo Kapoor. I had worked in a play directed by him in Jaipur, *Kanchanrang*. When we first came to Mumbai, Pinchooji helped us a lot. He even got us a place to stay as his guests at the NSCI Club. Every 15 March he would come in a *kaali-peeli*, black-and-yellow, taxi to present a bouquet to me. He never kept a car. The note always read, 'God bless you, my darling!' This bouquet presented by him, which for me was the most fragrant of all bouquets, will have a special place in my birthday memory forever.

Ila Arun, born February 18th. It may be 5 March on my passport, 15 March for my friends, but for me, it will always be 18 February now.

* * *

It is the season of *patjhad*. I sit on the balcony, one and a half months after the new year. For some days now, we had been seeing the bare trees from our balcony, with falling leaves being carried away by the breeze, and new leaves springing off the branches from green shoots. Moments past have been turned into dreams. Will they ever come back again? Will our mother never return to us, her smiling face and all that vibrancy, has it been lost forever with her? I am reminded of a *ghazal* that Ghulam Ali Sahib loves to sing:

> *Go ki khushboo ki tarah phela tha mere charsoo*
> *Main use mahsoos kar sakta tha, chhoo sakta na thha.*

(The fragrance had enveloped my being/ I could feel it but alas, could not touch it.)

Chapter 3

School: Because and Therefore

'School is a building which has four walls with tomorrow inside.'
I had read this somewhere and the words have stayed with me.

Not only one tomorrow, but tomorrow and tomorrow and tomorrow. School for most of us is a memory we do not want to forget. It is also perhaps the first place where your abilities are recognized, where you get an opportunity to blossom, to step into that tomorrow.

My earliest memory of school is of my nursery school, MVD Bal Mandir. It was just opposite St Xavier's School and Maharani's College. Since we lived just behind Niros, the only decent restaurant in Jaipur. this was the closest school, a few minutes' walk from our house. Also, it was one of the few nursery schools, since the concept of a nursery was not readily accepted at that time. My mother, I suppose, needed a little time off for household chores so would send me off packing. I think it was run by the same management as Mahavir School, perhaps a feeder school for regular school but was a reputed institution. It was a co-ed. Though I was very young, I have two vivid memories from those days. Prime Minister Jawaharlal Nehru was visiting. I remember the excitement, since some of us, including me, were chosen to welcome him at the airport. Fondly addressed as Chacha Nehru by children, he was a dedicated supporter of children's education, always looking for ways to ensure that the education they received gave them a head start in life.

Schools in India, especially at that time, were very strict about the uniform code and neatness. Our uniform was a white blouse and a maroon skirt and since it was winter, the uniform included a maroon

23

sweater. As we stood in line, the teacher suddenly approached me and gave me a slap without any warning. My transgression was that I was wearing a multi-coloured, half-sleeved sweater. 'You are in the front row and not in uniform,' she shouted. Apart from the slap inflicted on a three-year-old, there was the humiliation of being hauled up in public. She took off my blouse there in the cold in public view and made me wear the sweater under the blouse. The only thought I had was of my mother. She had perhaps not noticed the entry made in the school diary since the mornings were a mad rush with so many children to be readied and sent off to school. This incident affected me so deeply that I still remember that teacher's name. I carry the hope that one day if I ever meet her, I shall remind her of her insensitivity towards a little child in her care. I wonder what Chacha Nehru would have made of this! Today, no teacher can get away with this. There would be legal proceedings by the parents. Fortunately, today there is an awareness of children's rights and parents do hold teachers responsible for their behaviour, something that parents in our childhood did not.

The other incident I remember is also to do with a beating. During the interval, all the children were made to take a nap in school. It so happened that my mother came to my school to deposit the fees. I opened my eyes and saw her enter the office. When she was leaving, I somehow managed to slip out of the classroom and follow her, creeping behind her, unnoticed. My mother stopped on the way to buy some sugar cane for us to eat after school. It was then that she turned around and saw me, and without thinking, gave me a wallop with that sugar cane stick. She was very angry, more so because she had to take me back to school. In retrospect, I feel the school should have been held accountable for the fact that a little child slipped out of the premises unnoticed, but that thought never crossed my mother's mind.

When I was old enough for formal schooling, I moved to Mahavir Mahavidyalaya, also a co-ed school. But for some reason, I attended that school for just a year. I was happy to leave since somehow it did not have any attraction for me, and even as a young child, I could see that as a school, it had no character. By that time, we had moved to Purohitji-Ka-Bagh and the hunt for a school began again. We were on the lookout for a school that was nearby, within walking distance of our house. A distant cousin, a teacher at a government school in a small town, happened to visit us since he had been transferred to Jaipur. He was going to join a school at Topkhana, which was just across the street from our house. He suggested that I join that school. It was a beautiful heritage building, but no one gave a thought to the fact that it was a boys' school! The students were all from a lower middle-class background, very different from us. They were sons of farmers and blue-collar workers. The only girl there was the principal's daughter. I don't know how I survived there and what I studied. I was terrified of going to school, trying to avoid any interaction with the students. I remember we had a common bathroom. I would stick around with the principal's daughter as much as I could. Fortunately, my mother realized the mistake they

had   made,   and as soon as there was a vacancy at Maharaja's Multipurpose Higher Secondary School, the school where my other sisters were studying, I got admission there. I think I was sent to Topkhana as an interim school because I had to wait for admissions to other schools. I don't know what my mother was thinking. Culturally and socially, it was a very different place. My cousin had assured my parents that he would watch over me, but how could he, when he was teaching? I think it was when my mother saw my progress report cards and my

Maharaja's Multipurpose Higher Secondary School

shoddy workbooks that she realized I was in the wrong place. Fortunately, this experience lasted only three or four months.

Then began the golden period of my school days. I had been through an ordeal by fire in the three previous schools and the Maharaja's Multipurpose Higher Secondary School, though a mouthful to pronounce, was a great place to nurture one's talents.

I joined in Class VI. By that time, my two older sisters, Sudha and Uma, had already passed out. My sister Rama was in Class X.

Maharaja's School had the distinction of being the first girls' school in Jaipur. Started in 1866 by Maharaja Sawai Ram Singh, the Maharaja of Jaipur, the building had been donated to the school by the Natani family at the request of the Maharaja. Descendants of the family still live in an adjoining *haveli*. The building is a heritage structure and is built in the Rajputana style of architecture, with a huge gate leading to four courtyards and rooms on either side, which must have been residential rooms once but have now been converted to classrooms. I believe in the beginning, when this was the only girls' school, there were around 5000 students studying there, and they had to have two shifts. Girls from royal families as well as daughters of expats studied in the school. An alumnus of the school, now teaching there, Priti Kalra, has this to say about the school. 'It is a school where caste and class divide has never existed.' Another alumnus, Shashikala Pareek, who has been a principal of the school, says, 'The school has stood the test of time. It is one of the most prestigious schools in the country and has contributed immensely to women's education for the last 153 years.'

We all walked to school, except Rama, since she was very pretty and all the boys would follow her! So, she was allowed to take the school bus. Sometimes, Jaggannath, the bus driver, would take pity on us and give us a free ride too, the advantage of a government vehicle! I also remember how he kept us amused. The horn of his bus did not work for as long as I can remember, and he would imitate a horn with his cracked voice to disperse people and vehicles. He never got any extra money for his efforts!

This was the school I joined, the school which I feel contributed immensely to my development not only in academics but also in extracurricular activities. I loved going to school and made my first close friends there. The teachers were dedicated and took a keen interest in the students. There was much to do in school and the freedom to do so. Having come from a co-ed school and then a boys' school, I had never had the opportunity to excel as inhibitions always held me back.

As mentioned earlier, Maharaja's School had three *chowks*, which were used by the students and the fourth as a stadium for assemblies and sports events. In the first courtyard, the girls' tiffins from home were left on a bench. I had two Muslim friends, Nafisa and Hasina. They were my partners in crime for a lot of mischief we did in school. We had stitching classes, which I was very poor at. We had to cut patterns on paper and then measure the cloth against it for a good cut. I remember Nafisa would measure the paper cutting of underpants or a pyjama for me, cover it with her massive thighs and when no one was looking, pass it to me. I don't think I would have got through the tailoring class without her. Hasina, on the other hand, was unknowingly feeding me with some delicious meals. The fragrance of her tiffin on the bench was a great temptation and I would steal two *parathas* from her brass *dabba* and eat them with her delicious pickles before she came out for lunch. After all these years, recently, there was a phone call for me from Pakistan. Imagine my surprise and pleasure when I heard the voice at the other end. It was Hasina and she wanted me to talk to her children and grandchildren. She introduced me to them as the girl who used to polish off her *dabbas* in school!

My mother would give us a substantial amount of food in our tiffin boxes. But the aroma of kachoris in the canteen on rainy days would entice me to wander around the canteen longingly. But I never had any extra money. Observing my furtive glances, the *canteenwala* suggested a deal. He said that if I could give him old newspapers for wrapping food in the canteen, he would give me four *kachoris* in exchange! This barter system worked very well for some time till someone reported me and I was called into the costume room by a teacher and in front of several people she informed everyone about my barter system, which she deemed some grave crime. I was asked to stop it. And that was the end of my kachoris. I do think that instead of being chided for this, I should have been lauded for my entrepreneurship. In these days of start-ups and *Shark Tank*, my venture would have been considered a 'business experiment'. I think teachers should not be harsh and judgemental. They must understand the psychological effect such humiliation can have on a young mind, especially if they cannot understand what their misdemeanour was.

Another canteen mishap that happened was at Maharanis' College. I was friends with a girl called Chitra Mathur. She suggested we share a credit account at the canteen, something accepted by the proprietor, Mr Popli. This canteen had delicious samosas and burgers. While I was very frugal and had canteen food only occasionally, Chitra ate every single day, gorging on snacks and tea, drawing up a huge bill and then disappearing. I was left to pay the bill! It was quite a large sum for those days. I don't remember whether I was spanked for it. I was always hesitant to ask my parents for money, but later I came to know that each child from the family would take a little bit of money from Kakaji's coat pocket. It used to hang on the door and very often he would shout out to my mother, 'Bhagwati, I am missing some money from my pocket!' My mother would shout back saying that she had not taken any money. I wonder whether any of my siblings suffered pangs of conscience when they heard this. Much later, they confessed to this stealing. In the bargain, my father's coat pocket would have holes in it! Later, we all started earning a little from doing radio programmes and could indulge ourselves without troubling our parents.

I am proud to be an alumni of the school. Being termed a Multipurpose School, it really widened our faculties. Besides the usual subjects, a multitude of courses were offered. Domestic science, tailoring, cooking, singing, dance, debates, sports and participation in National Cadet Corps, and the Red Cross, Girl Guides, we took up everything we could. And we paid nothing. We owe it to the government for giving us a school that gave us a holistic education. None of us would have been able to afford the fees demanded by these additional extracurricular activities elsewhere. We got them free at the school. We travelled with the school; we participated in sports tournaments all over the state as well as debates, dramas, youth festivals—everything mostly sponsored by the school. I was selected to participate in a mock session of the Commonwealth, of which the former army chief, General J.N. Chaudhuri was the president and I the vice-president.

I have enjoyed other political positions too. We didn't have any houses in school, but we had a parliament. There was a cabinet, for which candidates were selected by the teachers and students and were given the title of 'ministers'. We campaigned like one does in a real election. Posters were made, our voters were fed from the campaign funds if the candidate had any money! When I was in Class IX, I was elected the food minister and stood up in the

House to discuss the sanitation and the cleanliness in the canteen. I recall that we had invited the education minister of Rajasthan and he sanctioned funds towards repairing the leakage from the canteen ceiling after my speech! Other ministers put forth their own problems for discussion. Our elections were fair and civilized. If there were two candidates for the same post, they would decide through a discussion, not a vote, and then come to a majority decision. No chappals were thrown at one another, no abusive words used and the dignity of the House was always maintained. In Class X, I stood for the post of the prime minister (PM) and was elected unanimously. The PM's duties were to see that discipline was observed, that every student was in uniform, homework completed and to ensure that everyone got a chance to participate in all school events. I was prime minister for a year, albeit a mock prime minister, so I have no regrets that I will never have that post in real life!

We learnt so many things practically rather than from books. I went on several Red Cross camps, the first to Mount Abu, Rajasthan. We were taught how to work in the community, and they had clinics to teach us first aid. Then there were cultural activities. We learnt a lot about India and that there were people who were not as fortunate as we were. The camp had both boys and girls. So, you had the opportunity of listening to different points of view. No matter how much of a vigil the teachers kept, there were bound to be some mishaps! I made a friend, called Sidney, from Goa. The crucifix

With Lal Bahadur Shastri

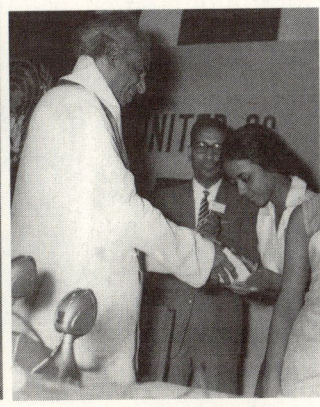

With V.K. Krishna Menon

he presented me, I wore for a long time, and I think it still graces a trunk in my parents' house!

At one of these camps, there was once a tragedy. One morning, we got the news that one of the participants, Pappinder, a girl from Indore, had passed away during the night. I remember it was raining and there was a chanting of Sikh prayers. We heard that she had juvenile diabetes and had not informed anyone. Perhaps her sugar levels went down drastically. Of course, none of us knew about diabetes, or for that matter about death. That is why that incident is still vivid in my mind.

On Gandhi Jayanti, each student had to spin yarn. We were given a spindle, *takli*, and for one hour, we were expected to spin. In government schools, we were encouraged to take part in a lot of activities. We were made aware of our surroundings, about the country and our social responsibilities. I do not know if any of these activities still exist in those schools. I remember how we knitted sweaters for the *jawans,* making our small contribution to the war effort during the war with Pakistan. I felt so connected to those war heroes that even later, during the Kargil War, I accepted an offer to go and perform for the *jawans* on the border. But the keyboard player, Raju Lalwani, chickened out at the last moment.

I took classical vocal music as a subject. My music teacher was one Miss Uma Bhatt. I was very good at it and scored high marks. I think my mother must have been secretly pleased at my prowess, since girls were expected to be good at singing and playing instruments as this was an assurance for a good matrimonial match! All my sisters either sang or played an instrument like the sitar. I must give my mother full marks for her perseverance. When you have so many daughters in a middle-class family, you can only give them whatever is within your means to increase their prospects of marriage. We

This is the only instrument
I have played all my life

were oblivious of her long-term plans and went along. We would walk to school from Purohitji-Ka-Bagh, quite a distance away and then after school, we would proceed straight to Chaura Rasta to Kala Sansthan for our music lessons. Each of us learnt something. I learnt Kathak, Sudha, the sitar, and Uma, vocal music.

Meanwhile, my interest in music was growing. I was often chosen for all the school competitions. I tell people that 'Pyasa kue ke paas jata hai, kua pyase ke paas nahin aata,' meaning that the thirsty goes to the well, the well does not come to the one who needs water. Your talent is first recognized in school. I participated in debates. A topic was given to you and the first practice was usually at school. We would come home with the topic and ask our father to help us out. He was a great reader and very knowledgeable. He had been the editor of a lesser-known newspaper, Prajapati, so was well-versed in current topics. I started debating in Class VI. Actually, it was my sister Rama who started debating and by association I was also roped in. Father would very systematically tutor us for it, and I remember his opening sentence: 'I would like to say that my esteemed opponent has raised her voice . . .' He came up with very relevant examples and we both became quite adept at debating.

I was good at some subjects but could not handle English and maths. Our English teacher was Miss Bahadur and I was quite impressed by her. I am not so sure about her being impressed by me! I never got more than 3 out of 5 in English. The passing average was 3.1/2 and today I am ashamed to confess that very often I tampered with the marks with a blade, scratching and adding another half on my report card. My mother could not be fooled so easily. She would run her fingers over the space and knew at once that I had changed the numbers!

My mother was only VIIIth pass, but she was able to tutor us even in subjects like maths, which we disliked. She used a Hindi book called Chakravarty to teach us maths. She would read the book and then explain the problems to us. Interestingly, she used real-life examples to teach us. Whenever we asked her for even Rs 5 for a picnic, she would apply maths! 'For you, it is only Rs 5, but multiply it by 5 for each one and what does it come to? 5x5.' She would use the 'therefore' and the 'because' in maths. 'If one of you walks 4 miles in one hour, how much will the five of you walk in the same time?' She was very involved in our studies. She was the one who attended all the parent–teacher meetings. But she always got the report cards signed by our father. She was always a little hesitant before presenting these to Kakaji since all her children did very well in extracurricular activities but never excelled at studies. Sudha was intelligent but got a supplementary I think because she got typhoid at the time of her exams. Then she went on

Gorgeous couple: my father Indra Narayan Pandey with my mother Bhagwati Pandey

to do a double MA, in English and Sanskrit. Tripti and Rama were average students. The two sisters who lived away from us, Deepa and Binno, did very well at studies I suppose because they were single kids and received a great deal of attention from their foster parents—our uncles and aunts. To add a little bit of drama, and perhaps some sympathy, I can say I studied under a lamp post. There were two young boys who were the nephews of the caretaker of the property. They were called Rupa and Panna. They came from Jobner, a tiny village on the outskirts of Jaipur, to help their uncle with household chores. They were very good students and would come after work and sit under the lamp post to study. My mother realized that perhaps they could induce me to study too. She requested them to teach me maths. So, I was given tuition literally under a lamp post by Rupa and Panna. They both did very well academically and went on to become officers in the cooperative movement. I shall always be indebted to them for giving me so much of their time, despite the limited study time at their disposal.

My parents were very good at Hindi and poetry and my mother taught us till we were in high school. I think she helped us with Hindi right till our BA. She seemed to have read everything that was prescribed in our course: Surdas, Rahim, Kabir and Sarat Chandra, among others. She instilled a love for the Hindi language in all of us and herself used the language so beautifully, with the most appropriate idioms and proverbs.

Dramatics was another sphere I began to enjoy. My first role was in a ballet called *Kumar Sambhav* and I was given the role of the sage Narad, the travelling musician and storyteller. Even though it was a small role and the only dialogue I had was to keep repeating 'Narayan, Narayan' to the tune of the *ektara*, I tried to understand the character and perhaps added some dimension to my performance. But my USP was that I could play the *ektara* in rhythm. I feel the teacher should have helped me understand the character better. Then there were some one-act plays and drama competitions in which I always came away with the 'Best Actress' award. While still at school, I started taking part in radio plays too and contributing to youth programmes on radio.

College opened up a wealth of choices. An exciting activity that I took part in for two years from college was the Republic Day parade in Delhi. I was selected to represent Rajasthan in the state tableau. We camped at Talkatora Gardens for a month, interacting with authentic folk dancers from all over India. I learnt about different costumes, languages, cuisines and realized at a very young age how diverse our country is. It kindled a life-long interest in folk music and dance, and I have used all these different traditions and languages with ease in my performances. The feeling of patriotism was still moving for us. My grandfather had been a Congress member,

My alma mater: Maharani College, Jaipur

In Talkatora Garden performing for the then Prime Minister Indira Gandhiji

and as you pass the President and see the flag of the country, along with thousands of spectators, it is a moment of pride and emotion.

Maharani's College was known for its English plays under the enthusiastic direction of the Head of Department of English, Miss Hemlata Prabhu. Another teacher, I think she taught sociology, was Mrs Maya Israni, who took part in plays for All India Radio. There was a lot of theatre activity and Mrs Israni decided to try me out. At that time, the college used to send one-act plays for inter-college competitions. So, I participated in one, directed by Mrs Israni, and went for a competition. The play was called *Dr Doklani*. Vinay Shukla, who later became a well-known director in Bollywood and directed the famous film *Godmother,* was selected from Rajasthan College to play the male role. The competition was in Gwalior, and I got the best actress award. I have one hilarious memory of a performance in a play, again directed by Maya Israni titled *Jhoota Khwab*. We all were nervous, including the director, because we were under-rehearsed. In one of the scenes, Manish Kothari and I,

With Indira Gandhiji

With the principal, Mrs Bhartiya, when I was the general secretary of the college

playing a Muslim couple, were lying on our bed. The director knew we did not know our lines and was probably biting her nails! We were speaking in Urdu, using words like 'Allah' and 'Khuda' in our conversation. At one point, while delivering a dialogue, I, in my confusion, shouted 'Hey Ram' instead of 'Allah'. The audience was in splits and so were we. But to my utter surprise, I still got the best actress award. I wonder what the other actresses did! Pinchoo Kapoor, a leading theatre director of Jaipur who was one of the judges, also had to hand me the award. I remember he came up to me, handed me the award and whispered in my ear, 'Atrocious!' I looked around in embarrassment to see if anyone had heard him, but since he was quite huge, I was dwarfed by him and no one heard the remark. I must have been what in Hindi is called an *'andhon mein kana raja'*, the best of the worst.

Later I had the opportunity to work under Kapoor's direction. We did *Kanchenjunga*, written by Nemi Chandra Jain. I played the mistress and Bharat Ratna Bhargava, my servant. I played the oldest character even though I was the youngest. The make-up was always improvised. I used to apply kajal on my teeth to make them seem discoloured. I never thought about age, only the potential of the character. The story was about the daily humiliation meted out to the servant by the family. When he wins a lottery, everyone starts running after him, pampering him. I had a beautiful dialogue that had to be delivered in the midst of a lot of chaos. This was lost in most of the performances, in the confusion of everyone speaking at the same time. Once, determined to get my word in, I must have raised my finger to warn them, when Bharat bit my finger! The next time we did that scene, Bharat recalling the last episode, burst out laughing on stage and could not stop. He remembers the incident to this day.

Then suddenly there was an exodus of directors and actors from the NSD. Mohan

With my friends Reena and Rajyashree

Playing the lead role of Jasma in *Jasma Odan*, directed by Bhanu Bharti, in Jaipur

Acting as Rani in the play *Shuturmurg*, directed by
Mohan Maharishi, with co-actors S. Vasudev Singh
and Vijay Bakaya

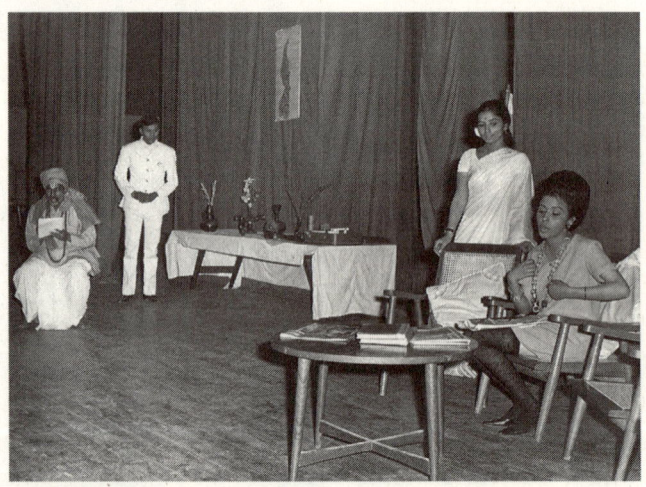

Acting in *Kutte Ki Maut*, directed by Pinchoo
Kapoor, with my sister Rama Pandey

Mahrishi did plays such as *Bhumija* with Meenakshi Sharma and
Rama. I was inexplicably drawn to theatre and would go and watch
the rehearsals with Rama. Once being short of actors in a *bidai* scene
for Sita, from the Ramayan, Mohan asked some of the audience to
come and join the group of girls. That was the beginning for me,
as a junior artiste, and I must have cried so well that the director
noticed me and from there I started doing major roles starting with

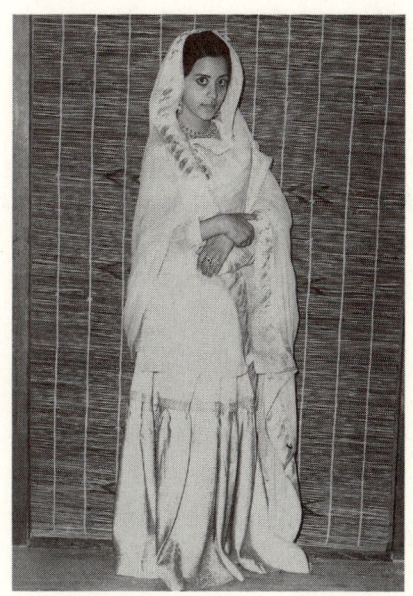

As Hajjo in *Azhar Ka Khwab*,
adapted in Urdu by Qudsia
Zaidi, based on George Bernard
Shaw's *Pygmalion*

As Priyangumanjari
in Mohan Rakesh's
Ashadh Ka Ek Din

Priyangumanjari in *Ashadh Ka Ek Din*. Then I did *Shuturmurg, Azhar Ka Khwab* (*Pygmalion*) and *Jasma Odan*. There was a lot of objection from my parents even though Rama had already been doing plays. There were some unique rules: no interacting with boys, no late nights. Of course there were late nights, 8 p.m., which was like midnight for them. Bharat and Mohan would come to drop us back on their bicycles. My mother would be pacing the terrace, waiting for me. And her first sentence would be, '*Jahaan se aai ho wahin wapas chali jao*,' which translated means 'Go back to where you have come from.' In later years, I would tease my mother saying, 'If I had done what you asked me to do, where would I have been now?' And my mother would have a good laugh.

So, I did not follow my mother's orders and stayed to follow my dream. School, college, home and theatre—these became my sanctuary and when the time came to bid my college farewell, I had already embarked on my journey into the myriad roles I was destined to play. Plutarch's words spurred me on: 'The process may seem strange and yet it is very true. I did not so much gain the knowledge of things by the words, as words by the experience I had of things.'

Chapter 4

Bonds: Mortgaged to Kashmir

I've never seen anywhere as beautiful as Kashmir. It has something to do with the fact that the Valley is very small and the mountains very big. So, you have a miniature countryside surrounded by the Himalayas.

—Salman Rushdie

Kashmir! It was a name that conjured up romance and beauty, with the heartthrobs of our generation Shashi Kapoor, Shammi Kapoor and Rajendra Kumar singing love songs to the heroines while dancing on the slopes of snow-clad mountains.

I could only dream about it. Little did I know that an opportunity would present itself very soon for me to actually visit the Valley. It so happened that the school announced that a trip to Kashmir was being organized. My joy knew no bounds. We were asked to take our parents' permission; the hitch being that we had to deposit Rs 150. I could hardly wait for school to be over so that I could go home and get their permission. With my head among the clouds of Kashmir, I confronted my mother, asking her to let me go. She gave me a painful look, a look all of us nine siblings were familiar with. Her litany was the same: 'It is not possible. Rs 150! Where will your father, the only earning member, produce this huge amount? Besides you are seven sisters, and each one will demand the same.' I could feel the sinking of the mountains, the avalanche of snow over my head—how could I let such an opportunity slip by? I begged and pleaded and my ever-resourceful mother had an idea. 'Why don't you ask Principal Mrs Bimla Sharma to let you go for free? Tell her you have brought the school many trophies and laurels which should buy you a free passage to Kashmir.'

A little confused by this suggestion and a little embarrassed too, the next day, I ventured to meet the principal in her office. Never having to deal with the protocol of such a meeting, I was going to walk straight into the office. I did not spare a glance for the *joshanji*, as the female peons were called, till she stood before me in her green lehnga, matching our uniform and bright yellow *odhni*. She blocked my way asking where I was going. An unnecessary question, I thought, since there was only one way to go. I told her I wanted to see the principal. She would have none of it. The peons in every office are the gatekeepers and the decision-makers for any entry for a meeting with authority. I went back dejected.

After a couple of more efforts, I found a solution; after all I was my ever-resourceful mother's daughter! I carried some gifts and again sought an audience with Mrs Sharma. Before the *joshanji* could say no, I unashamedly emptied my bag of goodies into her *odhni!* I don't remember what the bribe was, but it worked! I was let in!

With a great deal of trepidation, I crossed the *lakshman rekha*. Mrs Sharma looked up at me from over her glasses and asked what I wanted. There was an awe about our headmistress, Mrs Bimla Sharma. She was fair, with curly hair tied up in a bun. She looked intimidating but was known to have a soft heart. She asked me what the problem was. Tears come to me very easily. Whenever I feel hesitant or unsure, tears start rolling down my cheeks. This makes the listener soft towards my story. My appeal seems to be more desperate than the problem and disconcerts whoever is listening to my story. I started with my sob story, from the beginning. I pleaded to be exempted from the fee that was being charged. This was the story my mother had made me memorize; how we were seven sisters, with only one earning member, my father, who was a government servant. All the sisters were the pride of the school, having won every cup at every function, be it sports or debating, dance, music or acting. Then followed my own heartfelt plea. 'You have to do something for me. I cannot pay for the trip, even the mere Rs 150.' She looked up at me over her glasses and gave me a quizzical smile, saying, 'Rules are rules.' But she asked me to come the next day.

My mother was waiting for me and the first question she asked was, 'Did you get to speak to Mrs B. Sharma?' I first told her that she had been responsible for dragging my *izzat,* my dignity, through the mud, adding that Mrs Sharma had asked me to come to her the following day.

The next day, I walked into Mrs Sharma's office confidently. No *joshanji* stood in my way. Mrs Sharma began by saying that she had thought about my problem in every detail, but the only solution she had come up with was that I could get a 50 per cent discount, paying only Rs 75. She went on to say that she could not discriminate, since all the girls came from similar backgrounds. She would have to find an excuse and say that Ila had a special concession because of her contribution to the extracurricular activities in the school. That was the best she could do.

I felt on top of the world but had to deal with my mother. I told her half the battle had been won, one wall of the fort had been conquered. My mother mulled over this, and I knew she was calculating where she could get that Rs 75 from. Her usual response, when she was favouring one of us, was always, 'Don't mention this to anyone.' That was usually a sign that she would handle the problem and would not disappoint the pleader. Like something out of a magician's bag, she produced the Rs 75 and I was on cloud nine and already dreaming of Kashmir.

But as usual, there is always a twist in the story, some interference which takes you down a step or two. My younger sister, Deepa, who lived with my uncle, my father's brother, in Jodhpur, usually came over to spend her summer holidays with us. Though she was pampered by our uncle and aunt, her foster parents, she was always envious of the fact that she had been deprived of all her siblings' company and the good times we had together. She started crying, that if Ila was going, she had to go too. My mother

With my sister Deepa and brother young Piyush Pandey

explained to her that with great difficulty I had been accepted with a discount! She was not even a student of the school, so it would be impossible for her to join the school trip. But she had a card up her sleeve! Putting me in my place she condescendingly said that she was in a position to pay the Rs 150!

Once again, my mother made me the sacrificial lamb. I was to go and bell the cat and tell Mrs Sharma that my mother had said that I could go only on the condition that Deepa was allowed to go too as a guest. In my mind I thought this was being a bit facetious, but my mother was not one to relent. I sheepishly crept into the headmistress's room. She said, 'Now what is your problem?' I started my seven sisters' story again! She laughed and asked me to come back the next day. But luck was on my side, or should I say, Deepa's side. It so happened that the group was not meeting its target in numbers because of finances. So, Deepa became part of this group.

My dreams seemed to be coming true. Kashmir had caught the imagination of a whole generation of Indians. Doordarshan, our only TV channel, promoted Kashmir, though in black and white; Hindi films were shot on location in Kashmir, in brilliant colours and many of these became hits because Kashmir was one of the characters. For my adolescent mind, Kashmir was the place for romance. Before the journey to Kashmir started, my mind was already ripe for romance! When I look back at all these experiences, I realize how they became part of my emotional memory. My observation converted into dreams, retaining several moments which I later used in my writings: characters, words, accents and locations, which keep coming back to me as I write.

Most of us had never been out of Rajasthan and were familiar only with sand and dust storms and bare land. Not that my imagination was bereft of romance; we had our forts and *chhatris*, tales of valour and chivalry, enough to fire the imagination of a sensitive young girl. But Kashmir was to carry me to another sphere. Imagine a bus journey from Rajasthan to Kashmir, loaded with girls screaming and shouting, suddenly breathing the air of freedom, away from parental supervision.

We stopped at the Golden Temple in Amritsar, and I was introduced to the Sikh religion. In the shadow of the golden dome and the beautifully clean courtyard, we relished our *kada prasad*. It now strikes me as strange that most of us have such a poor knowledge of the other religions in our country. India is a multicultural and multi-religious country, yet we hardly encounter the rituals of other religions. The Golden Temple was my introduction to the history and culture of Punjab and of the Sikh religion. After Amritsar, we stopped at Pathankot and Jammu and then began our journey to Kashmir. The landscape and with it the world seemed to change. I looked at everything with rose-coloured glasses—the towering mountains, the streams and waterfalls shimmering over the slopes, the sounds of which still linger in my ears, the small wayside *dhabas* where we stopped for lunch, the taste of *rajma* with pure ghee and rice, a new flavour for someone who had never tasted *rajma*. The fragrances were different, the sounds magical, enticing, almost sensual, piling on my romance with Kashmir. The most inspiring person was Mrs Sharma. In school she was always a distant administrator, very formal in a starched sari and blouse. Now she was in a completely different avatar, almost unrecognizable in a checked kurta and salwar. And she was singing a romantic film song in the bus 'Aapki nazaron ne samjha pyaar ke kaabil mujhe.' We were tickled pink and the relationship changed at that moment. So, the romance of Kashmir had also brushed past her.

I still remember the caressing cold, and the smell of pine and fir on reaching Srinagar. I was in seventh heaven. Since we had gone on an exchange programme with a school there, we were put up in a municipal school. We faced several problems, one of them being a shortage of hot water since we were many of us. Always enterprising and creative, Deepa and I discovered that someone, I am sure on the side, was selling a bucket of water for four annas. I decided to make use of Deepa, my bank with several *chauanis*, or quarters! I knew that she had been given some extra pocket money by her guardians. As for me, after the Rs 75, my budget was over and my purse was empty! Whenever faced with any opposition from her, I would start my refrain that I had done her a favour by getting her along. She had no option but to buy a bucket which she shared with me.

Perhaps it was fate, or some call from the past, that my first relationship with Kashmir began at this first stop at Srinagar. Beyond the low wall of the school stood a magnificent mansion, in the typical Kashmiri architectural style. I could not keep my eyes off that structure, wondering what lay inside. Then I noticed that two equally curious young girls, my age, would peep out at us from behind the curtains.

They looked like the proverbial flowers in a garden, rosy-cheeked, heads covered with a scarf, their strange dress, a *phiran,* following us strangers with inquisitive eyes. A *shayar* has said '*Khubsoorti ko hamne aksar bhatakte dekha hai,*' meaning 'Many a time have we seen beauty wandering, oblivious of itself.' Surely, the poet was talking about these girls or perhaps of all Kashmiri girls. Soon we started talking to them. Their names were Zaitun and Shamim.

There are many thoughts which come back to haunt one now, when Kashmir has become a troubled area. For us at that time, it was ours, and we took pride in the beauty of Kashmir and its innocent people, away from the rest of India. Before we left, the two girls invited us over for 'high tea' at their home. We were girls from a Maharaja's Multipurpose background, unfamiliar with English phrases and idioms and at that time wondered what high tea meant. For us, tea meant a cup of tea with a samosa. What was 'high' about it? we wondered. But this was an experience beyond our imagination. The minute we crossed the threshold, we were in a wonder world: the wooden house, staircases that told many a tale with their creaking sounds to our footsteps, and beautiful carpets covering wooden floors. For a middle-class girl from Rajasthan, it was a dream. I can say that I was touched by beauty in all its myriad colours. I tasted their bread for the first time, imbibed the subtle flavour of the Kashmiri tea, *kehwa*, heard the word *dastarkhwan* for the first time. When we said goodbye, they gave us a gift—a red box of papier mâché. We were embarrassed that we had no gift to give them. We shed tears on parting, thinking we would never meet again. Years later, when Kashmir had become part of my life, with platonic relationships thrown in, I was destined to meet one of the sisters again. Over a cup of tea at the Srinagar Golf Club, where I was taken by my golfer brother-in-law Najam, whom I affectionately call B-I-L, short for brother-in-law, my thoughts went back to my first visit. Seeing the beautiful face of Zaitun before my eyes, I mentioned to Najam that my first friend in Srinagar had been a little girl called Zaitun. He gave me a quizzical look saying, 'Zaitun? There is a woman who comes to this club with her golfer-husband and her name is Zaitun!' And wonder of wonders, he saw a young woman and said, 'And there she is!' As if from a genie's bottle, she was facing me and being introduced. Who would have imagined that a fleeting meeting from the past would have had such an impact on both of us? She remembered me and had followed my songs from Rajasthan into the Valley. As for me, my memory of her was so vivid that when years later I adapted Ibsen's *Peer Gynt* and placed it in the Valley, my heroine's sister was named Zaitun, meaning olive. It is strange how some names and people stay in your subconscious.

As Ase in *Peer Ghani*

Our next stop was Gulmarg, with its rolling meadows and beautiful views of the snow-capped mountains. Then there was a climb by foot to Khilanmarg, about 14 kilometres uphill. The few who could afford horses hired them; the rest had to walk up. For me, it was again a matter of experiencing a horse ride accompanied by the *ghorawalas*, in their *phirans*, no less than the beautiful Adonis. Deepa said she would hire a horse. I asked her what she meant by that. She looked at me angrily and I unashamedly reminded her that I had brought her along. I surveyed the formidable mountain and announced that since I was older, I would use the horse to go up. So, it was decided that one of us would ride the horse on the way up and the other on the way down. Then started one more romantic journey. I imagined I was alone, the heroine on a horse, Sadhna, accompanied by a hero, Rajendra Kumar in the 1965 Bollywood film *Arzoo* shot in Kashmir. I was the '*phoolon ki rani, baharon ki mallika*', the flower princess, the spring queen. The horses followed their own path and often we criss-crossed other horse-riders. My *ghorewala* added to my imagination by using dialogues mouthed by Shashi Kapoor in the film *Jab Jab Phool Khile* (1965). Those 14 kilometres sealed my romance with the Kashmiri horseman! I even had ideas of getting off and walking alongside, talking to him. But he shattered my dreams by goading me on, 'It is going to rain. If it does rain, you won't be able to go sledging in Khilanmarg, neither you nor your sister.' I was brought back to earth, to real relationships with their problems. My sister, whom I had forgotten! I asked him to go down the hill as fast as he could to fetch her. He asked how he would recognize my sister. I hit upon a brilliant idea. I pulled off a sweater, a distinct green and lemon colour, knitted for me by my sister Uma, telling him he should wave that around shouting, 'The sister of this yellow sweater, the sister of this yellow sweater!' Sure enough, my idea worked and Deepa was soon with me, a smile of victory on the *ghorewala*'s face. Of course I had an ulterior motive too; Deepa was my cash box for the sledge ride! The finale came when the horseman produced some walnuts from the pocket of his *phiran* and offered them to us. I hoped I could get a ride back on the horse, but of course, the contract had been made and I had to forgo my wish.

The sledge ride was another unforgettable experience, Deepa and I and the sledge driver. Speeding down the steep hills, clutching on to a *phiran,* the wearer of which sang Bollywood film songs that reverberated through the snow-clad mountains, and with Wordsworth I could say, 'But to be young was very heaven!'

I imagined I was Saira Bano in *Junglee,* dashing down the slopes on a sledge, with the lovable Shammi Kapoor shouting 'Yahoo!' What more could a girl from the arid land of Rajasthan wish for? I lived my romance to the hilt.

The memories of the *ghorewala* had hardly left my mind when the *shikarawala* took his place. They are all endearing rascals. Gliding down the Dal Lake, with the backdrop of the hills and the houseboats, he sang *'Pardesion se na ankhiyan milana'*, a song sung by the charming Shashi Kapoor from the film *Jab Jab Phool Khile* with a twinkle in his eyes, while several *shikaras* crowded around us selling Kashmiri jewellery and trinkets. I had tears in my eyes, as if he were singing to me. He asked if we had ever met Shashi Kapoor and of course, we said yes. Whenever I met Shashi Kapoor years later at Prithvi Theatre, I wished I could have had the courage to tell him that I had had several romantic episodes in his name in the Kashmir of my childhood!

The horse rides, the sledges, the *shikaras*—these have been my strongest images of Kashmir, which no one can erase. Then a crowd of Kashmiris entered my life. Somehow Kashmiris were drawn to me and I to them. My first memory is of Rita Zibbu in Maharajas' School. I kept the green glass bangles she gave me for a long time. Then there was Rita Handoo, another classmate in school. Once again in my play *Riyaaz*, I recalled the name of Rita Handoo. There was Vijay Bakaya, who also worked in theatre. There was the Shivpuri family, who gave us that brilliant actor, Om Shivpuri. But these did not have the *jhalak,* the charm, of Kashmir; some came from Rajasthan, some from UP and Delhi and had no connection with Kashmir even though they may have spoken Kashmiri and dined only on Kashmiri cuisine. They were Kashmiris, and yet not Kashmiris, without that innocent fragrance, the *mehak,* the fragrance, of Kashmir. But they became good friends. Of course, Bakaya sahib's was an intellectual association, without the *ishq,* romance, of the *shikarawalas* and the *ghorawala.* I sometimes refer to him as 'the window of my wisdom'. This was also the time when I was introduced to Kashmiri cuisine by Vijay's mother and words like *kehwa, nun chai, yakhni, dum aloo* and *kadam ka saag* became part of my culinary vocabulary. For the first time, I ventured to try non-vegetarian food.

Of course, my vision of an innocent and peaceful Kashmir was disrupted by later happenings and something happened to the rosy-cheeked innocence of those *phiran*-clad children. It is as if they were caught between the devil and the deep sea and their alienation from their country was manifested in the immigration of those who fled that beautiful valley to settle in the hot plains of the country. And many of these were my close friends and I have lived with their sorrow for years now, sharing their tragedy of a lost homeland.

When I was at NSD, I met another Kashmiri who became a good friend, Shibban Ganjoo. NSD seemed to be a favourite haunt of Kashmiris: M.K. Raina, Bansi Kaul, Virendra Razdan, K.K. Raina. When I came to Bombay, three of these Kashmiris became my closest friends: K.K. Raina, Virendra Razdan and Binny Latif—two Pundits, one Muslim. They were the purest Kashmiris. Their first step out of Kashmir was to NSD, New Delhi. They even spoke the language. And for their holidays, they would go back to Srinagar.

I remember when I was shooting a song sequence for Tahir Hussein's film *Hamara Khandaan* (1988) in Srinagar, I was curious to see KK's house. I told Binny to take me there. He did, but I did not have the courage to go in and meet his family. Binny tried to drag me, holding my hand, but I had a strange kind of apprehension about their acceptance of me. I don't know why. I stopped at the top of the lane and looked towards his house. I wonder what middle-class norms held me back. I can still picture KK's father, affectionately called Bobaji, sitting at the window, with a *hookah*. I am sure they would have given me a warm welcome. I remember the locality, Habba Kadal, a colony inhabited by Kashmiri Brahmins. Within that was Ganpatyar, where KK's ancestral house was. And yet when later we went to Yousmarg, Virendra and I visited Binny's house, travelling on a rattling village bus, where I stood shoulder to shoulder with the local population, unwashed and unbathed, but carrying the smell of Kashmir, just like the Rajasthanis carry the smell of *gobar* (cow dung). I still remember Binny's mother and the lavish feast she laid out for us. They had been big farmers but were also enveloped by the happenings in Kashmir and were drawn into it willy-nilly like the majority of Kashmiris. His mother and his sisters-in-law were delighted to have us with them. That irked KK even more since he said that his parents had cooked lunch for the entire cast from NSD, including Manohar Singh, one of the best theatre actors to come out of NSD. The hospitality in Kashmir was way beyond our expectations. I am reminded of another high tea, this time in Lahore, at the house of Fauzia, a leading socialite of the city. Her dining table stretched across the large dining room and every inch of space was laden with delicacies. I believe that the hospitality in Kashmir and Lahore far outweighs the hospitality in other parts of India, perhaps matched only by the exuberant Punjabis.

The influence of Kashmir was so great that in my subconscious, I created many stories. By now the Kashmiri 'gang' had become a strong creative partner, especially KK. Living and working with them, I picked up quite a lot of the language, so much so that they could not discuss anything private in my presence. The first of my Kashmiri stories came out on the Kashmiri Channel, Kashir, *Maalded* and *Safed Jharne Ka Matmela Paani*. The second story was about how a simple, honest man can be corrupted by circumstance and society; a stream is clear but soiled by people around it. This depicted the corruption of Kashmir.

The call of Kashmir beckoned me continuously. One day, Wizcraft, the event management company, called me, asking me to perform in Kashmir for an event they were hosting for the launch of the Kashmir Channel, Kashir, for Doordarshan. By that time, in 1993, I had become famous through that one song that catapulted me to fame, 'Choli Ke Peechhey'. The audience clamoured for that song. But somehow it did not feel right. 'Choli Ke Peechhey' in Srinagar? So, I told them that I would first sing Kashmiri songs. I had imbibed so much of the ambience of Kashmir, their markets, the Dal Lake, the rural areas and had been there for various programmes. As I started singing in Kashmiri, the local population went crazy, singing along with me and cheering me on. After the show, the then Chief Minister Farooq Abdullah came to meet me backstage, congratulating me on my perfect accent. Little did he know that I had three perfectionist locals correcting the pronunciation every minute they were with me. Of course, the crowd demanded 'Choli Ke Peechhey', the song that they had come to hear, but I think that day, despite terrorism, despite the Armed Forces (Special Powers) Act, despite all the underlying hostility, I had conquered the heart of Kashmir.

When I sing, I like to carry the community with me. Being a folk singer and a performer, music for me is interactive. For me, the stage is a visual experience, not just an audio event. I had asked for some Kashmiri folk dancers to accompany my songs. Arun Jaitley was the Information and Broadcasting minister then. I sang 'Cholhama Roshe Roshe'. This song was originally sung by Shameem Azad, a very popular singer in Kashmir and the wife of the former Chief Minister of Kashmir, Ghulam Nabi Azad. Later, friend Binny produced a story for the channel which I adapted. So, my transformation into a half-baked Kashmiri continued!

My home was taken over by the Kashmiris, a terrorism of a different kind. All these friends were bachelors, so they craved their own kind of food. Fortunately, they were all good cooks, so very often, my kitchen was taken over by them and became a Kashmiri *dhaba*. Instead of our staple food, *dal-roti*, we were now gorging on *rajma*, brought specially from Kashmir, since according to them, the *rajma* we ate was not the right kind and did not have the right taste. We were introduced to *kadam ka saag*, again brought by some relative visiting from Kashmir, and also *rogan josh* and *yakhni pulao*. There were rehearsals in between, with the fragrance of Kashmir permeating the flat. Those were the days!

Kashmiri food, jewellery, songs, the people, and of course, *phirans*. I was very taken up by this piece of clothing associated with Kashmir, a unisex attire, which was becoming popular in winter with women from Delhi and the Punjab. In winter, the Kashmiris carry their *kangris* an earthen heating pot, inside it, quite a dangerous means of keeping warm. For me, I liked the printed *phirans*, the *chheent phirans* worn by women in the villages and the fields. Thanks to Binny, my wardrobe never lacked these. I learnt to distinguish *phirans* for different occasions, different strata, Hindu and Muslim *phirans*, festive *phirans* and the significance of colours in their attire. This came in very handy when I was designing the wardrobe for my adaptation of *Peer Gynt*. I could get the right clothes, shoes, the right musical instruments for the play *Peer Ghani* with the help of my sister and all my Kashmiri friends.

Kashmir came closer when my friend Vijay Bakaya joined the Indian Administrative Service (IAS) in the Kashmir cadre, finally going back to his roots. We went to visit him in his district, Baramulla. We drove through the avenues of eucalyptus trees, seen in all the pictures of Kashmir, by bus. It was so cold that the piping hot lunch at his house cooked by his wife was a relief. We tasted what the Kashmiris call *saag,* a leafy vegetable, neither spinach nor mustard greens; I still remember its fragrance.

It was here that we met a colleague of Vijay's, Najam. While I was still nursing my romantic dreams of Kashmir, my sister Rama realized hers! Najam and she tied the knot a few years later, in London, where Rama was working for the BBC. Of course, the furore over this inter-religious marriage is discussed in a chapter on my family and siblings. Through this marriage, Kashmir became a part of our household really and truly. We were destined to meet both Muslim and Hindu Kashmiris throughout our lives. I must have been a Kashmiri in a previous life . . . Or was it that discounted Rs 75 trip that had mortgaged me to Kashmir forever and I am still in its debt? There must have been a connection between the Kashmiris and the Kanyakubja Brahmins at some stage in history.

Kashmir loomed large in my life when I was adapting Ibsen's *Peer Gynt*. Kashmir and Ibsen, I lived with these two entities for months. I had already adapted *The Lady from the Sea*, placing it in Rajasthan—a contradiction in terms, the sea and the desert! In my mind, the desert became a metaphor, depicting the thirst of a woman, her desires and thoughts, her longing for the sea which unleashed her imagination. Otherwise, how could I justify *The Lady from the Sea* in Rajasthan?

What was happening in Kashmir was a source of concern for me, fanned by my close association with Kashmiris and how it was affecting the lives of my friends. I showed the devastation of these lives through Peer Ghani's life. They had nothing much to look forward to. They had lost everything—their homes, their livelihoods, their place in society and even relationships. Since Peer had nothing to look forward to, he lived in his imagination, making up stories of better times and perhaps a better future. He had been brought up on the stories his mother Ase related to him, about the glorious life they lived before they lost their fortune through laziness and extravagance.

KK's first reaction to my Peer being a Kashmiri was not positive. 'Why Kashmir?' he said. My answer was that even geographically, Norway was similar to Kashmir. The snow, the hills, the heavy clothing. It is the story of an innocent boy who, due to the lack of opportunities in his country, and the insecurities he encounters, is drawn into a life of dishonesty and devilish deeds against his own country and countrymen. KK thought I was going to sensationalize the story, but later he agreed that there couldn't have been a better location for our Peer Ghani.

I tried to bring out the tragedy of Kashmir, saying that the mother and the motherland will remain the same, it is we who change, who are hurting because of our actions and our guilt. I think the masterstroke in the play was my idea of casting the trolls as the counter-force in Peer's life.

In *Peer Ghani*, with K.K. Raina and Rahul Bagga

My greatest satisfaction came when the folk musicians we had called from Kashmir were so moved by the play that they said we should take the play to Kashmir. They lamented the fact that their children had gone astray and needed some message to inspire them.

Kashmir's tragedy is that there were no winners, where it was not just one community that had suffered, it was the entire state.

Jan Morris, the author, says, 'Kashmir has always been more than a place. It has the quality of an experience, or a state of mind or perhaps an ideal.'

Chapter 5

Bombay: *Aamchi Mumbai*

I came to Mumbai for the first time on a trip with the Red Cross from school. Just as I had dreams about Kashmir, its mountains and streams, so it was with Bombay, its sand and the sea. When a girl brought up under the shade of the *neem* and *babool* tree, yearning for each drop of water, sees coconut and palm trees, her heart will surely miss a beat. How does a man collect coconuts from that height? That what we see as a dried coconut was once young and green; that people can actually drink the water from that fruit, so sweet and delectable, was indeed a wonder for me. And of course there was the excitement of Bollywood. I imagined that just like the palm tree, I would see stars on the road! These were fantasies of girlhood: Dharmendra, Joy Mukherjee, Sadhana, Nanda, Dilip Kumar and who knows how many others. I saw the impressive VT, local trains and the sea of people rushing into them. People actually waited in queues for the BEST buses. We went on a sightseeing tour of Bombay, the Hanging Gardens, Kamla Nehru Park, Juhu, Sun n Sand, the Aquarium, Aarey Milk Colony—all the usual sights that schools and tourists are taken to. We took a trip to Pune, where I made many friends: Bapsi Daruwala, Hilla P. Wellington, Abdul, so different from any of the friends I had made in Jaipur, with different backgrounds, different religions. For years, we wrote letters inviting each other to our homes. I cried when we parted. These travels always fanned my instant crushes. I seemed to be in love constantly! My mother knew that every time I came back from a trip, I would walk among the clouds, lost in thoughts of those I had left behind. Some would-be *mooh-bola* (so-called) brothers, some sisters, some friends.

My mother knew my feelings, but intentionally ignored them and swept away any thoughts of romance. But crushes were definitely on, whether with the place or a young boy. If the feeling was not voiced, my mother had no problems. She used to say that Ila always gets a fever after every trip away from home. And it also comes down very fast. That is what she thought, but how the suffering soul controlled her obsession, only the one who suffered knew. I did not have either the years or the courage to cross the limits of social norms. My mother's constant reminder 'Avesh mein vivek mat khona' (Don't ever let your desires and emotions overrule your discretion) put a full stop to every overture.

Tell me who has discretion in adolescence?

It was time to go back, too soon. As the train pulled out of Dadar station, I saw Abdul running after the train on the platform. In his hand, wrapped in a banana leaf he carried something, some *taargola*, which he dropped in my hand. 'Don't forget me,' he shouted as the train gathered speed, and I was left with Abdul's heart in the shape of a soft, fragile *taargola*. I shed tears of sorrow in his memory and bit into not one but four heart-shaped *taargolas*. If only I could have preserved Abdul's *taargola*-like heart in a bottle! I never saw Abdul again, but surprisingly ran into his friend Raees. I remember when we went to Chowpatty Beach, on our previous visit, Raees had taken Abdul and three or four of us girls to have *chole bhature* at the Cream Centre at Chowpatty, one of the best-known places for this savoury dish. After several years, when I came to Bombay again with my sisters and met Arun, who was to be my life partner, he also took us to Cream Centre for *chole bhature* and ice cream and I recounted my first visit to this restaurant. Just then, believe it or not, a young man came up to us and asked me if I was Ila Pandey and when I said yes, he introduced himself as Raees! It took me a while to connect since he had changed quite a lot, but when I did, I was delighted to meet him. He was now the manager of Cream Centre! My mind went back to my past Bombay visit, and all the memories of my friends came back to me like a wave that seemed to touch my heart and wash away what seemed a lifetime; Abdul and his *taargola*, Bapsi, Hilla. Did I discern a hidden smile of satisfaction on Arun's face, when Raees refused to present us with the bill? The memories of my friends somehow find their way into my writing, perhaps unknowingly. But in the adaptation of Terence Rattigan's play *The Deep Blue Sea*, one of my characters is called Hilla.

On that visit to Bombay, Rama, Deepa and I stayed with my sister Sudha, at Mulund, in the eastern suburbs. But this to me was not the Bombay I knew, so I had to refresh my childhood memories of the Bombay I had visited from school. Every day we would take the local train to the city and would meet Arun there. Three girls and one handsome merchant navy officer. It was during the monsoons and we three would be in raincoats, carrying old umbrellas, drenched like Nargis, going to meet our Raj Kapoor! And he would be there, Arun, waiting for us at the VT station, under a very fancy umbrella with a fan attached to it. Being in the merchant navy, he had access to things we had never seen! It was as if we had won a lottery. From the time he picked us up at VT and dropped us back, we were his responsibility, to feed and shop and go sightseeing! We sisters had never had such fun and freedom. Three girls and one sponsor! Not once did any of us even offer to pay. Arun was related to my maternal aunt and had become close to my sister Sudha, who lived in Bombay. At that time, there was no overt talk of marriage, but Sudha trusted Arun and knew him well so he was a good chaperone for her young sisters in Bombay—young, handsome, modern and very different from any boy of our community. He was very interested in ballroom dance and Western music and always very well-dressed, perhaps because most of his friends were Christians. He was half a Christian himself! One of my aunts still teases him saying that he never missed an opportunity to look at himself in a mirror and comb his hair. I tell her that he still does, hair or no hair!

My maternal aunt always had Arun in mind for me. She said, 'I have a boy in mind for Ila. He is from our community, is in the merchant navy, earns well and dances beautifully, even better than Ila. Shall I carry a proposal for her?' This is how marriages were fixed in India, not in heaven as it is believed, but certainly with material considerations in mind! No one thought of asking the boy or the girl, whether they had anyone else in mind, whether they were agreeable to the match. That is why perhaps even today, I make Arun dance to my tune, or so I would like to believe! The four of us spent time together in Bombay as friends, without a whiff of what was cooking in Mausi's mind.

My script of Bombay carried on—the rides in local trains, sometimes climbing onto the luggage compartment with the fisherwomen, overwhelmed by the smell of fish. By the time we got off, we felt we had been born in a Koli family! Thinking back, I feel that any actor who wishes to act and observe life should travel in Bombay locals. The quarrels, the fight for seats, the romance, Hindus, Muslims, Sikhs and Isai, all bound together on what is known as the lifeline of Bombay. If the trains stop, life also comes to a complete standstill in Bombay, as we witnessed with the curbs on travelling during the Covid scare. There is no discrimination; rich and poor, working people and students, traders and conmen, *bais*, secretaries, bankers and beggars, all stand shoulder to shoulder, packed like sardines, with only one thought—to make it to work in time! You have to watch over yourself. I have used this experience in the locals in a song in my album *Titali*, 'Anyway, it is Bombay' I was reminded of a song learnt in school about Bombay locals. And I have included the train song in my album.

We came back with beautiful memories of our trip. One day, long after we had left, my sister Sudha asked Arun what he thought of her sisters. Arun casually said they were all nice. Sudha pursued the topic and said she was talking of marriage. Arun promptly asked, 'Which one?' He continued that if he were asked, his choice would be me. Of course, now that we are married, I have to believe that I was his choice.

Back in Jaipur, I got the news that I had been selected for a short course at NSD, in Delhi. I put everything else behind me and made my way to NSD. I had found my destiny!

Chapter 6

Home: Purohitji-Ka-Bagh

It is midnight. the whole world sleeps. Suddenly, there is an earth-shattering sound. It comes from our house, our terrace where we all slept at night in summer to escape the heat.

My father
Indra Narayan Pandey

My father's phenomenal sneeze, three times in a row! And somehow, I don't know why but when my father sneezed, there would be a sudden awakening and a thousand peacocks would start their call. They would raise hell with their shouting.

This was Purohitji-Ka-Bagh, the place where seven siblings spent their childhood, amidst birds, fruit trees and amazing companionship. It was here that Indra Narayan Pandey lived with his flowering bouquet of five daughters, *mogra*, *chameli*, *champa*, *raat-ki-rani* and roses—infusing an intoxicating fragrance into that world.

My precious home Purohitji-Ka-Bagh

The ravages of time, the same home today

Childhood! What connotations of innocence and excitement that word presents. Childhood is no childhood if you have not indulged in some kind of mischief. It is that time of life when you drive everyone crazy, and yet, in your mind, you are the centre of the universe. Your first steps into adolescence are tentative, yet full of fantasy and wonder. But with the passage of time, you start withdrawing into yourself. Adolescence is a time of flowering, just like the burgeoning of flowers in spring, the sensation of the drops of rain on your body while your mind wanders into forbidden spaces, romance knocks at your door. You dream of strange things; it is common for these changes to take place. In fact, if you don't display these feelings, your parents start getting worried about you, especially in the West, when you are a virgin at twenty! You don't have to seek far; even in India, several tribes in the Bastar area of Chhattisgarh as well as in the neighbouring regions of Maharashtra, Madhya Pradesh and Andhra Pradesh follow the tradition of the *ghotuls*. These are religious and social centres for tribal society and serve as village dormitories for unmarried girls and boys. The young adults here can date, experiment with sex before marriage with one or more partners and learn the culture and legends of their tribe.

Sawan aata hai, monsoon, with its flowering of buds, and the melody of rain on rooftops and leaves, how can a teenage boy or girl not feel the stirrings of romance? The senses start responding, your heart wanders and you await the appearance of your Prince Charming. How I wish I was a tribal or gypsy. I have always wanted to dress up like them, to dance and sing like them, in a society where there are no rigid rules and people are not so judgemental. There were several instances in my life, where I felt everyone in the family was hostile towards me. Your house is not a home any more but a jail. Their love and concern are like shackles on your feet. Your parents appear to be your jailers. Before you can take a step, my mother's clapperboard shatters into my fantasies, *Avesh main vivek mat khona*, don't lose your discretion in moments of passion. And the tidal wave of adolescence, the volcano of dreams fizzles out instead of erupting.

These feelings recede into the pages of my diary, in poetic language, very personal. But I feel that these feelings, however insignificant, which are recorded in every poet's or writer's diary, should be used by them when they write novels or plays. These memories can be conjured up easily if they delve into their childhood and this is what is called emotional memory in the writing world. Can we vouch for the fact that Sarat Chandra or Bimal Mitra's classics are merely fictional? Somewhere, sometime in their lives, they must have also faced these emotional barriers. Their writings are a result of either some experience they have gone through or that someone around them has. Their novels cannot be just the poetic imagination of these writers. Fiction is reality based. They say literature is the mirror of society; you combine both these facets. In all the plays I have written or adapted, I have used these life experiences—the good and the bad. It is not merely the relationship between pen and ink, but that between the heart and its stirrings.

My mother, with seven daughters, had to be always on her toes. As I have mentioned before, she was more alert than a warden of a girls' hostel. But her style was different, poetic and idiomatic. She could, without any warning, pull the rug from under your unsuspecting feet!

Jaipur was a small town and not much could be kept under wraps, not even the daughters of Indra Narayan Pandey. Several young men would be wandering around in the vicinity, like moths drawn to the light. It was difficult to fathom who was the favourite with which moth, especially where my older sisters were concerned, with very small age differences. It was a difficult choice. The four sons of one of our family friends were also in the running, being close to us in age and also from the same caste. If they so desired, they could have married any one of the sisters. But somewhere there was a hitch. In those days, young men in the

With my father Indra Narayan Pandey, mother Bhagwati Pandey and some of my siblings

administrative services thought they were the cat's whiskers. And their ambitious fathers would tout them in the marriage market to the highest bidder. My mother was aware of this and did not wish to venture down that path, where boys were being auctioned. But those boys were like-minded, they were good-looking, fond of music like us and with a good sense of humour. They liked to come to our house and we too enjoyed their company. There was a constant coming and going between the two homes. But my mother knew that the two families couldn't be related by marriage, so why build castles in the air? Why should any of her daughters 'fly the kite of unfulfilled emotions'? She would not say anything to the older sisters but would tell us, the younger ones, that these boys were older than us and that they should be addressed as Bhaisaheb, a term of respect for an older brother. That term, Bhaisaheb, put the brakes on the culmination of a potentially flowering relationship. One of the boys confessed that it required a lot of effort and patience to get to us. 'For a brief meeting with you, we have to first sit with your father and discuss politics, then cricket, making good our escape as we enter, we have to join your mother and aunts for a hand of coat-piece, all the while surreptitiously looking for you sisters. The next step is listening to your sisters' poems and writings and then on turning around we are confronted with the woes of your old family retainer. That is not the end; your brothers catch us to listen to their practice debates.' Now where was the time for romance? It just flew out of the window! And before any declaration of love could be made, they had already been addressed as Bhaisaheb!

We would all have a good laugh, but this is the fate of every middle-class romance. Our life was a mirror image of the stories of Sarat Chandra's novels. One cannot forget that memorable scene that is described so beautifully in *Parineeta*—that Shekhar Da came, played cards with *bahu di*, the stolen glimpse, the offering of *paan* with delicate fingers, these are not just a figment of the writer's imagination. These are the true-life descriptions of a budding middle-class romance, a lived past, which the writer recreates from his experience. Literature is surely a reflection of life. My mother never refrained from telling us that the kind of freedom she had given us, the education we had, and our introduction to the creative and performing arts, was more than any mother in our circumstances would have given. 'Now don't ever disgrace us,' were her closing words after every piece of advice. She would subtly convey to us that we could do what we liked, but an arranged marriage was a given, and that too an alliance that was only within our community. Anyone overstepping the line would upset my father. As I remember, there was no dearth of proposals for us sisters. If any of us had decided to elope, we would have had the whole of Rajasthan in our grip, every community represented in the son-in-law category. She always pre-empted all our moves and if she gauged that one of us was getting too close to a young man, she would have a long conversation with him, acknowledging that there couldn't be a better match than that young man. 'I understand your feelings,' she would say, 'but one cannot share the same water and alienate a crocodile. *Paani main rehkar magarmachh se bair nahin le sakte na*. If you take the wrong step, what will happen to the faith we have placed in you, the image that we have built up of you? Everyone will malign us, and their father would probably die by suicide.' We never knew what happened to many of the would-be suitors who literally leapt away to undeclared destinations and were never seen or heard of again. And we were left alone, holding that infamous clapperboard. *Aavesh mein vivek mat khona*! Now whenever I create such a character or play one on the stage or screen, my mother's face appears before my eyes and I recall those boys and their circumstances, creating characters based on my memories. How real they appear to me!

Our childhood was spent in Purohitji-Ka-Bagh. Three of my sisters were married while we were there, though because of the lack of space, the actual venue was the nearby MLA's Hostel. Childhood memories remain with you forever as does your first love.

The area was full of trees, many laden with fruit such as guavas, star fruit, tamarind, *phalsa*, mulberry. Some of the branches drooped onto our terrace. *Phir kya, mauja hi mauja*. What fun! My brothers Piyush and Prasoon would pluck the fruit off the trees and fill our little bundles with various fruits. The *maalin*, or the tender of the garden, would chase them with a cane made from the branch of a tree. She would shout abuses at them and at times the unlucky ones did get the end of the stick. There were many varieties of birds—parrots, black birds, *koel* and peacocks. Summer was fun time. The holidays were long and hot, so we could not go out during the day. The real treat was sleeping at night on the terrace on beds or mattresses laid out in a row. We could watch the stars and gossip till we fell asleep. There was a certain comfort associated with this dormitory. It was the duty of us sisters to cool down the scorching ground with water. Here, I must mention one fact which if I don't, my mother will step down to haunt me from wherever she is! She would say that I had also taken to lies like my sister Rama. After all, she had a reputation to protect and people should know that though we sisters did a lot of household chores, we had at least four helpers in the house. This was a status symbol for my father, which my mother was proud of. This was also one of the perks of being a government employee, where the pay was miniscule, but several perks compensated for that. Raghunath, my music teacher, Ramnath, the cook, our costume designer, whose wife's pure silver ornaments we always borrowed for all our fancy-dress competitions along with her authentic *ghagra-loogris,* not once deterred by the fact that they were not sanitized, or even washed. He would bring us her best clothes and my sister Rama and I would always go dressed in these clothes for the Teej celebrations in the grounds across our road and we always came back with the prize for the best fancy dress. And not only that—our pictures appeared in magazines such as *Kadambar*i and *Sarita,* because of the authenticity of our costumes. That is why I still wear these 20-metre *lehengas* for my shows, not caring whether I look plump because these give me an earthy feeling. I cannot dance without adorning myself with all the jewellery worn by village belles: *nathni, hamel, borla* and *chura.* I feel I am incomplete without this burden. We had a cook, a *maharaj,* called Hanuman. There was Giriraj and another man called Motiji. He was the barber to my brothers and father. He would come home to cut their hair, without a thought to any lines or styles, sometimes crooked, sometimes too short. As the haircuts were free, Kakaji had all done in one go. And my brothers didn't dare complain. It was the sisters who protested against these uneven hairlines and the parents were forced to have the boys' hair cut at Sartar Sahib's so-called salon.

Our life at Purohitji-Ka-Bagh was perfect for us children. My mother too had a good rapport with the landlady, Kakisa, and the two negotiated several issues between themselves, never involving the men. If ever we were late in paying the rent, my mother would 'adjust' with Kakisa. I remember when we first moved in, our drawing room had just a tin roof, which would be very noisy during the monsoon and very hot in summer. It was my mother's friendship with Kakisa that was instrumental in the landlord building a pucca roof over this room. This started a series of renovations, providing tin roofs over other areas, including on the terrace where we slept, scrambling down with our beddings when it rained, the provision of an extra bathroom downstairs.

There are several unfinished stories around Purohitji-Ka-Bagh, crying out for closure or completion. Our dreams took shape in Purohitji-Ka-Bagh, a home that contributed to our various careers and creativity in later life. Each one of us must be carrying some love story, our own guilt, some stolen moments, our own experiences while we grew up in Purohitji-Ka-Bagh. Perhaps they are using them in some way. I have several memories of that home. When we first moved to the house, there was a huge yellow-coloured *haveli* and a swimming pool. There were several rooms in a row and a large basement, where Kakisa would ask us to take our summer siesta to escape the afternoon heat. In front there was an extensive lawn with a courtyard, and I remember we children were asked to take part in a film that was shot there, *Manzil,* with Shekhar and Nimmi in leading roles and we were asked to be seen in the background playing football. We even appeared on the cover of the magazine *Parag.* Since my father was in the co-operative department, the co-operative auditoriums were under his charge. Often, he would get the mobile vans to screen films on that lawn, a sheer luxury for us and something we looked forward to.

All the inhabitants of Purohitji-Ka-Bagh would flock to see these films. I remember two films we saw, *Seema* and *Sujata,* in the open-air theatre of Purohitji-Ka-Bagh. There are many stories associated with Purohitji-Ka-Bagh, which I will use from time to time in my plays, unfinished stories, the protagonists of which have been lost to the remaining occupants.

Poori: An Unfinished Story

Poori was the girl who did the dishes at our home. This twelve-year-old girl, forced to work, would sometimes come up to the rooftop when she had respite from her work. I would also follow her up to the roof and we became good friends; ours was not a relationship of employee and employer, but a genuine bond of friendship, of shared feelings and desires. We would sit close to the water tank, which was also connected to the flush tanks down below. Every time someone pulled the flush, the round floating ball would rotate and with it our imagination, turning this round ball into a representation of the universe. We would burst out laughing and try to guess who the visitor to the toilet was. If Poori thought it was our mother, she would rush down to show her that she was still there.

It was on this tank that we sat and discussed our lives and dreams. Poori lived in the settlement of *kanjars*, a nomadic tribe, probably Kutchhis from the border of Gujarat, since they used to celebrate the Navratri festival with great gusto, with music and the *garba* dance. Sometimes on Poori's invitation, I would also join them in the dance. Their voices were melodious, but on high octaves. Poori was always dressed elaborately on these occasions. I picked up my first steps of *garba* with Poori and also saw the beautifully decorated mud vessels, *gharas*, lit with candles. The effect of this soft, flickering light from several *gharas* lit up my soul and stirred hidden longings in my heart.

Poori would add to my imaginative wanderings by telling me that their tribal societies were free of norms of morality and men and women could choose their partners '*naate baith gayi*' as they called it, which literally means she has chosen her partner and was in a relationship with him. I think this practice is common among several tribes, including the Gujjars. If a girl is unhappy with her husband, she can get into a relationship with any man she fancies. Listening to these stories I often wished I had been a *kanjar!* As a girl, these traditions appealed to my mind, since they were not chained to morality or social norms. But alas! I was a middle-class girl and my mother's clapperboard waved at me at every turn. If I had been a *kanjar,* or an adivasi, or any other tribe, I would have had a carefree life, unfettered by the constant clapperboard. Morality does not restrain the upper crust of society nor the poorer members of society; they don't spend their lives balancing what is allowed by society and what their own desires are. It is the middle class that is the upholder of morality and social norms.

Poori would tell me several stories, which would probably all end in disillusion and heartbreak. Though she was only thirteen, she was already married to a man who was a drunkard. Unfortunately, she was in love with another man. Her younger sister was in a relationship even though her family was looking for a bridegroom for her. Poori would bring packets of powdered milk wrapped in a newspaper and she and I would relish the milk while she told me stories, which were like fairy tales for me. I loved this powder milk. The milk was given to these tribals by the Christian missionaries, perhaps as an incentive for conversion. When my mother heard of this, she slapped me on my face and said, 'Don't you know that this milk is given by the padres to convert you?' This was proved later on when it was discovered that many a poor family had been enticed by this milk powder to convert to Christianity. That day, I decided I would stop gobbling up this milk powder. I don't want to comment on this, since I believe faith is a very personal choice. Yes, but I will never forget the song Poori sang with me accompanying her, on the water tank of our home: '*Bachpan ki mohabbat ko dil se na juda karna, jab yaad meri aaye, mil neki dua karna.*' (Don't tear away the memories of our childhood romance from your heart, whenever you think of me pray that we meet again.) I don't know who Poori was in love with, but it was I who shed tears for a lost romance! Whenever I visited Jaipur, I tried several times to find out where Poori was, but I never did find her. Once though, her sister came with her grandchild to visit us and took several selfies with me. But she could not tell me about Poori's whereabouts because she had eloped with another man.

Mano: A Tragic Story

Another tragic story concerns two sisters living in Purohitji-Ka-Bagh—Swati and Mano. They were Bengalis and I used to accompany them to the Puja *pandals* during Durga Puja. One year I took part in a performance of Tagore's *Chandalika*. Mano was very pretty, with curly hair, but at a very young age, she eloped with a man who was good-for-nothing, jobless and with no money. Soon after she had a baby girl. But one day we heard that she had died by suicide, hanging herself from a fan. Of course, there were several rumours; some said she was 'bad-charactered', others said she had an uncontrollable anger; some said that her husband was no good. But for me, she was still that pretty, innocent young girl I had known. Now that I have done a play by American writer Tammy Ryan titled *Baby's Blues*, I am reminded of the tragedy of Mano. Since she died by suicide soon after her delivery, perhaps she was suffering from postpartum depression, a condition still not fully understood in India. While researching for this play, I have discovered from many doctors that there are at least 65 per cent cases of postpartum depression in India. Yet, families are usually in denial about this problem. But for me, this tragic end left Mano's story also unfinished.

16 January 2022. Mumbai. I woke up to the sad news of Birju Maharaj's death. Social media was full of reports of this tragic event. As I pen down my memoirs, every event associated with my childhood in Purohitji-Ka-Bagh comes to the fore. I had met Maharaj-ji for the first time at Purohitji-Ka-Bagh. Since my entire family was passionate about music, dance and literature, there was always a chance of meeting one of the well-known figures in any of these fields. In those days, Rajasthan was still an important destination for artistes, because of the patronage of the Maharajas. The Langas, Manganiyars, the Dholanias and all the *maands* (royal bards) flourished because of the courts of Rajasthan. The lawns of Maharani's College and the auditorium of Ravindra Manch would come alive with music recitals and concerts, which carried on into the night. In those days, there was no deadline of 10 p.m. Audiences would arrive with blankets and thermoses of tea and leave only when the last notes of the Bhairavi echoed in the atmosphere. My sister Rama was always in the forefront when it came to meeting these celebrities. She would cross all limits, despite warnings from my mother, and somehow make it to any venue where she had a chance to meet these renowned performers. And I, as her tail, would quietly follow her to these meetings. She was even successful in inviting Birju Maharaj to our home for a cup of tea! My mother forgot all the warnings and the '*avesh mein vivek*' etc. and was delighted to entertain him. It was a known fact that Birju Maharaj was an accomplished singer too. He had learnt vocal music and could also play the *tabla*. At her

request, he even sang two thumris for her and a *ghazal* which I still hum constantly. '*Bhoole se kabhi ek bhool hui/ hum unki tammana kar bethe/ pachtata hai dil reh reh kar/ kya karna tha kya kar bethe.*' (One mistake/that of desiring him/I still regret constantly/what was it I wanted and what did I end up doing?)

My sister Uma used to sing his *thumris* in her melodious voice. My mother would often remind me that *even* though it was I who took to singing, Uma had the better voice.

I did not know that Maharaj-ji played the *tabla,* so without thinking, I took out the *tabla* and started accompanying him. How did I have the audacity to do that! I could see that he was watching me from the corner of his eye and giving me a whimsical smile. My mother told him that I had an interest in kathak and that I was taking kathak classes in Kala Sansthan. He asked me to demonstrate a mudra that he showed me. I must have passed the test with him because he told my mother that I should be sent to the Kathak Kala Kendra in Delhi to learn Kathak. But this suggestion was glossed over amidst laughter and that opportunity was lost. My mother believed that all these arts were like an extra pinch of salt in one's life and could never be a career. But destiny had chosen this path for me, and I did not give up, or who knows, today I would have been a housewife in some Kanyakubj household, stoking the kitchen fires. As luck would have it, Birju Maharaj's disciples have performed with me in several shows in India and abroad and I learnt a lot about him through their stories. How I regretted the fact that my mother had prevented me from being one of those disciples! We sisters often joked about the fact that the city of Varanasi was full of Kannaujias who were renowned performers: Lacchu Maharaj, Bindadin, Pandit Braj Mohan Mishra (Birju Maharaj), Shamta Prasad and Kishen Maharaj. All of them were Mishras, from our community. How is it that our mother never cast a glance in that direction, ignoring all these beautiful, melodious men? We would laugh and say how is it she only had these off-key IAS men in her vision?

Everything in life those days was associated with romance. Music and songs from Hindi films drew tears from our eyes as if all the sadness and heartbreak conveyed in the song was for us. My mind was like the *Chitrahaar* of Doordarshan, every moment associated with a song and each song a reminder of some tale of a fleeting romance!

On my previous birthday, which I spent with my brother Piyush in Goa, suddenly the fact of advancing age engulfed me. My life glided past me and thoughts of faces long receded from the subconscious appeared before my eyes. My first love, then the second and the third, after which I stopped counting! All those faces which had left a stamp on my impressionable mind. Several friends along the way, my friends from the theatre, a few teachers, some neighbours, and with these faces, all the incidents in your life which you will never forget. Recently, as we drove towards my brother Prasoon's home at Alibagh, in the midst of the seclusion of Covid, an old song drifted over the radio. *Chand aahen bharega/ Phool dil thaam lenge/ Husn ki baat chali to/ Sab tera naam lenge.* My mind was already delving into the past and this song brought back the past and the constant state of romance I seemed to be living in as an adolescent, always stopped by my mother's clapperboard.

We didn't have too many visitors at the time, except a few of my parents' close friends. One of them was Rakshpalji who, with his wife, Vatsala, would visit us. I still remember they had a Morris Minor. We used to call them Chachaji and Chachiji. They had two sons, but remember they were also in the category of *bhai*, brother. They would visit almost every Sunday and we would all sit down to musical afternoons, *mehfil*s, and there would be a chorus of songs, the favourite being my sister Uma's folk song, '*Dakia re, tu kagaz likh de*,' accompanied by Chachaji's rhythmic claps. We would visit them too. The great attraction in their house was a radiogram, on which Chachaji would play all the old songs of Kannan Bala, Pankaj Mullick and Sehgal. He loved to hear Uma sing his favourite bhajan sung by Juthika Roy—'*Aaj mere ghar pritam aaye.*' Rakshpal Chacha used to call me his daughter. There were two songs he always sang, especially for me, since I could not resist dancing to these tunes, especially '*Gore gore haathon mein mehndi laga ke, naino mein kajara daal ke*', and while appreciating my dance Chachaji would also remark that I had thin legs and large eyes, which I felt was an unkind remark about my appearance.

How beautifully has a poet depicted the passing of time '*Zindagi ka phalsafa bhi ajeeb hai, shyamme kat ti nahin aur saal guzarte jaate hain/Ek ghadi khareed kar haath mein kya bandh li/ Waqt mere hi peechhe pad gaya.*' (Life has a strange reality/Evenings are endless/ but the years pass by in a moment/Why did I put a watch on my wrist/ That time now tortures me constantly?)

Those days were special, yet today, like a goldfish in a glass bowl, searching for the unknown, my stream of consciousness constantly goes back to those moments.

One summer, despite all of my mother's warnings, my heart did feel the stirrings of my first romance. My parents had another close friend, and in the summer holidays, their daughter Sudha would visit her parents in Jaipur and would always drop by to see my parents. On one such summer visit, she brought her brother-in-law along. He was young, good-looking, his personality enhanced by the immaculate white *kurta-pyjama* he wore. At the request of his sister-in-law, he sang three songs, and as a creature of habit, I started giving the rhythm on the table. The first song was '*Jo vada kiya wo nibhana padega*', followed by '*Chand aahen bharega*'. I sang a song or two, and as they were leaving, he whispered, 'You sing well.' His sister-in-law said that they were going to be in Jaipur for a couple of weeks and that we should visit them. I was in a daze. I spent a sleepless night, wondering when my mother would take us for a visit. As I tossed and turned, I convinced myself that the songs were for me and only me! We did visit them, and I have no memory of how and when we communicated, but before I knew it, we had exchanged addresses. The episode was a replay of a romantic film scene. And while I lived in a dream world, the arrival of a letter a week later was the ultimate ecstasy! For many months I thought of little else but the songs he had sung, especially the phrase, '*Jo vada kiya, wo nibbhana padega,*' that the promise had to be honoured, which promise or why, I had no idea, but I felt bound by that promise. My family also started hinting, although jokingly at the time, that this boy was perfect for me. Of course, for them, any boy who was musically inclined was a match for me. Though this thought did cross their mind, I knew that Rama was there before me and my mother was conscious of the fact that any IAS officer came with a price, a price they could ill afford. But my romance refused to be dampened. When Sudha invited us to visit them in Gwalior, I was convinced that the invitation was specifically for me. More letters were exchanged and I would go up to the terrace, sit on the same water tank where Poori had recounted her love life and read each line several times to fathom if there were any hidden indications of his feelings. And I would always find something that seemed like a secret declaration.

My sister Rama happened to go to Gwalior for some competition from college and had contacted his family. It was he who took her around Gwalior and showed her the tourist sites and shopping centres. When she came back, she mentioned that he had asked after me. My hair stood on end!

Then as luck would have it, I too got an opportunity to visit Gwalior from college. I wrote him a letter and he actually came to the station to receive me. He took me to the Gwalior Fort, since he was a friend of Madhavrao Scindia, the Maharaja of Gwalior, from school, and showed me around the private precincts of the fort. All the time, at the back of my mind, the song was playing, like background music, '*Jo vada kiya, woh nibbhana padega*.' Definitely there was a connect between us, a sensation that gave me gooseflesh on that cold, foggy morning. When we were leaving, he told me I would have to do him a favour. I would have gone to the ends of the earth for him, so what was a little favour? But it turned out to be the most unromantic request! He wanted to send two little puppies for Sudha's younger sister. Not being a dog lover, I almost froze, but as I said, I would have done anything for him. He gave me an air bag, with the pups and little milk bottles for their feed. I was really at a loss and roped in my friend Madhu Tandon, who was a dog lover, saying that she would have to help me in the name of my *mohabbat*, my love. I was bold enough to say that I would take the dogs only if he allowed me to keep one, to keep his memory alive. He agreed, and as the train pulled out of the station, I was left holding the pups, seeing my love receding into the darkness.

At night, the pups wailed and squealed, and when the train attendant came to check, all the girls would start a loud Antakshari competition to drown out their whimpers. I don't know how we managed to evade being caught. We had a naming ceremony for the two pups, but somehow Madhu got it all wrong and named my pup Whiskey while the other one was Husky, which should have been my dog's name because of my husky voice! But this dog was indeed a long-lasting memory of him, since it lived with us for fourteen years!

And whenever he looked at me with his limpid eyes, I imagined it was the unconditional love of a particular human whom I had loved and perhaps lost.

Another memory that comes to mind is that on every Puranmasi, the day of the full moon, after the Purohit family moved out of their yellow-coloured *haveli* into their new home behind our house, we would all go to their house for the Satyanarayan *katha*. At that time, religion was not paramount in our minds. It was the *prasad* at the end of the *katha* that was the greatest attraction: bananas, guavas, *mawa* sweets, p*anchamrit, panjiri*. To partake of this feast, we would appear just 10 minutes before the final ritual, the *aarti*. If we were early, we had to wait longer and sit through the boring Sanskrit chanting of the pandit. Now when I look back, I realize how important it is to carry an audience with you, to retain their interest and to use simple language. Even religious chanting has to have a dramatic angle to retain the interest of the listeners, otherwise, like us, the devotees itch for the ritual to end. I have used these warnings from the subconscious in my theatre adaptations and presentations. Anyhow, this continued for some time, till at some point, the pandit stopped coming for the *katha*. Later we found out the reason for his absence. He used to go for the Satyanarayan *puja* to another house further up the road. No one knew at which point the lady of the house and the pandit came so close that one day they eloped, leaving her four daughters aghast. Not one of them had any inkling of the secret romance flowering before their very eyes. This took all of us by surprise too. How did this very ordinary-looking pandit, with no personality, with his boring way of talking and extremely slow pace, suddenly spring to action with unbelievable speed and smooth alacrity and carry off a lady in a swirl of romance? Since she was a widow, it became a real scandal in the orthodox society of Jaipur. But it left behind a trace of comedy since from then on, the story of the pandit's elopement was the prefix to every Satyanarayana *katha* in Jaipur. And for me, it was another reference for theatre!

I was still young but though I enjoyed the gossip, I also wondered why a widow is expected to be bereft of feeling and desire. And a pandit, or a Christian priest, who is considered the messenger of God, surely, he is allowed his moments of romance and innocent pleasures? In fact, Hindu gods and goddesses were known to indulge in dalliances with whoever took their fancy. Then why should the pandit be deprived? Traditionally, women have always veered towards swamis and gurus in their quest for peace but perhaps secretly also as a respite from their dominating and lacklustre husbands! Society accepts this. A distant aunt quite often missed family gatherings and her husband would say, '*Swamiji ke paas gayi hain*' (She has gone to meet Swamiji), without any hesitation. One day, she told me that her husband and she were now *bhai-bahen*, brother-sister. Now what was one to gather from that? Theatre is an excellent medium to portray such stories and question social mores and their hypocrisy. This keeps the audience at the edge of their seats and perhaps makes them think about such realities of life.

Purohitji-Ka-Bagh fell prey to the so-called development of cities and was portioned off into individual plots. It lost its close-knit community and all the festivals celebrated there with the participation of all the families who lived there. Holi, Diwali, Gangaur, Teej, the swings in *sawan, or shravan,* the monsoon season—there was always an excuse to get together. Kakisa would put up the swings herself and we would all fly in the air, high into the sky on these vehicles of joy. Later, my father would get the wooden planks and put up the swings for us. This was where our forays into All India Radio began and our theatre journey through Ravindra Manch. At first, this was all at an amateur level, but my passion opened up several doors for me. I had the good fortune of working with all the leading directors in Jaipur: Pinchoo Kapoor, S. Vasudev, Mohan Maharishi and Bhanu Bharati.

College life was also getting interesting. I had been unanimously elected as joint secretary of the Maharani's College Union and I realized that even elections at the college level can turn dirty and go way beyond just college politics. Local politicians interfere in college elections and students, instead of concentrating on their education, get involved in politics and indulge in vandalism and violence. Our beloved Rajasthan, which takes pride in its acceptance of all religions and celebrates every festival with gusto, unmindful of whether it is Hindu, Muslim, Christian or Jain, was suddenly divided during the university elections into gangs of Jats, Rajputs and Gujjars, who attacked each other over insignificant issues. When I was joint secretary, I remember a murder in the boys' hostel, which sent shock waves through the university. The unfortunate incident was the disgraceful culmination of Jat and Rajput rivalry during university elections. A gang of Jat students attacked the Rajasthan College hostel and with hockey sticks, mercilessly beat up a Rajput student, who finally succumbed to his injuries. Universities have become hotbeds of student politics. I feel that when students get involved in national politics on campus, they are wasting their time and their parents' money in activities that do not concern them. When parents send their children to the best colleges, the intention is to educate them and not to turn them into political *goondas*.

I had taken up civics in school, which in college advances into political science, one of my subjects in college. I did not do my master's since at that time there was no postgraduate department in music and dramatics. The department of psychology was started with just six students. I scored 70 per cent in psychology in my BA, thanks to my unofficial tutor, Vijay Bakaya, whom I have mentioned earlier. But the cut-off for admission to psychology was 85 per cent. So, my father procured admission for me in the Department of Public Administration, perhaps because he thought that an MA degree was a precondition for matrimony. I wouldn't be surprised if this task was also entrusted to his dear friend, Mishrilalji! As I entered the classroom I was convinced that all the boys were closer to my father's age than to mine! That was true of the law department too. It seemed that these boys never wanted to leave the university. The excitement I felt about joining a co-educational institution faded away immediately and my dreams of romance flew out of the window.

My name was called out every day for three months when the roll call was taken, but I never entered that class again! The boys in my class, I was told, looked around for me every time my name was called, but I never obliged them with an appearance! Three months later, I had an opportunity once again to join the psychology department when someone dropped out of the course. I was informed about this by the psychology professor, Mr Sinha, as I left the cinema hall Prem Prakash after seeing the film *To Sir, with Love* (1967)! By that time, I had received a scholarship from the Rajasthan Sangeet

Natak Akademi to join a short-term course at NSD. With God's
help, after years of yearning and begging, I had finally realized my
dream. Thank God also for the scholarship, since my mother was
sceptical and was not convinced that acting needed to be studied!
She reminded me that singing, dancing and acting was only a hobby.

Maharani's College contributed immensely to my growth and
perceptions. I have very fond memories of my alma mater. I had made
some very close friends. One of them was Rita Handoo and we came
close because of our shared love for music. She sang very well, but
she and I were very different in every other aspect. I loved dressing
up in flamboyant clothes, while she, even as a young college girl,
dressed only in white, like a Brahmakumari. We would do *riyaaz*,
practice, together and spend a lot of time talking. She would declare
that she would never marry a businessman, since they were all the
biggest *daakus*, or thieves. They would do anything, even sell their
country for profit. How prophetic she was! These days, all around us
we see nothing but corruption and scams involving businessmen and
politicians. She eventually married an air force officer and also did a
PhD in music. That girl turned out to be true to her convictions and
her music.

My mother was instrumental in turning our home at Purohitji-
Ka-Bagh into something like Shantiniketan, where each of us were
schooled in some art or music. Sudha and Rama played the sitar.

With my four sisters, two brothers, my aunt and my brother-in-law
R.K. Bajpai

Early morning, we would wake up to the sound of Umaji singing Bhairavi with her *tanpura*. That reminds me of the fate of the tanpura. We would all sit on a jute *khaat*, or bed, and often get up without securing the tanpura. As a result, that instrument had many a fall like Humpty Dumpty, but my father was always able to put it together again.

Initially, we walked from Purohitji-Ka-Bagh to school and were so tired and hungry by the time we got home that we would fall to the *nashta,* snacks, Mother had ready for us. Except on the days of *shravan*, when Mother would make us fast every Monday and we had to run to a temple before we were served our meal. Then we would get *parathas* and mango or *dahi*, yogurt. There were days when we would go straight to Kala Sansthan towards Badi Chauper.

At some point during my college-going days, I graduated from walking to college to taking a bicycle. It so happened that my father, who used to ride a bike to his office, acquired a car and started using that for his trip to the office. As a result, his abandoned bicycle lay in a corner of our house. I had a brilliant idea! Why should I not use this bicycle for my journey to Maharani's College? That was it. I appropriated the bike and my journey to college was a breeze. It gave me a sense of freedom, and like Hema Malini's Dhanno in *Sholay* (1975), I would fly to my destination, undeterred by the fact that there was no warning bell on the bicycle and all along I would be shouting at people who got in the way, '*Hato, hato, arre bhai hato*!' I guess I was better than our school bus driver, Jagganath, who had to manoeuvre a huge unwieldy bus without a horn! To this day, I cannot ride a lady's bike, having learnt on Kakaji's old gent's bike!

My companion on my rides was my friend Rajshree Rathore, the daughter of the famous writer of Rajasthan, Rani Lakshmi Bai Chundawat. She was beautiful, with the grace and elegance of royalty even at that young age. My mother would say that her slender neck was like the neck of a *surahi*, a clay jug used to keep water cool. Rajshree and I have retained our friendship to this day and one of the attractions of my visit to Jaipur is my visit to her place. Usually, when I go to Jaipur, I am on a tight schedule, but Rajshree comes to meet me wherever I am, even if it is for a short while.

In college, Rajshree and I started playing table tennis. She would come and pick me up on her bicycle and I would follow on Kakaji's bicycle. She would be smartly dressed in her sports shorts, while I trailed along in a skirt. Whenever I think of those rides, a wave of nostalgia engulfs me.

Purohitji-Ka-Bagh is only a memory now. But I had the good fortune to see it come to life in the Asian Paints advertisement 'Har Ghar Kucch Kehta Hai' and perhaps for the last time, I was able to relive my childhood in those rooms and courtyards and climb those steps that we ran up to gather fruit from the trees. With bated breath I opened the doors to each room, looked up at every loft and space, gazed at the bare walls which were once adorned with photographs of a large family and as I shut the gates behind me, I remembered the words of Swiss writer and philosopher, Pascal Mercier, 'We leave something of ourselves behind when we leave a place, we stay there, even though we go away. And there are things in us that we can find again only by going back there.' Once again, I was leaving something of myself behind in my childhood home, but perhaps I had found much more, which I was taking away with me after what seemed a lifetime.

Chapter 7

Clapperboard: *Muhavare Aur Lokoktiyan*

My mother never let go of an opportunity to convey some of her thoughts and her displeasure to us if she felt we were out of line. She had studied only up to Class VIII, but I would say she was more educated than all of us. She was a voracious reader and would read all the literature and classics she could lay her hands on. Pearls flowed from her mouth when she spoke or recited.

My mother, my clapperboard

She had also picked up a lot from local dialects and colloquial language of villages. Whenever she was displeased by something we had done, her admonishments were always some *muhavaras,* or idioms, to drive home her point. We used to get annoyed at that time, but now I realize how many of her idioms I have preserved in the recesses of my mind and which I now use to convey my displeasure to *my* daughter. And that she finds funny, but to my mother, it came naturally. Both my parents were fond of reading and writing; in fact, my father, who at one time did a stint with a local newspaper as editor, was fond of reading and reciting poetry. Piyush and Prasoon have probably inherited their booming voices and full-throated laughter from him. My mother loved reading Hindi magazines such as *Dharamyug, Manorama, Maya* and *Sarika.* There was no Hindi magazine that she did not subscribe to. Authors such as Bimal Mitra, Sarat Chandra, Prem Chand, Shivani, Harivansh Rai Bachchan,

Mahashweta Devi—these comprised her daily reading. She would not rest till she finished a book she had picked up. She would get all these magazines on instalments from the newspaper vendor since she did not have enough money to buy them outright. Her language must have been influenced by all this reading. We will always remember some of her idioms, sayings and teachings. And these would always come in our way of crossing our limits. One of her oft-repeated ones was *Avesh mein vivek mat khona*, never lose your discretion in moments of excitement. She would end her sentence with '*Main apne anubhav se kah rahi hoon*,' translated as 'I speak from experience.' I sometimes feel she had perhaps gone through some unpleasant experience that she didn't want to discuss, unlike parents these days who are frank in their discussions with their children. She probably thought that she would convey her feelings by reference. She would say, 'Never ask anyone for anything; always keep your palms facing down, never up.' *Phalon se lada vriksha hamesha jhuka rahta hai.* (A tree laden with fruit is always bowed down.) *Apne jaame main rahna seekho.* (Cut your coat according to your cloth.) *Tate panv pasariye jaiti laambi sor. Adhijal ghagri chalakat jai.* (An empty vessel makes the most noise. You have hardly acquired any knowledge, so why boast?) Her frequent warning, '*Har purush mein ek jaanwar hota hai*' (There is an animal in every human) would prevent us from crossing the lakshman rekha, that line of propriety. Like most girls, I must have had the stirrings of adolescent feelings, but before I took a step forward, my mother's clapperboard, with the words etched in chalk, would stop me in my tracks. My romantic film would call 'cut' and remain an untold story. I understood that no boy has the time for your platonic love. Before you know it, you are shown your place. If you see the rushes of my life there is no man in it, he is hidden behind the fog and the only thing I would see was the clapperboard. The three subjects I had in my BA would also frighten any young man: Sociology harped on the fact that Man is a social animal; in philosophy, Socrates and Plato teach you a different philosophy. Psychology was the most confusing, full of references to sex and human relationships, and Freud believed that even a pen is a symbol of sexual fantasies! In this eventuality, you are afraid even of your teachers. So, all my romances died natural deaths, contained in crumpled pieces of paper and unheard poetry, *sher* and *shairi*. I always imagined myself as Kalidas's beloved, Mallika, in Mohan Rakesh's play *Ashadh Ka Ek Din*. If you want to find me, or my first, second or third love interest, you will have to search the novels of Sarat Chandra or Bimal Mitra or look for me in the unfinished stories in Bengali literature. I would be that quiet, self-effacing, middle-class woman, vulnerable and withdrawn into herself, trying to prove her love, afraid of time, her feelings flowing like tears from a book. Such a heroine can be found in every street corner of small towns and villages and in every nook and corner of society. One wrong move or crossing the limit meant you were cut off from your home and family forever. That is why perhaps I never lost my discretion. Here, I am reminded of my close friend Nina Gupta, whose husband is Vivek. I tell her that just as well you never met my mother, or you might have been guilty of losing your *avesh mein vivek*. But on a serious note, a mother with seven daughters, each one of whom I can bet must have gone out of line at some time or the other, had to be all ears and eyes. My mother, without lifting the veil of modesty and keeping relationships in view, would caution us on behaviour and morality with her vast treasure house of idioms and sayings. But those sayings would have been inconsequential if this clapperboard had not been sounded before them.

The world is changing today. Children are exposed to a lot and made aware of dangers from people around them. Even parents talk frankly to their children, but despite this, many of these children go astray.

There are many issues that are not part of my book, but I am concerned about them.

Let me not stray from my purpose, my book, which is a memoir of my journey through my various roles on stage. Perhaps my mother's clapperboard will come down even on experiences and episodes in my story!

With my mother

Chapter 8

NSD: Drama and Beyond

'If there had been an Oscar for theatre, Ila Pandey would have got it,' wrote Vijay Varma, a local journalist in Jaipur, after seeing me in *Azhar Ka Khwab*, an adaptation of Shaw's *Pygmalion* in Hindi, directed by Mohan Maharishi, an alumnus of NSD, who had made a name for himself as a director. I was walking on air, though at the time I did not fully understand what the Oscar was! I knew that I had been recognized as a competent and good actress and the din of the standing ovation rang in my ears for weeks! I had worked in some very good plays with well-known directors from NSD. I was a great admirer of Mohan, having done leading roles in many of his plays such as *Shuturmurg, Ashadh Ka Ek Din* and *Azhar Ka Khwab*. Inspired by the accolades and the euphoria of being on stage, I dreamt of the impossible, and that dream carried me to the steps of NSD, a hallowed ground for all aspiring actors.

No matter how modest one tries to be, such reviews and praises do give one the courage to go forward. So, when I saw an advertisement in the newsletter of Sangeet Natak Akademi, Rajasthan, for applications for a short-term course at NSD, I applied without telling my mother or anyone else in the family. When I received a letter from them asking me to come to Delhi for an interview, my mother, bewildered, asked, 'What on earth is this?' I said, 'An opportunity to study without paying for it!' There was a sigh of relief from her since it was a trivial matter, related to education, but as soon as she realized that this was a scholarship to study theatre, she repeated her oft-used phrase, 'Is theatre anything to be studied? Music and theatre are like salt in *daal, namak ki tarah*, just a pinch is useful.' When

I did my usual sobbing and pleading routine, her answer was that she would put the proposal before my father the following morning. That meant that my file was stuck in the home ministry till then. Early in the morning, I heard my mother trying to convince my father. 'After all, what have we done for the girls? She is not interested in doing a master's. She will be bored sitting at home. Now she has procured this scholarship on her own strength, let her go for the interview. The selection is far off. It is possible that she may not get it. At least she won't hold a grudge against us for not letting her go. And look at it like this—there is no expenditure for us.'

My heart jumped for joy. I was so elated that for the first time I made their ginger tea for them that morning, different from my usual refrain demanding my morning tea, '*Chai pakai kya?*'

The day arrived for the interview. I was facing some formidable names in theatre, Ibrahim Alkazi, the director, Shanta Gandhi, Habeeb Tanvir. I was naturally very nervous. I have no memory of what they asked me and what answers I gave, but I do remember singing a Rajasthani folk song at the request of Habeeb Tanvir. I could see that Alkazi Sahib, an extremely attractive personality, was smiling at me. He asked me where I would stay if I was selected. I was completely at a loss for words and must have turned pale. He must have seen my consternation and said that if I had no place to stay, they could provide me accommodation in their hostel at Vakil's Lane. I think I told him that I had a sister living in Delhi. His answer was: 'Theatre cannot be pursued living with someone.' Alkazi Sahib sent me to check out the hostel accompanied by one of the students. It was a small single-storied house in Vakil's Lane. As you entered the gate, there were three or four rooms. The boys shared these rooms, and the dining room was in that block. I did not reveal to my mother that both boys and girls lived in the hostel! Her clapperboard would be whipped out and my dream of joining NSD buried forever. A little further, on the left, there was a tiny lawn, which led into another annexe with three rooms. This was the girls' wing. Rohini Hattangadi shared a room with a girl called Chhaya from Jodhpur, Jayshree, now a renowned Karnataka actress in both theatre and films, lived in one room. I was assigned a room with Saba Zaidi, who later worked as a costume designer for several Indian and international films. She had been a producer for several years in Doordarshan and has now migrated to Australia where she is a producer for television. This goes to show that NSD introduces its students to all the aspects involved in the performing arts so that later you can use this knowledge to pursue your career in this field. The choices are vast. You can take up direction in theatre and films or stagecraft, costume design, lighting or music. We had the opportunity to study and understand all these subjects. There were wonderful teachers, but once classes began, it did not take me long to realize that acting is not child's play. To approach a character that you are doing, it is necessary to be educated. Folk theatre requires you to know the mode and the tradition, the *vidha*, but when you study theatre, the horizon widens. You have to go beyond your way of thinking and your surroundings. In drama school you have to study traditional theatre along with folk, classical, modern, Indian, European, Russian, German, French, Greek; you get acquainted with the languages and traditions of several civilizations. This is not all; you must learn about everything associated with a performance: lights, sound, painting, poetry, music and dance. I was overwhelmed. Will I have to study all this? My idea of joining NSD was to get away from academics! I imagined drama school as a place where I would only perform plays and enjoy doing them. But I was confronted with a full-fledged curriculum, some of it quite out of my league. Girding my loins so to say, I took a deep breath and resigned myself to my fate—studying.

NSD had a motley crowd of students, intellectuals, with worn-out shoulder bags, hair astray and unkempt, their swagger, cigarette dangling from their lips. I felt a kind of complex among this strange crowd. I was a misfit with my traditional look, well-oiled hair and crisp clothes. '*Behenji*' was the word used for girls who came from small towns, though there were so many like me at the school. But the next day when Alkazi gave his welcome address, my perspective changed, and my spirits soared. He addressed every student as an individual, listening very attentively to each one's story, their family background, their experiences, the villages and towns they came from. He analysed their stories and explained how theatre was a vast field, encompassing every individual and his life and reproducing it on the stage. My confidence was restored.

I threw myself wholeheartedly into the exciting world of acting and stagecraft, discussing hitherto unknown subjects with my room-mate, Saba, listening to Urdu poetry, seriously reading scripts and books. Catching a glimpse of Alkazi Sahib in the corridors with his whimsical but affectionate smile and the occasional placing of his hand on my shoulder asking me how I was doing, was the highlight of my day. Since Mohan Maharishi was taking the course, Alkazi was an elusive sight and every glimpse of him added the proverbial *chaar chand* to my life.

As I have mentioned earlier, Mohan Maharishi had directed me in a few plays in Jaipur and I valued him as a director. One of the reasons for joining NSD was to have him as a teacher. Another reason was that all the students who came out of NSD, often talked about this great teacher and director, Alkazi, known fondly as Chacha (uncle) One of the things that struck me on coming face to face with Alkazi was the realization that each one of his students were clones of their teacher in their language, their mannerisms, their gait and gestures, photostat copies of the original. Imagine what an inspiring personality he had! A short man, but a larger-than-life character in our imagination!

I had made many friends by then, Om Puri, Rohini Hattangadi, Bansi Kaul. Naseeruddin Shah was also a student there. The Repertory had Raj Babbar, Nadira, Surekha Sikri, Uttara Baokar and many others who had already made a name either on the stage or on the screen in films of the so-called parallel cinema, which was making its presence felt at that time. Om Puri and Naseer were in their second year. We would visit Bengali Market for *chaat* and *chole-bhature* for which this market was famous. Many other groups from NSD would congregate there. Sometimes we would venture to the Triveni Kala Sangam café, though this was a little more expensive. This place was famous for its *parathas, aloo-gobi* and *keema*. The crowd here was a little different, comprising well-known painters and dancers, or members of the Press Club, who had established careers and so had a little more money than us poor students. Often our visits were to catch a glimpse of these famous personalities. NSD was first started at Ravindra Bhavan, Feroz Shah Road. The Sangeet Natak Akademi was situated on the first floor. This intersection at

Mandi House was the cultural centre of the capital, Delhi. Bhartiya Kala Kendra, Shri Ram Centre, Little Theatre Group and the Kamani Auditorium were all situated on the same road. We felt that we were surrounded by a hallowed treasure house of art. The only exception was the FICCI building, a far cry from the cultural ambience of that mystical road! For theatre, music and dance buffs, this area had a wealth of options. There were so many performances, art exhibitions and lectures that we were hard put to choose between them.

For the first time, away from home I had a chance to live in a free world, on my own terms and dictated by my own choices and aspirations. But my mother's clapperboard was always present in my mind. *Avesh mein vivek mat khona.* Sometimes we would take a scooter and go to India Gate. It was a pleasure to walk in the vast expanses of lawn, savouring the winter sun and the cool of the summer evenings next to the continuous pond.

The walk on the lawns of India Gate was a walk down memory lane and it reminded me of one incident that has relevance in this story of NSD. It was a memory from my participation in the Republic Day parade from school, an occasion which I have mentioned earlier. There was a long wait before we actually rolled down Rajpath for the parade. We sat, ready, perched on a tableau from 4 a.m. to 1 p.m. How was one expected to last out these nine hours without a visit to a toilet? I found a solution for my problem myself. On the pinnacle of the truck with the tableau, they had erected a structure like a temple without a deity installed in it. Whenever nature called, I would do my routine of greeting the audience on Rajpath, step down under the structure and do my bit! I must say that the *ghaghra* of the Rajasthani costume I was given, spread across the floor of the truck, provided a good coverage for my misdeeds! The thought of this makes me laugh, wondering how I escaped being caught.

I connect the need for toilets to another unbelievable story, a story about this unique teacher, Ibrahim Alkazi. He believed in the development of the total personality of every student who crossed the threshold of this remarkable institution with its charismatic principal. One day, as the story goes, he walked into the boys' dormitory to inspect their living habits as he was wont to do without any fanfare. He opened the door of the bathroom and was taken aback to see a huge six-foot student sitting on his haunches atop the toilet seat. Embarrassed, he shut the door, but sat on a bed, waiting for this boy to emerge after his ablutions. Heaven knows what the boy must have felt, perhaps squirmed at the thought, but Alkazi Sahib, in a very matter-of-fact way, told him, 'Young man, this is neither a jungle nor the banks of the Ganga, which you set out for with your *lota* in your village. This is a Western-style toilet. You have to sit on it like you would on a chair.' And to the astonishment, and I am sure, the amusement of the occupants of the room, he entered the toilet and sat on it to demonstrate.

This was Ibrahim Alkazi, who groomed young students from all walks of life, from small villages or towns, from farms or universities, and enlightened them on the small courtesies of life: how to talk, table manners, how to conduct oneself in public and also how to make the most of the opportunity that they had at the NSD. I would say he was a potter, who took the sons of the soil and moulded them into alert and aware human beings, breathing a new vision into them. He would explain the differences between *nautanki* and *natak*, folk and modern theatre. He emphasized the fact that it was as important to study to become an actor or performer as it was to be a doctor, engineer or a civil servant. Because as an actor, the student would have the opportunity to take on many parts, bringing to life personalities from all walks of life and he would have to have studied all these to be able to present them honestly. He insisted that we read the daily newspapers so that we remained connected to the social and political milieu around us.

One heard so much about this great man from everyone around and sometimes crossed him in the corridors, where he never failed to acknowledge you with a nod, and I thought, fate has allowed me to enter this temple of learning, but will I ever get an opportunity to sit at the feet of this God of theatre? Mohan Maharishi had started his classes from nine to five. We had the evenings free. One day Mohanji came and told me that the Shriram Centre in Delhi, another great cultural centre had chosen to do Mohan Rakesh's *Ashadh Ka Ek Din* and because I had performed the role of Priyangumanjari in the play under his direction in Jaipur, he said he would like me to do the role again. Since we were free in the evenings, I did not think there was any harm in doing the play. It was a good opportunity and since I had great regard for Mohanji, there was no question of saying no. I did not understand that he was moonlighting without Alkazi's knowledge. I had barely rehearsed for one day when there was a summons from Alkazi Sahib asking me to report to his office. I was taken aback and wondered why I had been called. A hundred questions came to mind and I could not sleep a wink. Somehow, I got through the night and reached his office the next morning. He opened the door, spectacles resting on his nose, two eyes peered at me as he said, 'Come and sit down.' He continued signing his files. A frightening silence enveloped me. I sat there watching the huge trunk of a tree that grew through the roof of his room. This, coupled with the vastness of the personality before me made me cringe. 'What were you doing at the Shriram Centre last evening?' The question, like a shot fired at me, made me choke, as if I had been hit by a bullet. Without a comma or a full stop, I blurted out the truth. Mohanji was my guru and he had asked me to do the part, which I could not refuse. In a few words he explained that I had come on a scholarship from the Sangeet Natak Akademi of Rajasthan to study the art of theatre, not to perform plays for the Shri Ram Centre! I was in shock. Tears started rolling down my cheeks. He continued, 'This is my first and last warning to you. If you want to perform at the Shri Ram, pack up your bags and leave the hostel. Go back to Jaipur.' Then very gently he handed me a tissue and even gave me a *jaadu ki jhappi*, which set me off again. He must have realized that I did not know that I was transgressing my commitment. His parting words were, 'Make sure you come to class on time. I will be taking that class.' I could not believe my ears! I forgot my tears and almost jumped for joy. None of the friends I had made at NSD and many who came before me had ever been taught by the great man! And I, a short-term course mendicant had the honour of being taught by him! I did not ask any questions, the whys and wherefores of the matter. I was delirious with joy. The next day, in class we were all handed the script of a Greek tragedy. He explained the importance of Greek plays for any actor, and the profoundness of thought that moulded a tragic actor. He had chosen the greatest of plays, *Oedipus Rex*, and I was asked to read the part of Jocasta. He concluded the class saying that he would decide on the casting the following day. Once again, I lay awake, hoping and praying that I would get a role and have the good fortune of being directed by him. The next morning, he announced that I was to do the main role of Jocasta. I could not believe my ears. My prayers had been answered. I was not only being taught by this great master but also being directed by him. I knew nothing of Greek theatre and had never read anything on it. Alkazi Sahib told me to go to the library and read all that I could find about the play and the character and work on my role. The story of Oedipus, performed in 429 BCE, is still the Bible of all those who study and perform in theatre.

From this day began my journey in theatre, my *natakon ka suhana safar*. The fact that Alkazi himself took classes for the short-term course was indeed an unprecedented event. And it so happened that as we proceeded with the play, the student who played the role of Oedipus was also asked to leave since he had carried on being part of the Shri Ram Centre play despite knowing that this was strictly taboo. And this resulted in another windfall for me! The man who took over this role was none other than the greatest thespian on the Indian theatre scene, the Amitabh Bachchan of theatre, Manohar Singh! By this time, Alkazi had taken up the challenge of producing this play and putting it on the stage. It was amazing to see his method of directing a play. Not being familiar with Hindi, he would plan his plays in English and yet he produced this most unforgettable of epics, *Andha Yug*, in Hindi.

I had never heard of the story of Oedipus. I was to learn the complexities of a relationship, the hundreds of little nuances that go into building a character onstage, the tragic end of unknown relationships, all through my rehearsals with Manohar Singh and Alkazi, the director. I started understanding the difference between just throwing lines or interpreting them and living the character. The play moved me so much that today I feel that if I can get the script of the NSD version of the play, I would adapt it and do the play with my actors, playing the role of Jocasta again! Those were the translations; I would write it in my words. I had heard of the Oedipus Complex in passing in my psychology classes in college but had not paid much attention to it. It was an irony that at NSD I started understanding subjects that I had taken up for my BA! I understood these only through the medium of theatre. It made me realize that theatre was a great education, a medium that forced you to explore the depths of words and ideas to their minutest details and I learnt this through the live experience on stage.

I must say that the short-term course also produced some students who later used their knowledge in their careers, becoming producers, directors and actors. Interestingly, there was even an IFS officer, Shashi Uban.

Everything in my life changed after my sojourn at NSD—my thoughts, my writing, how to read, how to live, how to conduct oneself and all this affected my performance. I went into the various aspects of acting and my views of the theatre world were completely turned around.

I recall three points of advice which Alkazi Sahib gave me as he admonished me in his office and these have become a mantra for me, not only in my professional but also in my private existence: those are professional dignity, commitment and belief in yourself.

Then there were those precious moments when our Guru, Alkazi Sahib, would place a hand on our shoulders as we walked down the corridors, adding to our confidence in ourselves, a moment shared by many a student who walked down those hallowed precincts. 'Hi, how are you? Good?'

Here I must mention one strange incident that affected me a great deal. I had just come out of Alkazi Sahib's office after the Shri Ram fiasco, wondering whether he would change his mind and order me to leave. As I walked past the cafeteria in the boys' hostel, I noticed a group of boys talking animatedly to a tall man who sat in their midst. Bhanu Bharati, theatre director and playwright, introduced us. As I passed by them, this gentleman looked at me and said in Bengali, 'Ma, you will die on the stage!' To me, at that time, it was like salt on a wound. I was still unsure of my position at NSD—whether I would be allowed to stay or asked to leave—and now this unknown man was addressing me as Ma, generally used for mothers. And he was predicting my end on the stage! I asked one of the boys who the gentleman was and I was told he was Ritwik Ghatak, who rose to become a famous film director in Bengal. The name meant nothing to me at the time. I was really depressed, and my ever-ready flood of tears disgraced me again. NSD being a small institution, word spread that Ila Pandey had taken Ghatak's remark badly. The next morning as I came to the breakfast table, the tall figure approached me and said, 'Don't you realize that I was blessing you?' My spirits rose and I still remember those words.

The performance of *Oedipus Rex* was a huge success. It was termed a studio production but had all the wherewithal of a full production—music, costumes, sets, a full-fledged production. After the performance, Alkazi Sahib called me and said that he could see that I had all the assets for becoming a good actor—perseverance, music, dance and acting—and that the short-term course that I was on the verge of completing was like touching the threshold of a temple. 'You have just touched the tip of the method. Don't imagine that you know a lot. To really go into the depth of acting and to understand the intricacies, you need to do a minimum of three years of study. This brings a maturity to your performance. You can do several roles.' I told him about my mother's parting words as I came for this course, that three months was more than enough to indulge in studying theatre. That all this was only to pass time and was like a pinch of salt in one's *daal*.

He laughed his famous sarcastic laugh and said, 'Go then and get married and produce seven daughters like your mother!' I was hurt by this remark and had no choice but to walk away. But it was an irony of fate that several years later, when I started my own theatre group and was performing regularly at Prithvi, I was at the Jehangir Art Gallery, having *parathas* at the Samovar with my husband Arun, when I heard that Alkazi Sahib was at the Art Gallery, displaying his impressive art collection. I forgot my *parathas* and Arun and hurriedly made my way to the Gallery. I was told that he was at lunch. I came back, finished my *aloo-parathas* and dashed back to the Gallery again. And there he was! I bent down to touch his feet, saying, 'Sir, I am married, but instead of seven daughters, I have given birth to a theatre group and have produced and acted in ten plays with my own theatre group, Surnai!' Alkazi Sahib knew that it was not easy for a middle-class girl in Indian society to wrest herself free of social norms and choose the path less trodden. With the same sardonic smile, he said, 'Well done! This is what I expected of you.'

I was ecstatic. I had got the blessings of two stalwarts of theatre—Alkazi Sahib and Ritwik Ghatak. Could one ask for more? These blessings spurred me on to excel in my work. I could never have imagined that I would play so many parts or be competent enough to adapt so many of Ibsen's plays and make a success of them. And the second blessing? I am waiting for Ghatak's prophecy to come true, though I will not be there to celebrate it!

When we performed *Jamila Bai Kalali*, an adaptation by me of Mario Vargas Llosa's *La Chunga*, at the Shri Ram Centre in Delhi, I invited Alkazi Sahib. He was effusive in his praise and wondered how we had discovered the playwright Llosa. He complimented me on what he called a superb adaptation. Whenever I got to know that Alkazi Sahib was coming for the alumni association in Mumbai, I was always there, disregarding the questioning glances of the graduates who wondered how I had joined the fraternity, when technically I was not a graduate.

Alkazi Sahib

My last memory of Alkazi Sahib will be a moment I will never forget. It was his ninetieth birthday and many of his students had come to Delhi from all over the country to pay homage to him. How could I miss this occasion? As my turn came to greet him, I knelt before this amazing guru and held his hand. It was common knowledge that by that time he had been diagnosed with Alzheimer's disease, yet I could have sworn that in that instant, as he held my hand for a long moment, he looked at me and he was there! Several people noticed his reaction and his daughter Amal Allana remarked on this later, saying that he held my hand perhaps in a flicker of recognition. What better gift could I have from a man I worshipped as my mentor?

'He alone teaches who has something to give,' said Swami Vivekananda, and my guru has given me a new life!

Chapter 9

Paradise 1: *Har Ghar Kucch Kehta Hai*

From booking a house to stepping into a completed one, it takes many years for people to settle down. It took us a few years too, but in those years, we travelled the whole world, like nomads, making a stop at various places and putting down our camps there, and then uprooting ourselves and trudging to another destination. We did not know where destiny would take us.

People always ask me whether mine was a love marriage. My answer is that like most Indian marriages, especially at that time,

Can you believe this is what I looked like at my wedding? So simple and innocent

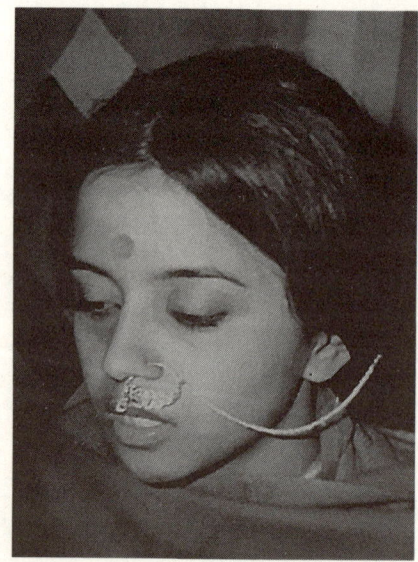

It's very difficult to leave your parents' house

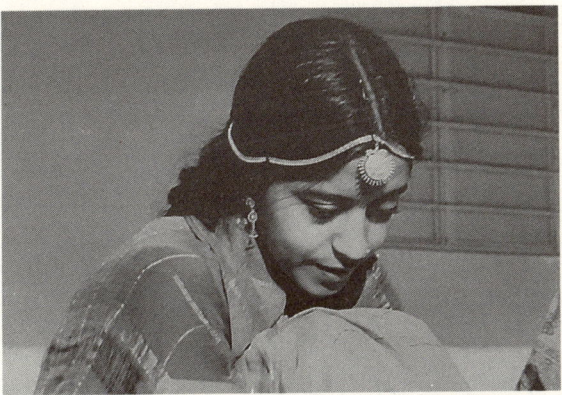

I think mine was a child marriage! This
picture is from my ladies' *sangeet* function

most of us went through an arranged marriage and love just came
along in our long journeys together. But one point or tradition in
a marriage that I did not find palatable was the change of name
for the bride. Several communities in India give the bride a new
first name too, completely obliterating her personality. Well, these
are the side effects of patriarchy! I was born Ila Pandey and could
not come to terms with the fact that I would have to change my
name, the suffix being my husband's name. My surname would be
Bajpai, but somehow I was averse to that since Atal Bihariji was our
foreign minister at the time and I thought that name carried political
connotations! Then quite out of the blue, a thought crossed my
mind: Nirmala Arun, the renowned *thumri* singer, actor Govinda's
mother. I remember listening to her *thumris* with my mother and
sisters. I discovered that her husband's name was Arun Ahuja, but
she had chosen to take her husband's first name as an adjunct to her
name. That appealed to me and I decided that I would also take my
husband's first name as my second name. Arun, the sun, paired with
Ila, the earth. And I think that name has been lucky for me!

After marriage, when Arun and I first came to Mumbai, we
stayed as paying guests at Mehra Mansion, in the apartment of a
Parsee lady, Manekbai. We had decided that Mumbai would be our
permanent home. There were two reasons for that—since Arun had
a seafaring job and I too loved being near the sea, perhaps because
I came from the parched land of Rajasthan, Mumbai was the best for

both of us. For me, it was a city rich in possibilities. Everyone knows that for any creative work—music, theatre, film or advertising—Mumbai was the best place to be if you wanted to further your career. I was interested in theatre, TV and films though I had not thought of film as a career. Most of the shipping companies had their offices in Mumbai and, as a result, all the international agents whom Arun needed for new contracts were available here. The other choice would have been Delhi, since I was familiar with it and it was close to home. But somehow, I felt that even the *aam janta*, the general public, lived in a highly politicized environment, which I found very difficult to deal with. The other aspect that I found unnerving was the class consciousness in Delhi. Mumbai was one city that accepted everyone and your address or occupation did not matter. One could always find a niche for oneself.

Arun didn't like long periods at sea. Many merchant navy officers don't mind an extended voyage, sometimes over a year, but Arun did not want to be away for more than six months. His next assignment was to be for six months, a voyage for which I would join him. We wanted to find a house before leaving so that we would have a settled home to come back to in six months.

So in 1979 began our search for a permanent home. It seemed like many others were also keen that we settle in the erstwhile Bombay, now Mumbai. Some of our friends jumped in enthusiastically, almost as if they were looking for a house for themselves. I was touched. Prominent among those who helped us were my director from Jaipur, Pinchoo Kapoor, and the renowned music director Kalyanjibhai. Every morning and evening, Kalyanjibhai would call us asking about our foray into the real estate market and the status of our house hunting. Since we were not familiar with the city, he often sent his son Ramesh to places like Santa Cruz and Vile Parle, saying, 'Show them some houses there.' This was going to be our first home, so I wanted it to be as perfect as possible. I did not want to buy a house in resale, since the whole history of the past owners would flit by in my overactive imagination. I imagined how someone had bought this flat with his hard-earned earnings and had to sell it because of some compulsions, happy or sad, one would never know. I had an unfounded superstition about the vibes of a house, what events had taken place there, some untoward incident, some tragedy. What was the energy one felt as you entered? When we move into a new home, we have a *havan,* a cleansing ritual by a consecrated fire, for *shanti*, peace. It is a house-warming ceremony and it is believed that one can turn around the Vastu effects, obliterating any negative energy contained in the house. For me, the first home must be a new building, which I can see developing from its foundations. That is difficult in a city like Mumbai because the moment the foundation is laid, builders start booking flats. A close friend of mine from Jaipur, Zafar Iqbal, who was the urban commissioner of Mumbai at the time, showed me a flat at Bandra Bandstand whose USP, according to the agent, was that Rekha had lived there in the next building. But the price was too high—Rs 9 lakh! Zafar said he would try and get a good deal for us. There was no way we could afford that flat without a loan. But in those days, middle-class families like us would not touch loans with a bargepole. I felt almost like a criminal at the thought of taking a loan! If I had bought that house with a loan, it would be worth crores today. I could have lived a life of luxury. But when we went to look at the house, there was an atmosphere of gloom since not a trickle of sunlight came through. Many of the flats we went to see somehow gave me a feeling of dejection, as if the flats themselves had been through sad times.

Ramesh showed us a flat in Bandra, which appealed to me, but I have never been able to understand the lanes of Bandra. In fact, I could not even take to the Pali Hill area, which was accessed through lanes of the *koliwadas* and *dandas,* fishing communities that had been the original inhabitants of these now-posh areas. Just a few moments there brought whiffs of the sea and with it a strong smell of fish. The soft sea breeze that I wanted to inhale came with the fishy smell! I imagined my body and clothes smelling of fish just like Matsyagandha in the Mahabharata and where would I find a Rishi Parashar to magically remove that smell? I was to be alone for long periods when Arun was at sea. I would go out to Prithvi and plays and other social events in the evening, and I would be afraid of coming back alone late at night in a three-wheeler through the *jhuggi-jhopdis.* I wanted to be in a place where, from my fourth-floor balcony, I could hear the continuous sound of passersby and their footsteps, and experience the feeling that there were always people around. The house also had to be near Prithvi Theatre. My demands for a house were always strange. When Arun took the flat at Mehra Mansions, I told him to make sure it was close to Doordarshan and near Kalyanjibhai's house. I couldn't think beyond that. I could have asked for a house in Chembur, near Raj Kapoorji, but I was adamant on being close to Kalyanjibhai and so chose Manekbai's flat at Forjett Street, down the road from Kalyanjibhai's house at Pedder Road. Smita Patil, who became a good friend after *Mandi* (1983), also lived close by at Forjett Hill.

The house hunting continued, with A.K. Hangal Sahib guiding us too. He wanted us to take a flat close to him at Santa Cruz and somehow in our wanderings we were shown a flat on the main road at Santa Cruz, close to where Hangal Sahib lived on 4th Road, in the street off the road from us. The building had the endearing name of Paradise Apartments! The foundations had been laid and the construction started. The location seemed all that I had desired. It was close to Hangal Sahib, a stone's throw away from the highway, the airport, the local station and a school, Arya Vidya Mandir! Santa Cruz was a good neighbourhood; I loved the name, since in my imagination, it reminded me of Santa Claus! The name means Holy Cross and one of the legends has it that a crucifix in front of St Teresa's church suddenly started blooming with flowers!

It looked like what the builder had shown us. Huge trees of bottlebrush on both sides of the road, which we were told were over a hundred years old. The flowers looked like light dusters or even like the brushes we use for our make-up these days! It is strange what unconnected thoughts come to your mind when you have the 'time to stand and stare'. This was a hundred times better than the smell of fish at the more upmarket Bandra! The soft sea breeze that I could now smell carried the fragrance of these flowers. I could also see that autos and taxis were available just outside the building.

But I discovered we were on the east of the railway tracks, considered slightly down market according to Mumbai standards. Of course, I had no idea of east-west, north or south, despite being the wife of a seafarer. When you go to buy a house in Mumbai, you consider this aspect, since the west is more developed than the east for some reason. Also, nowhere but in Mumbai do you encounter this snobbery about east and west. But I consoled myself by saying that we just had to cross the Khar Subway a few metres away and we would be in the west! So, I considered myself living on the west or should I say, fringes of the west. Crossing Khar Subway, you reached Wellington Club, St Teresa's Church and the beautiful bungalows of the Christians of Mumbai. There are Parsee colonies too and this mixture of communities living together in their own colonies is the special cosmopolitan environment of Mumbai, the USP of Mumbai. I have always had the desire to know about different cultures and communities, something that we missed in Rajasthan. So I was fascinated by the area. Just across in the west was the Arya Vidya Mandir School and in the east was the Sindhi writer and folk singer, Ram Panjwani's Sita Sindhu, a place of congregation for religious and cultural functions. I had the foresight to plan that this institution would be useful when we started theatre and would need a place for rehearsals and indeed for years we have rehearsed in the halls of Sita Sindhu.

This flat cost us Rs 2,30,000 and since it was under construction, we had to pay in instalments, which suited us. Arun, who bought the house, said that he could manage the Rs 2 lakh, but we were short of Rs 30,000. I asked my mother whether they could help us. She, as expected, said she would ask my father. As usual, the file went from the home minister to the CM! The reply came fast. They would give us a loan of Rs 30,000 with interest. I could understand their predicament since they had several other children who might need help. I gave them a deadline for the return and I am proud to say that I kept my promise and returned the money with interest on time. I do not believe in taking loans unless it is absolutely necessary and I feel loans should be returned before any reminder from the lender. This is a point of honour and trust, which should never be compromised. I have been a victim of this breach of trust several times. People have taken loans from me with the promise of repaying, but sadly, all those promises have been broken and the loans never returned!

Then we were faced with a dilemma, which I suppose most home buyers face—black money for builders. I knew nothing of this and it appeared that Arun was also clueless about black money transactions. He was an NRI, working for a foreign firm, so every financial transaction was in black and white. How does one obliterate the white to make it black? I had never heard of black as the colour of money. I knew of it only in terms of pencils and clothes and the colour of night! I love black as a colour for my clothes. The builder asked us for Rs 75,000 in cash. So, we took it out of the bank and gave it to him. I laugh when I think of how little we knew of the ways of the world. The builder also accepted it without question. How was he to know that this couple was so naïve? Much later, a family friend, who was a property consultant to the builder, just casually asked about the flat. When he heard about the Rs 75,000, as a bank transaction, he got really worried. I don't know what he did after so many years, but he somehow turned around the money, showing it as a loan. Then our white turned into black for the builder. After this, my preference for black clothes waned, since I finally understood the difference between black and white.

The *grihapravesh* (house-warming ceremony) was in October 1979. We did all the traditional rituals. My sister Sudha, who knew about these ceremonies, came over to take charge, and with my mother's remote control, conducted everything without a hitch. One of the rituals was to let milk boil over on the gas, something which in our growing-up years was considered a mishap and drew my mother's wrath!

Har Ghar Kucch Kehta Hai, beautiful words coined by Piyush for Asian Paints. There is no doubt that each house has several stories to tell, a story for each inhabitant. If walls could talk, they could recount so many moments of joy and laughter, of ups and downs, the highs and the lows, stories of depression and tragedy and the spirit of those living there, who overcome everything and continue with their lives within the many walls of the house. This is the apartment that we have lived in for forty years. So much has happened here, so many lives made, so many success stories that bear repeating. The name itself is Paradise. When we bought this place, we thought only of the pleasure this home would bring us. In my view, it was like paradise. It has proved very lucky for me and given me a lot of peace and my own space. A two-roomed flat may appear small to others, but for me, it is akin to paradise. My folk songs are embedded in every brick and slab and the walls have listened to every story I have written.

The table in the dining area has been the inspiration for five adaptations of Ibsen's plays and four new dramas. Every morning, from 4 a.m. to 7 a.m., till the house wakes up, it is this table that hears all my stories and registers my thoughts. This was my writing table and on this I saw the first rays of the sun coming through the window on my balcony, the hopping, chirping birds on those green trees. The tree-lined streets, the sound of feet on the pathway, so many songs have been inspired listening to those sounds and watching life go by! In this small space, between sips of tea, I have composed songs for ten albums—eight in Hindi and two in Bengali. Each piece of furniture has been the spot for my imagination to soar high, and perhaps been worn out in the process.

For the members of my theatre group, this was an *adda*, a meeting place. For friends like K.K. Raina, Virendra Razdan and Binny Latif, it was their home. There were several cookouts with different cuisines, dominating which was always the Kashmiri *yakhni* and *rajma*. The constant activity in the kitchen always ended up in a party. It was here that the most renowned artistes and singers like Padma Shri-recipient Allah Jilai Bai, the late Kalyanjibhai, Hari Prasadji, Shivkumar Sharma, Shabana Azmi, Javed Akhtar, Mrinal Sen and Jagjit Singhji came to share their talent and join us for a cup of tea or a meal—so many who left their creative mark on the walls and floors of the room, some who are no more with us but in the

With my friend Virendra Razdan

she instantly attracted the audience's attention towards her.

A scene with Lateef Binny in the Hindi version of
Albert Camus's play *The Just*, as *Jaayaz-Najaayaz*

real Paradise, though they will never be forgotten in this paradise.
I will never forget the concert of Allah Jilai Bai, when *gaddas* and
gao takias (mattresses and bolsters) were spread on the floor and
with four musicians in this tiny place, which seemed to grow in
size with its occupants, her songs too brought a bit of Rajasthan
into this paradise. Kalyanjibhai, who had been a friend before I got
married, made informal visits here, especially during Navaratri. He
had relatives in Vile Parle and when he went there for Dandia, he
would often take us with him and when he dropped us, he would
have to spend some time here. If we didn't accompany him, he would
still drop by. He was a night bird. He would ask me to bring out
the harmonium and sing long into the night. His wife, a very simple
and down-to-earth lady, would go into our bedroom and sleep on
the floor, which she liked because the marble floors were cool. Then
without any fuss, she would get up quietly and go into the car when
it was time to leave. I had no furniture in the house at the time.
I did not want to crowd the space since there was a constant flow
of visitors. I had only four pouffes, which I had got from Egypt.
The house was furnished by contributions from our theatre friends,
who would bring things like curtains and cushions from Fab India
and chintz sheets from the bazaar to sit on. Each new play added
something to our flat.

Kalyanjibhai played a huge part in settling us in Mumbai. Besides
helping us with the search for a flat, he also wanted to introduce us

to life in the city. He took us to the races for the first time. I had never seen racehorses before; only the horse droppings on the streets of Jaipur! He introduced us to the actress Binduji, an avid race enthusiast who owned a couple of horses, with her husband Champaklal. I am sure everybody could see that this young woman, all dressed up in Rajasthani attire, was from a village, without any knowledge of horse racing or the means to bet and gamble. I am sure that even the racehorses could gauge that! But Arun had class, he picked up the ways of betting very quickly. He would shout out to his horse and if his favourite one was left behind, he would call him a 'son of a bitch'. I wondered how a horse could be that since its pedigree came only from horses and mares, and not from canines! I did not even attempt to gamble, always being conscious of my mother's warning that one should stay within one's means. Arun also had to fall in line. He lost some money at the races and never went back again to the racecourse!

This is that house where world-renowned musicians like Ghulam Ali Sahib, whom I had met at Kalyanjibhai's house, came and sang for me and my friends. He became a close friend, and I was a great fan of his singing and I don't think I missed a single concert of his. He never sang in large auditoriums except for one or two exceptions, but always at private *mehfils* in people's homes. The music directors of Bollywood loved to listen to Pakistani singers, and at that time, they were invited without restrictions. This was the time when the renowned Pakistani folk singer, Reshmaji had also visited India. There are so many memories of Ghulam Ali Sahib. Many doors were opened to me because of Kalyanjibhai. Without him, I could never have had access to these rich homes, the owners of which were patrons of these musicians. I was fortunate enough to meet many other stalwarts of the Bollywood Hall of Fame through Kalyanjibhai—people like Laxmikantji and Pyarelalji. I went several times for concerts at Pyarelalji's house. He had a large hall in his home, which could seat several people. Then Ghulam Ali Sahib also started taking us with him for his private concerts. I have every cassette of his concerts, priceless collections of private recordings. I was very quick to acquire these cassettes. The moment a music company handed over a cassette to him, I would take it saying, 'Khan Sahib, you can get another one. This is my property!'

This home is one place where creativity flourished and people from the theatre world dropped by without any hesitation since they were welcome in my house at any time. My doors were always open for my friends and they all felt comfortable here since they said there was an atmosphere of simplicity without any show or pretence. Khan Sahib's fingers played over the keys of my harmonium, and we all joined in his impromptu singing. But I never had a *baithak* for him at my house. I knew that I could not afford his fee and that would be unfair to him. I also wanted to protect him from the evils of piracy, which I had been a victim of. He would often say that he would be quite happy to have a mehfil at my house if I wanted to oblige someone who would be of use to me, like police and government officers, officers of the Income Tax department, even doctors, but I did not want to take advantage of a precious relationship.

This was against my principles. He liked my home because of the simple atmosphere of informality. He would always ask my cook, Anita to make him simple moong *daal* and *rotis*. Since we did not cook meat in our house, he would sometimes ask his brother to get some *shalgam*, turnip, from the vegetable market and make *shalgam* and meat. His cooks were friends like KK and Razdan, who would cook the non-vegetarian meal for him. For this was not only Arun's and my home but the home of all my friends and they had open access to my kitchen. Ashok Bajpai, a distant cousin who lived at the Lovely Guest House near us, would come and listen to Khan Sahib and share the meals cooked by a team of Kashmiri cooks. Ashok unfortunately passed away recently. All these memories are the earnings of Paradise. I remember when we celebrated our daughter Ishitta's first birthday in the flat, we had no furniture and had to hire chairs. But that did not deter us from calling over seventy guests! We got Persian Durbar to cater for this party on Hangal Sahib's recommendation.

But the greatest pillar of this home is Arun. Whether the rays of sunlight enter the home from outside or not, we have a sun within the four walls. Arun means sun, and the earth, Ila, has no existence without the sun. An Albanian proverb says, 'The sun at home warms better than the sun elsewhere.' Arun and I did not match our horoscopes since as you have seen, my mother did not know when I was born. It is always difficult to write about people who are close to your heart, in fact, those who live in your heart. There are no words to describe such a relationship. So much can be written that I don't know where to start. The foundation of a building is its most important feature, and Arun is the true foundation of this house. He is also the ruler of all our hearts, the captain of our lives. T.S. Eliot has said, 'The home is where one starts from.' Truly, Paradise was the beginning of all my activities and success. My mother, being old school, never praised any of us, but she was always singing praises of Arun, in front of him, and in his absence too. She always said that I should be grateful to Arun because if he had not given me space in Mumbai, I would not have been able to do anything. 'All this theatre and films and you doing your own thing is only because of Arun.' She was right. Anyone doing anything in Mumbai has to have a roof over his or her head. Only then can they spread their wings and follow their dreams. I give all the credit to Arun, because he gave me that mental space, which is every woman's right. Marriage is not the be-all and end-all of a woman's capabilities and desires. The rich may have huge homes, cars, gems and jewellery, but the woman has no space for herself. She cannot express herself and is smothered under the weight of her expensive accessories. I did not have the accessories, but I had the space.

We share the same interests. Arun has given wing to my thought and imagination. He was behind me, motivated me and said that I was capable of great things, great possibilities. It is very important to have complete understanding and trust between husband and wife otherwise misunderstandings can cause havoc in a relationship. And the house can fall like a pack of cards. In my profession, I have more male friends than female, which can always be a bone of contention between husband and wife, but these friends are as close to Arun as to me. I am not interested in socializing and attending kitty parties. I can spend that time talking to Arun. We have similar interests and even though Arun studied engineering, he had a great interest in the creative arts and has even done a three-month course in film-making from London. He was planning ahead, thinking that after retirement he could help me in making a film, if I decided to do that. All sailors, after sailing for a long time, start their new life near the sea, always settling on seashores. Having spent a lot of time alone, they want to be with their families. From the beginning, Arun always found my choice of profession interesting. In fact, he has faced the camera for ads a couple of times like a professional actor. Director Mahesh Bhatt loves his face, but Arun didn't want to be an actor because he felt he didn't have the ability for it. But he understands everything about this activity and is the backbone of the Surani Theatre group, helping in all our productions and handling all the administrative work of the group. Whenever he returned from a voyage he had cassettes of popular singers like Farida Khanum, Reshma, Shafqat Amanat Ali and it was through him that I was first introduced to many of these singers—Indian, Pakistani and even Western. He introduced me to jazz and Western pop, which he had heard in his travels to the West. He watches all my plays at least five times and then comes home and gives his comments. He is my greatest critic, sometimes making me lose my cool. He points out all the mistakes, the lines forgotten, the errors in the lighting or music. I cannot convince him that because theatre is a live performance, there will be mistakes and each performance will be different. But Arun does not forgive me for mistakes onstage, expecting his wife to be perfect! Live performances allow you to improvise. But if, after a show that you are unhappy with, you come home and your spouse lists your shortcomings, it is the last thing you want to hear. Even the director doesn't pull you up, but Arun may even say that it was my worst performance! But then he is my anchor, the rock that I lean upon. All is forgiven and life goes on beautifully!

The following words which I wrote on our last wedding anniversary sum up our relationship.

Who says we did not have our quarrels and disagreements/That we lived in constant joy? No, there was an understanding between the sun Arun, and the earth Ila, that the sun would stand like a rock for the earth/ Never leaving it in darkness/ An unspoken love/An accepted compromise/Relationships are made of this/Where a few ups and downs are lost in an aura of goodwill.

Chapter 10

Act I: *Natakon Ka Suhana Safar*

Hindi theatre, despite its prolific literature, still stands alone and orphaned. The most unfortunate fact is that it has never had a dedicated audience like some of the other regional language theatre. No audience basically translates into no money! The Hindi-speaking public of Mumbai chases Bollywood rather than live theatre. Parents spend a couple of thousand rupees to take their children to malls to see some inappropriate film or they spend their time at home stuck to the TV, which has such a large choice of over-the-top (OTT) shows that you can spend weeks following them. Live theatre or classical music programmes are not part of their entertainment list. Sadly, Indian cities have a good audience for English theatre, rather than Hindi. For the well-to-do Westernized Indians, this is like their interest in golf, an expensive hobby. For me, theatre is more challenging than golf.

A golfer stands for hours on the course trying to hit a ball into a hole. Following him is a caddie whose only job is to ascertain whether the ball has indeed rolled into the hole. If you are involved in Hindi theatre, you are like the ball that falls into the hole with no caddie to pull you out! The actor has to bring his audience to the edge of this hole and convince them that this is not just a slushy mess, it is an unseen treasure house of enthusiasm, sensation, awareness, excitement and vibrancy. If you step into it, you will find the fuel to encourage and excite you.

If I go on in this abstract way, my book will be rejected by my readers and another project will be left unfinished. So let us move on to the actual topic, the theatre. There are so many spicy stories tied to the stage—stories of the green room, backstage tales, what happens in the wings—that if Prithvi Theatre were to recount these stories and whisper all the secrets it holds, the stories that emerge will carry on forever!

There are so many groups that have performed here. When I started performing forty years ago, most of the actors in these groups were either from the NSD or had worked with directors like Nadiraji, Dinesh Thakur's ANK Productions, Satyadev Dubey, Yatri Theatre and Indian People's Theatre Association (IPTA), etc. In those days, Prithvi was not popular with English theatre groups like Alyque Padamsee and Pearl's well-known productions. They had directed musicals, plays by American and British playwrights and of course Shakespeare, the Bible of English theatre. They preferred the theatres of South Mumbai since their audience was from those parts. Now English theatre also has a substantial audience in the suburbs.

Theatre actors form a close-knit community since they spend a lot of time together in the rehearsal room. When you rehearse a play for over two months, getting under the skin of a character, you go through a gamut of emotions. You identify with the mental make-up of the character and the relationships associated with your character. This is like walking on the edge of a sword. At times an actor cannot distinguish between the real and the imaginary world that he inhabits for those months of rehearsal. One doesn't know how and when these relationships are formed—some exploitative, some emotional, some attractions, some momentary, some reach a plateau, but there are several that are locked forever. We have seen many that lie shattered and fragmented too; homes broken never to be built again. The characters and emotions an actor represent onstage, which he is adept at portraying, often overtake his psyche and can wreck his life. Life on the stage churns up a host of images and feelings—emotions such as love, hate, creation, frustration, imagination, ambition, the applause and then the emptiness and loneliness. These are exacerbated by the lack of work and of course the prospect of a life of penury.

There were not too many options for an actor in those days. OTT, roles in advertisements or in TV serials were few and far between since there was only one channel, the official one, Doordarshan. There was only one attraction for actors to converge on the erstwhile city of Bombay—films and Bollywood. For most aspiring actors all roads led to Prithvi Theatre. But theatre was only an excuse. Appearing on the Prithvi stage was considered a stepping stone to the world of films. Prithvi Café, which generated a romantic ambience, was another haunt of actors. Directors, writers, music directors and well-known artistes were easily accessible at the café. Places like The Press Club, Madras Café and cafes like Prithvi were the *addas* for creative and talented people from the art and theatre world. We too, liked to congregate there because we lived and breathed theatre, it was in our blood. Many actors hung around Prithvi, hoping to meet one of these directors. Some came merely as tourists hoping to catch a glimpse of the glitter of the Bombay of that era.

It is not easy to lead the double life of an actor. That is why actors are generally believed to be frustrated and obsessed. To swing between the reality of life and your character onstage and then back into your own life can be a slow process. Many actors cannot handle this life of illusion and reality. As he steps off the stage, away from the bright lights, he is suddenly blinded by the darkness of the real world and loses his touch with reality, sometimes never to return to it. And yet people say suffering is the most powerful teacher of life, a suffering that an actor deals with daily in his life and work.

An actor's life begins in the green room, as he sits in front of a mirror, looking at the transformation as the make-up man works on his face, changing his personality and casting him in the role he has to play. The final stage, the moment you put on your costume, you become the character you are portraying. You take on the mental make-up of the person, remembering his lines, speaking his language and imitating his mannerisms. You have spent hours in rehearsal, converting the character's thoughts and soul into your own. Your entrance onstage makes you that character in front of an audience for a couple of hours. You make your exit and once again in the green room you sit by yourself, wiping your make-up off with coconut oil, seeing your real self in the mirror; the costume goes back on the hanger and with it, your character. Accepting that change and dealing with it can be very traumatic for an actor. Sometimes the illusion is carried home into your personal life and the struggle between your real self and the stage personality is very hard to disengage from. Those who can maintain their balance are successful, but those who are lost in the corridors of the mind and the stage disappear into that space. Many films have been made on the life of actors and artistes who have been lost in the whirlwind of the make-believe, between love and separation. When relationships are severed in life, they lie scattered like tiny pieces of crystal; picking them up and restoring them can be a huge task, resulting in pain, irreparable wounds and blood.

Society is more liberal now. Those days of hide-and-seek are in the past. Relationships are like a game of chess. The winner is one who has used his expertise in taking the queen out and no questions are asked. In fact, no one knows when the queen moved from one home to the other. No one knows whether the queen was abducted by the minister or the minister's wife seduced by the King! Anything can happen. Life is an open book. Relationships are flaunted not hidden.

Onstage it is drama played in the wings when at the third bell, wishing her luck, the director plants a kiss on the main actress's cheek, a kiss that would be the inspiration that carries her through her performance, also making her feel that the director was now hers for life! Even the director's criticism, the heroine's tears and the process of cajoling her and wiping her tears is part of the strange male–female relationships in theatre. These were some of the momentary perks that a director or actor takes away from his performances. But they vanish in a moment and those soft, fragrant rose petals of romance find their way pressed between pages of notebooks as dried and discoloured memories. This reminds me of Mehdi Hasan's *ghazal*: '*Abke hum bichhde to shāyad kabhī k̲h̲vāboñ meñ mileñ /jis tarah sūkhe hue phuul kitāboñ meñ mileñ*' (If we part this time, we will perhaps meet only in our dreams/ like dried flowers in the pages of a book).

The world of theatre is so different from most professions. There is no straight line to follow, no formula. It is filled with romance and struggle, truths and half-truths, and finally a few withered rose petals. Whether classical or *ghazal* singers, actors or musicians, as soon as they descend on the magical precincts of the stage, they are the performers out to dazzle their audience. But as soon as they leave centre stage, with the applause still ringing in their ears, they are faced with the reality of their lives. In those days, the minute their make-up was removed, actors would make a dash for the BEST buses or the local train to go home to their PG accommodation, grabbing a meal on the way or sometimes going to bed hungry. I was lucky. I had a home in Santa Cruz where two girls waited to serve me a hot meal. If Arun was not at sea, he would also wait up for me. I had my daughter Ishitta to come home to. Even then I am not ashamed to admit that after a performance, as I sat at the table, my dinner before me, with my family, I was among them yet far away. To this day, the passion, the character, the lines, the co-actors, the audience, the stage and its lights are not forgotten easily. You cannot break those bonds in a day or two and sometimes for weeks you live in that unreal world, intoxicated by its mysterious existence. Your mind is restless, wandering in the corridors of the theatre. But those moments slip away and cannot be recreated again—this double life is the romance of theatre.

Having given my readers an insight into my world, I wonder if there are questions in their minds about my life. Did I have any such experiences that I had recounted in my description? After all, I was young and lively and I think intelligent and attractive too. Perhaps I too had temptations and attractions in the unreal world I had chosen to inhabit. Were people attracted to me or vice versa? After all, I acknowledge that being carried away by my feelings and emotions is my weakness. Your second question would be: 'Did anything happen?' My reply is: nothing! My mother's famous clapperboard would drop down before me. *Avesh mein vivek mat khona*. But my mother was always wary of such deviations and never let us live our youth to its fullest, free from all restrictions.

When I started theatre in Mumbai, it was run in a very different style than in the present. There was indeed romance associated with it. Our bookshelves were loaded with literature and plays that we picked up from various bookshops from all over the world. We would gather all the props from our homes—carpets, chairs, crockery, vases, which we would then place on the stage ourselves. We were actors as well as backstage workers. The costumes came from our wardrobes and the money was mostly from the earnings that KK and I made from our TV shows or the rare film we sometimes got. Many of the props and furniture items came from the home of Anjulaji, a senior member of our group. Her large terrace at the Anchorage at Apollo Bunder, was our rehearsal space for many years.

Things have changed drastically for us in the forty-two years of our existence. Theatre is now only a means to get roles on TV or the big screen and be recognized by a larger audience. The young actors and actresses who join us now only want to be associated with names such as K.K. Raina or Ila Arun. We are their certificate of entry into a wider world. These days, directors do ask whether an actor has any stage experience and who are the directors one has worked with. This hope brings them to our doorstep. Often there are requests for a free ticket for a casting director and even during rehearsals; instead of concentrating on their role, some actors spend more time in talking to casting directors or making show reels that can be shown to directors, reels which appear on Instagram the next day. Aspiring actors approach us with great humility, saying that they will do anything to be part of the group; they will work backstage, help onstage with props, etc. or take up administration work like schedules, liaison work with actors, and being in-charge of tea and snacks. But as time goes on, they lose interest in the backstage and want to appear onstage and in the main lead only! So, though we can claim that our four decades can be looked at as a *natakon ka suhana safar*, we have been through some trying situations when an actor comes up to us at the last minute, informing us that he or she has been cast in an ad or an OTT series and has to leave almost immediately. Since it is a matter of money and survival for them, we have to let them go. Most youngsters of the present generation do not have any room for commitment. Their life is guided only by the bottom line, money, I guess, and rightly so.

We were made of a different mettle. One episode comes to mind to prove this. Several years ago, we were rehearsing on the terrace of a house in Juhu. Surnai was just a few years old and we were rehearsing for our second play, *Riyaaz*. We had been invited to Kolkata for a performance. In those days, theatre groups did not have the luxury of air travel but travelled in what was then the third class in trains. We had to leave in two days on a two-day journey. While we rehearsed, we saw our good friend, himself a director, coming towards us. Excitement in his voice, he told KK that he had very good news for him. He had come with an offer for a Sunny Deol-starrer, *Arjun*, being directed by Rahul Rawail. KK was offered the role of Sunny's friend, with substantial screen time. KK was thrilled. It was a big banner to work with. His life would be made if he took it on. He asked the friend when he was required. He said that the shooting was already on at Rajkamal Studios and he had to report immediately. KK was taken aback wondering why he was called when the shooting had already started. He had no idea about the script or the role, and what kind of friend he was supposed to portray. He paused before answering. 'I have a performance in a couple of days.' He was surprised at the answer. The friend said that anyone could take up his role in the play. It did not make sense that KK give up a film for a play! KK took this as an affront to his self-respect. How could his friend belittle his role in a play? It would not be easy to find an actor to replace him. His retort surprised all of us. He said that a director could find anyone to do the role in the film and film directors could also replace that actor at their whim. Actors were dismissed even at the editing table, but commitment and responsibility are essential for a stage actor. 'All the characters in the play take their cues from me and we are dependent on each other in a performance,' he said. Before the friend could persuade him further, KK said that he was a trained actor from NSD and had great respect for his profession. The friend asked KK to reconsider his decision, saying that it is not often that such opportunities come one's way. 'One day you will regret this,' he said. KK very politely told him that he never regrets any decision that he has taken. 'I am sorry to have missed this opportunity, but for me, a commitment is irrevocable.' Compare this etiquette of the past to these days, when after months of rehearsal, when the dates at the theatre have been confirmed and the production is ready to go onstage, an actor declares that he or she has to opt out of the performance since they have got a lucrative offer elsewhere. 'Our dream was to work on the big screen and we may never get this opportunity again. You will have to manage since I cannot do this play.' What can we do? Our heart bleeds and one just feels like abandoning all efforts and chucking up everything, but we also believe that the show must go on and a solution has to be found. And we are grateful that somehow we have never had to cancel a play despite the shenanigans of our cast.

What surprises me is that people pay thousands to join theatre classes with well-known directors and teachers, hoping that they will help them to get auditions and roles for films and television. But they lay no value on what they already have—a chance to learn from good directors on the floor, to improve their speech, their stance and their personality and that too free of charge. If we are lucky and find sponsors, our actors get paid too. An individual cannot step onto the stage at Prithvi without the backing of a known director, since the management wants to know who they have worked with in the past. Once they join a group like ours, they have easy access to the theatre. But their colours change after a couple of appearances on the stage. They owe allegiance to the stage as actors, but very often this very stage has no worth for them. These are the actors who do not last too long in the profession since they have forsaken the tenets of their profession—discipline and responsibility.

Another problem these days is their obsession with health and fitness—at the director's expense! Every new entrant in our group demands organic or health food and proteins—an expensive item for a theatre group. In all the groups I have worked with, including Nadiraji's, we were given a cup of 'cutting chai' and a couple of glucose biscuits in the break during rehearsals. As our group grew in stature, we tried to improve the working conditions of our actors. I assured them a comfortable air-conditioned rehearsal space and several cups of chai and *nashta*, snacks. We never had this luxury when we began our journey. Our rehearsals were in the foyers of temples or on rooftops of buildings, no matter what the season. But an actor's demands grow with every perk given to them. It's like you give them one inch and they take the whole yard.

We were lucky to have senior actors like K.K. Raina, Vijay Kashyap, Shilpa Mehta, Anjula Bedi and myself who we could count on.

But all is not lost as some of the following stories prove. Looking back over the years, I can happily say that the history of our *natakon ka safar* has several incidents, which bring out the commitment of our actors. There were many actors who are still associated with us who have made sure that the show goes on. I can happily say that not all our memories were sour or bitter. There were several moments of pure joy and pride, pride in the resilience of actors and their will power to go on despite difficulties, which still bring tears to my eyes. One such occasion, almost thirty years ago, was when we had been invited by the Haryana government to take part in a theatre festival at Ballabhgarh. The play was *Jameela Bai Kalali*. We had a group of very good actors, among them was National Award-winning actress Rajeshwari Sachdev. The other equally well-known actors were Rajit Kapur, K.K. Raina, Ravi Jhankal and me. It was close to Diwali and the hosts invited the press and actors to a Diwali night before the performance. We all were dressed up in our festive best. Rajeswari looked beautiful in a jute silk sari. The venue was decorated with ghee lamps and candles in all the alcoves of the entrance to welcome us, just as Ayodhya must have been lit to welcome Ram on his return from exile. This is a dangerous mistake that we often make on festive occasions without realizing that this beautiful illumination can, with a little oversight, take the form of a raging fire. It happened in a moment. At some point in a conversation, Rajeshwari must have leaned against the wall with a lamp in the alcove. Accidents happen in a second. She was engulfed by fire; her sari having caught a spark from the lamp. My husband Arun, who being in the Merchant Navy had been trained in fire drills, had the presence of mind to pull off his jacket and wrap it around her, thus putting out the fire. But by that time she had already got third-degree burns. She had to be admitted to the ICU. The doctor told her that she would have to stay in isolation at least for a month and a half to prevent infection. She was in great pain too. The doctor categorically told her that there was no way she could perform the next day. We were in a quandary. The organizers suggested that I sing some of my popular songs such as 'Choli Ke Peechhey' or 'Vote for Ghaghra', which had become all-time hits and were on everyone's lips at the time.

'Make it an Ila Arun Night,' was their suggestion. I was amused and told them that it was not so simple. An Ila Arun Night was not a preserve that could be pulled out from a pot! It was a huge affair, which entailed getting folk singers and dancers from Rajasthan. It was impossible to make their travel arrangements, their flights and buses, and rehearse with them a few times before the performance. I told the organizers that their budget would shoot up too. Other suggestions were offered—that we could just recite dialogues from the play or have poetry readings. In the meantime, I had talked to my niece, who worked for HBO in Delhi at the time and happened to be there for our performance. I persuaded her to help us out and told her that she would have to sit on the stage, with a veil over her face, without any movement and her co-actors would perform around her. The idea was to record Rajeshwari's dialogues in someone else's voice and play them on the stage. It was a formidable task, but there seemed to be no other solution. She agreed like a good sport and even started practicing onstage.

But we were in for a surprise or should I say, a shock? Rajeshwari's father, who had accompanied us from Mumbai, came with a message that took our breath away. Rajeshwari said she had taken permission from the doctor and she said the show must go on. Her father said we should go along with her decision to keep up her morale. I was amazed that a father would be able to convey such a message, despite knowing the precarious condition of his daughter. But he is also a theatre actor who has worked with IPTA and knows the etiquette followed on the stage in his time—that the show must indeed go on. Hats off to the courage of the father! How well he handled the situation when our Diwali turned into Holi and his daughter, like Holika, was engulfed by fire.

Rajeshwari came onstage in bandages. The doctor had advised that no actor should go close to her. The play was staged without a hitch and at the end of the performance when I told the audience under what circumstances the play had been performed, they rose together and the standing ovation went on for a good five minutes. I was so overwhelmed that I declared to the audience that I would sing 'Vote for Ghaghra' since Rajeshwari was in a ghaghra and this would be an ode to women, since this young actress had displayed the courage and the nerves of steel needed to be a leader. This is also a tribute to the discipline of an actor who will get on to the stage even with her last breath, making sure that no performance is cancelled because of her, no matter what obstacles come her way. If ever we write a history of Surnai, Rajeshwari's name will appear in golden letters.

Another actor whose name comes to mind is Rahul Bagga. Rahul is an experienced TV and stage actor from Delhi. We had started our Ibsen Festival and were casting for the play *Peer Ghani*, an adaptation by me of Ibsen's *Peer Gynt*. We had planned to cast two actors for the role of Peer, the young Peer and after the interval, the older Peer. Rahul was cast as the young Peer and K.K. Raina, who was also the director of the play, as the older Peer. I played Peer's mother Åse. In one scene, Rahul has to jump off from a height and despite our warning him not to do this, he got carried away and did jump and hurt his foot. But the next time it was more serious. In the scene he is having fun with his friends, teasing them and playing games. In the excitement, somehow someone must have pulled his arm a little too hard and his shoulder got dislocated. He was in great pain but tried to hide it. In the interval probably he told the other actors and they somehow managed to push the shoulder back into place. I am surprised they knew how to do it, because I had never seen anything like this. I did hear a loud sound from backstage which I was told later is the sound the ball-and-socket joint makes when it is pushed back. After the interval, there is a death scene where Peer comes back to see his mother for the last time. The mother gives him some advice and rues the day when he had chosen the path of destruction by turning into a terrorist. She explains the tenets of Islam to him and recounts a story which she had told him as a child. As she closes her eyes, Peer lets out a wail and starts sobbing. Now this was a scene we had enacted many times, but this time it was different. It was so intense, that I wondered whether Rahul had drawn upon some emotional memory which affected him deeply. In fact, I was tempted to open my eyes surreptitiously to look at him even though I was dead. When I came backstage after my scene, I wanted to ask Rahul about his reaction. I was told that he had been taken to Nanavati Hospital by my husband, Arun, because the shoulder had got dislocated again and he was in great pain. I was perplexed by the fact that his shoulder could come off and on like a Barbie doll's body parts! The doctor suggested surgery, but Rahul pleaded with him to postpone it since he had a show the next day. The doctor did fix his shoulder temporarily and he met me backstage after the curtain call. All the girls were weeping for him—all of them loved him in different ways—some as a friend, some as a lover, some as a brother and I as a son. He was known as my blue-eyed boy, a mature young man, extremely well-mannered and most of all, true to his profession. He insisted that he would do the last show the following day and then think of what to do next.

So, we proceeded with the show the following evening. One thing proved useful for Rahul's performance, his costume, the *phiran*, that is worn in Kashmir. In winter, Kashmiris carry a coal-fired pot called a *kangri,* drawing their hands inside and holding it under their *phiran.* The sleeves hang loose giving the impression that they have no arms. Rahul was able to keep his sling and bandage underneath the *phiran* completely out of sight of the audience, and no one guessed that something was amiss. At the curtain call when I told the audience about Rahul's accident, he got a standing ovation. The audience must have realized that acting is not such an easy or comfortable profession.

After a couple of days, I was told that Rahul has to be operated on. The problem was he had no medical insurance and of course he had no money for the operation. I took him to see Dr Anand Joshi, a leading orthopaedic surgeon, who was the doctor for several sportsmen, including Sachin Tendulkar. I requested him to give Rahul all the discounts he could to an artiste. The operation was successful and Rahul came home, but the financial beating that Surnai took shook us into realizing that all actors and performers must have medical insurance. But I strongly feel that the artiste must spend on his own insurance. Actors perform with their bodies and often get so carried away by their feelings that they lose their sense of space and height and can injure themselves. I will always remember Rahul and Rajeshwari and their dedication to their profession.

As I have said, every production has memories—some bitter, some sweet and some amusing—which bring a smile to your face when you look back on them even though at the time they have disrupted your performance. One instance that I remember concerns Vikrant Mishra, who had come to work backstage with us. His first duty with us was on the sets of *Namaste: Jai Sri Krishan.* We were performing at the Mysore Association Auditorium in Matunga, which has no proper green room. I was doing the role of a religious, middle-aged lady, who is always in a state of flux because of the idiosyncrasies of her family. I had a two-minute change in one scene. I had timed the change and pleated and pinned my sari and laid it on two chairs in the wings within easy reach. But when I came into the wings to change, lo and behold, there was no sari! I looked all around in panic. I had already taken off the sari I was wearing and would not have enough time to put the pleats in place in those two minutes. I looked a little further and what do I see—Vikrant Mishra, our great backstage helper, lying on my sari fast asleep, snoring. This is where my emotional memory came to my aid. Somewhere in my subconscious, I had an image of my mother, fresh from her bath, coming out of the room pleating her sari to attend to the various queries of her girls. She was oblivious of the fact that she would have been considered half-clad, like Mandakini, her petticoat showing and her pleats falling out as she gave instructions to the family members. I did the same and came onto the stage, petticoat showing, pleating my sari and continuing with my dialogue. This completely floored the audience who saw it as natural acting. I told them that the credit for this should go to Vikrant Mishra, who used my costume as a sheet to sleep on, when he should have been on his toes, attending to our needs backstage! I suppose one must also list the bitter memories, memories that shake your faith in actors. I would count that day as the blackest day in the history of Surnai. A young girl came to us, offering to be a backstage helper. Slowly she wedged her way upwards, showing great interest and endearing herself to us through her hard work. She even took on a couple of roles in our productions. As time went by, she began to ask KK questions about the NSD and its courses. After a few performances, she asked KK if he could recommend her for admission to NSD. One of the preconditions for admission to NSD is that you must have had some prior theatre experience. Her stint with K.K. Raina, a highly respected alumni of NSD, and me, was her passport to the school. KK gave her a good reference, something he doesn't do too often, saying that she was a competent actress and had worked with him in some productions.

After passing out from NSD, she came back to work with us while she waited for film offers. She joined us for the Ibsen Festival, doing a role in *Peechha Karti Parchhaiyyan*, an adaptation of Ibsen's

Ghosts. There is a scene in the play where the son of the house and the house help are seen as shadows at the back in an intimate embrace. I was the Rani, who watches this and sees a repetition of the same debauchery her husband perpetuated in the past. We will never know what actually passed between the actor and the actress, but something made her blow a fuse. She was hyper before the show and then suddenly she came to KK and me and said she was out of the show, four hours before we were to go on. In that moment she forgot that she called me Ma and KK her Pita and it was through his efforts that she had got into NSD. There did not seem to be a serious problem, since we were all witness to their scene and we told her we would sort it out after the show. But she did not listen to anyone and just walked off without giving a thought to what would happen to the show. What surprised us was the fact that she was fresh out of NSD, where students are taught the etiquette of the stage and the discipline necessary for an actor. KK is always ready to take up a challenge. He said he would tell the audience about the showdown and actually stand on the stage, reading out her lines from a script. But the show must go on! He would explain that a play is dealing with reality and something like this could happen in real life!

But luck does favour the good and this time it was on our side. We learnt that one of the actresses who had played this role in the first few shows was in Mumbai and actually riled about the fact that she had been replaced in this show. KK had to apologize to her and pander to her ego and she agreed to come down immediately to do the role. She rehearsed for a couple of hours and was ready to go on stage. The performance went off very well.

After the show, the consensus was to blacklist the girl who had let us down so badly. I remember how Nadiraji had the same crisis in her group. One of her actresses, quite well-known at the time, threw a tantrum and refused to do her role in a play. Nadiraji told her that she could leave, but she must not be seen in the Prithvi compound. Nadiraji would handle the situation and cancel the performance, telling the audience that her actress was not well. But the girl had the audacity to sit at Prithvi Café, in full view of everyone. This was an affront to Nadiraji and she took the decision to blacklist her. When Jennifer heard about this, she was very angry. She said this kind of behaviour shall not be tolerated at her theatre. The misunderstandings and quarrels between the actors were their personal problems and should not affect a performance. The show must go on. She put this actress on the blacklist and told all the groups who performed there that she was not to be part of any performance at Prithvi. She was also banned from entering the Prithvi premises.

Theatre has its own rules and culture. It cannot be treated as a stop for the longer journey to the big screen. It is not a *dharamshala*, a resting place, or a ladder to take you to other heights. It is a temple and you cannot play around with the sanctity of the theatre. Like any other profession, it has its conditions. It is an extremely demanding profession and you come to it after a very tough training, which takes a lot out of you. It is an ordeal by fire through which an actor passes either to be destroyed by it or to come out cleansed through it like gold. I am very emotional and sensitive about the theatre and also very loyal to it.

With all these difficulties, we decided that the new way of dealing with this problem was to insist on a double cast, which gives you the freedom to opt out of a performance at the last minute. But that option also did not seem to be the right one. If an actor was chosen to perform on a particular day and he was selected for some more lucrative assignment, he would assume that he could get away because of a double cast. This was not always the case because the second actor could have taken up another role too. We had a troublesome situation in an English play that we have done, *Baby's Blues*. We had selected actors after an audition. Bringing in actors from outside means they have to be paid. We had a double cast for a couple of roles, including the lead actress. Having a double cast means extra work for the director, as well as extra shifts, which bring up the cost. Dilnaz Irani did the first shows and she was amazing. She wanted to know if she was doing the second round too. We had to tell her that now it was the turn of the other actress. We went to Norway for the Ibsen Festival, and the performance was scheduled for our return. While still in Norway, I was shocked to get a call from the second actress saying that she had got a role in an OTT series and could not do the role. When I told her she could not do this she asked me, 'What would you do if you were offered a choice between a theatre performance and a series that paid you good money?' I replied that she was asking the wrong person. If I was in that predicament and had already committed to a set date, there is no way I would have taken up the series. I would regret it and feel that I had lost out, but I would never go back on a commitment. She unashamedly told me that she was opting out since it was a question of her career. Disheartened, I rang up Dilnaz, requesting her to step in. Of course, Dilnaz had to be coaxed and we had to listen to her excuses. We have by now reached a stage when we are always begging actors and actresses, almost touching their feet to ask them to oblige us. And who are these people, actors who begged us to take them in and called us their gurus? Now we tell them that they are our gurus since at the drop of a hat, they will make fools of us by leaving us high and dry on the day of the performance!

I again say that the profession we have chosen is a very demanding one. It takes a lot out of you, but I can honestly say that we have done some good work. The plays we have taken up have been different and we have taken the trouble to have the best production values in our plays. We have never taken shortcuts or compromised in either the acting or the sets and lights. The characters in the plays have been interesting and while portraying them we have learned a lot. The stories we have recounted have been thought-provoking. We work towards perfection and in the forty years we have lost some and gained some, in Harivansh Rai Bachchan's words: *Kya khoya, kya paya*? What have we gained, what lost? We cannot really fathom. There have been several ups and downs in the forty-two years of our theatre group. We have lost some of our precious actors like Virendra Razdan, who became popular in his role of Vidur in the Mahabharata.

I had performed in Hindi all my life, and though I do speak English, I am conscious that it is with an Indian accent. So, it was a surprise when one day, after the international success of *Jodhaa Akbar*, I got a call from the UK Asian theatre group, Tamasha.Theatre Company. They were going to present an adaptation of Federico Garcia Lorca's *The House of Bernarda Alba* titled *The House of Bilquis Bibi*. I was offered the role of the protagonist, Bilquis. I accepted it, taking it up as a challenge, though I was a little apprehensive. I was more confident because I was familiar with the script, having taken part in Govind Nihalani's production of the play as a teleplay called *Rukmavati Ki Haveli* in Hindi, where I played the role of the eldest daughter. I went to London, accompanied by Arun, who was my dialogue coach, taking my rehearsal every night after each performance. I worked really hard since I had to mug up each word and line, not having the luxury of improvisation in a language I had never used onstage. But to my advantage, there were so many accents among the cast members, that I realized I would fit in! I did have a problem coming on cue with some of the accents I could not understand—Welsh, Scottish, Irish and a potpourri of Asian accents. The play is a tragedy, but for me it had comic moments before the third bell, as I recited my lines to myself. It was a revelation for me to see the workings of the theatre world in the UK. Every aspect of the performance had been mapped and readied before the rehearsals began—the lights, a model of the stage, meetings with the artistic director—even the costumes and accessories were discussed with each actor and finalized. In our productions, all these are taken up much later, alongside rehearsals. We just do not have the professionalism to plan so far ahead and of course there is always a paucity of funds.

After a month of rehearsals, we had a straight run of fifteen shows at the Hampstead Theatre. We then moved to the town of Oldham which has a large Pakistani population and our last shows were at the quaint town of Harrogate, which reminded me of Matheran. I am happy to say that the shows went off very well and I did not have to improvise at any point, thanks to Arun!

Another international event we took part in was in Shanghai, where we were invited to perform at the International Theatre Festival in 2014. We chose *Death Variations* by Norwegian playwright Jon Fosse. Once again, I took up the challenge of performing in English. But this time I was surrounded by my own friends and colleagues. I also had support from brilliant actress Aadya Bedi who had made a name for herself on the English theatre scene of Mumbai. This was the first time that Surnai ventured into English plays. Later we did *A Doll's House*, directed by Pushan Kripalani, for one of our Ibsen Theatre Festivals. This was the first time we collaborated with actors from the English theatre. Since then, we have produced another

English play, *Baby's Blues*, by American playwright Tammy Ryan. Now Surnai can proudly say that we are a bilingual theatre group!

It has been a difficult but marvellous journey. How can I even attempt to put it in a nutshell, to tell my story in a few words or even in a few chapters?

Chapter 11

Act II: Surnai

The year-long celebrations for the fortieth anniversary of Surnai started on July 2022 and continued till July 2023. Starting with our inaugural performance at Prithvi, on to the National Centre for the Performing Arts (NCPA), for the finale on 30 July 2023, we were on a 'high'. There was only one thought in our minds, only one passion—that of turning this event into a memorable occasion. Surnai Theatre and Folk Arts Foundation has survived four decades! I have written about how my mother did not even remember our birthdays; in fact, she always told us that the birthday of girls was never celebrated in our family.

But the birthday of a theatre group was a different matter, a cause for celebration. The fact that we had kept the group going for forty years against all odds, was indeed a milestone. The years had been spent in going out with begging bowls. To save money, which we did not have, we rehearsed on people's terraces, in their flats, and in temple precincts but never gave up on our dreams, that of presenting 'good' theatre to audiences. We never compromised on our work.

Today as I sit at this table, the same table that has seen me write ten adaptations of plays and four original ones, I wonder how we have managed to survive, how we can proudly declare that this *natakon ka suhana safar* has been a journey of challenges, of proud moments and despondent ones, of ecstasy and heartbreak, and I wonder, what did I lose or gain?

When and at what point did I decide to start my own theatre group? So many thoughts come to my mind, an outpouring of memories, being churned in the mixie of the mind, which seems inadequate for such quantities of food for thought. As I write the story of my life, it passes before my eyes like a film, and I realize that three-quarters of the script is my life in theatre! Without this, my life is incomplete. The strange coincidence is that as I sit down to write in my red diary, the first written word that attracts my attention is this quotation, 'Suffering is the most powerful teacher of life.' How true that is! All the obstacles and disappointments we encountered made us more determined to achieve our goals.

So let me tell you the story of the birth of Surnai, 'a soulful voice of the performing arts'.

I had already made a name for myself in my *janmabhoomi*, Rajasthan. My audience considered me a sensitive yet entertaining performer. So, when I came to Mumbai I felt lost. It was a dazzling city of glamour. How was I going to have an identity of my own in this city, which boasted the leading talent in the creative field?

Now before my editor demolishes my extensive memories, I will cut my story short by plunging into my own 'jump cuts'!

I came armed with names of people I had met in Jaipur and Delhi, many of whom were from the stage or the music world. I felt I needed to tell people that I was in Mumbai to work, to be part of a theatre group where I could hone my talent. I knew A.K. Hangal, who was like a family member and because of my association with NSD, I had met Nadira and Raj Babbar. A.K. Hangal had been a member of the theatre group IPTA, the oldest theatre group in the Hindi-speaking world, having been established in 1943. Hangal Sahib was keen that I join IPTA, but somehow since my school-going days I believed that IPTA was aligned to the communist ideology, and I did not have the inclination to be a member of any group including IPTA, which I felt was aligned to a political doctrine. At that time, IPTA had many well-known members who believed in socialism and wished to use theatre to change the mindset of society and to bring about an awareness of social issues.

Then I met Nadira and Raj Babbar. I knew them from my stay in Delhi. Nadira seemed to have carried the ambience of Delhi with her and I felt completely at home. To this day when he meets me in public, Raj always tells everyone that he had started his career in television with Ila and he had earned Rs 22 for it! He had been part

of a Doordarshan programme with me. Nadira's house was at Juhu
and one had a clear view of the ocean. How I loved to watch the sea
from her balcony!

Theatre and money never go hand in hand. That is why most
theatre preparations start in peoples' homes. The initial play-reading,
the selection of the cast, familiarity with the script, all of this happens
on the home front. Till such time when the play is blocked and
rehearsals start in earnest, there is no question of spending money on
rehearsal space. Nadira's home was a haven for all actors-in-waiting
who had graduated from NSD and were eagerly awaiting a chance to
graduate to the Mumbai stage. Raja Bundela, Satish Kaushik, Anita
Kanwar, Girija Shankar, Ramesh Manchanda and Alok Nath would
all gravitate towards the Babbars' Juhu home. I did three plays with
Nadira Babbar: *Yahudi Ki Ladki* by Agha Hashr Kashmiri and Hindi
translations of Maxim Gorky's *Lower Depths* and Arthur Miller's
A View from the Bridge.

Like all debut actors, my life also started at the bottom, from
the lower depths! In that play, Nadiraji cast me in the role of the
old woman, Anna, who lies in her bed throughout the play, with no
dialogue except for an occasional moan of discomfort and pain. In
a corner of the stage at Prithvi, I lay on a bunk, calling out at my
cue. When I got the role, I was disheartened. The scenario was very
different when a few years ago, Nadiraji and Raj had come to see
me at the YWCA of Delhi, offering me the main role of *Jasma* in
the folk play *Jasma Odan*. What a come down to this role of an old
woman with no dialogue! Unfortunately, beggars can't be choosers,
so I accepted the role, thinking that this way at least I was getting the
chance to be associated with Nadiraji's theatre group and have the
support of the actors' community.

There were other perks too! Tea in tiny cups with a couple of
glucose biscuits, along with several reprimands was the order of the
day. There was never any question of actors' fees. I would cross the
rail overbridge near my house to the west, from where I would catch a
BEST bus 231 to Juhu. But it felt good to be with my colleagues from
Delhi and the NSD and my memories of north India were revived.

Despite my disappointment with the role, I realized that I learnt
a lot from this enactment. The moans were my dialogues and I had

to time my sound with the dialogues of other actors since their lines were dependent on my groaning cue! If I coughed at the wrong time, I would disturb the scene. I had to be alert all the time. Timing and volume and the consistency of the ailment were critical. In the three-hour play, there was also the possibility of falling asleep, lying on a bed at the far corner of the stage and not groaning on cue, thus throwing off the actor who waited for my cough! Thanks to Nadiraji's training, when the review of the play came out in newspapers the next morning, I was the only actress to get a mention, albeit a two-liner, but I was there. Those were the days when newspapers reviewed plays and performances and the morning after the show, we would run to the newsstands to get the newspapers. If we got a good review, we would keep the newspaper cutting in a file in the cupboard, like I did for this one. But heaven help the critic who gave one a bad review or no review, he would be cursed for not having understood the play and the newspaper discarded in the dustbin! Since actors were not paid for a performance, these reviews were our payment, keeping our enthusiasm alive. These days, there are no reviews and no payment!

There was something in Nadiraji's persona that attracted one. She was beautiful, a strong personality, sardonic and biting with her actors; her sarcastic remarks were sugar-coated pills. But she was a good-hearted soul. She was a wonderful singer, with a hearty, infectious laugh. The more I got to know her, the more I appreciated these qualities in her. My relationship with her was one of respect tinged with fear but without any complaints.

I was then cast in Nadiraji's *Yahudi Ki Ladki*. The role was small, but I got to sing a song too. The main role was given to Anita Kanwar, a fantastic actress and a good singer. We were invited to perform at Jhansi. We all got into a train in the third-class compartment, which has now been discontinued. Before we reached Jhansi, Nadiraji spoke to us about how we were to conduct ourselves in Jhansi. She told us to be careful in how we dressed and generally to stick to the decorum of a small town. This was before television had come to small towns and people were not exposed to the Western style of dressing and to ladies smoking. But despite these warnings, an unpleasant occurrence took place at Jhansi. We were rehearsing in a village on the outskirts of Jhansi. One of the actresses went to her room for a smoke. She had already been the cynosure of the villagers' eyes because of her dress, which would be considered inappropriate for a village. She did not realize that a bystander who was watching the rehearsal had followed her. Before she reached her room, he tried to molest her. Her shouts for help sent all the actors in the group to her aid and a disaster was averted. There are several incidents like this that are a part of one's theatre experience brought on by indiscipline among participants. Many actors and actresses say that this is their personal matter, but they forget that while you are in a group, you have to follow the dictates of the person in charge and not your individual preferences.

The last play I did with Nadiraji was *A View from the Bridge*. Nadiraji asked Satish Kaushik to direct the play. Alok Nath played the role of my *chacha*, who was very possessive about his niece. I remember one day I took my usual bus for Juhu and noticed a very attractive young girl, dressed in a *ghaghra-kurti*, Delhi-style, her hair done up in a bun with a *parandi* dangling down, a Gurjari sling bag on her shoulder. We came face to face on the bus and exchanged greetings. She was none other than Neena Gupta. She, like all actors, happened to be going to Prithvi too. She asked me what I was doing and I told her I was going for a rehearsal for Nadiraji's play. She told me that a friend of hers, Alok Nath, was also in the play. I told her I would tell him how I had met her. I got to know later that Alok and Neena had a very close relationship while they were at NSD and later in Mumbai but had broken up some time ago. It so happened that I needed a frock for my role in the play. Nadiraji asked me if I had a frock. I said that I did not have one. Anyone in theatre knows that all productions rely on costumes and properties borrowed from friends and family because of lack of funds. Alok piped up saying that a friend of his had left a red frock hanging on a peg in his flat and would that do. Nadiraji gave a knowing smile and asked him to bring it the next day. Much later when I met Neena on the sets of *Mandi*, I told Neena about her dress. She dismissed the frock and the incident with a loud laugh and that was the end of the conversation!

Everyone looked forward to the cast parties at Nadiraji's home, especially the young actors who got to drink—no not the usual tea, but something that they longed for but could not afford! Some of the girls also drank. The food at her place was delicious too. I was a vegetarian in those days and solely a tea drinker, a *shakhahari* and a *chai-hari,* and that too the *kullarh-wali chai.* I tasted meat much later and I have only started drinking white wine a couple of years ago.

After these plays, I realized that this was not the way to go if I wanted to establish my own identity in the theatre world of Mumbai. I was unsure of what I could do and how to set about it. I had earned a name in Rajasthan through my rendering of Rajasthani folk songs and music. I wanted to do something with the knowledge I had of the folk medium, which was not possible if I stayed with Nadiraji's group. You cannot sow your seeds on someone else's land and hope to reap the benefits. When the seed of your thoughts is planted on your own soil, you can plough it for better results. It is a difficult task, one that could sap you, but then to achieve something you have to give up part of yourself to your dreams.

Then one day I met Jennifer Kapoor, who had just started Prithvi Theatre in her father-in-law's memory. When I told her about my theatre activities in Jaipur and my achievements in the world of folk music, she gave me a bit of advice, which helped me make up my mind. She said if you have not come to the Mumbai stage using it as a stepping stone to more lucrative creative fields, if you want to do the kind of theatre you envisage, and if you want to be recognized in Mumbai, then it is essential to have your own group, which means you have to work to build it up brick by brick. It is easy to start your own group but another matter to sustain it. She said that for any project to succeed, the intent had to be honest. The process meant choosing like-minded members and infusing them with a passion for theatre. An activity like this has to counter several obstacles and work under extremely difficult circumstances, mostly without any remuneration. It was going to be a daunting task fraught with risks. She also said that it would be wise to register the group once I have made up my mind. She added that I should do something new to make a name for myself. She confessed that she was tired of seeing repeat performances of plays performed at the NSD, some of which had been onstage continuously for several years.

With this resolve was born our theatre group Surnai—upgraded and rechristened Surnai Theatre and Folk Arts Foundation a few years ago. We were lucky to get two dates for our opening, 9 June 1982, at the NCPA and 11 June, at Prithvi. But the need of the hour was money! I rang up, Zafar Iqbal once again. He was a good friend and had been associated with theatre while in college at Jaipur. He assured me that he would help me in collecting funds, but I had to first get the group registered because without that no one would give any money. I was advised to produce a souvenir for which I could collect money for ads. Registration meant going into government offices and waiting around to meet the relevant officer, if he deigned to oblige. I have always been apprehensive about entering the portals of government and like to keep my distance from them. So, I appealed to my father, who was familiar with official procedures, and he helped me get Surnai registered in Jaipur. That started the ball rolling. Zafar introduced me to some real-estate companies, mostly in Maker Chamber in Nariman Point and I would go into those offices and collect small sums, Rs 500 or Rs 1000 or at the most Rs 1500. I felt I was collecting ads from grocery stores! But my bag was being replenished with this money. By the time I finished, I was done with Maker Chamber and the very mention of those buildings would suffocate me. But I must say our souvenir turned out to be a work of art. I called upon all my friends from the literary world as well as Ashok Bajpai and his colleague Shankar Bose. Both were working for the *Times of India* and were familiar with the editorial format as well as art direction. We collected Rs 45,000, which was a large sum in those days and with that money were able to invite forty folk artistes from Rajasthan on our own strength.

A new theatre group, Surnai, was born out of our commitment and the fire in our hearts to present 'meaningful' theatre to our audience. Our byline was 'Surnai, a soulful voice of the performing arts'. The *Natyashastra* says that the primary goal of drama 'is to transport the individual in the audience into another parallel reality, full of wonder, where they experience the essence of their own consciousness, and reflect on spiritual and moral questions'. Quoting the same treatise, Daniel Meyer-Dinkgräfe, lecturer in the Department of Theatre at the University of Wales, says that the function of drama and the art of theatre is to restore the human potential, man's journey of 'delight at a higher level of consciousness'.

A tall order for a theatre group just cutting its teeth on the Mumbai stage, but we were a determined group of dedicated actors, ready for our trial by fire to prove ourselves in the tough world of theatre.

Chapter 12

Ibsen: In Love with a Stranger

If I cannot be myself in what I write, then the whole is nothing but lies and humbug.

—Ibsen

Suddenly he entered my life, a stranger from across the seven seas. I, a child of the desert, was like a doe, thirsty, searching for water, searching for true love. I followed a mirage in the desert, a recurring dream that took me beyond my ordinary life, searching for words for my thoughts, poetic words of romance and beauty.

The love of our adolescence, one's first love, they say is never forgotten. But it is also said that the love of our youth can go astray, governed only by the heart and not the mind. But forty years down the line, my love is mature, governed by the mind.

When this stranger crept into my life, I was obsessed by him, without ever having set eyes on him. I had not heard his voice nor had the fortune to be enraptured by his look, his eyes. I had only read his words—once, twice, three times, then ten, and I kept reading them, sinking deeper and deeper into his stories. Every word he wrote drew me to him and through him to society, a society he had watched and observed all his life. He motivated me to be the voice of women, women who did not dance to my songs, women who suffered through no fault of theirs, women who needed to be empowered through his writings.

Who was this man? A simple, short man, with a tall vision, a Norwegian called Henrik Ibsen. I was introduced to Ibsen by Alkazi

Sahib's son-in-law, Nissar Allana, in 2010. He was holding an Ibsen festival in Delhi, termed 'Ibsen in Tradition'. He needed to present at least one woman director at the festival and he contacted me. He knew me as a folk singer and actor who was well-versed in folk culture. He tried to convince me to direct an Ibsen play. I was not ready to take on this responsibility. At the time I was not familiar with his plays. I had seen a version of *A Doll's House* in Jaipur, in Hindi as *Gudia Ghar*, directed by a friend, H.P. Saxena. I learnt that it was written 150 years ago and had shocked the narrow-minded society of Norway at the time. He had shaken up their complacency and with it provided women the world over a new perspective on life.

At that time, Hindi theatre adopted plays of Anton Chekhov, Molière and Bertolt Brecht, adapted or translated into Hindi. Shakespeare, the most performed writer in the world was not as popular, perhaps because his English did not lend itself to easy translation. I myself was more inclined towards the Indian writers since I was more familiar with them: Dharamvir Bharati, Mohan Rakesh, Nemi Chandra Jain, Bhisham Sahni, Girish Karnad or Sanskrit playwrights such as Bhasa, Kalidasa, etc.

But once I started reading Ibsen, I could not stop. They say love is blind, but I can say that Ibsen opened my eyes and I hung onto every word of his. I was so fascinated that I took up the challenge and agreed to direct a play for the Delhi Ibsen Festival.

Devouring his plays, I went deeper into his mind, I felt myself being overpowered, submerged in his thoughts and ideas. He desired to change the concept of theatre. He steered the themes away from the innocuous farce of the French playwrights and brought the audience into people's homes and exposed them to the dark secrets of realistic bourgeois families. Many of his plays deal with the issues of women's empowerment. I felt I owned his words, his thoughts and could read between the lines and I tried to interpret them as best as I could.

As I began understanding him, and accepting his thought process, I decided to adapt him in the Indian context, to the life of the Bhartiya *nari* in Indian society. My pen wouldn't stop and over reams of paper Ibsen's words, in Hindi, were dancing before my eyes. I placed his characters in different locations, different costumes and mouthing Ibsen's dialogues in different dialects of India. His words gave me a direction to address the problems women face, surprisingly the same problems that Norwegian women were confronted with, almost 200 years ago. It seemed as if nothing had changed. I used his words to talk to women from every stratum of society, rural or urban, middle-class or royalty, working women and housewives, literate or illiterate, suffocating beneath the *ghughat*, veil, or confronting a hostile world after having crossed the limits of so-called propriety. I used Ibsen's language as a support to give full weight to my words. I wanted to shake up Indian society just as Ibsen had done, but would my words be the voice of women in India?

The stranger I fell in love with enticed me first with his play *The Lady from the Sea*. I called it *Mareechika*, a mirage. In the play, Ibsen's lead character, Ellida, after years of subservience, revolts against her position as a wife and mother, saying that she has the right to choose her own destiny. As we are aware, most women in our society do not have the freedom to take a decision on their own lives and actions. Not so long ago they did not even have a right to education. Now when they are being educated, it is the parents who decide which subjects they can take, something that will be an asset in the marriage market! After graduation, most girls are married off and have to accept husbands chosen by their families. And this is in a country which we know from our epics allowed *swayamvars*, gatherings of eligible bachelors, from which a young girl could select a husband of her choice. We know from the Ramayana that Sita garlanded Ram and chose him as her husband from among several princes. But slowly Indian society moved away from these traditions and with it came the change in the position of women. But just as Ibsen called out to the women of Norway, I too have tried to awaken the women of my country by calling out to them in Ibsen's voice.

I drowned in the magic of Ibsen, more because I was not only the writer but an actress who was using his words and my own interpretation in roles that suited me. I created a character for myself in *Mareechika*, a narrator, *bhopi* in Rajasthani, who talks about all the female characters in Ibsen's plays. Ibsen's women represented varied social strata with different issues facing them. My daughter Ishitta played the main role of Ellida, Rampyaari.

My tryst with Ibsen carried on with the adaptation and performance of *Peer Gynt* as *Peer Ghani*. The play was set in Kashmir of the 1980s, when the youth of Kashmir lost their way and joined the *jihadis,* or the militants, who brainwashed them into believing that their future lay only in militancy and martyrdom. This was very well received. In 2017, I was invited to share my experiences at the Lillehammer Literature Festival in Norway. It happened to be the 150th year of the performance of *Peer Gynt* and one of the themes of the Lillehammer Literary Festival was the focus on India. I was obsessed with Ibsen, the love of my life. They took me to Galle, the place where Ibsen was inspired to write *Peer Gynt*. Peer Gynt is as familiar to the Norwegians as Arjun is to us, a character both real and the hero of our folklore. I travelled over the fjords and valleys with him, and I started understanding his character, his compulsions and his language. I also decided that the best way to understand Ibsen was to follow in his footsteps, literally and figuratively.

I still cannot get over my trip to Lillehammer. It is etched in my mind as deeply as the scripts I write. I had left Mumbai on 28 July 2017 and arrived in Oslo around 4 p.m. Then began the most magical journey I have ever experienced. Two hours of the drive to Lillehammer was dreamlike and romantic. It was raining and there were lakes on both sides, and at every step, I was haunted by thoughts of Ibsen. Lillehammer is a hill station where the Winter Olympics were held in 1994. It was time for rehearsals with renowned theatre actor, Kåre Conradi, and the same evening we performed a scene from *Peer Gynt* before an audience of 2000. The spirit of Ibsen was surely with us, as Kåre as Peer Gynt appeared on stage, speaking in Norwegian, while I as Åse, his mother, addressed him in Hindi! It was a magical moment for us and for the audience; words cannot describe the emotions that carried us through and indeed words were not needed! Art has no language and this collaboration proved that. We got a standing ovation and we were wordless with wonder. Another surprise awaited me as the next day in a beautiful theatre, as part of the Indian festival, there was a screening of my film *Jodhaa Akbar* directed by Ashutosh Gowariker. I was asked to share my experience on the making of this film and also to familiarize the audience with the story of Emperor Akbar and Jodhaa.

The next day was a dream come true. I was taken to the famous Peer Gynt Road to Galle. This was the journey Ibsen himself took in 1862 when he travelled all over Norway collecting folk tales and stories from Norwegian culture. Locals still call it Peer Gynt's kingdom. And it is here that Ibsen was inspired to write the tale of Peer Gynt. I couldn't have asked for more; I was actually following Ibsen's footprints. I had been living the visual poetry of Ibsen while I was adapting *Peer Gynt* and now I was reliving his thoughts on the shores of Lake Galivanted, an amphitheatre that he peopled with trolls and mythical creatures. What a fabulous journey in this rediscovery of Peer Gynt, my Peer Ghani! I consider myself lucky and blessed. For me, it was a pilgrimage, a homage paid to Ibsen at Gudbrandsdalen, like taking a dip at the Sangam! Overcome, I became Åse and could not resist reciting my lines. I called out to Peer in the mesmerizing wilderness of Lake Gala. Like many actors before me and many who will follow. For every year in August, on the shore of this lake, there is a production of *Peer Gynt*, while the music of composer and pianist Edvard Grieg floats over the vast waters of the lake. As I left, I was literally floating on these magical waters.

I returned to Oslo on 2 August and embarked on another mystical journey to Flåm in a small train. Forest-covered mountains, the sound of streams and waterfalls and spectacular lakes—Norway is indeed blessed with an abundance of water. And at a stop on an ancient bridge, a tourist attraction, the voice of Solveig wafted across the mountains and waterfalls and a lady in a red gossamer dress stood atop a rock, an ethereal Solveig reminding one of the tragic figures of Ibsen's stories. Then on a misty, cold day, once again I was transported to Ibsen's world in a ship that took us on a tour of the fjords, the famous fjord which Ibsen mentioned in *The Lady from the Sea*. Spellbound, I could not take my eyes off the fjord and imagined Ellida, my Rampyaari from *Mareechika*, emerging from the waters.

I travelled to his birthplace, Skien, imagining Ibsen's childhood in those streets and in his cottage. And then to my surprise, I was invited to the Ibsen Festival in Oslo for two years running. I was overwhelmed when I was asked to be part of a panel to discuss and share my thoughts on my adaptation of *Peer Gynt*.

I was obsessed with Ibsen; I visited his house and saw the chair he sat on while writing; it is believed that to be a good writer, you must spend at least an hour writing. Ibsen wrote for one and a half hours every single day of his life! I read his books and those written by others about him; I visited the Ibsen Museum and looked through the vista of his life. Then I sat at his grave in Oslo, offering my tribute to a man who had become so much a part of my life. If this is not love, what is? It is indeed rare to follow a writer to this extent, that you are able to retrace his steps from his birth to his grave!

Then came *Peechha Karti Parchhaiyan*. an adaptation of *Ghosts*, in which I played the main role of Yashodra, Ibsen's Mrs Alving. My Yashodra was the widow of a feudal lord from Rajasthan. A strong woman, the pillar of the household, she was still unable to rise against the injustice meted out to her as a woman and the wife of a debauched man. I became that woman, as I wrote the play, completely immersed in her character. I lived the life of Yashodra and as I said my lines on stage, I could feel the pain of a mother, the torture of a wife betrayed. My words, Ibsen's words recreated in another language, conveying the same emotions. It was a unique process indeed! That is why my love for Ibsen became deeper, since I lived his characters for months, writing and rewriting them till I felt I had perfected the character and its language and emotions.

As I said my pen would not stop and I went on to *Hedda Gabler*, as *Hardit Kaur Gill*. Hardit is the spoilt, pampered daughter of General Gill. Her desire for the power and dominance that she enjoys in her father's home overpowers her and leads her to a tragic end. This time the family was from the Punjab. I adapted the play against a Punjabi background, since I felt the story fit very well in that social milieu.

We opened our Ibsen Season 8 with my adaptation of *An Enemy of the People*, which I have titled *Ajaatshatru*. Though this play was written in 1882, it is still relevant in society amidst the corruption and dishonesty in our political and social system. *Ajaatshatru* deals with water pollution and the destruction of the environment perpetuated by selfish, corrupt politicians who manipulate nature to suit their own interests and fill their pockets. In India, where tradition has been to worship nature and protect it, we are hurting Mother Earth by exploiting its resources—the seas, rivers, the air and mountains. Our tradition teaches us to venerate *agni* (fire), *jal* (water), *akash* (ether), *vayu* (wind) and *dharti* (the earth); instead, we are destroying them.

I do believe that my adaptations of Ibsen having very strong women protagonists have been very well-received by the Indian audience. Surnai has been holding the Ibsen Festival in Mumbai for the last eight years, inviting groups to perform Ibsen in several languages. Our journey began in 2010 when my adaptation of *The Lady from the Sea* as *Mareechika* was performed at the Ibsen Festival in Delhi. Since then, we have come a long way in our Ibsen journey. Our performances of Ibsen's plays in Hindi have earned accolades all over India and their echoes have reached Norway too. I am lucky too to have retained my relationship with the Royal Norwegian Embassy in Delhi and the Norwegian Consulate in Mumbai for over ten years. I am happy to say, in all humility, that in recognition of my 'obsession' with Ibsen, the King of Norway, His Majesty Harald V has honoured me with the King's Order of Merit–Knight 1st Class, an award presented to me in Mumbai.

In 2018, I was invited to the Ibsen Conference in his home town of Skien. It was the highlight of my relationship with Ibsen. To cheer me on were Surnai members: Arun Bajpai, K.K. Raina and Anjula Bedi. Later in Oslo for the Ibsen Theatre Festival, we watched a memorable performance of *Peer Gynt*, with the ninety-one-year-old Toralv Maurstad playing Peer Gynt. There were nine actors playing Peer Gynt! And Toralv was felicitated as the first Peer Gynt when the play premiered.

My pilgrimage in Ibsen's footsteps still carries on and my Ibsen adaptations will forever be infused with the heady beauty of Norway and its mysterious vistas.

Chapter 13

Act III: The Show Must Go On

It was 11 June 1982. Our inaugural show *A Musical Sandstorm* was to open at the Prithvi Theatre. We arrived at the venue with our group of forty folk artistes. The Mumbai monsoons had started and there was torrential rain. It seemed that the city was drowning in the deluge. Then to top it all, the lights went off. In a way, it was a boon since we could not see the auditorium, which had only ten or twelve people seated inside! Was our inaugural show going to end with a whimper, even before it had begun?

I managed to find Jennifer and asked her what we should do. The only sensible decision would be to cancel the show. Jennifer looked at me and said something which I have never been able to forget. She said, 'You say these performers were from villages. Which village in Rajasthan had electricity? They are probably used to performing with lanterns. You cannot disappoint the few people who have come to watch the performance in this weather. I will open all the doors to the auditorium. I will allow you to light candles as a special favour. The show must go on!' The folk artistes did not bat an eyelid and stormed onto the stage in candlelight. It was a spectacular performance for us as we gave it our all. To our ears, the auditorium seemed to ring with the applause of a thousand hands! We had done it like true theatre troopers and we took a firm resolve to face all obstacles to carry on our work.

Fast forward to July 2023. We were celebrating our fortieth anniversary. Throughout the year beginning June 2022, we had been performing at various venues. The finale was to be flagged off on 21 July. We were again at the Prithvi. Once again heavy rain and thunder and lightning were the background sounds for our performances. The only difference was that the auditorium was packed to capacity and there was a long queue clamouring for tickets! For an actor, there couldn't have been a better way to know that we had arrived! The rain did not deter us nor did the sound of thunder, which was in competition with our voice boxes.

We did seven shows in three days and I was in all of them. The show on 23 July was special since it stirred up so many memories. All our actors who had been with us for the last forty years were present, raring to go on to the stage for cameo performances from our various plays. K.K. Raina, Anjula Bedi, Vijay Kashyap, Ravi Jhankal, Rajit Kapur, Rajeshwari Sachdev and her husband, Varun Badola, Shilpa Mehta, Gaurav Amlani, Ruturaj Shinde and Ishitta Arun—they were all there to join in the festivities. There were folk artistes and singers from Mumbai—the stage like the auditorium, was so full that there was no place even for a pin.

I was worried about my capacity to deliver. My mind went back to Ritwik Ghatak's prophecy so many years ago: 'Ma, your end will be on the stage!'

Was today that day? I had prepared myself with a strict exercise regime, yoga and diet. And that day my body and breath held out! The three days of celebration at the Prithvi were a resounding success, a *dhamaal* that would live in our memories forever.

This time there was a difference—we had prepared a children's play. Though we had been taking theatre classes with children off and on, Surnai had never included a children's play for a public performance. This play was the culmination of a workshop for children, *Guru-Cool*. The play was called *Hamid Ka Chimta*, my adaptation of Munshi Premchand's *Idgah*. We were overwhelmed by the response when we advertised for the workshop. Parents called to make sure their child was on the list. Mothers were there on the day of the performance helping us with costumes and props.

For me, that day was a milestone in more ways than one. My granddaughters Amaala and Alaaya were also acting in *Hamid Ka Chimta*. Jennifer would have been very pleased to see three generations of my family on her stage at the same time: my granddaughters, daughter Ishitta and I.

All the members of Surnai put their heart and soul into that performance. Director K.K. Raina, Salim Akhtar at the lights and Sanjoy Dazz in the music room worked hard to achieve the perfection we always strive for.

The grand finale, the *mahayagna*, was a few days away, scheduled for 29 July at the Tata Theatre. After many years I had picked up the gauntlet for a live performance of my music shows. Over the years, I have performed close to 250 live shows in India and abroad. There was a different kind of audience for these shows. It was an audience covering many generations, many languages and many ethnicities. Language and age were no barriers and from five-year-olds to their parents and grandparents, all had danced to my folk and film tunes. I danced at the weddings of some of the richest families, and my voice was heard in the tiniest dwellings in towns and villages. I received the love and respect of thousands of people who listened to my songs. I am humbled by this because this kind of love demands a huge responsibility.

The last time I performed live in Mumbai was in 1996 for Sony TV. This was following the great success of the song 'Choli Ke Peechhey'. It was a huge show and the only singer who had performed for Sony before me at that time was Lata Mangeshkar (Lataji). There were several celebrities as guests: Subhash Ghai, Amitabh Bachchan, Jackie Shroff, Kalyanjibhai, who had all come at my request. The performance was on the grounds of SNDT University in Juhu, a huge open space rented out for performances. The show began late. Unfortunately, a new rule about outdoor performances had just come into being—the use of loudspeakers and sound amplifiers was not permitted beyond 10 p.m. I had put in a lot of effort to make this a special performance. I had folk dancers from Bastar, from Gujarat, and Rajasthan, and top models from the fashion world. I had choreographed the show *A Musical Sandstorm* and I made an entry in a bullock-cart singing 'Mela mein le chaal sajana'. The entry itself got a standing ovation. I had recreated a village *mela* scene, with balloon sellers, shops selling bangles and accessories, and even animal performances—*bandar-walas* and bear dances. There was no PETA in those days!

It was inevitable that a performance of this magnitude could never start on time in India. The performance was only halfway through when the police arrived and disconnected the wires of the music system because the deadline for such shows was 10 p.m. No amount of pleading helped. The irony was that there were several senior police officers in the audience! With a heavy heart, I stopped the performance midway. But it was my responsibility to complete the recording for Sony so I decided that the show must go on and the next day I completed the performance at my own expense and handed the recording to Sony.

I mention this performance here because this was my last live public performance in Mumbai. I was invited to perform overseas but never in Mumbai. Since then, live performances have been few and far between and the quality has deteriorated immensely. The pandemic put a stop to whatever was left of any performance. In the last ten years, I have not done anything in the way of live performances of music and I thought that this was the right time to bid farewell to my live shows. I was not retiring because that word does not exist in my dictionary. There is a lot of young talent coming up in India, discovered through reality shows and competitions, so it is time for the old guard to make way for younger performers.

One of the main reasons for my giving up my music shows was my discovery of Ibsen. I was fascinated by this playwright and read almost all his plays that had been translated. I decided to devote myself entirely to adapting his plays in Hindi and placing them in the Indian context. The stage became my priority and so music took a back seat.

But while we were planning our fortieth anniversary celebrations Avni, the chief choreographer and dancer who was with me for all my live shows, suggested that I should include my songs and dances for one show at least. She reminded me how she was still earning because of my songs, which featured prominently in her dance classes and in the choreography she did for weddings. And I, the original singer had opted out of music shows! I usually brushed it aside with a laugh. She assured me that I still had an untapped audience for my music, among the Marwari and Gujarati youngsters whose mothers had danced to my tunes at weddings and festivals. She said that all her students were yearning to dance with me onstage and all I had to do was to say 'yes'! The idea set me thinking. From 21 to 23 July 2023, we were celebrating at Prithvi. But we had actually started our journey on 9 June 1982 with a programme of folk music and dance called *A Musical Sandstorm* at the Tata Theatre with forty folk artistes. Why not a repeat of forty folk artistes for our fortieth birthday for the finale?

This was going to be an ordeal by fire. Even though I was better known now than I was when I stepped onto the stage in Mumbai, I was also forty years older! Things had changed a lot. I was a celebrity now, with a treasure house of my own songs, both original folk compositions and songs I had sung as a playback singer in films. Yet, to get on to the stage with the same energy and vigour would be a stupendous task. It is a well-known fact that with age a singer's octave goes down a notch. This happens also through overuse of the vocal cords. My voice had been used to deliver dialogues to the last person in the audience without using a microphone. In the course of our fortieth-year celebrations, I had just finished doing an act as Gandhari from *Shabd Leela*, a play I had adapted from Dharamvir Bharati's letters to his beloved partner, Pushpaji, interspersed with scenes from his famous play *Kanupriya* and *Andha Yug*. I selected one of the most powerful scenes in this play for my performance, the scene where Gandhari curses Lord Krishna for his part in the tragic war. This meant a full-throated angry declaration, which always affected my voice. After the decision that I would indeed have my live music performance, I decided to go slow on the volume, or it would be a toss-up between the curse and the loss of my voice! To still keep the impact of the curse, I decided to use the expertise of my composer–singer son-in-law Dhruv to record part of the curse in his studio, with the intention of using the recorded version on the stage to save my voice and get by for the two shows. But can an actor's performance ever be restrained by what happens the next day? This was not a film where a lip sync would be effective, but a live performance. When the cue for my dialogue came, the recording floated over the sound system but along with that and louder, with full force and emotion, my curse for Krishna came out in a deep-throated voice, shaking the very foundation of the auditorium. I was also singing live at Prithvi and because of my nervousness, I had got singers to support me. But their voices were used to microphones and I could hardly hear them. It was the folk singers from Rajasthan whose support took the performance to a higher level and Prithvi Theatre rang to the sounds of all our past folk plays and past memories—*Jameela Bai Kalali*, *Mareechika*—and the audience swayed to our music.

But the impending live show of 29 July hovered over my mind. There was no medicine—antibiotics, anti-allergy, inhalation, that I did not try. Yoga, a silent retreat, no spices, every method to ensure that I could carry off the grand finale. My thoughts were riddled with memories of a performance by the popular singer, Talat Mahmood, who was to give a live performance in Jaipur. Alas, his throat gave way. He used every method to recover his voice—spoons of honey, warm water, but his voice did not respond. There cannot be a worse disaster for a performer—a huge audience waiting to hear him, his fans and followers who came with great hopes and he could not oblige them. Applause is a performer's life, his audience, his very breath. He is kept alive by his fans, who can put him on a pedestal or abandon him in a moment, the light of a lamp that is left to fade away slowly. Both success and failure can be dangerous for an artiste if he does not know how to handle them. It is said that failure is the mother of success, but to fall and rise again and then recoup and carry on is a difficult task. You need determination and moral strength and a belief in yourself to pull yourself together and stand on your feet again. This encouragement is provided by his audience.

To say that I was nervous about the grand finale would be an understatement. Would my voice give way, would I be off-tune and off-note? I sing and dance simultaneously, so many things could go wrong. Suppose my legs crumbled under me? But in all this I appealed to only one Being, Vishnu, and kept reciting '*Om namo bhagvate Vasudeva/ Om namo bhagvate Vasudeva*'! I felt his strength and support. And my moral strength carried me through as did the trust of my audience.

I am a maverick once I get on to the stage in my music performances. I forget to follow instructions. My entries and exits are my own and my co-stars and even the director have to hold me back. Avni Shah wanted to create the Ila of the past, making a spectacular entry dressed in all my folk finery, laden with heavy silver jewellery, including heavy anklets, for the '*Morni*' song from the film *Lamhe*. Several suggestions were offered for my entry. I listened to all of them. But I was nervous. My legs were hurting and I hoped I would be able to complete the show. I went to the Tata Theatre a few days before the show and practised going up and down the stairs of the auditorium several times. This was to test if I could do this without losing my breath and what would the effect of this exercise be on my song. Supporting singers have now become part of my live music programmes. I have many who are like an extension of my voice; Inka Vyas, Sonika Sharma Vijaylakshmi and Saveri Verma. They stand at the back and accompany me and sometimes take over. It is seldom that a performer sings and dances at the same time as I do. Most live shows have a few live songs, but the rest is lip syncing to pre-recorded songs. I spoke to the huge audience telling them that whatever was happening on the stage was live, not hampered by recordings of either music or songs.

I remember that an American pop singer had come to perform in India. He had a huge fan following here and people were falling over each other to buy tickets for his show at the Patil Stadium in Navi Mumbai. He arrived with planeloads of equipment, a huge entourage that stayed at the best hotels in Mumbai and people spent Rs 14,000–15,000 for tickets! I was horrified, but what could I say when members of my family and close friends too had 'wasted' large sums on the show, only to find out later that his entire performance was on a track!

At the NCPA, my audience and I were on top of the world. I sang all my old numbers and my listeners shared my enthusiasm and clapped at the beginning, in the middle and at the end of each song. The popular songs from my old albums 'Resham Ka Rumal', 'Assi Kali Ka Lehnga' and 'Morni' were the hot favourites. Three generations had danced to these songs at weddings in Marwari and Gujarati households. And today, sixty-year-old grandmothers to the five-year-old students from Avni's class were dancing with abandon at the Tata Theatre!

I sang a few solos accompanied by Dhruv. Shilpa and Ishitta as the master of ceremonies kept the audience in good humour alternating between Hindi, English, Marathi and Gujarati. The performance that had given me sleepless nights finally went off very well, way beyond my imagination. In the blink of an eye, my forty-year journey in theatre was over, contained in the four days of celebrations, leaving me with a new energy, a new passion, a new confidence.

After all the excitement, the following day left me with a feeling of emptiness, a listlessness that usually follows days of excitement. Each moment of joy, all the arguments, the quarrels, the compulsions and the faces of all the actors who had journeyed with me rose before my eyes, happy faces who seemed to egg me on saying 'Cheers! The party has just begun!' All I can say is 'Cheers to Jennifer. The show must go on!'

Despite being riddled with obstacles, uncertainties and difficulties, the forty-year journey seemed to have gone by very fast. The greatest boon from these activities was that we were all kept busy and healthy. A busy mind and body are the way to good health. The gym of the mind is stronger than the gym for the body. I pray to God to give me the strength to dance like Sitara Devi, at ninety, to sing like Asha Bhonsle and be on my feet like Vyjayanthimala!

I thank God also for giving me the strength to sustain theatre for so long. Several of the artistes who had graduated from NSD, many with a PhD in drama, had to give up theatre to join other professions to make a living. It is impossible to live on earnings from theatre. I wish Indian theatre could be self-supporting, and actors, directors and others in this profession could have some state help like in many Western countries. Sometimes I regret that I did not register Surnai as a repertory company with the Department of Culture so that we could avail of government funds. Many of my friends are given some stipend annually so they can perform regularly, but there is nothing new coming out of these groups. The funds given by the government make it mandatory for them to perform regularly. One performance can leave a group gasping for breath and life. There is a mental and physical fatigue especially if you have no money in your coffers. Freelance artistes like us are walking on a razor's edge.

But then perhaps in retrospect, I did the right thing. There is a freedom to do something new since we are not bound by deadlines. The creative hunger has scope to experiment and present something fresh to theatre audiences, the challenge to produce plays that force people to think. Surnai was born with the help of friends and well-wishers. There were always people who gave us rehearsal space, props from their homes, costumes from their wardrobes and most of all the goodwill to keep us going. We would put in our own money to produce plays when the begging bowl did not work. Our director, K.K. Raina, who trained to be an actor but had to take up the mantle of a director, was the one to inspire me to put in all the energy and stamina in reading new plays and adapting them. I think we had a good rapport and we complemented each other. In the course of the forty years, we have touched upon several issues, come up with new ideas and presented them in many genres—mythology, folk, comedy, modern—each had a thought that would move audiences and convey a message.

They say literature is a mirror of life and that is why I was conscious that our plays, both adaptations and original, evolve with the times. As I wrote, my pen seemed to convey what I had wanted to say—to women, to politicians, to the youth and senior citizens, and to the *aam janta*, the common man. Women's issues have taken centre stage in all my original plays and adaptations, and I have tried to present these issues in an interesting way. This is what is called theatre.

Theatre and politics both try and get their views across to their listeners, and they have one thing in common, both wear a mask. But I believe getting a message across to people is more impactful through theatre than politics because there is no agenda involved in the former. In politics, you are mere puppets, misleading the voters with false promises, but through theatre, you are only trying to create an awareness without thought of the fruit of your endeavours, just like the message of the Gita, duty without rewards.

A Chinese proverb says, 'Better to light a candle than to curse the darkness.' Theatre can entertain and also bring about change. But change does not happen in a moment, mindsets do not change overnight. It is a constant effort, and we have tried to say something in every play, we have lived each scene of a play we have enacted. But before succeeding in creating an awareness in the audience, you have to first search your soul and discover yourself.

That is the role of a writer.

Chapter 14

Paradise 2: *Is Ghar Ke Andar Kaun Rehta Hai?*

Then came the other precious gift, the person who made this house feel like a home, who brightened up our life, the person whose arrival made the house resound with voices—our little girl, Ishitta, the person who is gifted with the power to captivate everyone's heart. When Ishitta was born, my elder sister had suggested the name Ishitta and in the true sense, Ishitta lived up to this name. Without her presence, Paradise seems deserted and bereft.

I had always wanted only one child and that too, a girl. On my sea voyages with Arun, I fell in love with Japan. It was like a toy country. The Japanese people, short-statured, with features to match, soft spoken and always smiling, looked like the dolls you get in Japan. I had rarely seen such beautiful people. At that time, Japanese toys, especially dolls, were very popular all over the world, especially in India. I am sure many of you remember the song, '*Le gayi dil gudia Japan ki*' (My heart has been stolen by a Japanese doll.) from the film *Love in Tokyo*. 'Cult' dolls like the Barbie had not come into the market till then. Even before Ishitta was born, whenever I went to Japan, I would bring back one or two dolls. Perhaps the child in me never grew up! The clothes for girls were so attractive that I could not resist buying them. I ended up buying dresses for all ages for a girl. The joke would have been on me if I had had a son. He would probably be in frocks till the age of eleven!

When I was expecting Ishitta, we decided that Arun would have to make a voyage because there was a new turn in our life, which would require us to be financially secure. So, closer to the delivery, I went to stay with my mother in Jaipur as Arun joined

145

his ship. In our time, girls were hesitant to display their extended bellies during pregnancy, especially before the elders of the family. Call it modesty or foolishness, but I was embarrassed about appearing before my father and my brothers in that condition. How different from today's pregnant mothers! For Page Three, pregnant women especially get photographed, displaying their big bellies and proclaiming to the world that they are excited about motherhood. They know everything about pregnancy and motherhood, along with the husbands who participate in their day-to-day progress. My mother said that the stomach needed to be covered to shield the baby in the uterus from the evil eye, the *nazar* of envious people! So, I lived in loose 'maxis' as they were called in those days, which my sister in Mumbai sent me, custom made by a tailor in Mulund, a triple-X size, which ended up making me feel as if I was carrying my tent with me around the house.

Ishitta decided to arrive at an inconvenient but auspicious time. I say inconvenient because she was born during *pitra paksh*, the fifteen days consecrated to remembering our ancestors and parents who have passed away, and the household is busy with rituals and the feeding of Brahmins. But children born at this time are also considered lucky, especially on the day she was born, *matrunavami*, the ninth day of *Shraddh* dedicated to rituals for deceased married women and unmarried daughters who have passed away. A girl born on this day is considered especially lucky since she comes with the blessings of all the women who we believe, have gone to a better life. Preparations for our *puja* were going on. The clock showed the time as 12.05 p.m.

While the ceremony was going on, I had a feeling of uneasiness and called up my sister Tripti, who worked in the tourism department and had her office next door. Tripti called the doctor and was on the phone with her, constantly updating my condition. I had chosen a nursing home close to my parents' home and not a large hospital because of the privacy it afforded me. I was a known face in Jaipur and I wanted to ensure that journalists and stage artistes of Jaipur did not find out about my confinement. I did not want any newspaper reporters chasing me and my newborn baby in a hospital. I did not want my mother to know either since that would disturb her *puja* and cause a commotion among the old women who had been invited to the *matrunavami* feast. So, it was my unmarried sister and I, an equally ignorant first-time mother, who were trying to handle the situation.

Tripti's constant frantic phone calls must have irritated the doctor, so she laughed and said that she should bring her sister to the nursing home, Sahay Nursing Home. I got a few essential things and put them in a bag. I decided to take the back route through the bathroom door so as to go unnoticed by the women who had been served their lunch. But Tripti was nervous and decided to tell my mother. She of course dropped everything and started chasing me. The women did not want to be left behind either, so they abandoned their *thalis* and this bevy of older ladies too started running to the hospital. I still cannot help laughing when I recall this dramatic scene—a young pregnant girl, rushing to the hospital, carrying a bag, being chased by her somewhat overweight, 'healthy' mother, clutching on to her sari, followed by three or four old women also panting and puffing their way after this relay team! This must have been quite a scene for passers-by!

The doctor was waiting for me and I was wheeled into the labour room straight away, while my mother and her entourage waited outside, no doubt praying for a boy! At the back of her mind was the fear that a delivery in Jaipur only brought forth girls since her two older daughters who had come back to Jaipur for their delivery had two daughters each! But had she forgotten that after her seven daughters, she had insisted that Jodhpur was not conducive to the birth of sons and had come to Jaipur and brought forth two sons!

But while she and the other women prayed to several gods for a grandson, I was praying to Durga Mata, that it has to be a girl, otherwise what would I do with all the frocks and dolls I had bought from Japan?

I had taken time to read a few books on prenatal care and had done some exercises to prepare myself for the delivery. One of the exercises, besides mopping the floor on my haunches, was that of throwing a whole pack of cards on the floor and picking them up one by one! Whatever the reason, I had a fairly easy delivery as I ran straight to the delivery room, and without too much of crying and shouting or cursing my husband, which I believe several mothers in labour do, and contrary to my mother's hours of prayers, a lovely baby girl, wrapped in a white muslin sheet, was handed over to my mother. I will never know whether the tears that fell from her eyes were those of relief or disappointment. Whenever I teased my mother on this subject, of her preference for sons, she would say that this was a figment of my imagination and that I should become a writer. Well, this blessing seems to have come true and today, four decades later, as I write this book, I am reminded of her remark.

The baby was brought home to my parent's new house, Indrangan. The naming ceremony took place with great pomp and ceremony and my sister named her Ishitta, though her name from her horoscope was Kusum Kumari Bajpai! For three months, Ishitta was showered with love and attention from her grandparents and her aunts, and since then she has always thought of Jaipur as her home. Then it was time for her to set foot in her own home, Paradise, which has been the only home she has known till she married and moved into her own place.

She was carried in a bamboo basket, all the way to Mumbai, in a train, accompanied by the old family retainer, Nandu. I don't know why my mother sent him along, since he was completely inadequate in helping me with anything. Probably he was sent as moral support or just to see Mumbai It was my mother's belief that a little baby should not be taken on a flight since the air pressure gives them a severe earache. The basket was layered with a tiny mattress made of straw and decorated with colourful flowers, a cradle on the lines of what European women farmers carry their children in when they go out to the fields. I got down at Bombay Central station, like an English lady carrying her beautiful fair-skinned baby in a basket, thumb in mouth and not a single hair on her head! Dressed in a light-yellow gown bought by Arun in Japan, she looked like a Buddhist priest. On her tiny feet shone the silver anklets given by my brother Piyush. How was I to know that this little baby, who had the peaceful look of the Dalai Lama, would later follow the Buddhist faith and bombard us with the chant of *namyo ho rengyo* for hours on end!

I still remember our first entry into Paradise Apartment, when we crossed the threshold with our little girl, the Princess of Paradise, as Arun called her.

And today, while sitting in Paradise and writing about the same Princess, it seems that I am sitting on a pile of memories. What do I pick up from that pile? I feel I have the right only to re-write those aspects of her life that I had seen and those that I had control over, a word Ishitta may not like!

From the age of three, then thirteen and then twenty-three, we saw this vivacious, mischievous, little girl grow from a baby into a self-confident woman. At the age of three, she had already been the heart-throb of the public with her Vicks ad—*gale mein khich-khich*. She was a child brought up in the wings in the true sense of the word. Mischievous, with a mind of her own, and brought up in a literary environment, listening to the *sher-shairi* around her, she developed a passion for rhyming at a very young age. She would ask visitors to the house whether they would care to listen to her 'mushroom'. I don't know where she picked up this word, which no one could understand. I think it was a combination of *sher* and *mushaira*.

In a later chapter I have recounted the lines she came up with during the shooting of Shyam Benegal's *Yatra*, a couplet which Shyam used as her dialogue in the series. She once wrote:

समंदर के किनारे बैठा हूँ मैं लहरें आती हैं चली जाती हैं
आती हैं चली जाती हैं पूछती हैं मुझसे क्यों भई क्यों बैठे हो।

I sit on the seashore, waves come and go
Asking me 'Why do you sit here, my friend?'

Once a man begging at a traffic light, kept putting his hands before us, so the driver quickly pulled up the window glass. She saw this and was obviously moved by it. She wrote:

गरीब लोग कहाँ से आते हैं भीख
माँगते हैं अमीर लोग जिन्हें देखते ही अपनी खड़िकी का कांच चढ़ाते हैं।

Where do the poor come from, asking for alms,
And the rich see them and roll up their windows?

It was as if she was born to write. She had the writing bug and was thinking of new things all the time. Her interest and her knowledge of music were phenomenal. She endeared herself to all who came to visit, especially Ghulam Ali Sahib, with whom she would have conversations in her baby language. She was a child who gathered her knowledge not from books but from the environment she was exposed to, a comment Shyam Benegal made when he wrote to her school asking for leave for her for the shooting of *Yatra*.

I imagine that Ishitta's baby talk and conversation have also been recorded by the walls of this house. Her tears and laughter, the stories she created, her songs and music, her journey from her school, Arya Vidya Mandir and then college at St Xavier's are all part of her life at Paradise. As long as a child is young, they are easier to deal with, but when they enter their teenage years, a spirit of rebellion takes over. Luckily, as for most daughters, her father was the favourite. Whenever he came back, he was Santa Claus, loaded with gifts. During his stay on shore, it was his responsibility to take her to outings, to parks and entertainment hubs. All her entertainment outside the house was taken care of by Arun. Our friends also contributed to her growth with their affection and advice; she was a child growing up among adults.

Then came the phase when she did not like any advice from her mother. We had all gone through this phase in our lives when we believed that our mother was the obstacle to the realization of all our dreams. Little do we realize that there is no greater friend in life than a mother. I remember my mother's oft-repeated warning, 'I speak from past experience.' She never let us know what that meant—I can only guess that perhaps she did have some unpleasant encounters in life and was warning us to shield ourselves against that. I also tried to use the same words, but they did not have any effect on my child.

Life revolved around the known since we did not have much exposure to the world outside our given circle. There were no computers in our homes and no Internet to browse. Then the trend of cybercafes started and they sprouted at every street corner, drawing excited teenagers to a world hitherto unknown. This worried me since Ishitta also expressed a desire to visit these cybercafes with her friends. I, out of sheer ignorance, wondered what they were doing there. I had visions of them accessing information that might mislead them. When the computer reached every home, I would sit close by, keeping an eye on what the kids were watching. I called this the third window of the house which could be very dangerous since parents could not keep a watch on the material children were accessing.

Well, Ishitta reached college, and like every young person, some wrong steps were taken and some proved to be the right steps. I am proud that my daughter has achieved a lot without any help from us. She entered the Miss India pageant without any recommendation and grooming, since I had no idea about such competitions, only about debates and drama. I did help her in debates and she won many prizes. I could teach Hindi, I could teach her literature, and singing, but Miss India was something which would never have occurred to me. But she managed very well, got physically fit, and dancing and singing, she made her way to the ninth position! That was the year when Priyanka Chopra was Miss World, Lara Dutta, Miss Universe and Diya Mirza, Miss Asia Pacific. Very few people know that Ishitta is a very good singer and has the advantage of both language and melody. She could be on top as a singer, but for that you have to be focused. I remember what Amjad Ali Khan Sahib had said about his music, that when other children were playing marbles, his father had placed the sarod in his hands and from then on there was nothing else but *riyaaz* for him. That kind of excellence requires dedication and *sadhana*, devotion. I can't say much as I too lacked that focus when I was growing up!

Considering Ishitta was an only child, she was never indulged or spoilt. Kalyanjibhai's words echoed in my ears and Anandjibhai's face in front of my eyes, telling me that Dilip Kumarji had advised them not to install an A/C in their house, since children, especially daughters, should not get used to luxuries which they may not get in their marital homes; they should be able to adjust to every kind of environment, in every season. All these luxuries should only come from their own earnings. Ishitta never complained about the fact that she had to share her room, her space and food with all the people who came to stay at our house. I don't remember taking people to restaurants very often, so we were always home, eating whatever was placed before us. I marvel at how she has become such an excellent baker, graduating from simple home-cooked food to sophisticated, gourmet cakes!

The environment at home also proved helpful in shaping her personality. She met so many famous personalities within these four walls. Film-maker Mrinal Sen, *ghazal* singer Ghulam Ali Khan Sahib, Anita Kanwar, Soni Razdan, Neena Gupta. Actors who worked with us were at our house often and living among them, under their tutelage, Ishitta was exposed to much more than most children who never get this opportunity. She took up a job with B4U and became a very successful anchor. After that she continued to do successful anchoring in many television series. Then video albums like Sonu Nigam's *Bijuriya* and *Aai Ka Dajeeba* came her way, giving her a new image. But she was doing this only as a hobby and not as a career.

And while doing this, going through several ups and downs, a day came when Ishitta took an important decision in her life. She told us she that she wanted to get married. With this a new person entered our family and the small Paradise Apartment, Dhruv Ghanekar. He also brought music with him. He is an internationally known musician and has played with several well-known groups. But we all joked about the fact that it was as if Vicks had married Hajmola, since Dhruv had been selected for a Hajmola ad, and Ishitta had been the Vicks, *gale mein khich-khich* girl!

I have been in favour of living a very simple life. I have not had grandiose dreams about my lifestyle either, not pining for a bigger flat, an expensive car or branded clothes. I come from a normal middle-class family, and I never let myself or my daughter forget this. The rooms in the house resonated with the sound of music, literature, drama and advertisements when my brother Piyush lived with us, it was the era of advertisements in Paradise; then came the time of plays and theatre and after the arrival of Dhruv, the era of global music.

Ishitta is the soul of Paradise. The truth is that Ishitta's name is written on every visible space in Paradise, especially on the wall of her room. She had been very impressed with Javed (Akhtar) Bhai's poem 'Woh kamara yaad aata hai' and wrote the words on the wall of her room. I did not have the heart to erase the lines written in her handwriting. She said that it was as if Javed Bhai was describing her room, every single thing in the room in which she had grown up—her door, her window, her books. I think she was in Class XII at the time and I was surprised that she had such an amazing knowledge of Urdu poetry and could relate to it emotionally. Whenever I got the room painted, I made sure that the writing was not erased. Once the wall was damaged and the poem disappeared. We called the painter back and asked him to inscribe the words in his handwriting!

This was the poem that Javed Bhai recited especially for her at her wedding sangeet, bringing tears to Ishitta's eyes. Then Ghulam Ali Khan Sahib enthralled the audience with his *ghazal* at the sangeet. These two great personalities had a deep influence on Ishitta's personality. The visitors to Paradise, an open house for many artistes from the performing arts, had a significant role in shaping the personality of the all-rounder, Ishitta. I say all-rounder because she always surprised us with her new ideas and enthusiasm for whatever she took up. Once she declared that she was going to start a new line of living room furniture. Before we had taken that in, she was designing interiors for luxurious homes, one of her clients being choreographer Terence Lewis. She also designed two new restaurants, from the walls and décor to the furniture and the accessories.

There are memories of many people peeping through the doors—Paradise echoed with the melodious laughter of the next generation, Ishitta's two daughters Amaala and Alaaya, who fortunately were able to spend a lot of time in this house. I used to wonder whether Ishitta would be able to cope with the phase of motherhood. But I am proud to say that she is a better mother than I was, alert and cautious in her duties as a mother. She pays more attention to her children than I did.

This Paradise has been a witness to many a flourishing relationship and captured their feelings in its warm embrace.

Many people and personalities have been made in this house—and many more have contributed to making this house a home. My elder sister's daughters, who were older than Ishitta, spent a lot of time here during the monsoons. They lived in Mulund, but during the three months of the monsoons, the Central Railway tracks would invariably be flooded and they could not get home. So, through school and college, whenever the trains were suspended due to flooding, they would come to my flat since we were on the Western Railway, which in those days did not experience flooding. A house full of three girls reminded me of my childhood in Jaipur; somehow the chattering and laughter of daughters always brighten up a house. We celebrated the monsoons with hot *chillas* and *pakoras*. At night, they borrowed my *ghaghras*, many from my costume wardrobe, and slept in Ishitta's room. Ishitta grew up in their company and they took full responsibility for her homework and also doubled up as babysitters when needed. Ishitta also could not do without their company and missed them when they were not there. These two girls have done very well for themselves and the older sister, Swati, is head of the department of haematology at Manipal Hospital in Bengaluru and the younger one, Shruti, has been the head of HBO.

I was a struggling artiste then and was looking for work. These girls came to my help, taking up all the planning for Ishitta's birthday, inventing new games for more than fifty children, packing return gifts and handling the children. One of the benefits of the younger sister being in the company of older sisters was that the values of the family were passed on to the younger children. Ishitta was very sad when both the sisters got married and left Mumbai.

I don't know why, but as I sift through my memories, I feel like apologizing to Ishitta today. It could be because I was busy or simply ignorant. Unknowingly, I had neglected many things while she was growing up, which I now regret. From getting her homework done to fulfilling many important motherly responsibilities, I admit that I have made mistakes. Mothers today go through more difficult times than we did. They do not have the advantage of joint families nor dedicated family retainers to help with housework or babysitting. Mothers have to deal with everchanging methods of education and the stress of long hours of study.

For Ishitta's schooling, on the advice of Pandit Shivkumar Sharmaji's wife, I chose Arya Vidya Mandir School. She said that I should not think of admitting her to any of the new international schools that had sprung up, since these schools lay emphasis on the results and could leave a child struggling with several complexes and a feeling of inadequacy. This school concentrated on a holistic approach to education and laid emphasis on Indian culture and language. The students are introduced to our past and our roots—a philosophy that appealed to me. The aim of the school is 'to ensure that their students leave school as successful, happy individuals grounded in human values'. (This is the motto of the school.) A quotation of screenwriter and journalist Nora Ephron, 'Your education is a dress rehearsal for a life that is yours to lead,' stayed in my mind. I was familiar with dress rehearsals, mistakes and mishaps through which you learn.

Arya Vidya Mandir has played an important role in shaping Ishitta's personality. This is the same school where Aishwarya Rai studied and when she greeted everyone with a namaste from the stage of the Miss World competition, the world was stunned. She brought the Indian form of greeting and Indian culture to the world stage. When she went to college at St Xavier's, Ishitta was initiated into the cosmopolitan culture of this prestigious institution. It is said that the company you keep and the opinions of your peers have a strong influence on your growing-up years. When a child comes from a sheltered environment into a space where he or she has multiple choices, the choice could be the wrong one. This is the time, I feel that we need to have a hand on the shoulders of our teenagers, rather than holding their fingers in childhood. Time has changed so much before our eyes. New ideas come up every day on the Internet. As a result, there is bound to be conflict between two generations. Parents' thoughts seem outdated and irrelevant to their children, and in truth, we have been left far behind. When I see working mothers raising their children along with managing their jobs, I realize that they are far ahead of us. Ishitta is a good example of that.

During her tumultuous years, there was one person who guided her to choose the right path—Arnab Chaudhuri, my late sister Uma's son-in-law, married to my niece Ashima. Arnab, who headed Channel V and later Disney World Channel, was the master of animation films. He made the landmark film *Arjun: The Warrior Prince*. He was Ishitta's mentor and guide and gave her advice with a loving, personal touch. And she listened to him. The fact that they were neighbours in their new home in Goregaon worked to Ishitta's advantage. Unfortunately, he passed away at a young age. But he was a frequent visitor to our home, leaving his mark on the biography of Paradise and an irreplaceable spot in my heart. I miss him a lot.

There are many such personalities whose mention is necessary here, who showered immense love on Paradise. Leaning against these walls, we have laughed and cried, dampened the paint with our sobbing disappointments and banged the walls in frustration! These walls have deciphered my thoughts as I have contemplated on my behaviour towards my mother as a girl, and now my daughter's behaviour towards me and the relationships that change with marriage and motherhood. All this is written on the walls of Paradise.

One of the greatest contributions to this house came with the arrival of my brother Piyush. He wrote telling me that his job as a tea taster in a tea company in Kolkata did not appeal to him. There was no excitement in just sipping cups of tea! He wanted to do something creative. And find some new possibilities in Mumbai. He asked if he could come to Mumbai. This was a blessing for me. To spend time with my precious brother, whom I had not seen for a long time, was a chance I did not expect. There was no contact on the ship with Arun, no phones on board the ship, and letters took weeks to reach. When Arun called me and I told him of Piyush's desire to come to Mumbai, he was really happy at the news. They had got to know each other and got along fairly well. So Piyush came to Mumbai and took up a job with a construction company. But this was like jumping from the frying pan into the fire. The sips of tea at least gave you time to think, to let your imagination run wild. After all, many great poets and thinkers have composed, written and published their work over a hundred cups of tea. But can you do anything creative surrounded by bricks and mortar and the sound of grinding machines and cranes? The hunger for something creative grew and luckily I was able to introduce him to our friend Satish Bedi, who was very close to Ranjan Kapur in the erstwhile OBM, now O&M Advertising company. Ranjan gave Piyush a job with OBM and Piyush's innings in the creative world began in Mumbai. OBM had its office at Apeejay House at Churchgate, a five-minute walk from Churchgate Station and our apartment was within walking distance of the Santa Cruz Station. So, the commute was not difficult for Piyush since he bought a first-class pass. He stayed with us for five years, sharing Ishitta's room and that is why they have a special relationship. Ishitta refers to Piyush as her 'real' Mama. It was a wonderful time. Because of him this small house was enlivened by many parties with his colleagues, and his birthday celebrations. Virendra Razdan, KK and Binny pulled up their sleeves and got into the act of cooking.

It was a relay race of cooking vessels. One pot was hardly taken off the fire and another quickly took its place. The aroma of *kheema, rajma,* Gomaji's *dhansak*—Gomaji being my secretary, Meena's father—dissolved into the rooms of Paradise, the smell of warmth and camaraderie. I especially remember Charu Sharma, who had a great appetite. He could polish off twenty *rotis* at one go! If he had come to our house without notice, my girls would have left their jobs. I had to tell him that his dining with us would disturb the routine in the kitchen and though I loved having him over, he should inform us before visiting since my girls could not cope with his appetite at such short notice! He took it sportingly and started giving us prior notice and would also get loads of noodles, a dish he used to live on as a bachelor. Soon noodles became the favourite dish of all the bachelors who ate with us. Perhaps I should refrain from giving away Charu's secrets since he has now married into the Mahindra family!

There are so many recollections of my friends, of Meena and Anita, the two valuable additions to Paradise, whose stories need to be told. But how can these be squeezed into one book? Those really were memorable times, the real *acche din* for Paradise and me. As the character Andy Bernard says in the NBC comedy television series *The Office*, 'I wish there was a way to know you're in the "good old days" before you've actually left them.' But I think I knew!

When Piyush left us after five years and shifted into his own house, he took a slice of Paradise with him. The Athenian statesman Pericles has said, 'What you leave behind is not what is engraved on stone, but what is woven into the lives of others.' Piyush's presence has indeed been woven into our lives; he has many homes now, but to this day, with one call saying, '*Bhaiya*, your favourite *daal* has been cooked today. Come!' he is sure to be there. I think each step leading into my apartment, recognizes Piyush's footsteps, the door knows his knock!

Later when Piyush got married to Nita, after the big reception on the vast lawns of the United Services Club Mumbai, we had a small family get-together on the terrace of Paradise. The party carried on late into the night and after the couple left for their own home, the rest of the family just spread mattresses and sheets on the terrace and watched the stars and gossiped till the wee hours of the morning. Purohitji-Ka-Bagh was recreated on the terrace of Paradise! Sharad Purnima dinners were always on my terrace, and as is the custom, white was the colour for this beautiful night. All the dishes served were white, for a change no turmeric in the cooking, and you had to dress in white. I remember my mother happened to be in Mumbai once on Sharad Purnima. She and my sister Uma were staying with Piyush, and not having white saris, my ever-innovative mother came for dinner draped in Piyush's white sheets, with Uma in tow!

It was here that the touching and emotional lines for Asian Paints were coined by him, *Har Ghar Kucch Kehta Hai*. And now I can say that *iss kamre mein Piyush ki kalpana jhalakti hai*, that Piyush's imagination still glimmers in this room. And Paradise does talk to us, in the *ghazals* sung here, the poetry recited and appreciated, the *thirakana* of dancers, the dialogues of our plays, yes even in the arguments and disagreements that the walls resound with. For us, Paradise has been regained in two cities: first in Bombay and later in Mumbai.

Chapter 15

Broadcasting: Akashvani, BBC and Jingles

In those days, there was not much organized activity for children and no theme parks where a weekend could be spent. The only means of entertainment was the radio and the national channel, Akashvani, was the most listened-to programme. It was one of the largest media organizations in the world. Since my father was the registrar in a co-operative bank, he used to go for talk shows related to farming and farmers. My mother, though not well-educated in the conventional sense, was a great reader and well-versed in issues related to women. She would often be asked to speak in programmes for women. My older sister, Rama, used to take part in radio plays since her college days. It seemed natural that I would also be drawn to Akashvani. I started with a children's programme *Mukul*, for which I was paid Rs 5, a princely sum in those days for a child. Then I went for a programme, *Sangeet Shiksha*, conducted by the music teacher at All India Radio Jaipur, Askaran Sharma. I was part of a group of girls sent for a general knowledge programme from school. I had no 'knowledge' of general knowledge but could not get out of it. I remember I answered only one question and that was also wrong. The question was, what is the currency of Great Britain? My hand went up first since I had done a lot of cramming for this programme and thought I knew the answer. 'Lodder,' I said. My school lost some points and of course I became the joke of the class. I was pulled up on my return to school, with the teachers saying that I had been selected because they thought I was good. Now when I travel abroad and handle dollars, the voice of a child still calls out to me, saying, 'Lodders!'

As I joined college, I began writing for youth shows on subjects that might interest them. I also took interviews with youngsters. An audition got me selected for radio plays. I went up a notch when I started earning Rs 11 as a casual announcer for Vividh Bharti. This was a chance to get away from home and make Rs 77 a week!

Things changed when I got married and Arun was stationed in London as chief engineer on a ship. With my experience in radio, a friend got me a position as an outside contributor for the BBC. My first programme was *Visitor to Britain*. After that, many family members, who visited London did that show, which paid you £25. But I would remind them that I was the first one on the BBC! The producer of the Hindi programme, Mr Verma, told me that I could come for any programme as an outside contributor as long as I was in London. I was called by different producers for talks on various subjects. You were given a subject which you had to interpret, paraphrase and present on the spot. I even spoke on subjects such as the share market *Mudra Mandi,* of which I knew nothing! I wrote and presented programmes on tourism, which took you to all the landmarks of London, on sports such as soccer, boxing and cricket. The ones I enjoyed doing most were those on music and culture.

The most interesting one was a series where the concept and the name was derived by me, *Amma Ke Naam Chhitti*. It was based on Indian immigrants and the problems they had adjusting in an alien culture. There were fourteen episodes of 15 minutes each. Dedicated to immigrants, all over the world, this show brought out the alienation of these people and how even those who had been in Britain for a long time still held on to their roots and missed everything they had left behind. They could not let go of superstitions, like believing that if a cat crossed one's path, it brought bad luck. London had so many cats that a superstitious desi could be left waiting on the sidewalk forever! There were problems using the pot in the bathroom, the surge of water reminding them of the Ghaggar river! The motive of this show was to make immigrants aware of the problems and how to learn to assimilate with the local whites. The series became very popular with the Indian populace. I presented episodes which showed how Indians tried to keep their traditions alive, the shock at being faced with new customs and manners and the fear of being laughed at, all put forth in a light-hearted manner. Many of the immigrants came from the small towns of UP, Gujarat, Rajasthan and Punjab for menial jobs to sustain their families back home. Young brides would come after a mock marriage with all sorts of absurd things like trees and even handkerchiefs! When they arrived in London, they were completely lost in an alien society. There was a vast cultural gap. When two cultures interact, ignorance of the rules and customs of the other can lead to hilarious episodes. After the popularity of the first four episodes, the producer, Evan Charlton, told me that this programme was going to be promoted in India since it had become very popular. They would print posters and distribute them globally and for that, they were going for a shoot to Covent Garden. This happened to be my favourite place in London.

He asked me to play the role of a woman buying vegetables. When we arrived, he asked me to select vegetables at a shop. I was to select them by handling each piece and pressing it to make sure of its freshness. In India every housewife seems to follow that practice. I saw some tomatoes and started pressing them, at the same time saying, 'How much?' The vendor came at me furiously shouting, 'What are you doing, lady? You Indians, you don't know that you are not supposed to touch the vegetables?' I was taken aback. But when I looked for support from Mr Charlton, I saw he was directing the photographer who was clicking photos rapidly. I realized that this was all staged for the shoot and I had been tricked into following his instructions. I still remember I was wearing a red silk sari with a purple blouse with mirror work. I had the photo till very recently. But today, when I am close to writing my memoir and want to use the picture, it is nowhere to be found.

London is one of my favourite cities and I have wonderful memories of my visits there. As I write about cats on the London streets, I am reminded of a cat that Arun had to mind for some time—cat-sitting! My meeting this ginger cat is one of the most heart-warming episodes of my London connection, this unexpected meeting with an amazing woman. Our friendship started at the London airport, as I waited despondently to check in my excess baggage. When Arun left to join his ship, I stayed in London for a couple of days. As usual, like most Indians travelling abroad,

I decided to do some last-minute shopping for gifts for people at home. Coming from a large family, I couldn't buy gifts for all my siblings, but I bought a few things for their children. My mother always had requests for gifts for all and sundry; an attache case for a cousin, an umbrella for a neighbour, saris for my *mausis* and nail cutters for my father and his friends, as a result of which I spent almost all the money I had. So, I arrived at the airport and went to the check-in counter of British Airways. Of course, my luggage was way beyond my allowance. The girl at the counter was very brusque and insisted that I pay for the excess baggage. I pleaded with her and told her I had no money to pay. My uncontrollable tears let me down as always. I had noticed a girl watching me from afar. She caught my attention because of her ginger hair. Suddenly she came up to us and asked what the problem was. The girl at the counter told her that I had eleven pounds of excess baggage. Obviously, she was senior to the lady I was dealing with. She said that they should check to see if this could be offset against my hand baggage. But alas, that also was overweight. Anyhow I paid for the excess baggage but did not have money for the excess hand baggage. The ginger-haired girl took me aside and asked where I was from. When I told her that I was an Indian, she became very excited and told me that she had been to India and loved it. She was even more thrilled to know that I was from Rajasthan. 'I have travelled by bus from Delhi to Jaipur and I remember there was a place called Kotputli. The bus stopped for a short break. I had a cup of tea. I cannot forget the aroma of tea, urine and cow dung!' I couldn't imagine how anyone could sing praises of that smell. I bowed my head in shame because I realized she must have had a tough time since we did not have any *sulabh shauchalayas*, or public toilets, at the time. Now the PM has been insisting that every house in the smallest village should have bathrooms. In Rajasthan, the women would spread their *ghaghras* behind a bush and that was that! As it is I was embarrassed that I did not have the money to pay for the excess baggage and now I was even more ashamed at what the girl was saying. But she very kindly said, 'Listen girl, I will help you since I owe it to Rajasthan. I'll pay for you and you can repay me whenever you can.' I was not ready to accept that, but I had no choice. I told her that I would repay her since my husband comes regularly to London on his voyages. 'This is my address but don't send me the money, instead send me textiles from Sanganer. I love the printed ones.' I was proud that the vegetable dyes of Rajasthan were appreciated by foreigners, and that sending her the textiles was a way to promote Rajasthan. And all this conversation because of a small town called Kotputli! So, she added six pounds to what I had and that was enough for the excess baggage. The girl at the counter looked at us quizzically, but the girl assured her that we were friends. This was the beautiful beginning of my friendship with the ginger-haired girl, Dodie Mcque, and of course, she had to be from Ireland!

She was a fascinating woman. She rode a Bullet motorbike and ran a tour company called Ginger Cat Tours—Ginger being the name of her cat, whom she adored. She was obviously a great seamstress too, since she showed me her tour van, the interiors of which she had furnished herself, using her small sewing machine for stitching the entire upholstery and furnishings.

She was a great conversationalist and had fascinating stories to share about her travels. I could listen to her endlessly. The next time Arun went to London I sent her a whole lot of textiles. Arun called her and she came on her Bullet 560 cc, from Belham, where she lived. She insisted that Arun stay in their home and when he hesitated, she said that he could repay them by looking after their cat, Ginger, a job that he would be doing and they would pay him for that.

She has given up her Ginger Cat Tours now, but whenever anyone from my family visits London, they always make it a point to call her and she looks after them and entertains them. I call her my soulmate in London.

I worked at BBC for over six months. But just as I was offered a permanent position there, Arun got news of his transfer from London. There was no option for me but to leave. However, fate had decreed that this job was for one of the Pandey girls. After a few months, Ramaji applied for the job and was taken in, working for over six years as a permanent contributor in London.

On my return to India, my life took a new, unexpected turn. Vividh Bharti had just been introduced by All India Radio (AIR). This station relayed mostly film songs and it was slated to be a commercial channel that would be supported by advertising. Radio had been like my maternal home. Whenever Arun left for his voyages, I would pack up and make my way to my parents' home in Jaipur. And every time I came to Jaipur, even for a short stay, I would call up my acquaintances at AIR. They would ask me to do something for them and I would present at least three or four programmes for them. I had the same kind of rapport with the BBC too!

Since the concept of a commercial radio station was new, they were looking for companies that would procure ads for them. The local market had to be explored for ads. At the time, Blaze Advertising was the only company that was doing print ads. They had an office in Jaipur too, which was making slides for ads. When you see ad films and 30-second ads these days, it seems strange to imagine that in the beginning advertising only worked on stills and slides! Blaze then realized that they needed local talent to establish a rapport with traders and shopkeepers. Most of them had family businesses that were doing well without much advertising, except perhaps in the regional newspapers. Blaze had an enterprising young man, Kailash Bhargava, who was familiar not only with the markets of Rajasthan but also knew most of the actors, writers and other creative people in Jaipur. Unfortunately, he died young. But for me, he was a godsend. It was because of him that I was inspired to make my first sponsored ad for radio. He was also responsible for me establishing my own advertising company which he also named, Ila Arun Publicity! I am amused by the fact that in a family of creative and artistic people, how did my company get such an absurd name? It appeared as if I was selling myself and my name! Actually, to give Kailash the benefit of the doubt he had no choice. He literally went from shop to shop looking for ads. One day he discovered that the Rajasthan Small Scale Industries was looking for a company to promote their new brand of wool. Through his sources, he found out that they were going to ask for tenders from companies. He instantly put in a tender through some insider and that tender was for my company which he had to name on the spot. So, a new company was born, bearing my name, but without my knowledge. I don't know how Kailash promoted me, but thanks to him I got that job to make an ad of 30 seconds! The Small-Scale Industry was trying to market their new brand of wool, Mayur, after the success of their wool made from the hair of two species of goats, whom they had named Sita and Gita. I had to highlight the old brand and then make a tag line saying that now after Sita and Gita comes the new brand, Mayur!

I was given a brief on the USP of the product and was told that the entire ad could not exceed 30 seconds. This seemed to be an impossible task for someone like me, a theatre person, who had been nurtured on plays lasting no less than two hours and songs and recitations of at least 15 minutes. To explain the benefits of the product, along with the address and phone numbers of the Company in 30 seconds to a target audience was fraught with difficulties for me. But before this, a logo had to be made for my company, which as far as I could gather had been given the ad unofficially! I had no idea what a logo was. But the ingenious Kailash persuaded my brother, Prasoon, who was still in school, to create a logo for my new company. Prasoon loved to draw and took a great deal of interest in anything creative. He came up with a brilliant logo, which somehow managed to overshadow the pedestrian name and gave my company some dignity and professionalism. My company was on its way, the first professional publicity company in Jaipur!

I became the first businesswoman in the family too! Ours was a simple Brahmin household, not known for its business acumen. My mother used to tell us about my father's business venture, a shop selling sanitary fittings opposite Jodhpur station. He named it Indra Narayan and Company. Theirs was a conventional Brahmin family, learned and of simple habits, who followed all the rituals of their caste. No one expected them to indulge in trade and that too of something as mundane as sanitary fittings! But compulsion and need are two great equalizers, having no religion or caste. It started badly. My father had no idea of business and it was not long before he sold the business to someone else. The new buyers kept the name Indra Narayan, and their business was so successful, riding on my father's name, that it still stands opposite Jodhpur station, perhaps one of the oldest shops dealing in sanitary fittings!

When my father found out about my business proposition, he tried to dissuade me, but by then it was too late. I wrote the copy for the ad, praising the qualities of Mayur wool. 'Rangon ke badal umde, man mor machye shor/ sajan mujhko lado pyare Mayur

oon ki dor . . .' Then I gave a voice-over, *'Aha Mayur oon ki dor.'*
The first ad established the name of the company. There was a lot of
discussion among the shopkeepers and other small companies about
the benefits of a radio ad and they agreed that the ad should be made
only by Ila Arun Publicity! Kailash realized the benefit of bulk ads,
since the Jaipur public was still to understand the economics and
numbers and were still trying to figure out why they had to pay so
much for radio ads. But I was enjoying it now, having acclimatized
myself to quick delivery and interesting lines. We would hire a studio
at Akashvani, finish the ad quickly and then spend the day's earnings
on a picnic, often joined by Kailash! In those days, Jaipur did not
have that much merchandise or big manufacturing businesses.
The market sold locks, underwear, oil, soap, incense and the like.
I became an expert at selling these through my ads. Ila Arun Publicity
was advertising for fragrant *agarbattis*, soaps that removed spots,
vests that absorbed sweat and strong locks! I remember one ad for
Jhago soap, which I really liked. I worked on it and had the jingle
ready with the chorus joining me, repeating, *'Jhago, Jhago.'* But there
was nobody to sing the chorus! Our budget could not pay for any
singers. So, I approached my two brothers, Piyush and Prasoon.
This was the first time my family realized that I was working on
ads seriously and that the Pandey family had a start-up working
from the house! The chorus that Piyush and Prasoon sang in their
powerful voices sounded way better than my expectations! For me,
the greatest challenge was to announce the long, and to my mind
funny, addresses in a 30-second ad! Imagine delivering a dialogue
like this—*Lalji Sand ka Rasta Dukan number 11 Bhatton ki Gali
Johri Bazaar Chaura-Rasta Jaipur* in 14 seconds!

I can proudly say that my ad agency progressed very well. The
result was that Piyush would keep asking me if there was any work
for him for voice-overs and if there was, he would happily do it
for the extra pocket money that he would make! Can I say that it
was the beginning of the stirring of thoughts about advertising in
Piyush's mind? Perhaps yes! When Arun heard of my start-up, he
bought a recording system from Japan, with two microphones and
a spool. That gave a spurt to our company. Now I wouldn't have
to pay to use the studios at Akashvani. We could record 10- and
14-second ads, not requiring music, at home. Prasoon, who had a

solution for everything told us that we should do all our recording at night when there was silence. Luckily for us, the city of Jaipur seemed to go to bed by 8 p.m., so we could start our work by 9 p.m. But we hadn't factored in the howling stray dogs at night! Their barking and growling in the silence of the night cut through every wall and door of the house. Prasoon's ingenuity sparkled again. He used every spare mattress and quilt he could find in the house— believe me, in our large family there was a huge stock of these. He stuffed them on all the doors and windows and lo and behold, we had a soundproof studio right in the house. I was reminded of this much later when I went to record with A.R. Rahman Sahib and Remo in Goa for *Trikal* (1985). In the initial stage, they all recorded at home and always late into the night with home-spun ways of keeping the sound out. Now of course Rahman Sahib has state-of-the-art studios and music schools. It made me value my brother Prasoon more than ever! The routine in our home changed. All the housework, such as cooking—the most piercing sound being that of the pressure cooker, eating, the washing of dishes had to be wrapped up by 8 p.m. Everyone was cautioned not to make a sound and we had to station someone to keep a watch on all the comings and goings. Often when there was some delay, the whole household had to remain hungry till midnight when our recording would get over! So, we worked within our budget, and with the multiple voice-overs, Piyush's interest in this field grew. We never imagined in our wildest dreams that both boys would go on to become such prominent personalities in the advertising world.

But the waves of the ocean were about to sweep Ila Arun Publicity away and make it disappear with the wind. I had to join Arun on the ship and when I returned, we settled in Mumbai, where I got totally involved in what was my prime passion—theatre. I am convinced that if I had stuck to that line, my publicity company would have been among the top such companies in India.

My long association with the ad world and radio continues. I am still doing voice-overs, and sundry compositions, often for friends and acquaintances. This confirms my belief that a strong, striking voice is the road to success. It should never be suppressed or strangled.

I would like to pay a tribute to the much-loved voice of the late Amin Sayani Sahib, a voice that came over the radio, a voice that spelt magic and romance. We would sit around the radio listening to his show *Binaca Geetmala*, which was broadcast every Wednesday from Radio Ceylon during 1952–88 and later from Vividh Bharti. We listened to the programme as much for Amin Sayani's voice as for the countdown of the top-ten film songs of the week. He made more than 18,000 jingles and almost 54,000 radio programs. We shall miss him, but his tireless, caressing voice will be an everlasting memory in the Indian psyche.

Chapter 16

Folklore: From Bullock-Cart to Limousine

'Those who wish to sing always find a song,' said a wise man. How right he was! I had found a song, many songs, in my daily life. In fact, my life has been a soundtrack! My mother often told me that from early childhood, I was mesmerized by rhythm—the sound of someone brushing, the clanking of a train nearby. I would watch the workmen working on a building site, listening to the sound of their pounding and scraping. And all these sounds would set my feet a-dancing, dancing and more dancing, *thirakna*, as my mother would say. I am sure most children love to dance. But I was a little different in my obsession. We did not have the luxury of a radio or a gramophone. My ears, always listening for sound and rhythm, were attuned to the singing of the women and men around me. Rajasthan seems to be infused with colours and rhythm—the women who came in as household help would be humming songs under their breath as they washed clothes or cleaned the house. Since it was a large household, several kilos of wheat and *daals* would be purchased from the wholesale *mandi* and a few village women would be called to the house to clean these grains. The swish of their *chhaajlas* (soops), the grinding of the *masalas*—so many rhythms pounding your consciousness. My oft-mentioned guru, Raghunath, sang, uninhibited and loud, as he dropped me to school. All the festivals— Holi, Gangaur—had their own songs and music, and the *dholak* for wedding songs. I would run to the window to hear the invocations of people begging for alms. My feet would be tapping to their call, their sound of music. There was little film music played at home. We would go to the home of my father's close friend, Rakshpal Sharma,

whom we called Chacha, to listen to music on his radio. He told my
parents that he would never forget that little girl, Ilu, who would
dance to two songs, 'Gore, Gore haathon mein mehndi lagake' and
'Raja ki aaye gi baraat, rangili hogi raat.' He loved the hip shaking
and the rolling of the eyes of a child so engrossed in her movements
that she was unaware of her audience! But some of his words,
mentioning my thin legs, my wheatish complexion and my ordinary
looks would dampen my dancing spirit. Another uncle, tempting me
with hot sweet jalebis, would ask me to sing a Rajasthani song, 'Mari
chatta hogayi.' I have no recollection of where and how these songs
and this music entered my consciousness. I would give thanks to
my birthplace, my 'motherland', Rajasthan, where daily life seems
unthinkable without music. Every truck driver, labourer and bullock-
cart driver, both men and women, use songs while they work, perhaps
to relieve the monotony of their labour.

The desert sands beckoned me, as did the fragrance of neem
and babool trees. I would be lost in the sweet fragrance of the sand,
glistening after a monsoon shower. I looked at every movement, the
changing of seasons, the flight of birds, the ripple of water, every
action as a musical symphony.

I used to study at M.V.D. Bal Mandir. My father, as a government
officer, was entitled to two orderlies, or helpers. Raghunath was from
the Gujjar community. His starched turban and dhoti-kurta and
his proudly cultivated moustache gave him a bearing of authority.
He used to take me to school on a bicycle. As I sat perched on the
handlebars, his face close to my ears, his voice would reach out beyond
my unstable seat, singing Rajasthani songs. He was completely
oblivious of his environment, belting out his songs to the amusement
of passers-by. I would be embarrassed and would report him to my
mother saying that she should admonish him for his loud singing,
which drew attention to us. A couple of times I asked him to stop,
but of course, the complaint of a child had no effect on him. Soon
I got so accustomed to his singing that many a time when he was
on leave and Ramnath Meena came to drop me, I found this bicycle
ride very tedious. Sometimes I would start singing Oraaa...h, a long
stretched-out call, 'chhoti si lugai, tharo devar lagoon chhoon, tharo
mundo to dikhade mein kayin lere bhagon choon', which translated

means 'O little woman, I am your brother-in-law/ Why don't you reveal your face to me?/ I am not going to run away with you!" I remember that people stopped to listen to me, wondering what a little girl in uniform was doing singing a somewhat raunchy song. Then Ramnath would complain to my mother, wanting to know who was teaching me these inappropriate village songs. My mother would sometimes reprove me, at his prompting, but when I started singing Rajasthani songs in public, I realized that Raghunath's *Oraaa...h* had become the prefix to my folk songs!

He would start on one scale, take the *Oraaa...h* up to a higher scale and then almost as if he were throwing a rubber ball, the tone would be brought to the ground and come rolling down. This was his style and somehow, I made use of it in my singing.

Later, I used this as a signature to my folk singing. The *Oraaa...h* became part of several songs in my private albums. In fact, many music directors would ask me to use this in my songs. I have loved folk music, from any state. Because of my husky voice, no one could have imagined that I would take folk songs to such heights of popularity, that people would be singing them not only in India but all over the world, that a day would come when my folk songs, written and composed by me, would be played in every home, at several public functions. In every school, every wedding and at college competitions, they would dance to my songs and win awards. I could never have imagined this. I could not resist beating the rhythm at a wooden table, on doors and desks till my mother would shout out, 'Don't make such a racket!' On the other hand, my older sister, Uma, who had a beautiful singing voice was always asked to sing at all household functions. The family said her voice brought on serenity, while mine was only noise. That was an era of high-pitched voices, when listeners preferred soft and controlled female voices, just as they expected women to be suppressed and voiceless. But, listening to Raghunath's songs, the spirit of Shikhandi, the transgender warrior in the epic, Mahabharata seemed to have entered my soul, a spirit that perpetuated the full-throated voice of women's freedom. I suppose mine was a male voice in a female body, a forceful voice that refused to suffer in silence. In song and in theatre, I have believed in giving vent to my feelings and belief that 'a woman with a voice is by definition a strong woman', as Melinda Gates says.

My passion for music was fanned by many little incidents. As I have mentioned before, I had already learnt the methodology of music in my school and college. Several accolades came my way in competitions and performances. Then my participation in the Republic Day Parade state tableaux, twice, exposed me to the folk music of India. We spent a month at Talkatora Gardens during this time. We watched dancers and musicians from different states, we savoured their cuisine and we picked up words from their languages. That is how I learnt a lot of the folk tunes from India. We would have a campfire where I would dance and sing with them. I made many friends. One was a girl from Assam, from whom I learnt many a folk song of Assam, a few sung by the renowned singer Bhupen Hazarika. Their clothes, their accessories, their languages, coupled with their simplicity and innocence, unknowingly drew me to them. I went beyond my own frontiers and sought out folk music from African and Arabic communities, a rhythm that seemed akin to our tribal music and yet was very different in intonation and scale.

When did music become such a passion with me? I was never encouraged to sing either by my family or in my school and college where I was known more for my talent in acting. I was singing for myself, living in an imaginative world of song and dance, the same little girl who would stand up and dance to every sound she heard. But all these sounds from many sources were the rhythms that made me dance till they metamorphosized into a medley of songs!

My songs were composed standing on the balcony of my house, travelling in a car, on the spur of the moment as I talked to people or when I needed a filler in my plays. Strangely, the tunes and words came to me together, and then would be interpreted and put to music by the musicians. I did not sing according to a scale and had to find my note on the harmonium later. It was spontaneous music. I remember when I was composing for my album, *Chhappan Chhuri* I included a song, '*Jhoola Jhoole*'. When I sat down to record the song, Shambhu Senji, a renowned Rajasthani musician, who was playing around with the notes on the harmonium, said that the song was in Raag Kirwani but the lines were short of one beat! I had used this *raag* unknowingly as I always do. This *raag* is light and playful and is used in *thumri*-style compositions. That is why perhaps I used it for this song. I was wondering how I would change the line to fit the beat! I looked at him hopefully and before I could say anything he had found a way of getting around that missing beat. Since this was a song where a young girl was pining for her lover, we could cover the beat with a *hitchki,* hiccup. Now there is a big difference in the connotation of hiccup, a mundane word in the English language, which when translated into *hitchki,* turns into an emotion, a word of love and longing. Instead of changing the line, he suggested that I hiccup, a *hitchki,* to complete the line! I am an expert in sounds and sighs, so the *hitchki* was an interjection that was added to my dictionary of sounds!

I later learned that Michael Jackson also composed his songs in the same way. He did not know how to read sheet music. He would dictate the song into a tape recorder, singing the song and giving the beat of each instrument. He claimed that music came to him from above. 'The lyrics, the strings, the chords, everything comes at the moment like a gift that is put right into your head and that's how I hear it,' he said. Perhaps that was my music too, music from the heart, which just flowed out of my mind.

Opportunities came to me unexpectedly and took me one step closer to my destination. My sister Tripti, who worked with Rajasthan Tourism and Himmat Singh, a well-known exponent of Rajasthani culture, organized a cultural evening of Rajasthani music in Jaipur. As I sat in the audience, completely absorbed in the sound of music, I heard my name being called out and I realized I was being invited onstage to join in the singing. I walked up, Raghunath's face before my eyes as I sat down on the stage, a novice among the traditional singers of Rajasthan. I still remember the song: '*Sahu mahri e dholni mein daalo dhol*'. The folk artistes, the Manganiyars and the Langas looked on in wonder and I knew that this memorable moment was going to be a turning point in my life. I had been accepted by their community as one of them and I was assured of their love and support. I never looked back and as I left the stage, walking on air, I raised my eyes in salute to Raghunath and his regal moustache!

A few days later, much to my surprise and delight, the Rajasthan Tourism Department asked me to record a special cassette for tourists visiting Rajasthan. I took several artistes with me to Delhi and in a studio at Daryaganj, working through the night, we recorded the whole cassette, without the support of any music company. I sang every single Rajasthani song I knew, the folk artistes accompanying me with great enthusiasm. The cassette was named *A Musical Sandstorm*, a name that we used later for our first show in Mumbai. I had visions of planting my own flag in the world of folk music and later tried to market this cassette on my own strength. But not everyone has the luck of Gulshan Kumar and T-Series and my attempt at starting a business in music cassettes fell by the wayside, a fate shared by many others before me! But I was proud of this attempt. The cover, a sketch of me and the folk singers, by my brother Prasoon, still a schoolboy, was eye-catching. We decided on a marketing strategy, that we would sell the cassettes through agents at every bus stand, railway station, hotel and tourist destination frequented by travellers. This was not a bad plan and should have worked. But none of us had any concept of marketing and no idea of how to keep count of the production and sale of our merchandise, which ended up in total disarray! Even if I say so, that cassette was a pure form of the voice of the desert, without any modern embellishments. These cassettes now lie in caskets, battered boxes of my home and heart, waiting for their resurrection. But for me, this recording was a milestone in my music journey.

Many offers started coming my way. When Rajasthan Tourism launched their special royal train, Palace on Wheels, I was asked to record some Rajasthani folk songs to be played on the train. I sang many of my own compositions and some songs from the repertory of the Manganiyars and Langas, who were gaining popularity in north India. Not only were their songs included in this collection, but I used several folk instruments, hitherto unknown outside Rajasthan such as *morchung*, Sindhi *sarangi* and *khartaal*, etc., which added a different dimension to the singing. Much thought went into finding a title for the cassette. I decided on the name *Sound Track*, which seemed to fit the association with a train. The train was launched on Republic Day 1982, and it was the first luxury train launched by the

Indian Railways. My cassette was played on this train as background music and the cassettes were to be sold on the train. The cover, once again designed by my brother Prasoon, drew a lot of attention. Rajasthani folk instruments were used as visuals—the *dholak* was the steam engine, the *surnai* the funnel and the *khartaal* used as the train tracks! People would ask me what my mother had fed on to produce such talented offspring, and my reply would be that my mother was a woman from the middle class who ate whatever was available, usually leftovers. The vegetables in Rajasthan were not the fresh green vegetables of her home in the Gangetic plains of UP, but the roots and seeds from a desert. I give credit to the land of my birth where every particle of sand and those who tread on it have music, dance and poetry in their blood. So have my siblings, nurtured by the vibrancy and colours of Rajasthan.

My journey was also special. From the tiny footpaths of villages, from bullock-carts to the buses of Rajasthan Roadways, I finally landed in Mumbai, only to encounter the crowds of the local trains of this city. Incredibly, this husky voice from the desert found recognition in this city of glamour and Bollywood. Purely by coincidence, two opportunities came my way, where I could use my knowledge of folk music and find my way into the music scene of Mumbai The first was when I was asked by Manju Singh, the producer of the Doordarshan programme, *Showtheme*, later called *Showtime*, to be the compere for two episodes of this series. I had known her and the director, Virendra Sharma, from my Delhi days. Each episode was based on a theme and film songs were selected and played to go with the theme. The episodes I was presenting were on village life and its environment: a postman, the drizzle of rain in the fields, swings hanging from branches of trees and other aspects of village life. As I went through the brief, I suggested that why not change the format a little and introduce folk songs instead of film songs. The idea appealed to them and they gave me the liberty to sing my own songs on the programme. Two of my songs were great hits to such an extent that people started asking about this new singer, Ila Arun. The aficionados of folk music welcomed me with open arms and I was a celebrity in Mumbai! Umesh Mehra offered me a role in his film *Jaal* (1986). Subhash Ghai Sahib approached me for his film *Karma* (1986), which unfortunately I could not take up since I was too young for the role. But later, as I have mentioned before, he signed me to sing for his film *Deva*, an Amitabh Bachchan starrer, which for some reason remained incomplete.

Once again purely by chance, while visiting Shabana Azmi at her home, Janki Kutir, I met Mahesh Bhatt. Shabana had told him about my singing, and he asked me to sing a Rajasthani song. I started my song as usual to the beat of the table in front of me. The song was '*Sahu mhari e*,' and Mahesh Bhatt was sold! He called me to sing the song for his film *Aghaat* (1985), with Jagjit Singhji as music director.

I could not believe I was actually singing in films and thought that this was just in passing, an interlude before I discovered my niche. But once again opportunity crossed my path and I was drawn into a wider, more exciting world of music.

Chapter 17

HMV: His Master's Voice

But the most exciting outcome of all this was that I was approached by the music company, HMV. There is a saying in Hindi that the thirsty are drawn towards the well, but in this case, the well itself came to the thirsty, a unique happening indeed. Opportunity was actually knocking at my door, an opportunity that greater artistes than I longed for! Even in my wildest dreams I could not have imagined that a reputed music company would approach me with a proposal for an album of my own—HMV, the company that was known as the label that laid the foundation of the Indian music industry. I went to meet Sanjeev Kohli, the general manager of HMV, at their office in the Fort area. He introduced me to the VP, V.K. Dubey.

As a school-going girl, I had seen two ads connected with music and broadcasting, the HMV dog and the cute little baby in the Murphy radio ad. Both were associated with tragedy. The dog listening to the gramophone was Nipper, the fox terrier, who actually ran to listen to his dead master's voice, which had been recorded on a phonograph. By now I also had a dog, if you remember, who ended up being called Whiskey in a family of teetotallers. He seemed to be the only one in the household who appreciated my voice and I think, listened to me with soulful eyes and one ear cocked to my songs! By this time, we had acquired a radio, our only source of entertainment at home. It occupied pride of place in a room, covered with crocheted doilies. I was thrilled at the idea that if I sang for HMV, Nipper the dog would listen to me, like Whiskey, and my songs would be broadcast on the radio, not necessarily Murphy, in our sitting room!

The discussions were fruitful and it was decided that I would create an album of Rajasthani music for the Company. I was given a free hand to decide on the strategy and the concept for this album. The only suggestion was that since I was still new and relatively unknown, I should use the services of Shambhu Sen, whom I have mentioned earlier, a well-known music director from the Shekhavati region of Rajasthan. The Sen family was known in Rajasthan and Shambhuji's two sons, Lalit and Sameer Sen also worked with the father. HMV said that using famous names would be good for the sale of the cassettes and their experience and knowledge would be the icing on the cake.

I knew nothing about contracts and did not even check to look through the details. I was told that the company would sign me against royalty. Of course, I had no idea what that meant either. I was familiar with a similar-sounding word—loyalty, something I expected in all my relationships. But in such professional associations, one does not get loyalty and of course even the royalty was less than my expectations.

However, my loyalty towards my music prompted me to put my heart and soul into my first commercial album. I called it *Banjaran*, gypsy girl. The opening lines were composed with the memory of the lives of the gypsy tribes whom I had observed while travelling in Rajasthan. Another song *Satolia* was composed keeping in mind a game popular with children in villages, *satolia,* or seven tiles. Raghunath's *arrrrrrr* sounds featured prominently in this composition! Released in 1983, it was the first folk album to be recorded in India! Someone told me that it is available online now for Rs 3999 on some site.

The songs for this album were all songs I had heard at weddings, festivals or *melas* or my original songs which I had composed for my plays. I remember HMV sent the photographer Rakesh Shreshta, the chronicler of Bollywood, who has photographed every star and here he was coming to my home in Santa Cruz, to photograph me! He did not carry any other equipment except his camera. I was surprised that he was not even carrying a light! He wanted a good skyline as a backdrop, so I told him to come up to the terrace of our building, Paradise Apartments, which was the tallest building in our

With Aishwarya Rai in a scene from the Bollywood film *Jodhaa Akbar*

In the British film *West Is West*

As a deadly antagonist in the OTT web series *Aarya 3*

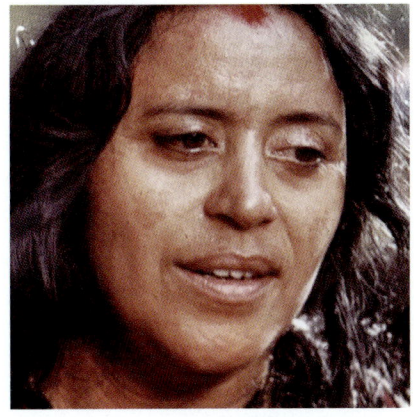

As a mentally traumatized victim in a scene from the film *Ghatak*

Jacket cover of my music
album *Chhappan Chhuri*

Jacket cover of my music album
Vote for Ghaghra

Ethnic Ila

The *Bichhuda* Girl

Jacket cover for the music
album *Mela*

Jacket cover for the music
album *Banjaran*

A personal photo-op with the
Mahanayak Shri Amitabh
Bachchan

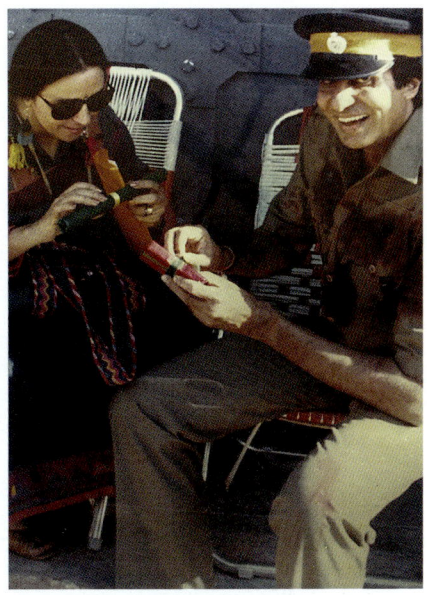

On the official release of my
album *Chhappan Chhuri* by
Amitji on his film set

Jaya Bachchanji at
my niece's wedding
with my brothers Piyush
(seated) and Prasoon and
his wife Gayatri Pandey

With my mentor and cinematic guru, Shri Shyam Benegal

With Shabana Azmi

With Rekhaji and Vidya Balan

Love playing Holi at Janki Kutir

Admiring Rekhaji's affection
for my daughter Ishitta

With Sushmita Sen in the web series *Aarya 3*: Foes in reel life but like a daughter in real life

With another guru, Shri Govind Nihalani, remembering my dear brother Om Puri

Precious picture with Ghulam Ali
Khan Sahib and Zakir Hussain

With Jackie Shroff, a true
well-wisher and evergreen friend

Surily dosti with the great
singer Anup Jalota

Bappi Da singing at
Ishitta's wedding

The King and Queen of Paradise, Santa Cruz, Mumbai

With the Princess of Paradise,
Ishitta Kumari

Table for two: Celebrating our
wedding anniversary

Ex-vice president Bhairon Singh Shekhawat (fourth from the left) and A.K. Hangal Sahib (sixth from the right) at Ishitta and Dhruv's wedding reception

Ishitta and Dhruv at their wedding

Naani Bhagwati's blessings are always with Ishitta and Dhruv

The full Pandey family cannot be captured in one frame,
some are still missing

Ishitta's selfie time with Piyush mama
and Nita mami

My eldest brother-in-law
and his family from
Bhopal

With my daughter Ishitta, son-in-law Dhruv, granddaughters Amaala and Alaaya, and my husband Arun

Three generations: with my daughter Ishitta and granddaughters (left to right) Alaaya and Amaala

The late Arnab Chaudhuri (in red) always brought a smile to our faces

Celebrating Christmas with my adorable granddaughters

Actor–director K.K. Raina
and me in a Henrik Ibsen play
Ghosts (Hindi adaptation as
Peechha Karti Parchhaiyan by me)

Ravi Jhankal and me in Ibsen's
Norwegian play *The Lady from the Sea*
(Hindi adaptation as *Mareechika* by me)

K.K. Raina as Colonel Vikram and
me as Sanyogita in my original play
Yeh Raaste Hain Pyaar Ke

Playing the lead role in
Jameela Bai Kaalaali

Surnai's Fortieth Anniversary Celebrations

(Left to right) My friends Avani Shah and Shilpa Mehta have been dancing to my tunes from the beginning

Performing my most famous song 'Resham Ka Rumal' onstage

Selfie onstage with Surnai actors

Celebration continued with folk artistes

Nayak nahi, khal nayak hoon main

Nawazuddin Siddiqui and me in the important roles of transgenders or eunuchs in the film *Haddi*

As a judge in the reality show *Junoon Kuch Kar Dikhane Ka*

Playing an eighty-year-old grandmother in the children's film *Gauru: Journey of Courage*

Nostalgia time: (standing left to right) Jagjit Singhji, Chitraji, Talat Mahmood, Bhupendra Singh, Talat Aziz

Gary Lawyer, Alisha Chinai, myself, Mitali Singh and Nandu Bhide

With the Norwegian Ibsen actor and
my dearest friend Kåre Conradi at the
National Theatre, Oslo

Norway: Home away
from home

Receiving the highest Norwegian
civilian award to a foreigner:
King's Order of Merit—Knight
1st Class from the then consul
general Ann Olstead for 2018

With my hero Henrik
Ibsen's statue in Norway

Paying my respects to
Prithviraj Kapoor

Being featured on the
Harmony Celebrate Age
magazine cover

With my best friend–backbone and
co-author Anjula Bedi

Family bonding: Nadira Zahir
Babbar, Juhi Babbar,
Ishitta and me

area at the time. But he looked around and still was not satisfied with the skyline. I had got myself ready for the shoot. I had no make-up man or costume designer and had used my own *ghaghra* with a black backless *choli*. In my hand, I held the *ravanahatta*. According to legend, the *ravanahatta* was used by Ravana in his worship of Shiva and after the war between Rama and Ravana, Hanuman returned to north India with a *ravanahatta*. This folk instrument is used by street musicians in Rajasthan, especially the *Bhopas,* travelling storytellers, who relate the story of the folk hero Pabuji. My idea was to show my back with the title *Banjaran* written on it. I would turn my head to the left, showing just a part of my profile, leaving the listeners in suspense about the identity of the *Banjaran*. I had on chunky silver jewellery and a heavy *ghaghra*. Yet, on the spur of the moment, I told him that perhaps we could use the height of the water tank and he agreed. Both he and I scrambled up the perpendicular ladder standing against the water tank, I gathering my *ghaghra,* the *ravanhatta* and clanking jewellery in my hands, where Rakesh got not merely the skyline but the vast blue sky! And there the cover picture of my first album was clicked by Rakesh Shreshta! I could think of only two people who climbed up a water tank for a shoot, Dharmendra in *Sholay* and now Ila Arun in *Banjaran*!

The cassettes sold like hot cakes and won the hearts of not only the Hindi-speaking public but those who spoke Bengali, Tamil, Punjabi and other languages of India. I was touched by the response of the owners of HMV, industrialist R.P. Goenka and his wife Sushilaji— Marwaris living in Kolkata who showered me with love and respect. There was no social media and the means for the promotion of my cassette were limited, yet the sales went way beyond our expectations. Riding on this wave of popularity, I was signed up for another album. This time Shambhuji requested me to use his son Lalit as the music director, while he himself would stay in the background. Now there was a reversal of roles. He said that my name would help in promoting Lalit! I was a naïve newcomer and did not realize that actually I was the music director myself, having composed the songs, set them to music and decided on the presentation. All that I needed was an arranger to complete my songs! But I did not think about the credits

as long as the work done was good. Lalit was supported by his father
and his two brothers. I remember those days when I would go to the
Sen home at Aramnagar to rehearse for my numbers, Shambhuji's
wife, whom we addressed as Bai, would feed me delicious *laapsi*, a
sweet made of broken wheat, similar to porridge, sweetened with
jaggery and washed down with hot milk. We spent hours talking
about Rajasthan, a land we had all left behind, but which was still
home to us. The atmosphere exuded music and warmth! I named
my second album *Chhappan Chhuri*. I loved all the eight songs
I recorded for this album, but one song 'Resham Ka Rumal' was
highly appreciated by both of Lalit's brothers, Sameer, one of the best
rhythmists in the industry and Sanjeev, a famous *tabla* player, sought
after by music directors. Sameer was always called upon to take the
responsibility of setting the rhythm to most Rajasthani-based songs
and whenever a *dholak* maestro was required, it had to be Sameer.
Half of Rajasthan seemed to be there to support the Sen brothers—
their uncle Dalip Sen and several others took charge. Dalip and
Sameer Sen were the rhythmists and did such a superb job with the
percussion instruments that since then three generations have danced
to their beat! The whole of Shambhuji's family was there, all great
rhythmists whom no one in Mumbai could match. Then there was
Shakoor from Sikar and Roshan who accompanied every song in
Bollywood that required the *chhaap* and *dhaap* of the *dholak*. Liaquat
Masterji was on the sarangi and most of the other musicians were
also from Rajasthan. The result was amazing. Two songs 'Resham
Ka Rumal' and 'Assi Kali Ka Lehnga' broke all records and could
be heard at all weddings, school and college competitions and all the
village melas! And are still playing after thirty years!

I must mention here that the provocative cover of *Chhappan
Chhuri* was designed by my brother Prasoon and his friend Sonal
Dabral. The photo shoot took place at Gautam Rajyadhaksha's
house, a beautiful bungalow on Hughes Road. He was a master of
photography and worked mostly with Mickey Contractor, the king
of make-up men, probably the best in the business and sought out by
Bollywood and the modelling communities. Both these men worked
wonders on anyone who posed for them. Rekha, Aishwarya and
other actresses would only be photographed and made-up by them.

The most ordinary faces, including mine, were turned into things of beauty. The brief given to them was to make me look sensuous and bold, with prominent eye make-up and hair in thin braids. With Mickey and Gautam working on the photo and make-up, I was upgraded and moved into the world of glamour. I was transformed into a beauty.

Prasoon and Sonal had just passed out from the National Institute of Design (NID) and were full of new ideas and designs. They listened to the songs several times and then decided that the cover had to represent the spirit and flamboyance of the gypsy women of Rajasthan. The colours they chose for the cassette were the vibrant bright yellows, greens and reds, which immediately caught the eye, compelling people to pull the cassette out for a second look! *Chhappan Chhuri* changed my life and the two songs I have mentioned, took the music world and my fans by storm. I am proud that these songs were written and composed by me.

I had observed the nomadic tribes from close range. Their itinerant lifestyle, their colourful costumes and their food, was a source of fascination for me and gave way to my creative and emotional sensitivity. I would write poetry and compose my own songs listening to their singing. They were not traditional songs, but my own compositions inspired by their activities, using their language and their rhythms, the same rhythms popular in Rajasthan. My songs were not borrowed from the traditional repertory of folk songs but grew out of the very soul of the desert, songs to which I gave life and the folk form. I was intoxicated by the spirit of Rajasthan and lived and breathed its culture. As I grew up in Jaipur, I was familiar with the *ragas* and songs for special occasions and seasons. I was able to use all this knowledge in my music. I believe that the more involved you are in your culture, the richer you become.

Suddenly I was flooded with offers for live shows. Rarely was a ladies' sangeet or wedding planned without one day dedicated to my performance! I had no manager and no event planner. My clients approached me themselves and the shows were planned by me. I did several shows for the RPG group, both personal and corporate. The Goenka family is one of the most cultured and genteel families I have come across in my life. Humble and courteous, never once did they make me feel that they were the bosses of the company I was recording for. In fact, they gave me, a mere singer, so much respect and consideration that sometimes I did not know how to handle it.

HMV has been the 'dream' company for the greatest musicians of India: Bismillah Khan Sahib, Bhimsen Joshiji, Ustad Vilayat Khan Sahib, Ashaji, Lataji, you name them and they were in the honours list of HMV. The company has the largest collection of classical and film music, a treasure-house of the heritage of India. As for me, I gave them the same loyalty that their dog Nipper had given his master's voice!

I consider myself the common man's artiste. I sing for the *janta*. But after the release of *Banjaran*, when the acclaimed critic Subhash Jha called me the poor man's Reshma, I did not take that as a compliment. In fact, I was upset by his remark. Later I realized that he meant well. He turned out to be quite a fan of mine. I myself was a great fan of Reshmaji. I had heard her several times and would listen to her in wonder. She was from the tribe of gypsies and the minute she started with the *alaap*, it would send her listeners into ecstasy. I remember listening to a cassette in which she recounted her journey into Pakistan, saying that though she was from a nomadic tribe from Sikar, she earned a name for herself in the world of music by sheer determination and *riyaaz*, practice She was undeniably my role model. I was neither from a gypsy background nor from a family of musicians. My parents were settlers from UP who did not have anything to do with music and referred to musicians as *mirasi*, a derogatory term, denoting the lower castes. If only I had been born in such a family, I would have lived and wallowed in music! Though to be fair to my mother, she was a woman way ahead of her times and saw to it that all her children were tutored in the arts—music, dance, poetry and writing, but only as a hobby!

'Resham Ka Rumal' is the story of a young village girl who calls out to her beloved, asking him to return home as she had waited long enough at the door looking out for him. Each accessory she adorns her body with also echoes her desires. A door had been my accompaniment since childhood since most of my songs were composed to the rhythm of my improvised door-*dholaks*! I cannot even fathom how these songs have travelled far and wide to all corners of the world, that my 'Assi Kali Ka Lehnga' has twirled and danced its way to places I have never seen! I can claim with certainty that my songs were not just songs but shone with the legacy of the folk tradition, so much so that young people were drawn to their ethnic origins and the fashion scene changed to the same ghaghras and cholis, the jhanjhar and churas worn by women in villages. When I saw city girls dancing to my songs, their ghaghras pirouetting to my music, I was happy that at that moment they were connected to their roots through my songs. I felt I had been successful to some extent in bringing the new generation from pop culture to folk tradition.

These songs became so popular that a time came when the Manganiyars, Langas and Kalbelias, who were commissioned to entertain tourists in hotels, started receiving requests to sing Ila Arun's songs. They had no choice but to add my songs to their repertoire. What could be more gratifying than watching people acknowledging and accepting something you have created and enjoying it with abandon? These songs are mentioned even today when people meet me.

One of the most popular songs I sang and one of my favourites, was 'Morni baaga mein bole'. which had been composed for RPG's film Lamhe (1991). The story behind the rendition of this song needs to be mentioned. Almost at the same time as the release of Chhappan Chhuri, HMV signed a film with Yash Chopra. The story was based in Rajasthan. Yashji wanted to record a song on the sand dunes, a duet, with Lata Mangeshkar and another strong voice similar to Reshma. HMV sent him my cassette. There is no comparison between Reshmaji and I, but he detected a newness in my voice. He invited me for a sitting in his house. In those days, the sitting for a song was a very important affair and was attended by the producer, director, music director and the singer. Sometimes even the stars of the film would stop by for a while. That is where I met the duo Hariji and Shivji. They listened to my songs and then asked me whether I knew a song titled 'Morya aacho bolo re dhalti raat mein,' which had been made popular by singer Afroz Bano from Jaipur. I said I knew only a verse or two. Surprisingly, Shivji knew the whole song which he sang for me. I too sang after him. After two or three rehearsals, Shivji combined this with one of my songs 'O Re Dhola' and created a new song, a beautiful composition, 'Morni baaga mein bole aadhi raat mein', which was used for the climax. Half the song was sung by Lataji and the other half by me. Yashji wanted Sridevi to dance to a voice of the desert. For me, this was perhaps the most exciting day of my singing career, when I had the opportunity to sing with the Nightingale of India, Lata Mangeshkar. I spent a sleepless night. As I have mentioned, recordings in those days were very different from now. Today, there is one engineer to supervise your recording and he just dubs your voice. Sometimes even the music director is not present. His assistant indicates with four fingers raised, telling you where to stop and where to begin.

I rehearsed this song twice with Lataji and Shivji and Hariprasadji at HMV Studios. I was so nervous that my throat was parched, my lips dry and my heart in my mouth. I had a bad throat, which seemed to become worse as I waited with bated breath. But somehow the recording went off very well. Lataji was obviously satisfied since she asked me who my guru was. I whispered my teacher Raghunath's name! The recording was a live one. The musicians sat outside behind a partition with their own microphones. There were two cabins for the singers—one for Lataji and the other for me! If I remember correctly, the song was recorded in one take after two rehearsals. I was still in a state of suspended reality. It was beyond belief that the melody queen of India would sing with an earthy Rajasthani voice! This was the golden moment of my life, a moment, which comes to the fortunate few, which I could now claim to be! There were more surprises in store for me. Not only did I sing the song with Lataji, but I got the chance to enact the scene on screen with Sridevi! This was also nothing short of a miracle for me and it seemed that my luck was holding out! The reason was that when the film was launched at the Centaur before the whole film industry, HMV suggested to Yashji that instead of other dancers performing at the launch, he should use me and my group who always performed with me and whom they had seen onstage with me in my live shows. I would sing three songs from my album and then the song 'Morni' would be presented. Yashji agreed and I stormed onto the stage singing 'Mela mein le chaal sajana,' in a bullock-cart with two of my actors as bulls, wearing costumes and bullock heads borrowed from Maganlal

Dresswala! *'Resham Ka Rumal'* and *'Assi Kali'* followed in quick
succession and my dancers and actors made a dramatic exit while
the blowers blew sand and leaves onto the stage, creating the desert
for the entry of Sridevi, Anil Kapoor and Anupam Kher. Sridevi and
I danced to two lines of *'Morni'* and the launch was complete. I was
showered with accolades. In the audience was the crème de la crème
of Bollywood—leading music directors, producers and directors who
noticed me and realized that I could dance, sing and act. It was as
if for me, one moment had been turned into a hundred years. I did
not even need to make a show-reel. Bollywood opened its doors to
me and I suddenly became a commercial actress overnight! After the
show, Yashji told HMV that he would like to film the song with Ila.

So, there I was in Jaisalmer, in the biting cold of winter on the
freezing sand dunes, shooting for *Lamhe*. I had been on cold sand
dunes often, but for Sridevi, who was from the south, it was a new
experience, and I remember her being really cold and wearing socks
to keep away the chill. The dance director Saroj Khan was there
too, the best choreographer in the industry at the time. She gave me
the freedom to choreograph my own movements and came in only
when Sridevi and I had to coordinate our steps. The bonfire was lit
and a romantic ambience was created. It was shot so beautifully,
that there was a spontaneous applause at the end. Sridevi danced so
gracefully, oblivious to the cold, that all of us were left speechless.
It was a lesson for me that a dedicated actress does not get fazed
by circumstances and situations. Watching her, I also did my best
and the song and dance were instant hits when the film opened in
theatres. During the filming, Saroj Khan said that Lataji had sung
more of the song than I, so there should be an equal division and
without any discussion on the spot she made me lip-sync a line of
Lataji and the cameraman caught it on camera. She said the music
director will have to record that one line in the studio. That was
easier said than done. I could not match Lataji's scale. Yashji asked
Hari Prasadji to deal with the problem. I was called to Sunny Studios
for the recording. After several attempts, I do not know how Hariji
used his expertise to turn the music around, it was magic, as if he
was meandering through several paths to get to the destination! This
change cannot be heard on the cassette in which this line is sung by

Lataji. You can only see it on film. Hariji's ingenuity has infused life into that song. This was another learning process for me—how to turn something around to enhance its effect. I am also grateful to Sarojji for having given me that extra time onscreen, a chance that very few actors get; their lines and presence are usually cut instead! This was a historic moment in my life.

My costume for the song, one lingering memory, was my own and it is still with me, used for all the performances of 'Morni' for my live shows. I must have acquired it from my usual sources, the wives of Raghunath or Ramnath and the *choli* I picked up locally. My folk artistes supplied the traditional *chuda*. My *lehenga* is on its way out, but it is taken out and repaired for a performance, few and far between now!

I was still living in the euphoria of 'Morni', while around me a new trend for music was setting in, a new genre called Indipop. HMV asked me to include that in my compositions and to give myself a new image. They wanted me to use my deep voice to sing Indipop like Usha Uthup. I bowed to their demand and put a new album together, calling it *Titali,* butterfly. Once again, the photo and make-up were done by Gautam Rajadhyaksha and Mickey Contractor. I was presented in a totally different avatar. I wore Neena Gupta's red dress and I felt I could match all those Indian pop singers who were singing to Western tunes. I introduced several international musical elements which I thought would enhance the presentation. This colourful, fluttering butterfly did attempt to fly with its velvety wings but could not really take off. I was disappointed that my beautifully crafted work did not reach my audience. I was reminded of a children's song, '*Titali udi, ud na saki/ train mein chadi seat na mili*', meaning that the butterfly took off but could not fly/it boarded a train, but no seat was available! My *titali* had indeed missed the train! There were plenty of Western singers who had become popular in India by that time and I was trying to compete with them in a totally different language, *khari boli,* which I later realized was unacceptable to listeners of Western music, especially since I had already established my identity as a folk singer. Besides, there were already several Indian singers who were singing Indipop—Shweta Shetty, Sunita Rao, Dalip Tahil, Alisha Chinai, Gary Lawyer, Colonial Cousins, etc.—and the Indian audiences loved them. There was also a craze for singers from the West, like Abba, Tina Turner, Grease, The Doors, etc.

Titali was a well-made album but perhaps it was burdened with too much Western spice, making it a tasteless offering of Indipop for the Indian palate! It was a different kind of music, which unfortunately did not appeal to my fans. They had got used to my ethnicity, the folk genre that I had started out with—a soulful voice, the voice of rural India. It was unfortunate that my fans rejected me and the new generation did not accept me!

But before I could make another album with HMV, my life took another unexpected turn. Before Subhash Ghai's film *Khal Nayak* (1993) had been released, the song which I had sung with Alka Yagnik, '*Choli Ke Peechhey*', had become a superhit overnight and with it, my position in Bollywood and the music world took a quantum leap!

Chapter 18

Controversy: *Choli Ke Peechhey Kya Hai?*

Rows of shoes outside a door—the door of Parasmani, the home of the most popular music director, Lakshmikant of the famous duo, Laxmikant–Pyarelal—shoes of different colours, sandals, chappals— and then the tell-tale ones, white! Strange that these shoes still remain in my memory, white shoes, the symbol of status in the film world. It was an intimation of something serious. What lay behind the closed door, and why was I summoned to these exalted precincts of the film world? I had got a call from the renowned director Subhash Ghai, asking me to meet him at Parasmani since he wanted me to sing in a film he was contemplating. It was 1993. I had no idea what to expect. In those days, the music of a film was the most important element of its popularity. When a song was being composed, everyone connected with the film was part of this sitting. So, the shoes belonged to the financier, the director, the producer, the composer, the singer and the most worn-out chappals usually belonged to the lyricist! For me, it was a real test of my talent and courage. Alka Yagnik was there and seeing her I felt a little more relaxed. I sat down and joined this group of 'greats'. How fortunate I was to be part of this *mehfil* of the best talent in the Indian film industry! Pencil in hand and holding on to my diary, I waited for my entry! Anand Bakshi, the lyricist suddenly said, 'Write!' My pencil barely touched the paper, when the first line was recited by him, "*Choli Ke Peechhey Kya Hai*'. Did my pencil falter, or did I frown or look up? I don't remember. But there was silence for a few seconds. Behind me I could hear a slight giggle from Alka. But I think that moment brought forth my theatre experience. With a degree of nonchalance, I waited, my eyes fixed on my diary,

188

waiting in the wings for my next cue. I did not realize that I was the focus of all the people in that room; they too were waiting, waiting for my reaction to this bold first line. But for me, with a strong folk tradition behind me, these lines were mild! I was used to songs sung by village women, uninhibited, raucous, singing from behind their *ghunghats*, oblivious of the suggestive *kurti-kanchhlis* revealing their assets! I had sung songs in several languages, in Punjabi, Hindi and Bhojpuri with overt sexual innuendoes. Then there was the *naktora*, a group of marriage songs from UP. Since women did not accompany the *baraat*, they gathered at the bridegroom's home and had a ball singing traditional wedding songs, which described every detail of the relationship between the new couple. The *samdhis*, the in-laws, were not spared either and the leg-pulling and teasing would make even the most hardened blush! Unfortunately, these traditional songs have been forgotten in the blaze of Bollywood numbers now being sung at every marriage function.

There were several sittings, a great learning experience for me. The song grew. Laxmikantji was a great composer, but when he hummed a tune, it sounded so ordinary that not in your wildest imagination could you picture how extraordinary the end product would be. Pyarebhai was the soul of the composition. There was such a wonderful rapport between the two that Pyarebhai would immediately pick up the song and put it to music, producing an amazing orchestration. During the course of the recording, Subhash Ghai asked me to put in my own folksy interjections. That was all I needed! So, my chorus was the '*oohs*' and '*aahs*' of folk songs which gave an amazing fillip to the already naughty lyrics! When Subhash Ghai heard my improvisations, he was so excited that he thought I should also dance onscreen to the song. As usual, my small-town sense of propriety came to the fore. Afraid of what the possibilities were with the '*peechhey*' of the '*choli*', especially with Saroj Khan as the dance director, I once again had the temerity to refuse Subhash Ghai and Saroj Khan. But Neena Gupta, who performed to my lines, stole the show with her sensuous rendition of the number. So much so that whenever there was a live performance with Bollywood celebrities, with '*Choli*' as the requested number from me, Neena was always in demand! She became part of some of the live shows, which travelled in India and to Dubai, dancing to my tune! I would say that the song is beautifully recorded and the credit goes to Laxmikant–Pyarelal. It is not obscene even in the film. It is like a folk number. Madhuri Dixit has excelled in the rendition. And Neena made it look so real even though she was lip-syncing.

The song was recorded and released before the movie came out and had already made waves by the time *Khal Nayak* hit the movie halls. I was suddenly catapulted to fame or infamy, depending which side you were on; there were several discussions on the song, people calling out for my blood, court cases being filed against me in remote towns of India, accusing me of obscenity; the police from the Santa Cruz station arrived at my doorstep one morning, saying I had not responded to a summons sent to me, a word that I had never heard before! My family members thought I was compromising my sense of propriety to make a break in films. I turned a deaf ear to all these snide remarks.

1993, the year when well and truly, my mother's clapperboard came down on me or rather should I say crashed over my head! My reputation and propriety literally 'went for a song', an innocent song, '*Choli Ke Peechhey*', which was now heard everywhere, from loudspeakers for weddings, on every music channel, and sung by every Romeo on the street. And it was in my voice!

My mother shook her head in dismay, reminding me again and again of her constant warning '*Avesh mein vivek mat khona*'. She was convinced I had lost my *vivek,* my conscience, to the improprieties of the film world. And indeed, she was not the only one in the family. My sisters too pointed the finger of indecency, surprising me with their response.

I always wonder why the fallout of this song dragged me into a controversy! I was only the singer! The song was written by Anand Bakshi, the dancers were Madhuri Dixit and Neena Gupta and Tips the music company! Tips loved the song and the popularity with the negative publicity sold thousands of records. Why on earth was I singled out for impropriety? Of course that brought me into the limelight, though for the wrong reasons! And I became the '*Choli Ke Peechhey*' girl. Audiences loved the song and there were demands for it at every live show, in India and abroad. I was included in every Bollywood show. '*Choli ke peechhey hai kya?*' Much to my amusement, several *choli* songs were offered to me. One of the most ridiculous was a song brought to me by Dalip Sen. Each day of the week was associated with a different kind of *choli*! The last straw was an advertisement for some footwear, where the copy was *Chappal ke neechhey kya hai*, what is behind the slipper? Sometimes I wondered whether I was a singer or a tailor, being questioned about *choli* styles!

If I look back over the years, the seeds of the song were sown many years before 1993, in the soil of the village on *Showtime*! How was I, an unknown singer in the film world, a raw newcomer to Mumbai's world of glamour, selected by the great director Subhash Ghai, to render a song in his new film? It was a star-studded affair with the likes of Sanjay Dutt, Madhuri Dixit, Jackie Shroff and Anupam Kher in lead roles.

The brickbats kept coming. A lawyer filed a complaint somewhere in Rajasthan and I had to appoint a lawyer there to represent me. By then I had understood the game; it was a publicity stunt for the complainant. This was not the first song that had double entendres. We have had several songs, which could have attracted the same kind of publicity. In fact, even Meerabai mentions Radha's *kanchukki*, her *choli,* in her songs. The controversy was blown out of proportion. I had several press interviews where I gave examples of so-called 'obscenity' throughout Indian myths and art. The *sringar ras* in Indian art and music, contains elements of eroticism, mentioning the *choli* or the *angana* as accessories to enhance a woman's beauty. I would give several examples of folk songs in Punjabi, Hindi, Bhojpuri and Marwari, which had all the naughty nuances that were being condemned in this song.

I reminded the moral brigade that every young girl, including myself, had encountered these questions from the eve teasers who hung around girls' colleges. Anand Bakshi had only answered that question with dignity. '*Choli mein dil hai mera*'—the *choli* contains my heart—he wrote, admonishing the vicarious and lewd comments of boys and men. I said that it was only my sensuous voice and my style of singing which drew the attention of listeners to what was behind the *choli*! Tips loved it and in fact commissioned me for another song.

At the end of the day, *Khal Nayak*, 'Choli Ke Peechhey' and I had the last laugh. *Khal Nayak* walked away with almost all the awards in the various categories of the Filmfare Awards. Best film, Best director, Best actor, best female actor, etc, and 'Choli Ke Peechhey' was adjudged the best song of the year, with Alka Yagnik and the beleaguered Ila Arun chosen as the best female playback singers! The lyrics, battered by many citizens of India, including forty-two political parties calling for a ban on the song, got Anand Bakshi the best lyricist award. The so-called vulgar dance won Saroj Khan the best choreographer award!

So, though 'Choli' was condemned by many and loved by many more, I was riding high on it! Not that *choli* was a flag of my popularity or my career, but my own albums too were once again in the limelight. The sponsors of these shows realized that many of my private albums were really popular with Indians abroad so I was invited to join almost every live show for several years. Many years later, Subhash Ghai asked me how much I had earned on the back of this song. My whimsical reply was that though he gave me peanuts for the original song, I had earned popularity and many live shows after the phenomenal success of this song. I had also earned an audience for my plays, since people came in large numbers, expecting that somewhere, sometime this song would be spouted from the stage!

People have asked me what I am: a singer, an actor or a writer? I say I am all of these put together, because I act when I sing, and sing when I act, since both a singer and an actor have to grasp the rhythm and tone of her performance. I remember, Kalyanjibhai used to tell Alka Yagnik to watch my expressions when I sang since a song is brought to life with the singer's eyes and face. Since I am used to performing on stage, I cannot help but convey my emotions and feelings when I sing, oblivious to the camera.

The success of this song brought me many live shows and several requests to sing at weddings. I cannot even count the times I had to sing 'Choli Ke Peechhey'. People would ask for encores and I, carried away by the rhythm, would take several *chakkars*. This is much easier in a film since you have several takes, but live onstage it takes a lot out of the dancer. My brothers would say that I would have an early burnout but with my limited knowledge of the English language I did not understand this warning, and I danced for hours onstage, trampling on all the complaints and sniggers that had come my way. 'Choli' got me real recognition. I went on world tours with the stars: Saif, Amrita, Rishi, Shah Rukh, Akshay and Juhi Chawla. And when *Lamhe* was released, there would be a special demand for 'Morni' and 'Choli'. I took two dancers with me, Avni Shah, and Meena, so my balancing act was good. Avni danced to 'Morni' and Meena took on Madhuri's act in the 'Choli' song, while I did Neena's seductive dance. I was riding a wave of popularity with the audience demanding more songs from me. And as is my wont, I would get so carried away that I would sometimes sing three additional songs after 'Choli' without an increase in my performance fees to the absolute delight of the organizers, who had paid me for only two songs! They realized how popular I was in places like London and Washington. I cannot forget Washington. The Indian diaspora knew all my songs and would demand songs like 'Payal Uttar Doongi' and 'Resham Ka Rumal' and they would be dancing in the aisles!

I think it was after the popularity of 'Choli Ke Peechhey' that the RPG group invited me to perform at the Siri Fort in Delhi. It was a two-day show of massive proportions, in memory of the late Prime Minister Rajiv Gandhi. I was to do the opening show, a matter of great pride for me. Pandit Shivkumar Sharma was performing on the second day. I was told that Rajiv's widow, Sonia Gandhi, had specifically asked for me and would be there for my show. Since I was a great admirer of Rajiv Gandhi, I was thrilled to be part of the show with Sonia Gandhi in the audience. The programme started but Soniaji was nowhere to be seen. There were different explanations. I was told that she was not well so could not attend. Someone said that at the last moment she had been told that since Ila Arun had courted controversy after 'Choli', it was not appropriate for a person of her status to be seen at this show! I was hurt by this attitude. After all, why should the *choli*, a women's essential attire, be the subject of a national debate? The song had been a runaway success and yet the press looked for every opportunity to rake up a controversy. I had repeatedly answered them pointing to the fact that through generations the subject of folksongs had been a lot of teasing and good-humoured vulgarity. Light-hearted playfulness with double entendre was used in folk songs to bring a feeling of informality. My fans, on the other hand, were saying that the credit for the popularity of folk music in schools and colleges, at weddings and festivals, goes only to Ila Arun! Why then in those days, was my singing belittled and I branded an outcast, a singer to be shunned? All India Radio and Doordarshan, the official channels of the government, also followed with a ban on the song. It struck me as a cruel joke that everyone enjoyed that song, but when they wore their hat of officialdom and represented a lobby, all those in power pulled on a mask of disdain, even though their wives and families clamoured for my song. This attitude only showed the narrow-mindedness of those at the top. It did not affect my popularity in any way. Government officers then felt that morality demanded that they promote only classical music to display their superiority.! I thank God that folk singers are given a lot of importance these days and sought after even for official functions.

Despite my disappointment and the pall of controversy, the show was a huge success. But the next day when I went to listen to Shivkumar Sharmaji, I was shocked to see Soniaji there. How could she have recovered so fast from her illness? She hadn't come for my performance but had recovered enough in twenty-four hours to attend Shivji's concert! I was really upset and went and sat down far away from her. Goenkaji came to me and escorted me to Soniaji saying she had asked for me. I had no option but to follow him. I greeted her and she sincerely apologized to me for her absence the previous day. She was so gracious that as usual I could not control my feelings. My weakness is that when I am faced with a situation where I should be confronting a person, my emotions get the better of me and I am at a loss for words. Tears come easily to me and embarrass me in public. Soniaji sensed this. I was touched by her gesture. She need not have said anything to me, but she made it a point to explain herself and the reason for her absence from my show.

As a result, all the 'naughty' film songs started coming to me. Bappi Lahiri asked me to sing 'Guttargoon' and 'Chad gaya uppar re!' 'Choli' brought the audience out in droves. I can say that this 'choli'was just my size! I had suffered the repercussions and yet earned the glory with 'Choli'.

I remember that when I performed at weddings, very often the elders of the family would come to discuss the programme with me and each time I knew what the warning would be. 'Ilaji, please don't sing that song. We have our *samdhis* and orthodox family members so it would not be appropriate.' I loved their beating about the bush, not being able to say the name of the number, knowing full well that during the performance the requests for '*Choli*' would outweigh any sense of impropriety! And so, it did. I would sing my popular folk songs but after the third number, the women of the family would call out for '*Choli*'. Very often even the bride would join in the dance and the would-be mother-in-law would do *nauchawar* on her! So much for Indian morality or should I say hypocrisy. There would be the usual *nok-jhok* with the *bhabhis* and the *devars*, between the *saalis* and the *jija*. When I told them that I had been asked not to sing this number, there would be an outcry.

'*Choli Ke Peechhey*' became such a topic of discussion that Jagjit Singhji once jokingly said that often he would be asked to sing '*Resham Ka Rumal*' and other folk songs after his *ghazals* and he would wonder when the audience would come to '*Choli*!' As I have mentioned, Daler Mehndi has added this number to his medley of songs. Several commercial artistes have exploited the popularity of this number in their shows.

Now after thirty-one years, '*Choli*' has been 'recreated'. I had just about got used to remixes and 'inspired by', but 'recreated' was a new word in this genre. The film is *Crew*, produced by Balaji Motion Pictures.

I received several phone calls, some lambasting Tips for having destroyed the original song, others telling me that I should be grateful for the fact that the song was aimed at the younger generation which had taken to it immediately. A young couple came up to me in Jaipur and said that they had just heard the song and they were disappointed that such an iconic song had been tampered with. But I am confused, and don't know if I should be unhappy or proud. The irony is there is no controversy this time! This time I am questioning the propriety of recreating the song!

'*Choli*' was like an answer to the lewd questions of men, the eve teasers who throw all kinds of insults at young girls in public places.

It was about telling them to look beyond the obvious. But the newer version has the captain announcing, 'Your Captain speaking. Please tighten your *choli*.' I object to that. When you destroy the mystery of the song, it turns vulgar. And not a squeak from the moral brigade! Perhaps I should be happy since this has proved that the old *choli* can fit every size, in every generation, that the *choli* is the same, but the generation has changed! In fact, many people have assured me that this is a rebirth for me. I will be drowned in offers for shows and the Indian Singers' and Musicians' Rights Association (ISAMRA) will support me when the question of royalty surfaces! So, I am also thinking of recreating myself for the younger generation.

I think the time has come for me to do my own remixes and recreations of my old songs! Then perhaps I can hand myself an envelope, something worthwhile, a time capsule of my songs. I am a positive person and have always lived with hope in my heart. I believe, 'No matter how hard it is/ No matter how hard it gets/ I am going to make it!'

Courageous words at this stage of my life.

Chapter 19

Tips: A Million-Dollar Idea

'*Choli Ke Peechhey*', the one song that catapulted me into the public eye caused a storm in my career. The song was released by Tips and after the success of this one number, the Taurani brothers wanted to sign a contract with me for future albums. I had also become a wee bit wiser. I thought that so far, I had signed a contract that included royalty for the album. I decided on a lump sum, though probably the best way is to have a combination of both, a signing amount and royalty. That is how you retain your loyalty to a company. But when royalty cannot be seen, your loyalty also is thrown out of the window, and you are forced to sever your association with that company. But one thing I can proudly claim is that all my albums with HMV have been successful, both creatively and commercially.

The first album with Tips was *Mein Ho Gayi Sawa Lakh Ki*. This title was my choice, a subtle reference to my decision that I would not sell myself and my music cheaply any more! This album contained the song '*Bichhuda*', which became a real hit. This one also had '*Holiya mein ude re gulal*'. My second album with Tips was *Mela*. The number which was selected for a video was *Nigodi kaisi jawani hai*. After that I did *Khichdi*. I had used different genres of music and the opening song was a comment on the condition of music at that time: '*Khaale khaale bhaiyya aaj culture ki khicchdi*'. A number of songs from this album became all-time hits: '*Tum mujhko chhoona naa*', '*Haath mein bottal.*' The next album called *Haule Haule* had two directors, Karthik Raja, music director Ilaiyaraja's son, and Jawahar Wattal, from Delhi, known as the pioneer in the non-film music field.

My last album with Tips was 'Vote for Ghaghra', which became a runaway hit selling 8 to 9 lakh copies.

The advantage with Tips was that they gave me the best of musicians, arrangers and music directors in India, and they never compromised on quality. Often even film music does not get such distinguished musicians. With the advent of MTV and the demand for videos, the Tauranis commanded a great deal of respect in the industry. I was lucky to have a very good rapport with both the brothers. They gave me full support and it was because of their vision and their confidence in me that my music videos came into being. There were several videos of Western singers, performers like Michael Jackson. But this was not usual in India. By now people were watching MTV. The trend for videos brought in many directors from the advertising world. The direction of a video was the easiest way to get a foothold in Bollywood, the final aim of most ad film directors. They looked for popular singers for whom they could make videos. Mahesh Mathai, Rakesh Om Prakashji—they all sent their show reels to me showcasing their work. Even today I can say that my writing table drawers are full of show reels of well-known ad film directors. Mahesh Mathai directed two of my videos, 'Bicchuda' and 'Haath Mein Botal.' These days videos are shot in just one room, but my videos were shot on location, outdoors and in the case of 'Haath Mein Botal,' overseas in Prague! All thanks to the Tauranis, who did not interfere with the creative aspect of the song.

'Haath Mein Botal' was directed by Mahesh himself and the other song 'Main Dilwali' was directed by Sanjay Gupta. Mahesh had his own production company Highlight Films and my brother Prasoon had just joined him. All of them from the ad world knew how to tell a story in 30 seconds. A music video has to be at least 3 minutes and is effective only if there is a story to be told, a story that unfolds till it reaches a climax. The concept for the song 'Bicchuda' was mine, and the song was composed by me. I had seen Rajasthani women tattoo their husbands' names on their arms; besides the husband's name, the only other name used was that of the many gods in the vast Hindu pantheon. Besides that, they could not dream of any other tattoo. Once at a *mela*, I had seen a woman getting a scorpion, *bicchoo,* tattooed on her arm. Adivasi women often have tattoos all over their face and arms. This was the make-up that they used, a permanent adornment of their faces. Beauty is an attitude! When I saw this, I thought that a scorpion is poisonous and its sting very painful, so why did the woman want a tattoo of such a creature on her body? I thought perhaps it is a symbol of love, a woman's suppressed desires that trouble her and this is her way of bringing out her hidden longings, 'Bit by the love bug', as Tina Turner sings. In the video, I had used a lot of sensuous sounds, sounds exaggerated by the beat of the *dholak,* sounds of ecstasy, which shocked my musicians who had only seen the staid side of me. During a take some of them could not stop giggling and the take had to be cut! Mahesh chose this song. He sat down with me to understand the lyrics, since Hindi is not his language. My brothers were familiar with the language and the ethos. They added a lot of creativity and a little of their own *mirch masala.* Creativity does not have any obstacle, no hesitation in telling a tale with all its connotations. Despite the fact that their sister was performing! I remember how Prasoon sat in a studio and made many sketches with the *bicchoo* crawling all over the place. I had to restrain him and his runaway imagination! Mahesh had first thought of Aishwarya Rai for the video, but her mother politely declined saying she had other plans for Aishwarya and her aim was to be a star on the silver screen. And indeed, Aishwarya did prove herself as one of the most successful actresses of her time. He then approached Malaika Arora and she agreed immediately. The three-minute story that was created was quite bold. A young couple is on a honeymoon trip to Jaipur, where the bride notices a young tattoo man, a tall, good-looking villager, a macho man. His image is imprinted in the bride's mind and instead of thinking about her husband she starts to fantasize about this unknown man. He tattoos her arm with a scorpion, but at night he appears as the dangerous scorpion in her dreams. When the bride is sleeping with her husband under a mosquito net under the stars, she dreams of the tattoo man and when they awaken, the husband notices that her body is riddled with thousands of scorpions. Every artiste adds his subjectivity to his creation. The story now rises away from the village and reaches an international level. There were so many layers to the story because of the three minds working on it. 'Bicchuda' was shot by the late Ashok Mehta, whom I had met on the sets of *Mandi* and *Trikal.* He had professed a desire to shoot a video with me and agreed readily when I asked him. MTV acquired the video and premiered it at their own launch in India. We were invited to watch the launch on a huge screen at the gardens of the Taj Hotel at Apollo Bunder. This was the first Indian music video that was launched by MTV so my video had a global reach. My folk songs were seen and accepted by the international community by now. Generally, only one or two songs in an album become hits but I could not believe that all ten songs from this album became unprecedented hits! I went on to make many more videos with Tips.

After 'Bicchuda' the next song selected for a video, was 'Nigodi Kaisi Jawani Hai'. Folk music, no matter from which part of the world, is a meeting of souls. When I had composed the music and got ready to rehearse with Lalit Sen, some of the other musicians familiar with Western music commented that this was the reggae style of music. I had never heard of reggae before this. But not wanting to appear ignorant, I nodded knowingly, saying that was my intention!

We had to decide on a story line for 'Nigodi Kaisi Jawani Hai'. I declared that this time I would weave a story around the song. The idea came upon me suddenly. Earlier when I was being photographed by Gautam at his bungalow, I noticed his bai watching us. I wondered what thoughts would pass through the mind of a woman who day in and day out watched this glamour world from afar. Perhaps she also wished that someday Mickey would caress her face with his brush so that she would be transformed into a beauty, perhaps more beautiful than the scantily dressed models who posed for photographs. She could dream that her days would change. I thought of just such a character and the idea was applauded by all those involved. Jerry Pinto, the well-known director from the ad world, was to play the part of the photographer in the video. Three models were part of the cast: Achla Sachdev, Anu Kuttoor and Maheep Sandhu. I decided to play the part of the bai! The high point was that the most sought-after young choreographer, Farah Khan, choreographed the video on Ashok Mehta's request. I remembered that Farah had met me at the King's Hotel in Juhu where she and Nikhil were dancers at the night-club, and she was the choreographer for the launch of my album Titali. This time I requested her to choreograph my new video. And she agreed despite her busy schedule. I am grateful to the late Ashok

Mehta, an old friend who agreed to shoot, direct and produce this video, which got the Channel V award.

'*Nigodi*' of course was a runaway hit. I went on to make another video '*Resham ka kurta jaali ki chunariya*'. This remix for Tips was directed by Bobby Khan, another brilliant director in those days.

I want to share the story behind the making of '*Haath mein botal gale mein guluband, kahan gaye the*', which was directed by Mahesh Mathai, assisted by Prasoon. I had heard this *mujra* song sung by an aunt at some celebration in UP. The first line got stuck in my subconscious and since I could not remember the next lines, I composed the song and the music myself. I wanted to experiment with a different kind of music. I thought of putting my song in the blues genre and was fortunate to get Ravi Khote, a well-known singer and stage actor, to sing this amazing number. The folk song and *mujra* was moulded into blues music. The song of course was unique, but the video broke all records. The words were those of a wife who questions her husband when he comes home late. She wants to know where he had been and whom he had spent the night with.' *Sautan ki zulfon ka baal tere kurte pe, hum to pade the akele tum kahan gaye the/Sautan ke honton ki laali tere gaalon pe hum to roye the aakele tum kahan gaye the.*' (The strands of hair from my rival are on your shirt, where have you been, the red from my rival's lips is on your face where have you been?) The interesting thing was that my part was shot in India on a set dressed up to look like a *kotha,* but the team went off to Prague to do the rest of the shoot. My brothers Piyush and Prasoon are known for their humour in the ads that they shoot, presenting unusual and sometimes unacceptable stories. This was one of the most expensive videos ever made. They created a story, which shocked the sensibilities of that generation. The suggestion of homosexuality was a subject before its time. It was a taboo subject, that an unfaithful man would go to a man when he was cheating on his wife. But the way they dealt with the story was sensitively done, and when the viewers realize the truth, the video makes a totally different statement. The relationship was left unspoken. In the opening scene, a girl sits in a graveyard, laying a wreath on a grave. Suddenly, the sound of a shot breaks the silence. The story then goes into a flashback. A couple is shown, a man and another figure with long hair, who we realize later is a young man, the husband's lover. When the young boy finds out that his partner is a married man, in a fit of jealousy, he shoots him.

To bring this subject to viewers was a very bold step and though it shook the audience, it heralded a change in the mindset of the viewers. Society, including me, was in denial on this subject. I met a gay couple at one of the literature festivals and they came up to me saying that they were grateful to me for having the courage to show a homosexual relationship over twenty-five years ago. I was embarrassed that they said this since I did not know about homosexuality at that time and did not know how to deal with it either. I can truly say that my folk journey led me to connect with people from different backgrounds and cultures.

When they returned from Prague with the video of 'Haath Mein Botal', Prasoon and Mahesh Mathai had a special screening for those concerned. I can still see the look of shock on the faces of the Taurani brothers, who never questioned us on anything that we did for our videos, but I could see that this was a bit too much for them. But it is their greatness that when we explained that this video would go viral and do well commercially too, along with opening the eyes of the audience to another version of sexuality, which was usually swept under the carpet. Ramesh and Kumar Taurani gave us an open chit and they spent a lot of money on the shoots and the musicians though I myself was not paid much. But they didn't compromise on quality. I was in seventh heaven creatively, confident that I had made a mark in the world of videos, presenting something which my fans and listeners were happy with. The current videos are all made in a studio, where the four corners are turned into five corners and the video is shot in that tiny space. The big singers who are not actors step into the fray with a bevy of scantily clad girls clinging on to their feet and neck. But there is no story to the video, no layers and no climax. Then came my next album *Haule Haule* from which two songs 'O Mere Bairagi Bhanware' and 'Kash Haule Haule' were made into videos. The director for these was my brother Prasoon Pandey, who had started his own company for ad films, Corcoise. The highlight of these two videos was that the most celebrated choreographer of the film industry, Saroj Khan, choreographed the songs and the videos were shot by ace cinematographer Ravi Chandran.

My last video was '*Vote for Ghaghra*', where the camera was wielded by no less than national award-winning cinematographer Santosh Sivan, who has now been awarded the Cannes' Pierre Angénieux Award, the first Indian to be bestowed with this honour, and believe it or not, the video was edited by Rajkumar Hirani! This song is close to my heart, one of my favourites, since this was the first time I experimented with rap in Marwari. This video focused on the menace of eve-teasing and women's empowerment, a subject close to my heart. It tells the story of a village belle who is working in the fields and is accosted by a young man. She feels humiliated but decides to fight back, paying no heed to the fact that in a village she would be harming her reputation. She accuses the man, telling him that just because he is the son of a minister, does he think she should be afraid of him? Her garments of modesty, her *chunari*, her *choli* or her *ghaghra* should not be taken as a symbol of weakness but of her immense power as a woman. Her courage shakes the political world from the village to the capital Delhi. All those in power try to gag and threaten her but she does not relent. She gains the support of the villagers who want her to stand for election with the *ghaghra* as a symbol. In seven and a half minutes, we told a wonderful story. It broke all records and is marketed as the 'must-have hits of Tips'. Today this number has made waves in the film *Crew*, where the box-office has been twirling with my *ghaghra* to dizzying heights.

Tips was keen on making my next album too. I had already composed ten songs for it and they had been approved. But for some reason, they gave up this idea. I have no means of knowing why this project was abandoned. In hindsight, I think, they had understood that the music industry was facing a crisis and they would not be able to sell the albums. They requested me to stop recording any further. But as usual I was not able to gauge the future and felt betrayed by Tips. I decided to go ahead and record the album since I had worked so hard at this collection. I approached my brother Piyush, who talks only cricket terminology and told him that my album had been stalled. He said, 'Don't be disheartened, go into the field and play the innings on the front foot.' He forgot that his sister is not a cricketer. I went out on a duck and had already lost a lot in the process and to this day it lies buried in other memorabilia that is collecting dust in the many boxes that house memories.

Both my music companies have been supportive and I still have a good relationship with them. Tips is like my family and there is mutual respect for each other. Even today when I am in a crisis in my theatre activities, I run to Kumarji for help and without asking any questions they have always obliged graciously.

The crisis in the music industry reared its head and it appeared as the greatest threat to music and films. This was the word 'piracy', which shocked the industry into stunned submission. Many projects were stopped in their tracks and there didn't seem to be any way to stem this tide.

Unfortunately, this beautiful album, which could not see the light of day, had all the top musicians collaborating with me such as Sivmani, Salim Suleiman, Tauqfiq, Piyush Kanojia, Tovi and Pari, Dhruv Ghanekar and Ashutosh Pathak and many more. The compositions were made by Ali Ghani and the lyrics were written by the late Ibrahin Ashq. I still carry this disappointment in my heart, hoping that one day I will be able to resurrect it, but I am happy that I have done some exciting work with Dhruv, my son-in-law, who is collaborating with global musicians. I am now working on Dhruv's new album *Voyage* with four folk and jazz fusion numbers among which '*Dheema Dheema*' has been made into a video and another song, '*Neemri Nimoli*' produced by Dhruv for Coke Studios.

Perhaps I am re-inventing myself?

Chapter 20

Piracy: The Other Side of Glitter

Folk music, film music, recording companies and live shows—my musical voyage has been beautiful. I have done several musical shows, travelled all over the world, have been part of many cultural exchanges and everywhere I have performed, my audience has given me enormous love and respect, a love which has been my inspiration. My musical voyage reads like a story of success. I sometimes marvel that I have been so blessed that I have not had to struggle to get to my destination. Opportunity has knocked at my door and I have accepted its offerings! Doors kept opening for me and the process of learning something new kept me going. Perhaps I could have achieved much more if I had been focused and believed in my abilities instead of being discouraged by my family about my chances of becoming a singer. I could have perhaps been a playback singer if I had pursued music after college. Instead, I swung between music and theatre, wanting to wear two hats at the same time. There were days of depression, humiliation and frustration, which I suppose every artiste goes through.

Every morning by 9 a.m., I was riding high since there would be a flood of offers for performances and I would be building the proverbial castles in the air, planning what I would do with the millions I would make. By the afternoon, many others would have jumped into the fray, middlemen, event managers and the like, and the bargaining would start. Come 5 p.m., when offices closed, I was a pauper again, my begging bowl empty, hoping for a better tomorrow!

Imagine my shock and amusement when someone sent me a YouTube report on a channel called Next 9 Channel, where the reporter talked about my grand lifestyle, my opulent apartment, my collection of expensive cars and my treasure house of heavy jewellery! My net worth in 2020, according to this channel, was estimated to be close to 80 million USD! 'She attracts attention at every event she attends, because of her fabulous jewellery and expensive attire!' I have no idea how these snippets are reported on channels, without any verification of facts or an interview with the celebrity. However, I am thrilled to know that my two-roomed apartment in Santa Cruz (E) appears like a mansion to people and my 'collection' of cars is usually borrowed from my brothers. And the icing on the cake, a younger me—'66-yr-old Ila Arun …'!

Many of the shows that were offered to me, I was told, would be sold as charity shows, so there would be pressures and emotional blackmail, which I did succumb to quite often. I was told that this show would get me more contracts in the future. An artiste is intimidated by these suggestions. As for me, I do not perform alone. I have a team of musicians, dancers and singers who are professionals and have to be paid. One might think that for me music could be a hobby since my husband, Arun, would always be there to support me, but for my accompanists, this is their bread and butter.

An artiste's life is not all gold and glitter as imagined by those who see them from the outside. We walk hand in hand with stress. In our decade, many new music companies sprung up out of nowhere. Where there was only one company, now there were several, big and small, like Meghna Sound, Venus, T-Series, Tips, Rainbow, etc. Many of them were fly-by-night operators and did not last too long, but others discovered new ways of selling their products. Cigarette and *paan* stalls, small bookshops, juice shops, all became vendors for music cassettes. Mumbai at the time had only one go to place for good music, Rhythm House at Kala Ghoda, the cultural hub of south Mumbai. They stocked every kind of music, Western and Indian classical, film music, folk music, in every format—records, cassettes and videos. All roads for music aficionados led to Rhythm House. They had cabins in which you could listen to the music of your choice before buying it, or just for the pleasure of listening. The dream of every musician was to have their records or cassettes displayed on the shelves of this classy outlet. Online music has snatched this old-world pleasure away from us. I was one of the lucky ones to have my cassettes on their list. Later, they started selling theatre tickets also from this shop, a double whammy for me! The girl at the counter was Nita Daru, a very helpful and pleasant salesperson whom every theatre organization knew.

Suddenly, Rhythm House started seeing less footfalls since every small *paan* and cigarette shop, juice and cold drink stalls, became vendors for music. I remember going to Delhi and stopping at a fresh juice stall. When my order was handed to me, I was barely able to hold it! This shop gave the largest glasses of juice—and cheap cassettes! I did not understand at the time that I was drinking away my royalties with my glass of juice! This shook the music world, both music companies and the artistes. One had no idea how many cassettes were sold and of course there was no question of royalty! Sales were up but the royalty did not match the sales! A new word came into the lexicon—piracy.

Being the wife of a seafarer, I had heard this word often with pirates at sea. But this was the first time I heard this word in connection with music, films and books. I realized that this was a business, like fake notes, where machines were working overtime, operated by a few gangs. They got hold of music and films as soon as they were released and went to work on them, distributing them to anyone who had even a tiny outlet! This was real injustice to artistes like me who had given their blood and tears to compose and sing songs for music companies, almost selling our souls for our work. These companies in turn would finance these albums and put them out in the market and yet our royalties evaded us.

The music companies were in a quandary, unable to understand what was happening, while our music was being nipped in the bud even before it took off. Later, we discovered that some of the known music companies had started their own sister companies under false names and their vendors were producing copies of music albums and films and selling them at very low prices. We were working on trust and could not believe that we were being taken for a ride. I can only conjecture why this was happening. Perhaps the music companies were not able to make big profits and they were always on the radar of the Income Tax authorities and this was a way of evading tax. This was to hit me directly soon.

It came to my knowledge that a very popular album of mine, which was being played in every household that listened to music, had been copied and sung by one Shikha Varma (name changed) for some unknown company. I saw a dwindling of my royalty but could not do much about it. Shikha was a new singer who had emerged out of Delhi. She was a good singer; that is why I could not understand why she needed to steal my music to get ahead at the beginning of her career, copying my style for some unknown music brand.

I was livid and people goaded me on to file a case against her. But I have always dreaded getting entangled in court cases and am generally wary of lawyers, courts and judges.

Then one morning, as I was catching a 5 a.m flight to Delhi for a show, one of the members of my group pointed at a figure far away at the check-in counter saying, 'There is Shikha Varma' I had not noticed her. I could easily have confronted her and had a show down. But as usual, my mother's famous warning about '*Aavesh mein vivek* . . .' hammered at my brain and another of her favourite sayings rang in my ears: '*Paathar dare keech mein/ucchal bigade ang*', meaning that if you throw a stone into slush, some of it will rise to dirty you too. It would not affect the person you shouted at but would leave a bad taste in your mouth. I was still trying to calm myself down when suddenly someone wrapped her arms around me from the back. It was Shikha, who touched my feet and very shamefacedly apologized saying, 'You would be justified if you want to beat me up in front of all these people. But my grouse was that despite being a good singer, I was not getting a break. When I was made this tempting offer, I did not look left or right and just accepted the proposition. My dreams needed a push and your album provided me that so I recorded the whole album, which was a great mistake on my part.' As usual, I could not control my tears and said, 'Did you have to clip my wings to fly high? Surely you know that piracy is a crime. To pass off someone else's creation as your own, to copy someone's songs and sing them in your voice and to claim the lyrics as your own, falls in the jurisdiction of piracy and is an offence. You are lucky that I have not filed a case against you. That could send you to jail.'

She kept on repeating that she was wrong and that I should forgive her. I could not do much at that time at the airport, so I let it go saying with a wry smile, that I had forgiven her, but that I would not forget this betrayal. How could I forget that I had lost a fair amount of royalty because of her piracy? I can say that we are good friends now and I always go to her place during the Ganpati festival and one thing I must mention that at my daughter's wedding sangeet, her singing infused life and verve to the evening. She has also sung for my son-in-law, Dhruv. By now I have forgotten her transgression but do rag her when I meet her, asking her why she did what she did. I often tell her, 'The truth is you are a far better singer than I am and have a better range. I was singing only simple Rajasthani songs; you did not need my songs to be successful. You are much younger than I am and many tempting offers will come your way, but you must use your conscience before you make any decision.'

One day I got a summons from the court saying I was to appear in a case of piracy. I was scared, wondering what crime I had committed. The summons warned that if I did not show up, I would be liable to be jailed! On making a few inquiries, I discovered that there was a gangster who was selling pirated albums with impunity, and no one had the courage to take any steps against him. But later I was told that HMV had filed a case against him and I was the state witness.

I was angry because I had not been consulted or even informed. It was only when I arrived in Delhi, that I was told that HMV had filed the case. The whole thing was handled shoddily. The company should have given me the travel expenses and someone from their side should have accompanied me and stood with me in court. I was so nervous that I took two people with me for support and had to pay their expenses too. I was already the aggrieved party, having lost so much of royalty due to piracy! I had taken my brother-in-law, Pramod Bajpai, a lawyer himself, who briefed me saying I should not say anything. My lawyer would handle everything. I was irritated and said what kind of custom was this that though I was the witness and had made losses and yet was not allowed to speak? The lawyer did not know the whole story, he could make mistakes and what was the guarantee that he would win the case for us? If he lost, what state would I be in? But I was told that the rules of court were such that the lawyer had to speak on my behalf till I was called to the witness box. I was trying to hide behind sunglasses, and the first thing he asked me to do was to take off my glasses. I thought that was an affront to me, but Pradeep's little pinch from the back stopped me from opening my mouth. The gangster stood before me nonchalantly, no remorse either in his body language or his look. He was the winner, having made a lot of money from my pirated albums!

I could not wait to call up HMV on my return to Mumbai. I told them that I was very upset by their conduct. They had just thrown me before the court as a state witness all alone, without informing me or even asking me if I was available at the time. Since they were the complainants, they should have taken care of the case and appeared in court with me. The case mercifully was thrown out of court. I have no idea what consequences HMV had to bear, but despite all that happened, they still remain my favourite company, and I am happy to say that after so many years, I still get cheques of royalty from them!

Talking of temptations, there were several in my life too. I was asked to do many shows which I did not agree to. But one of the most tempting offers which I can now reveal to my readers came from the proprietor of a very well-known music company. I met him at the old Centaur hotel, now known as Sahara, at Santa Cruz. He was no other than Upavan Kumar. I had already done four albums with Tips and had a very good rapport with them. I did not see any reason to break away from them. As I have mentioned before, loyalty comes before royalty for me, an aspect that all my family believes in.

I was contacted by one Mr T.P. Jain, whom I had known from Delhi Doordarshan. He had been transferred to Bombay Doordarshan and was scripting films for them. He then joined T-Series, as a consultant, or so he told me. He called me up to tell me that Upavan Kumarji wanted to meet me. I was taken aback since there were several rumours, true or untrue about this gentleman in industry circles. I did not wish to deal with anyone without verifying their antecedents. I was quite happy following the straight and narrow path of my musical journey. He had tried to put pressure many times to persuade me to meet him, but I evaded him. Then some well-wishers told me that perhaps I should meet him. It may lead to something. Very good singers and musicians queue up outside his door and it is unheard of that he approaches an artiste himself. So, I decided to meet him. The time was set for 7.30 p.m. At 8 p.m., a harassed Upavan Kumar entered the hotel, wiping the sweat off his brow. 'I am sorry,' he said. 'This meeting would have been cancelled. I am very punctual, but I had not anticipated the Bombay traffic. I was stuck at Milan subway, so I have left my car there and come here in an autorickshaw.' I was speechless. The owner of this big music company had left his luxury car and come in a three-wheeler to see someone as insignificant as me! The pressure had begun even before the discussion!

He had a congenial way of talking. He said that my voice would suit the singing of *bhajans*, 'Why don't you give it a try?' He did not sign up an artiste for a single album, he was known to make bulk contracts. He wanted his artistes to sing everything, bhajans, their own songs, songs sung by other singers and that is how you were made part of his repertory. This was a very big offer for me. His offers were so tempting that very few would have had the temerity to refuse him. Everything would come on a platter—a flat, a car, money, all that one desired. At one point I was tempted. My tiny two-roomed flat flashed before my eyes. This was my ticket to a bigger flat and an upgradation of my lifestyle. In between sips of coffee, I was building castles in the air—the model and colour of my new car, and of course my flat in the posh locality of Juhu!

I am sure that many other well-known singers would have jumped at this opportunity. But for me, my mother's clapperboard came crashing down on my dreams. He was insisting on my acceptance at that moment. But I said I needed some time to think about it. 'I will definitely do an album with you,' I said. I could not say no to him but nor could I agree in that instant. He gave the appearance of being a simple man, calm and composed but persuasive. If I had agreed, I would have been handed a key to a flat at that moment, or perhaps an entire building! I did not have time to regret or ponder over my decision, because four or five days later, we got the tragic news that Upavan Kumarji had been killed in some kind of accident. I was saddened by the news and remembered that evening when such an important man, the owner of a renowned music company, had come to visit me in a three-wheeler, for a meeting that lasted just two hours! Perhaps his intentions were good; perhaps he wanted to change my life. Today he himself was gone. Life is indeed short and unpredictable.

I could not forget Upavan Kumarji's visit for a long time. His rushing in, wiping his forehead and sitting down was an image that stuck in my mind.

Things were changing for artistes. We were being called for more shows than ever before. The Maharajas had been patrons of folk singers such as the Langas and Manganiyars, but now even those who sang film songs were being approached to perform. Weddings became a great source of earning for artistes since in a five-day celebration, one evening was always set aside for singers and one for film stars.

This was the 1990s. Those were the days when fame brought with it a lot of attention, sometimes from the wrong channels. Many unknown 'relatives' would creep out of the woodwork. They were not related to you in any way, but in the Bambaiyya language, they were known as 'bhai'. I called them 'colonial cousins'! Most artistes in the industry were afraid to work openly. The moment you showed signs of success and were earning well, somehow this gang would trace your journey and your wealth, and the singer or actor would get a menacing call saying, 'Bhai is asking about you.' The hidden message was that you would have to pay 'bhai' a percentage of your earnings. You had to comply with their demands, or else . . .

I thank God that I never did receive such a call, but nevertheless, I too lived in fear like the rest of the industry. I thought it wiser to stay at home without any earnings rather than be noticed by these dangerous 'bhais'. This was perhaps the most trying time for the industry. Many actors, singers and producers were plagued by these threatening calls. In my mind,' 'bhai' in the Indian context was a brother, who was supposed to protect you and give you money and gifts on Rakhi and Bhai Dooj. What kind of 'bhai' would extort money from a sister?

But I carried on my work in small ways. This was the phase when on the one hand artistes were trying to stay away from the income tax (IT) department because of the 'black money' payments, and on the other hand, threatening calls were making life impossible for them. It was rumoured that actors and performers were hiding their money in overhead tanks and buckets! They spent eight to ten hours working and sweating, and could not understand how and at what point their earnings suddenly turned 'black'! A performer's working life is very short and they have to work hard to sustain themselves when they are eased out. Strangely at that time, the star makers and breakers were also these 'bhais' and even builders who tried to make a quick buck while the going was good. They worked hand in hand and held Mumbai city to ransom for several years. That phase is happily a thing of the past. This is because there is more transparency since most work is done online, including the payment of royalty, and the cult of black money has also largely receded. There was a time when a large percentage of dealings with builders involved black money. With demonetization, we have also started being paid in so-called 'white' money and we no longer live in fear of the IT department and our 'bhais', and we can sleep in peace!

Yet, some dangers still remain as obstacles to our making money. Many shows are offered to us, half of them without any remuneration—shows for the IT department, for the police, for doctors, and of course, any number of charity shows for NGOs. Since we have to keep good relations with them, sometimes there is no option but to agree. Sometimes I do retort: '*Arre bhai,* all my life what have I done but charity? To such an extent that I have become a "charity" myself! I need the money to sustain my own theatre group, Surnai Theatre and Folk Arts Foundation, to pay my struggling actors who work hard to entertain the masses.' I have had to go around with a begging bowl, much against the grain, so that we can do meaningful theatre. How many people actually put in money in that bowl? I dislike the word 'donation' and again think of my mother's advice: 'Your hands and palms should always face downwards . . . never asking but giving.' If I were to follow my mother's teachings, how would I sustain myself and my activities?'

I imagine a world without piracy, where artistes would get their royalty, where actors would be paid for the films they do as well as the 10 per cent which is their due for dubbing, where producers never go back on their word. If this were so, no artiste would be needy, and his art alone would be his life and work. Each individual looks for means to earn a living, whether it be a designer, shoe-maker or goldsmith who sell their wares for money. We artistes are selling our art too and often dying as paupers, so why is there no lobby or sympathy for us? We are addressed as *bhaands and mirasi*—words considered derogatory in high society. But *bhaand* is in fact a very large community of folk artistes from Kashmir, while the title of *mirasi* is given to a very talented tribe of musicians from Rajasthan. These communities are respected in their surroundings and many of us want to learn from them. They are asked to perform at high-end weddings and functions yet are looked down upon by the very clientele whom they entertain. And they die in penury, with no money even for their last rites.

Several famous stars and musicians have fought the demon of poverty in their last days and have gone to their grave without having any money for hospitals and doctors. The government boasts about the help it has given to many sectors of small-scale industry and agriculture, but it has not given any thought to starving actors who keep the population entertained through an industry that contributes crores to the economy. I can only talk of my community of the performing arts. There are several other neglected groups who are struggling to make ends meet. I am not referring to myself, but to those of my colleagues who have joined this field because of their passion and who are more talented than I am but are unable to make an honest living out of their profession. We work on a daily basis, and these earnings, believe me, only last for a day! We have no retirement benefits, no pension, no provident fund to fall back on. I have been lucky to have the support of my husband, Arun, and I have not had to struggle for my *roti, kapda aur makaan* (for food, clothes and a roof over my head). I have also not gone beyond my limits, limits that I had imposed on myself. We had decided that we would live in a small, manageable house and not in one of those towers where you would have to pant up the stairs if the lift stopped working for some reason. I am happy where I am. I too could have had a farmhouse, but I had no such desire. Singers and musicians exist only for their work and are satisfied only with the applause and the *wah . . . wahs!* I think we need a business partner who would handle our affairs and save us some money! Singers abroad make a killing with a single song. Why is it that an artiste in India, a land with a 140-crore population, can make ten or even twenty albums and yet find it difficult to survive? Forget being a millionaire, he or she cannot even be sure of two meals a day. A singer has no idea of finances and cannot even imagine that the music company is making enough money from his work to sustain his family for a lifetime and also to leave them with intellectual property rights forever. And the actual protagonist gets hardly any share of this fortune!

Actors are in danger too from fly-by-night financiers and producers. I remember the problems director Kalpana Lajmi ran into when she was shooting for her film in Bhopal. After a couple of days of shooting, the producer was not accessible. Cheques started bouncing so much so that the actors and the film equipment was locked up in the hotel for non-payment of bills! The harassed director said she did not have either the resources or the time to file a case against the producer. She said if any of the actors or crew wanted to file a case, they were welcome to do so. Which of us could take up that challenge? These small-time producers know this and get away with their fraud. The film *Haddi* too went through the same problem, but the director, Akshat Ajay Sharma, was lucky to be bailed out by ZEE5. I have come to the conclusion that keeping in mind these obstacles, I would rather do small roles in a big-banner film rather than big roles in small films with dubious, unknown producers!

Can the entertainment business not be transparent? So that everyone is content, and the music companies and producers also make a profit after the money they have put into a project. There is a saying in Hindi: '*Ek haath se taali nahi bajti*', that you need two hands to clap. A steady rhythm should be created where both parties gain something. One hand can only make a tightly closed fist, which benefits no one.

Naushadji and Sanjay Tandon were the pioneers for the protection of copyright and justice for the artiste. Several artistes joined their IPR, the Association for Intellectual Property Rights, but that did not help either. The same problems confronted them. No one could keep a track of their royalty. I would like to mention here that Javed

Akhtar and his forum raised this question in Parliament for several years and finally they were able to pass a law that would benefit both producers and artistes. If the actor gets even a quarter of the earnings of a producer, then it makes for a good collaboration. But I would advise artistes to be alert too. People will ask me what is the moral of the story and I say even though my life has not been a struggle, I have gained wisdom from years of experience and realize that every artiste should be aware of what is his due and fight for his rights.

An artiste, I feel, is always apprehensive about the pressures that can be put on him to toe the line. I have already mentioned the police and the IT department, but there is another sword of Damocles hanging over his head—politics. You are expected to promote a party and sometimes asked to campaign for it too. If your ideology is different from theirs and you have rejected their offer to join their rallies, then rest assured, you and your art will die a slow death.

Many actors and artistes have joined politics and won elections too, but they have not been able to handle that unfamiliar world. It is not an easy task. You have to mouth the words that are given to you, the propaganda that you do not know anything about. It is difficult to follow their style of work. In the language of music, we are used to singing in *tritaal kaharva*. When we perform, we do not step out of line as far as the *sur, taal* and *alaap* is concerned. Politics is conducted in a fourth *taal*, the *ara chautala*, with no known rules or ethics. Those who have given up the discipline of music have been successful as politicians. But those who could not follow the unspoken language of politics and tried to air their own views were smothered by the political arena. They would have been better speaking their own words and language in the performing world. I tell my CA that a singer or actor's life is like a flame, lasting for a short while and then enveloped by darkness. And yet people expect us to help them with fund-raising or in performing for charity. And in our waning years, there will be nobody to handle us!

I wish to relate another strange phenomenon from my experience. Each of my cassettes has eight to nine songs. All the songs were good as far as I was concerned since I had put my heart and soul into each number. But unfortunately, only three or four of them would become popular, those that had a dance rhythm or those which were made into videos. The slower numbers, which exuded romance and talked about emotions and feelings were not that widely heard. I would say that since you have bought the whole album and spent money on it, do listen to all the songs to get your money's worth. Listeners don't seem to go beyond three or four numbers. 'Vote for Ghaghra', 'Resham Ka Rumal', 'Choli Ke Peechhey' and 'Bicchuda' became my most popular numbers. Perhaps I should have focused on only four numbers and not wasted my money and time in recording eight of them. I wish I had learnt some gimmickry instead of *muhavaras* from my mother. All these beautiful and romantic songs captured in recordings were finally left to die of suffocation in their cassettes, which became their burial caskets.

The first lines of my first album, *Banjaran*, were appropriate for my own eventful life and were dedicated to this nomadic community: '*Meri zindagi ka bikhar jaata tana/ Arre o re julahe, meri zindagi na bun/mujhe chalte chalte jaana . . .*' (The threads of my life are crumbling/ Don't gather them together O weaver/I have far to go, on and on . . .)

The entire film industry is plagued by the issue of piracy. But after my own experience, though I lost my cassettes to piracy, the end result was that I never went back to a juice shop for a drink of fresh juice.

Chapter 21

Recording and Live Shows: A Step Forward

On one hand, my folk albums were being played in every nook and corner of the country, and on the other, I was working with well-known music directors for my albums, which were doing well on their own strength and had been recognized by music lovers and professionals alike. Several music companies were coming to me with offers. I was doing many live shows too for both private and official functions. I had the audience's acceptance and their affection, which cannot be counted or recounted in a few pages. All these memories flood my mind and I would need several volumes to describe my experiences. When I say that great producers worked with me, I am talking of people like Raju Hirani, who edited my video 'Vote for Ghaghra', and sound recordists like Bishwajeet Chatterjee, now a successful sound designer, and Daman Sood and Ravi Chandran, the director and cameraman for 'Haule Haule'. I was fortunate, to have the best talent in the industry to work with me. They turned a rough-cut recording into something admirable. So many people had a hand in producing a classy product that it is difficult to name all of them. I would not have been able to bring out such gems without their help.

Offers came to me for playback singing for the silver screen: from Anu Malik, Anand Raj Anand, Bappi Da, Rahman Sahib and Laxmikant–Pyarelalji to Rajesh Roshan. Never in my dreams could I have expected that such great directors both established and the emerging ones would ask me to sing for them. Then one day the unexpected happened. I got the opportunity which I, like every singer of the time, fantasized about. I got a call from A.R. Rahman Sahib, asking me to come to Chennai to record a song with him.

My heart seemed to stop and my joy knew no bounds. Rahman Sahib was known for his unconventional style of working. Everyone who has worked with him comes prepared to spend a few nights sitting outside his studio. I would call it 'Dark Nights with Rahman'. But the songs that emerged from those nights of waiting would transport you from darkness to the most glorious aura of light! While you waited, a tiffin would arrive for you with steaming hot *dosas, idlis* and *rasam*. Sitting outside the studio, devouring the delicious fare from the tiffin box, I became a great fan of south Indian food.

Many years have passed since that day when Rahmanji's secretary, Noel, called me. I was in a state of euphoria. But I prepared myself for the dark nights that I would have to endure. When you sign a contract with Rahman Sahib, there is an unwritten commitment that you mortgage your sleep to his time. It was very exciting working with him. His astounding understanding of music could turn a simple song into a great composition. To watch Rahman Sahib work on his music at such close range was indeed a golden opportunity for me. I went to Chennai at least seven or eight times after that. I sang a solo, '*Rang Rang Dole*', for him in the film *Mr Romeo* (1996) which became a hit. I sang the Tamil and Telugu versions of this song too. It is always a pleasure working with him since he has a special way of recording with the singer. He gives you a tune and tells you to play with it and come up with a composition. At that time, he had the disadvantage of not being too familiar with Hindi, but he has such am amazing understanding of music, which coupled with his vast experience, ends in immensely powerful and memorable songs. Now of course he has sung songs in Hindi himself. As I sat before him, he would play a tune and hum the beginning and then tell me to put words to his melody. I would write the words and almost immediately he would complete the tune and the song would be ready. Every song I sang for Rahman Sahib, received much appreciation from the film fraternity. One day, I was called to a studio in Mumbai. When I entered, I looked around for the music director, but he was nowhere to be seen. It came as a surprise when I was told that he was sitting in London and would direct me through a video conference call. This was the first time I had ever made a recording like this, but now of course many recordings are done online. This was a song recording for a film *Chamki* and the song was about a mosquito. Unfortunately, the film was never released. When he called me the next time he said, 'Forget the mosquito. This time the song is on a bed bug!' He said he wanted a composition that could be set to the kind of sound I had used for Subhash Ghai in *Choli, Ku, ku, ku, ku*. I thought about it and out came a sound *chik, chik, chik, ring, ring, ring, ringa*, which I ended with my oft-used *aahaa*. Rahman Sahib was happy with my sounds. Alka Yagnik later sang the words for the song. I wonder why the music industry gave me songs featuring all the blood-sucking insects! I was going through a phase when I was getting songs featuring birds and other creatures: pigeons, partridges, peacocks, parrots and scorpions. And all the sounds of sensuality used in my folk songs came to the fore.

Before I knew it, after singing so many songs for Rahman Sahib, my voice actually made it to the Oscar stage, when Rahman Sahib got the Oscar for his music in *Slumdog Millionaire* (2008). I also have a certificate that proclaims my participation in the Grammy Awards. This was beyond any dream that I could ever have had.

I had sung *'Choli Ke Peechhey'* with the brilliant duo of Laxmikant–Pyarelal. With its success I was offered several songs by them: *'Payal utaar doongi'* for *Mohabbat Ki Arzoo* (1994) and *'Mere maula, mere malik'* in the Sufi style for *Hamara Khandaan* (1988). After my song with Anu Malik for the film *Jaal*, I sang many numbers with him in films produced by K.C. Bokadia. I have no words to describe my association with Anu Malik and his brilliant compositions. I had a long association with Maya Govind, who was from UP, and made me sing songs from that state, which are replete with naughty references, teasing and double meanings. The most popular was *'Darwaza khula chhod aayi'* for the film *Naajayaz* (1993), with music by Anu Malik.

I then had the good fortune of working with Bappi Lahiri, whom I call 'King Midas'. Not only was he laden with gold himself but all those whose lives he touched as a music director, also struck gold. Bappi Da, known as the Disco King, reigned supreme in both south Indian films and Bollywood. He gave the music for several Amitabh Bachchan starrers, like *Sharaabi* (1984). The song *'Aaj rapat jaeyo'* still lingers in the minds of thousands of listeners. I sang *'Chad gaya upar re'* for Bappi Da, with Kumar Sanu and Alka Yagnik in the film *Dalaal* (1993). I sang several songs with Kumar Sanu, Kavita and Alka. In fact, most of my hit songs, beginning with '*Choli*', were duets with Alka, so much so that I call her my better half! Though I sang many numbers for Bappi Da, I did many more live shows with him.

Some of my other hit songs were with music directors such as Rajesh Roshan, for whom I sang '*Lamba lamba ghungat*' in *Karan Arjun* (1995). There was '*Kiti, kiti*' with Dalip Sen in *Maidan-e-Jung* (1995), '*Sun o bedardi*' in *Janta Ki Adalat* (1994), '*Kesar ban jaoongi*' in *Zakhmi Dil* (1994), '*Sakhi mujhe jaana*' in *Smuggler* (1996), '*Bin barsaat ke*' in *Zaalim* (1994) and '*Main ho gayi atthara saal ki, Sarkayi lo sarkayi lo khatiya ki jaado lage*' in *Raja Babu* (1994) by Anand Milind are some of the songs which are sung by every tractor driver, the labourer who carries bricks on his head, the mason who builds homes in villages, the people who can relate to these songs and my heart is filled with satisfaction that I am touching the lives of the masses of India.

All my live shows with Bappi Da took place in Bengal during Durga Puja. He would take a group to perform at the puja pandals and I had the opportunity to get acquainted with the small towns and villages of Bengal. The Durga pandals in Bengal follow the traditional way of decoration and pujas. There are cultural programmes and literary readings and the atmosphere is one of devotion and rituals. The clothes and make-up of the Bengali women, devotees of Durga Ma, are a delight to the eyes for first-time visitors.

The largest show with Dada was at the Salt Lake Stadium in Kolkata, teeming with over a lakh people. I was there with Neena Gupta and Madhuri Dixit and I cannot forget the spectacle of a lakh people with torches beaming in their hands, listening to the songs and music. Dada was a star himself and he was accompanied by some of the most popular stars from Bollywood. Govinda was always included in Dada's troupe. These stars performed to some of the current Bollywood hits like '*Morni*' and '*Choli*'. Since this was my first performance in Bengal, I was really impressed with the audience at all the concerts we gave. Whether it is sports or music, once they have accepted you, they become your fans for life and shower you with love and complete involvement in the performance.

I did more shows with Bappi Da, going to Ludhiana and three times to Dubai. By now there was a family bond between us, and I was invited to his house every year for Saraswati Puja on Basant Panchmi and on his birthday, which he loved to celebrate in grand style. He was truly a show man and loved dealing with the press. His gold chains seemed to get heavier each time I saw him. I would joke and say, 'Dada, why don't you give us a tola too?' And he would laugh and say, '*Arre baba*, everything is yours, Ilaji!'

It is sad that he left us so soon. But then so many of the musicians are no more with us. But memorials to them are there at every turn. When you pass Juhu, you see Laxmikant Chowk, and Anand Bakshi's name; at Peddar Road, you are reminded of Kalyanjibhai. And now even Lataji has a memorial in her name. For me, these are golden memories of a time when I had close associations with all of them, and I thank my god for having given me a golden opportunity to work with them. I have only seen the bright side of life with them.

Laxmikant–Pyarelalji took me on a tour to Antwerp, in Belgium, for a wedding in Bharatbhai Shah's family. I can never forget how shocked I was to see that Laxmikantji always carried a *peekdan*, a spittoon, with him since he was always chewing betel and tobacco. Somehow, he always got the permission to carry this vessel with him wherever he travelled.

The city of Mumbai is dotted with shrines to music and the film industry. Just the other day, I was called to Mehboob Studio in Bandra, where the song '*Choli Ke Peechhey*' was filmed, the song that was the beginning of success in my film career. Several memorable films were shot here: *Mother India* (1957), *Kaagaz Ke Phool* (1959) and *Guide* (1965). Later it was the location for some of the evergreen songs from films. I am sure many of the doyens of Bollywood have preserved the staircase and rooms of Mehboob in their memories. I remembered the singers' section of Mehboob Studios. After the success of '*Choli*', I had the occasion to visit this section several times. There were two entrances to the studio. The front entrance was for singers and music directors and the back entrance was for the accompanists, which included great maestros such as Pandit Shivkumar Sharma and Hariprasad Chaurasia. There is a photograph of Goddess Saraswati in the singers' recording room to which all musicians and singers pay obeisance before the start of every session.

After a long time, recently, Alka and I had to go to Mehboob Studio in connection with a book release of the encyclopaedia on films by Amit Khanna. The wheel of time had changed the face of the studio. I was saddened by this scene. We bowed to the dust-covered floor of the once-revered studio. We cleaned and dusted the microphones and stood at the singers' section, each lost in the memory of what had once been a vibrant workplace. We had a mock session of 'Choli' before we began revising the lines of the song.

I have lost count of all the recording studios I have been in. And each visit has a story. But one thing is constant—the loss of little items of jewellery which is of my own doing. I never leave the house without putting on several pieces of jewellery. It has become a habit with me. Perhaps these are like my security blanket and I feel safe only when I am clad like this. Whenever I put on headphones and got ready for a recording, the sound recordist would stop and look for some sounds which disturbed the recording. It took some time for the technicians to realize what was causing the disturbance: the long earrings, the bracelets and bangles on my wrist, and even the multiple rings I wore. Now every time I enter a studio, I spend some time decluttering my persona and divesting myself of all the knick-knacks I cannot do without. Of course, I often forget to retrieve them from the drawers or shelves of the studio. As a result, every studio I have worked in has some piece of jewellery of Ila Arun's lying in some nook and corner of the room. But a story I heard about something similar in a recording studio in the US amused me. It was the day they were recording the song 'We Are the World' at the A&M Studio in Hollywood. This was to become the most iconic song in this genre, with forty-five of the best singers lending their voices to this song to focus the world's attention on Africa. After several takes, the recordist and the singers could not understand where a tiny tinkle of sound was coming from. All the great singers put their heads together and finally realized that the sound was coming from American singer and songwriter Cyndi Lauper's hanging earrings. This episode was caught on video and remains one of the memories associated with the off-stage discussions on that historic occasion.

I can only say that we women are often victims of our accessories. In fact, just a few days ago, I got a tiny little packet sent through Wefast, a pair of earrings sent from the studio where I was dubbing for the series *Aarya* with Sushmita Sen.

After the success of '*Choli*', I was invited to be part of a world tour comprising Bollywood stars. Film shows were rare at the time and stars were not that visible as there was no social media, so a star-studded show drove overseas Indians berserk. There were over seventy Bollywood celebrities. The group was managed by the Morani brothers and their partners in various countries and it was purely a business deal. The showstoppers were Shah Rukh Khan, Saif Ali Khan, Rishi Kapoor and Juhi Chawla. Rishi and Saif were accompanied by their wives, Neetu Singh and Amrita Singh, respectively. Model and actress Ashwini Bhave had blasted the screen with her dance rendition of my solo number '*Payal Utaar Doongi*', so she was also part of the group. Strangely, the Morani brothers did not give me that much importance, but their overseas partners were looking for me. They had a Gujarati partner, Brahmbhatt, who had asked for me, saying that my fans were getting impatient for a live performance from me so Ila should be part of the group. '*Morni*' and '*Choli*' were extremely popular but so were my own songs from my personal albums. Brahmbhatt told the Moranis that if they were not agreeable to my coming, the partners would book me separately on their part. As usual, I was getting paid much less than the stars. But I had put down my conditions that I would get two club class tickets, since Arun would have to accompany me. I also insisted that two of my own dancers would come with me since they knew my songs so well that they gave authenticity to the presentation. So Avni Shah and Meena Rathore came with me too. I had prepared three songs with the Bombay dancers, part of Lollypopji's group and two more popular dancers, Pappu and Malu, were also with us. They were going to perform to three numbers, since I was given permission only for three songs. '*Morni*', '*Choli*' and '*Bicchuda*'. '*Bicchuda*' looked really good while Avni and I had choreographed '*Morni*' and '*Choli*'. By the time we reached the US from London, there was a demand for two more of my songs, so '*Resham Ka Rumal*' and '*Payal Utaar Doongi*' were added to my repertory.

The Moranis were shocked to see how crazy the NRIs were for my songs. This was because Washington, DC has a huge population of Mathurs from Jaipur, who were familiar with my songs. They arrived in large numbers for the show. There was no dearth of fans from the Gujarati and Marwari communities in Washington, DC, who filled the hall to capacity. I could not believe my eyes and ears when I entered the stage. The reception for me was amazing! The Moranis realized that Bollywood stars were not the only centre of attraction at such shows. A folk artiste like me and classical singers can draw an audience on their own strength, often surpassing the crowd-pulling capacity of stars.

My own albums were no less popular than 'Choli'. I was in demand at weddings and functions abroad too. I have done around 200 shows overseas. Steel magnate Lakshmi Mittal invited me to London to perform at his wedding anniversary and then to Kolkata for his son's wedding. I have travelled to many countries: Bhutan, Nepal, Russia, Canada, Sri Lanka, Indonesia and several European countries without an entourage of Bollywood stars and my shows have been resounding successes. I travelled with a group of over thirty artistes. There were always several traditional musicians from Rajasthan in their finery. We invariably attracted a lot of attention at airports. When my show was sponsored by the Indian Council for Cultural Relations (ICCR), we had a larger group since their aim was to promote Indian culture and music abroad. When the Canadian prime minister asked the ICCR for a performance, it sent me. We had seven performances in various cities of Canada.

I have decided that wherever I go, whether in India or abroad, I will always learn a song in the local language. Looking at India's varied language pool, you can imagine how many languages I have sung in. I have sung in several European languages too. This brings the audience closer to me and keeps them happy too. If many among my audience who do not understand Marwari can listen to my songs, surely, I can go one step towards them by singing in their language, albeit only a line or two. Sometimes I would have three or four shows continuously. I remember one occasion when I did back-to-back shows starting in Delhi, then Agra and the finale was in Indore for the Dainik Bhaskar group.

I was indeed honoured when the director of Dainik Bhaskar himself, Girish Agarwal, came in his plane to fetch me from Agra since there were no convenient flights between the two cities. This was my first flight on a private plane and I walked out of the aircraft feeling like a superstar, perhaps even royalty, while thousands of people gathered at the airport to catch a glimpse of me. I felt I had a great responsibility to live up to their expectations. When we went to inspect the venue at night, the collector of Indore came up to me. He said that they were expecting a huge crowd at the open-air venue and that I will have to tread carefully. I was told not to step into the crowd as I always do, since that could drive the crowd into a frenzy which could lead to some untoward happening. I was amused and told them that I was not such a great singer that the crowd would get unruly trying to get to me. But he said I should take this warning seriously. He told me about a show of Kishore Kumar at Khandwa, in Madhya Pradesh. The crowd went out of control and the police had to resort to a lathi charge. Things became so bad that women were molested and there was total chaos. He said he wanted to warn me to be alert since I was a superstar in Indore. This did please me, but at the same time, I was a little worried. I was given a time limit and told not to interact with the audience since once excited, the crowd would be very difficult to control. I saw huge barriers being placed before the stage. Perhaps they had been told that I do not stand in one place when performing, like most trained singers do, but dance all over the stage. But I am a folk dancer and singer, and my songs are full of vivacity and movement. I prance and pirouette around the stage, unmindful of my surroundings. I am out of control, as my choreographers often tell me. I feel my folk show is more like a rock show. Neither my technical director nor I, can predict my entries and exits onstage. Just like the sea or a swimming pool beckons you to take a dip, so the sight of my listeners turns me into a singer possessed.

I had so many creative ideas of my own that my stage show was no less than a Filmfare Award night or a Femina Miss India show, even though I say so myself. I would enter the stage on a bullock-cart, a rickshaw, sometimes on top of a truck or a golf cart. I have even emerged out of a well once! I am obsessed by my work and forget everything else once the programme starts.

Our show was to begin at 7 p.m. I reached the venue four hours in advance, thinking I could make a peaceful entry and sit in the green room. To my horror, there was already a crowd gathered near the gates. Since it was a free show—the ticket came with a copy of Dainik Bhaskar, every citizen of Indore seemed to have come for the show. Somehow, I managed to evade the audience and hurriedly made my way to the make-shift green room in a tent. But when I peeped out, the *maidan* was more than half full. People were standing in long queues, as if waiting for the *darshan* of Chaumunda Devi. I felt sorry for all those who waited to see Choli Devi and spent hours standing in the sun. My heart melted seeing this enthusiasm for my performance. For me, half the joy of singing is my interactions with the audience, but I had been strictly warned against any such actions. There were special police forces called in from other *zilla*s, and I could see the Collector himself supervising the arrangements. A couple of times I was tempted to step down into the crowd since I am a singer for the masses as I always say, happy only when I interact with my audience. But the height of the stage had been raised by order of the Collector and the massive barriers put paid to my intentions.

The show was literally a thundering success. It gave me great satisfaction to see the appreciation of folk music among the masses. I always give my best and never take shortcuts in my performances. I want to live up to the expectations of my fans.

There are so many memories associated with my live shows— some sweet, some alarming. One of the most difficult and I would say bordering on the dangerous show was in Kolkata. This was soon after 'Choli'. As I have mentioned before, Kolkata had many shows during Durga Puja. Promotors would come to Mumbai from Kolkata and book the dates with popular stars, six months in advance. Once I was also booked for a show together with Alisha and Neena Gupta, who had danced to the 'Choli' number. Actors Shakti Kapoor and Kader Khan were to provide the spicy bits of comedy. The sponsors would give an advance as surety. If the stars did not get the advance, they would not leave Mumbai. I was always nervous since I did not know how to deal with these problems and could always be taken for a ride with sweet talk and promises. The show was at Durgapur. Alisha and I, along with the musicians, arrived at Durgapur on an earlier flight. Neena, Shakti and Kader were to reach by 2 p.m.

We arrived at the venue well in time. We were ready for the show when we were told that the rest would be late. We heard whispers that they had some problem with their payment. It was getting late so the organizers told us to start the show and informed us that the other stars would join us later. We had sung two numbers when we got the news that the other stars had backed out and were returning to Mumbai. They were told that they would get their full payment once they reached Kolkata, but the organizers went back on their word. The matter was taken to the police and Neena and the others were sitting at the police station! During the show, the organizers told us that the Bengali audience could shower love and affection on their artistes, but they were quick to take drastic action if they felt they had been shortchanged. They were known to set fire to venues if they did not get their money's worth. They kept the attention of the crowds by sending local singers to entertain them, while backstage, the police bundled us into their jeeps to take us to safety. It was like being evacuated during a war! I was in my heavy costume for 'Morni', with jewellery that weighed a ton. It was not easy for me to get into a police jeep, with sirens blaring, adding to the tension and confusion. Avni and I somehow got into the jeep and we both tried to get out of our costumes in the back seat of a bumpy police jeep, stuffing everything in our bags. We were told not to reveal ourselves to the crowd, who might turn on us. We got out of our cumbersome costumes in the cloakrooms at the airport and we got on to a flight for Mumbai. Later, we got the news that the audience had indeed set fire to the *pandal*. We were lucky to have escaped the wrath of the infuriated audience. This was nothing short of being an ordeal by fire for all of us.

This episode shocked me, though I have had the same experience many times. I did not know how to deal with it. I had lots of work in hand, but earnings—almost nil! I am embarrassed and hesitate to put this down on paper, but perhaps without revealing names, I would like to mention that very often an envelope that I was handed and told to open only when I got home, turned out to be empty, loaded only with disappointment. Many a time as I left the recording studio, I was told that the payment would be sent to my apartment. Several years later, the money is still on its way, I suppose. Soon the artistes in this industry found a way to deal with this betrayal. They hired managers, event companies or middlemen to negotiate their fees and to follow up on the payment till it was released.

I knew nothing of these wily ways of the world. I would take the envelope, and as a courtesy, put it in my bag, without even looking into it. When I opened the envelope at the first red light, I was left wringing my hands. I never uttered a word or called the producer, accepting this empty envelope as an appreciation of my work. One producer handed me an envelope with the tiniest image of Ganesh, not once but twice. They sit lost, invisible, in my *puja* room, among the many images that I pray to every morning. As I bow my head, I try to erase the negative thoughts that pass through my mind at this injustice. I consoled myself by remembering the saying, 'All that glitters is not gold.' My fee was the love and my popularity with the public. My cassettes were selling like hot cakes, so what if my treasury was empty? People were my fans on the strength of my creativity and art. I was so busy I had no time for myself.

'*Bicchuda*' was at the height of its popularity. Tips didn't spare any efforts to produce my albums and release them. I was getting a lot of work. The top directors of the silver screen and several producers called me to either sing for them or to compose and sing and later even to act in films. Often my own songs were picturized on me.

Lucknow was another city that welcomed folk singers like me. At one show, the auditorium was packed with 18,000 people. I always opened my live shows with a recording of my song '*Mela mein le chaal sajana*'. The stage was set up as a carnival space and I would make a dramatic entry in a colourfully decorated rickshaw. This was my favourite curtain-raiser. The rickshaw puller was one of our actors, Shankar Sachdev, who enjoyed his entry with me, pulling the rickshaw with great aplomb. All the folk musicians and everyone from the group would be onstage, either as a vendor or a buyer at the stalls. There were bangle-sellers, hair accessories, balloon-sellers, jewellery stalls and I would jump off and on from the rickshaw to buy something that caught my fancy. All this drama was created around my song.

Despite the rehearsals, where all our moves were designated, the excitement of all the action made the musicians forget their roles as actors and they would all start watching me instead. I would try and communicate with them through gestures, suggesting they get back into character, but all in vain. As I was trying to direct the crowd on the stage, I happened to jump off and had the horrible feeling of a wardrobe malfunction. My *ghaghra* seemed to be slipping. I realized to my horror that the drawstring of my heavy *ghaghra* had snapped. The song was being played on the speaker and the end of the song was the cue for my exit. I tried very hard to turn my face away to tell Shankar my predicament, but he could not understand me. I even boxed him five or six times, telling him to exit, but to no avail. It was like a comedy of errors when finally with a wrench, I caught hold of the handlebars and guided the rickshaw into the wings. It didn't take me a minute to pull out the string and tie it over the *ghaghra*. Fortunately, we wear tights or *churidars* under the *ghaghra,* so are well protected from accidents with costumes. All this happened in the blink of an eye, and I was back again before the audience could fathom that there was a problem. I got a stupendous ovation for this number. The show carried on flawlessly. The narrator entered and I was back onstage with a change of costume for the 'Morni' number. The director K.K. Raina, not happy with my unscheduled exit, asked me why I had left the stage. When I told him about the mishap, he and the lights designer Salim doubled up with laughter and congratulated me on my presence of mind.

Live shows throw up many unforeseen problems and goof-ups, which provide us with several evenings of amusement and topics of conversation once the crisis is over. An actor has to learn to deal with problems that require split-second solutions, to use his intelligence and training to improvise and innovate, to be aware of the problems of his co-actors.

I remember a show in Udaipur. A section of the Maharaja's palace is rented out for weddings. I had gone for a performance there. I noticed that there was a grand staircase, with about fifty steps, at the venue. Usually, the stage is set up below the steps and once it is decorated and lit up, it gives one the feeling of being in a royal courtyard. The stage was fine and would be a dazzling backdrop for my performance, but they had made the green room at the top of the steps. This was bad planning, especially for me, since I have costume changes after two numbers, sometimes after each number too. If you see my green room in the course of a show, you will wonder whether you have entered Maganlal Dresswala's costume shop. Every inch of wall has some costume along with all the accessories hung with it. There was a time when I would have ten changes of costume and jewellery. The changes had to be done within a minute or two so that I was ready for my entry in a non-stop performance. I concentrated more on my costumes than the song I was singing, because I am a showman through and through. Every detail was taken care of by me, and I saw to it that the coordination of sets, costume and accessories was perfect. I would go to great lengths to find the perfect match. Now I have cut down on the number of changes, but still, it requires split-second timing. For the show I had selected a song from the film *Mr Romeo,* which had been filmed on Shilpa Shirodkar and Prabhu Deva. I had choreographed my entry in a *palki,* or a palanquin, in which I was to be carried down the grand staircase. This became a trendsetter and Bollywood directors started using *palkis* for their heroines. I felt like a maharani, but I did not take the fifty steps into consideration. The palanquin they had chosen was the original, belonging to the Maharaja. It was beautiful and regal but so heavy that all the bearers found it difficult to walk down the steps. So, we chose to walk down a ramp that was hurriedly installed for us, but even that proved to be a difficult proposition. The minute I was lifted up, the palanquin swung forward, then to the right and then to the left. I sat nervously inside the palki, holding on to a pole, hunched like a monkey. Despite eight strong folk artistes carrying me, it was a scary ride. If there had been a camera trained on the inside, it would have taken shots of me pathetically crouching with my heart in my mouth. But somehow my entry was on time and lip-syncing, I started my dance routine with the Bollywood dancers. I did not hide the fact that two or three songs were always pre-recorded, though even for these I would take the mike and sing at least a couple of lines live. Then I would discard the mike and dance to the song. I did not see any harm in dancing to some of my own songs which had been pre-recorded. The audience got a bonus, listening to my songs and seeing me dancing to them. Dancing and singing together, specially to my kind of rhythm is virtually impossible, since the voice would break at some point. Those were the days when folk singers, film singers, musicians, my dancers Avni Shah, Neeta Bhimani, Poonam Gandhi and their group would dance to my traditional numbers. The group travelled with twelve musicians, the show director, the technical director, a compere, a host of people who had a role to play in the success of the show.

The moment the lights come on I cannot wait. A kind of headiness takes over and I jump into the fray. I am not a singer who is staid and disciplined, who can perform sitting in one place. I am a performer who entertains her listeners, both audibly and visually. When I dress up for a show, I am ready to dance for four hours. Often, I get messages on the walkie-talkie asking me to shorten the programme. The organizers tell me that I should cancel the songs I have selected and instead sing some of the songs the audience is demanding. This usually throws us in disarray. We are dressed according to the sequence we have selected, so there is a lot of confusion on how we should present the number that is the audiences' choice, in a costume designed for another number! Not that the audience knows the difference. Sometimes in our eagerness and passion I have carried the show for three-and-a-half hours. People would wonder at my stamina, little knowing the condition I would be in the following day, feeling as if I needed to be carried away on a stretcher! But this would last only for the next twelve hours. Rejuvenated, I would be up and ready for the next show. Sometimes people would ask strange questions. I remember in Hyderabad one of the event managers asked KK which bottle he should put into my room. Both KK and Salim were shocked and asked him if he was in his senses. They told him that I do not take any stimulants and that the best he could do was to put some hot water and ginger tea in my room. The poor man apologized profusely saying that many artistes take some spirits to boost their energy and that he thought he should provide Ila Arun with some energy stimulant. Forget outsiders, even my sister Rama, who used to compere my shows, once asked my helper Meena what I fed on to sustain myself. People were curious to know what I took to boost my energy rather than appreciate the fact that I had the energy to perform continuously for three hours or more without any booster. How do I tell people that I do not even take a vitamin pill to sustain myself? Very often, lacking time to have a full meal, like most Rajasthanis, I make do with a dry *roti* with some Bikaneri *bhujiya*.

My brother Piyush warned me saying that I should not drive myself so hard that I end up in burnout. I did not know the meaning of burnout then, but now when my bones ache and make cracking sounds, I know the meaning of his words. Yet I still say that even today, if the lights come on and there is the bang of the *dholak,* these bones will break into dance without a thought of burnout.

New ideas kept springing into my mind, and I was always looking for dramatic expositions onstage. I follow Einstein's axiom, 'Anyone who has never made a mistake has never tried anything new.' We had been called for a show in Pune. I felt I had exhausted all my ideas for my first entry. But my mind was working overtime till I found a solution. I told Salim to make a well on the stage, and I would come out of the well, singing. The height of the stage was about six feet. Salim laughed and said that he could do this but if it misfired, what would we do? I told him to go ahead and that I would handle it. So, the well was constructed and the show began. Avni was on the stage and I was all ready to make my entry from the well. Two or three people were there to help me to negotiate the ladder leading into the well from below. The song had started, when some of the pleats in my *assi kali-ka lehnga* got caught on a nail on the ladder. Half the song was over, and I was still struggling to release my *lehnga* from the clutches of the ladder. I don't know how, but I managed to pull the material off the nail and made my entry, still a little dazed from the ordeal. But the moment I heard the audience's thunderous applause, I forgot all else except my performance. Sometimes some of my way-out ideas involving my shows do lead me into trouble— my entries and exits, my insistence on jumping into the auditorium, my acrobatics, my constant change of costume, have caused a lot of backstage chaos.

Like the show in Dubai. When I was asked to come to Dubai for a show, I thought of the similarities between Dubai and Rajasthan and planned the show with the desert as background. I was booked for four shows at the time, in Delhi, London, Dubai then on to Greece. For the Dubai show, I thought of my entry on a camel. The audience would be happy with the association since I was singing 'Morni' and the film *Lamhe* had been shot in the desert. The sponsors were a bit surprised and said that they had never had such a demand before. The camel was awkward in its movements, especially when sitting down and getting up. In fact, I did remember the occasion when one of my sisters had fallen off a camel in Jaisalmer because she clutched the camel's neck in fright and the camel, startled by this grip, threw her off. But I had ridden on a camel several times and also made an entry for a show, riding on a camel. So, I stuck to my demand and a camel was booked for the show. When I came to see the venue, I realized that the show was in a hotel and not on the sands of Dubai. There was an air of excitement regarding the show. It was decided that the camel would come from afar and the spotlight would follow it. I, like Sridevi in *Lamhe*, would be riding on the camel. The camel would have to come down a sandy slope and reach the stage set up near the swimming pool. There were two rehearsals and every move was fixed. There was another rehearsal before the show, where we encountered some problems. I had to sing the *alaap* from 'Morni'. The trainer of the camel was walking alongside, and the camel managed to come down the slope without a mishap. Avni was sitting on the stage with the actor who played Anil Kapoor's character in the song. The show started and I came down the slope, riding on the camel and singing the *alaap*. In the darkness, from the sands of Dubai, the audience heard my voice and went wild. They wondered where the voice was coming from and where was the Ila Arun they had come to see. The technical director, with the noise and confusion around him, shone the follow light right in the eyes of the camel which frightened him so much that he refused to move. Meanwhile, the song had started being played on the stage. The camel-keeper started scolding him in Arabic and also gave him a few hits with his stick. Somehow, we reached the stage, but the camel's hooves, meant only for the sand, started slipping on the mosaic floor. I sat on the camel's back shouting out the lyrics of the song: '*Mhare hivde mein begai re kataar re*'. *Kataar* means sword and in truth, the sword of Damocles was indeed hanging over my head, sitting perched on the back of a frightened camel. That is where my actor's training came in useful. It had been decided that I would enter on the camel's back singing the *alaap* at the end of which I should reach the stage, get off the camel's back and join Avni in the dance, just like in *Lamhe*. But for that the camel had to sit down. But he was so frightened that he refused to follow the commands of his trainer. Thank God there was no PETA at the time, otherwise they would have trolled me for ill-treating the camel! Half the song was over before the camel could be controlled and made to sit down. Avni and the dancers were dancing to the song when I joined them, more than halfway through. The musicians, used to such gaffes, played the interlude twice and I improvised and the show went off so well that the audience thought that was all part of the performance. I always remember Jennifer Kapoor's words in such circumstances: The show must go on. Of course, I had to listen to my director's scolding, warning me that he would not allow such a risky entry again. But somehow, the showman within me did not quite agree with this. I have watched shows of stars abroad, like Tina Turner and Michael Jackson, making their entries lifted by a crane, or walking on a tight rope. I have also sung '*Assi Kali Ka Lehnga*' hanging from a crane. But now when I see the panic in the director's eyes, I feel I must tone down my wild nature. I have always had a hunger for adventure in the creative field. Of course, sometimes the arms and legs don't support me, but what about my crazy heart, which tells me to go ahead?

HMV called me to perform at a corporate show in Chennai. I was shown the venue, Marina Beach, which they said would be a great setting, with the waves in the background. The stage would be set up on the beach. While they were talking to me, my mind was already racing ahead. The sea, the sand and the horizon were too tempting for me to forgo this wonderful opportunity. I always make a quick survey of my performance location, and I had noticed a rock within sight. I told them I would sit hidden behind the rock in a boat and then make my entry onstage on a boat. The organizers were apprehensive and warned me that because of the high tide in the evening, this would be an impossible feat. But I could not let go of this idea. But when we went on to the beach in the evening, the tide was so high I realized that the people of Chennai had been right. Director K.K. Raina, who is always wary of what I might do next, turned towards me and said, 'Just as well we didn't go ahead with your idea. You would definitely have had a quick immersion!' I told him I was very disappointed, that my entry from the rock would have been really romantic and the audience would have loved it. But that was not to be!

I have composed many songs for the festival of Holi, which is played with great gusto in Rajasthan, the land of colour and festivity. Songs such as '*Holiya Mein Ude Re Gulal*' and '*Mujro Chhe*' are some of the favourites. It is not just the rituals, but I love playing Holi too. The play of colours, the liberties you can take with people who you would not dream of offending, all these appeal to my slightly mischievous nature. But one day I did go too far. When we perform Holi songs onstage, we play with dry colours. At one point, I got so carried away that I went up to the musicians and smeared colour on one of our very staid and quiet musicians. The colour got into his eyes, blinding him for a while. He suddenly could not see the chords in the middle of his playing. I have never forgiven myself for that blunder.

One more incident comes to mind with the mention of Holi. Once again at Dubai, I decided to use earthen pots for a dance number. At the last moment, I thought that it would add to the visual, if I filled the pots with some coloured water. So instead of the dry colours, the dancers would drench me in wet Holi colours. This was for the climax of the last song. I always wear white clothes for Holi songs since the colours show up so well on white. Holi is fun only when you are drenched in colour! I have spent thousands on my white Holi costumes, which are only for one-time use. My mind goes back to the Holi parties at Raj Kapoorji's house or Subhash Ghai's celebrations. Or the celebrations with Maharani Gayatri Devi, when the only colour used was the natural bright orange of the *tesu* flower, which looked like an artwork on the mandatory white clothes for the royal celebrations. In India, I have used the *pichkaris*, colour spray guns, onstage and the audience has loved it. But the colours from the *pichkari* do not have the same effect since it only targets a part of the clothing. Water pouring slowly from a pot would cover you entirely with colour. As soon as the water from several pots started trickling down, the man who had supplied the sound equipment, came running on to the stage, shouting in Arabic, and started gathering up his mikes and monitors which were in danger of being drenched in Holi colours. He thought we were insane to have even thought of a scene like this. I was apologetic and embarrassed. I realized, as I had several times before, that though you get carried away in a live performance, you have to keep your senses about you. But I never learn my lesson, because a live show somehow compels you to go beyond the limits of pure craziness. I am creating new scenes in my mind, which sometimes cause misunderstandings and often lead to disaster. Even my mother's clapperboard cannot restrain me sometimes.

The ICCR sent me to Poland and Germany. I had the occasion to be invited to Armenia by none other than Deepak Chopra, who requested me to sing Bappi Da's '*Jimi Jimi*'. I was sent the words of an Armenian song before I reached Armenia. When I got there, I worked with their ballet dancers and choreographed '*Jimi Jimi*' for a live performance, in which I sang and danced to the number. The audience went wild and several shirts were ripped open in their madness. Till today, I believe Bappi Da and Mithun and the songs of *Disco Dancer* are very popular with the Armenian public. Our shows in Poland and Armenia were successful way beyond our expectations. We were treated like VVIPs and the officials in Poland were so helpful that they assisted me in getting my visa for my personal visit to Switzerland. If this is not cultural bonding, what is? I have tried to understand the traditions and culture of every country I visited. I especially enjoyed my stay in Armenia, where I had time to do a little bit of research on their folk music and dance. Music, dance and sports are a good way of meeting and getting to establish a bond with different cultures. I always sing at least one song in the language of the country I visit. I remember how when I sang a Bhutanese song '*Meetho Lage*' in Bhutan, shirts came off in the audience and people were dancing in the auditorium. I have never understood this medium of appreciation.

Wherever I go, I like to dress up in the costume of that country. I once had a dream to collect the costume of every country I visited and then make a museum to display them in Mumbai. But now I have nowhere to house them since every piece of land I purchased has run into some problem or the other. As for my collection of costumes, they are lying buried in some box or the other, tucked away in a loft.

The hold of our folk traditions on Indians living far away from home was a revelation when I was invited to Holland. Our hosts who came to receive us at the Amsterdam airport came to me and asked

me, 'Jijji, have you come alone? You should have brought our Jijaji
too!' The welcome they gave their Jijaji, Arun, when they found him,
was overwhelming. I stopped in my tracks. This was how relatives in
the heartland of UP would speak. The accents were pure UP, and the
language retained some of its archaic nuances. Fascinated, I asked
them how they knew some of the words and was told that they
were from Suriname, which had been a Dutch colony. Thousands of
Indians were transported from UP, Bihar and Purvanchal as labour
to work on the sugar cane plantations in the Caribbean and parts
of South America. Thus, their mother tongue, *khari boli*, flourished
on the shores of the Caribbean Sea. The settlers in Suriname were
crazy about Bollywood and its music, so they evolved a new genre
of music, with words taken from Avadhi, Bhojpuri and the language
of Purvanchal which got the name of Chutney music. It was a
combination of Bhojpuri, English and Creole and started out as
religious music, sung by labourers working in the sugar cane fields.
They used Indian instruments such as the *dholak*, the harmonium and
the *tasha*. Now it is the popular music of the Indo–Caribbean people
and has even incorporated reggae beats. This was the first time I had
been exposed to Chutney music. This music was significant because
it had combined two languages of two immigrant communities. The
African community did not understand the words but amalgamated
the beat into their music. Chutney music is very popular in Trinidad,
Tobago, Guyana, Jamaica and Suriname. The Indian diaspora in these
countries has preserved their language and traditions, bit by bit, as
if in a foreign land, thousands of miles away, they wish to retain the
fragrance of their country through these memories. Not only had
these people worked hard to extract the sweetness of sugar cane from
the earth of Suriname, but they had also succeeded in stirring in a bit
of sweetness in their music and songs. Then one day when we were
being taken for a tour round the city, I heard a familiar word *lalwa*.
Though I knew this word as a term of endearment for a son, I found
it fascinating hearing it in those surroundings. I was compelled to use
it somewhere in my music and when I made my album, *Haule Haule*,
I included a song, '*Lalwa lalwa sab koi pukarein / Lalwa toh gaye
videshwa/ Ho Rama/ Arre Ganga Maiyya tohka pukarein, ajao apna
deshwa mein Rama*'. This is a comment on the lives of these overseas
settlers and their alienation from the land of their birth.

My trip to Germany with the ICCR was an episode I would like to forget. One Mr Sodhi was deputed to be our escort during our stay in Germany. The show was in the evening and our hosts insisted on taking us to see the town and to do some shopping. The other members of the group were sent off in a bus and only KK, Arun and I were accompanied by Mr Sodhi in his BMW for a round of Berlin. I never like to be separated from my group before a show, but we could not protest too much. He took us for lunch to his restaurant and we had just set out from there when at a crossing, his car was hit by a huge trailer-truck.

Somehow, I bore the brunt of the crash. My seat belt snapped and the airbag hit me on the face so hard that my face turned black. Some other unknown object crashed into me and my arm had multiple fractures. I must have lost consciousness. I don't remember much after that. When I came to my senses, I remember that I was lying prone on the ground at the signal, surrounded by the police. KK and Arun were in a state of shock. The police called for an ambulance, and I was taken to the best hospital in Germany. The orthopaedic surgeon said I would need a surgery. I could think of nothing but the show in the evening. I remember I kept telling all the doctors who attended on me that the show must go on. Most of them did not understand what I was saying. I was then taken into the operation theatre and before I was given anaesthesia, an elderly nurse came to me and I told her to hurry up with the treatment since I had a show in the evening. She must have understood the word 'show', since she started pointing at my face saying, 'Kaput! Kaput!' Then to convince me she took out a little mirror from her purse and showed me my face. It was a shock to see that my whole face had turned black and blue. There was no question of my appearing on the show. KK and Arun were also being treated for their injuries at the hospital. Arun had to sign a form for permission for the operation, which must have scared him a little.

The Indian Embassy sent a message saying that the show must go on without me since I had been on a radio programme to promote the show. Fortunately, Saveri, my back-up singer, was with us. The show did go on, with Saveri singing for me. I shed many a tear at my misfortune. The previous night I had performed for a select few at the Embassy, but I was not able to sing before the Indian inhabitants of

Germany. My son-in-law Dhruv and Ashutosh had recorded a new number specially for the show, *Mahne Aave Nahin Nindiya*, which was played onstage while my group of dancers, in maroon costumes, faces covered and carrying candles danced to this song. There was an atmosphere of gloom and they were all weeping. They are my *jaan* and I theirs; we are bound by many years of work, our work which is our passion. KK then came on stage and told the audience about my accident. There was an audible sigh from the audience who then told KK to carry their good wishes to me for a quick recovery.

The show went off very well even without my presence. The folk artistes took over and managed to satisfy the audience. The dancers, with Nita's choreography, shone as always. But I shall always regret that I could not dance in Germany. Another blow was missing the concert in Rome the next day. I had always nursed a desire to visit Rome specially since my BBC days when I had written and spoken a lot on Rome. The Indian ambassador to Italy had met me in America and had said that I should perform for the Indian Embassy in Rome. My group performed in Rome without me and did a wonderful job I believe.

I spent six days at the Berlin Hospital. But the next show was in Stockholm and there was no way I was going to miss that. I pleaded with the doctors to allow me to perform, but since I had a bandaged hand, they were not sure they could give me permission. They did not put my arm in a plaster, only in a bandage. I told them they could put my arm in a sling, and I would manage. I would hold someone's hand with my injured arm. They agreed, telling me that there should be no movement with the hand, since the wound was still fresh. We performed at Stockholm. I covered my blemished face with some special make-up. No amount of ice packs could help lighten the bruises on my face. I was still on antibiotics too. But once onstage, nothing mattered. The '*Choli*' song floored the audience, as I walked with my hand in Babu Khan's hand. But when we reached the coda, the climax, I freed my hand from Babu Khan's and danced with abandon. The *dhaap* on the dholak by Pyarelalji in that song, made me forget all the promises made to the doctors at Berlin. The audience gave me a standing ovation, but I had to pay the price later.

Dr Anand Joshi, who treated me in Mumbai, told me that my hand had swollen up because of my having taken it out of the sling. I was under his treatment for almost two months.

Though I did disappoint the audience in Germany, at least the fans in Stockholm were happy.

There have been goof-ups even in some of my recordings. I remember one particularly. Raju Lalwani had played so well for the recording of 'Resham ka hai kurta mera jaali ki chunariya', that we left the studio with a sense of achievement. The next day when we went back, the assistant recordist told us that he had recorded another song on the spool over mine by mistake. All our efforts had been wasted, besides the money going waste. Angry though we were, there was nothing we could do about it. We had to record it again. The company did not charge us for the extra time and the musicians repeated their commendable performance and the number was recorded again—an exact copy of the first.

There is one story of my musical journey which I am a little embarrassed to recount. But it is such an essential part of anyone's travel in India that I think it needs to be told. Now we all have the luxury of air-conditioned vanity vans. But when I first started my shows, we had never heard of those. At most you were provided a tent with plenty of hangers. There was always a full-length mirror, with loose bulbs hanging over it. In my tent I insisted that I have large pots with plants and greenery. But one of the pots should have only mud. Salim, our technical director, was in charge of my green room and he used to tell the sponsors that Ilaji likes to be surrounded by greenery in her green room. But they still could not understand why one pot had no greenery. They must have thought it had some Vastu implications. With the PM's emphasis on shauchaalyas in every home, things are improving slowly in rural areas and slums, but that was not the case twenty years ago. You must have understood by now why I needed one pot without greenery. Rajasthani women use their ghaghras for this purpose, spreading them out in a semblance of decency. I unfortunately could not do that, so I had to make do with the large pots filled with mud. I guess you can count this also as part of my innovative setting for a show. This secret was only between Salim and me, but today I am sharing it with my readers too!

My rhythmic folk journey had been progressing without any real obstacles, except for the slow speed of the bullock-cart on which I was mounted. But it was gathering speed and soon I would graduate to a limousine. Though this travel in a limousine was short-lived, who would have imagined that live shows would give me the chance to enjoy that joyride? I am happy that I got more than I had ever dreamed of. 'Believe in your dreams,' says singer Bon Jovi, 'if you don't, who will?'

Chapter 22

Reality Shows: Real or Unreal?

It seemed that life was taking me from one reality to another—this time to reality shows. I accepted these shows since they took me back to my childhood and youth. I had lived every moment and every note of all the songs I had ever sung. I was lucky to have got the exposure I did, otherwise I would have been like the proverbial frog in a well. If I had not crossed the boundaries of my state and had not trusted my voice, despite peoples' opinion, I would not have reached this far in my journey. We did not have any openings at the time. There was only Akashvani and then a little later black-and-white TV made its appearance, first in Delhi then Mumbai. These two cities held the fortunes of all artistes and musicians in their grip. Times changed and with it the world of television. I had several appearances on TV and the day came when the trend for reality programmes caught the producers' fancy. These were mostly talent shows for music or dance and suddenly the most sought-after performers were youngsters who were looking for an outlet for visibility in this field, hoping for fame and money through their talent.

Mumbai was the city of dreams for most youngsters who wanted a break in the music world. The reality shows would become their platforms for their entry into this field. I was a judge on three such shows: *Fame Gurukul, Junoon Kuchh Kar Dikhane Ka* and *Maati Ke Laal. Fame Gurukul* followed the format of the UK show *Fame Academy*. The producer was the same one who handled *Big Boss*, Endemol Shine India. The creator of *Junoon Kuchh Kar Dikhane Ka* and *Maati Ke Laal* was Gajendra Singh, with whom I had done a couple of TV shows before this. He was a very creative person, a visionary in the field and had conceptualized some of the most popular shows on television. The format for *Fame Gurukul* was decided by the foreign creators of *Fame Academy* and we had to follow all the rules set by them. I was brought into the show by Tarun Katial and Anup Kumar Verma. According to the format, the contestants would eliminate each other. Besides these, there was a panel of three expert judges: Javed Akhtar, Shankar Mahadevan and the late singer KK. The three judges listened to the participants and then gave them numbers. They would give their comments on what they thought was good and what the contestants needed to improve. The next step was the elimination by the peers, sometimes despite the highest scores. Then there would be voting by the public via SMS, which would be the final decision. I was given the position of the headmistress and had the power of veto and could stop the elimination of a contestant if I felt he was an outstanding participant. I think I used this power a couple of times and it was always to save the most popular participant, Arijit Singh. He was a small-town boy from Jiagunj, Murshidabad District, West Bengal, and did not get too many SMSs from his home town. Since he was a threat to the rest of the singers, the axe always fell on him. I have no way of knowing whether the judges gave him a good score or not, but he was eliminated twice over. This is what is touted as fate generally, but it saddened me when I could not save him in the third elimination, and I saw him leave the contest. It was not only I but all the judges there thought he was exceptional. He had mentioned that Sonu Nigam was his role model and we surprised him by inviting Sonu on the show to encourage him. When Pandit Jasraj heard him at *Fame Gurukul*, he told him that whenever Arijit left the show, he would accept him formally as his *shishya,* disciple. When Arijit came on the show, he brought along a *surmandal*, the Indian harp. Music was his life. At that age, it was obvious that he would be an outstanding singer and I had a special attachment for him. The system of SMS failed him and he could not be the winner in that competition. But he had won my heart and the hearts of thousands of young people watching that show.

That night of his elimination I was so disturbed that I could not sleep. The reality shows have a lot of positive points, but they are not without flaws. Young people get a lot of exposure, but I did not like the process of elimination in front of thousands of viewers. The system of SMS was an extremely dangerous one especially for those youngsters who came from remote towns and villages, without any contacts or money. How were they expected to garner votes from their supporters who had no access to technology? Smart phones were also a new introduction to communication. The cell phone companies that earned money from the messages were also inadvertently supporting those who had the largest number of SMS votes. These youngsters were stuck in a vicious circle, a *chakravyuh*, formed of the TV channel supported by the sponsor, the sponsor surviving on the advertising and the ad world depending on consumers. No one could have imagined that Arijit would lose. The boy who won was Qazi Touqeer from Kashmir. Kashmir was a sensitive political issue at the time. The fact that a boy from Kashmir could actually be selected to join the contest was in itself an anomaly. The TV audience was bowled over by his simplicity and the innocence his face radiated. Just his personality and his circumstances had already guaranteed his victory. The stories circulating about Qazi's family and his struggle were enough to touch the hearts of the Indian public. Once the audience gets carried away by emotion, the voices and musical notes are deadened by the flood of feelings.

Yet, it was Arijit who won the race in the music world and has even reached international levels. He is the most followed Asian singer on Spotify and went on to win seven Filmfare Awards and one National Award. My blessings will always be with him.

The next show I judged was *Junoon Kuchh Kar Dikhane Ka*. Gajendra Singh had a unique idea for this show. It was based on Sufi music, folk and film music. There were three judges: Rahat Fateh Ali Khan came from Pakistan to judge the Sufi singers, Anand Raj Anand for film music and I was the judge for the folk section. Surprisingly, there were some Pakistani contestants too. When it came to voting, the SMS from the audience was the decisive vote. I was glad of one thing, that my contestants were procuring the largest number of votes. But again, something strange was conveyed to me. Anand Raj Sahib, along with the producer, told me that I should appeal to the public to give the same affection and preference to singers from across the border, as my singers were getting. They wanted more votes for Ali Abbas from Pakistan, who was in the Sufi section. My appeal made such an impact that the next time my participants got fewer votes than the others. As a result, Malini Awasthi and Kalpana, both excellent singers, were very upset with me for having spoilt the chances of my own 'children'. I also got carried away by emotion for our neighbours and pacified them saying that we were getting plenty of votes in any case, so let the others also get some in their favour.

These shows were a new experience for me and I have very fond memories of those days. My argument against the means employed for these shows sprang from the fact that they were not always in the realm of 'reality'. There were some unwritten rules, which took away from the transparency of the show. Sometimes we were asked to mouth lines from scripts handed over to us. I was forthright in telling the sponsors that I believed in telling the truth, that a reality show should be just that and I will say what I think is appropriate for the moment. These young people have come with dreams in their eyes, their luck in their hands. I should not make any mistake that would discourage them, because my responsibility is towards them rather than any channel or sponsor. And I can honestly say that I tried my best to work with honesty and integrity.

Maati Ke Laal was a very different show. Since it was made by Doordarshan for the Kisan Channel, they did not need any sponsors. The programme was a contest for rural India with contestants singing folk songs from their own state. There was no question of SMS votes. Anu Kapoor and I were the two judges, and I spent three months listening to folk music. I relived my childhood in Rajasthan and also discovered that our country was blessed with such talented children. Most of the parents of these participants were folk singers or had knowledge of classical music. The children usually took part in the chorus or group singing in their towns and villages.

The parents of these children were trying to give them the chance they never had because of lack of money and the means to go ahead. They wanted their children to get exposure to a wider world with more opportunities. They saw these programmes as the channel through which they saw their children gaining access to a world they themselves could only dream of. This in itself is not wrong, but a great deal of caution has to be used when exposing children to this unreal world. Children get a taste of winning at an early age and find it difficult to deal with failure or rejection later. They can go astray, become arrogant and neglect their training—the very reason why they had come for the show. I feel that the word fame is in itself an illusion. Parents should not encourage their children to get into such tough competitions unless they are mentally ready to win as well as lose. These competitions should be taken as a game of chance, all played with the spirit of sportsmanship. The old system of the *guru–shishya* tradition was a much better way for talented children to become masters of their craft. There is no shortcut to excellence.

There are many good reality shows these days and so much talent is being discovered and groomed. There is a mine of talent in this country and each show is throwing up gems for the world of music.

A few years later, DD Urdu asked me to host a reality show. I thought for the Urdu channel I should do something different, not the usual folk that people had come to expect from me. Having seen the dejection of the ones who did not make it in my previous shows, I decided that in my format there would be no losers. There were three positions in the winner category, and no one was eliminated from the show. Each participant was given a certificate of participation and appreciation signed by Ustad Rashid Khan, Waseem Sahib and Kavita Krishnamurthy.

While ruminating on several ideas, my mind zeroed in on something new. I thought that people sing *ghazals* and there is such a good audience for this genre, but the emphasis is on the singer, not the poet or the lyricist who gave birth to the *ghazal*. My show should concentrate more on the poet, without whom there would be no *ghazal*.

I had learnt music for over ten years, but in those years, I got to know music, just know it, without actually living it. I knew that there were seventy-two *thaats* of which mostly ten were used. I knew that the *thaat* was not the thought, but the thought from which emerge the *raag* and *raaginis*, the emotional rendering of music. I knew the difference between Hindustani and Carnatic music, the time for each *raga*, the morning *ragas*, the evening *ragas*. I was able to recognize them all. This knowledge came in very useful for this programme.

I selected the opening lines of a *ghazal* sung by Ghulam Ali Sahib and written by Pakistani poet, Saleem Kausar, '*Main khayal hoon kisi aur ka, mujhe sochta koi aur hai*'. This seemed just the right title for what I wanted to convey through the programme—the importance of the poet and *shayar* who writes the *ghazal*. A *ghazal* cannot exist by itself. As I like to put it, it has the support of classical music on its left and on the right the *shayari,* the words that give it life. A *ghazal* is first written, the thought and words of a poet, and then when the *raag* joins it, a *ghazal* is born. The idea appealed to everyone involved with the show. And my *khayal* became a reality—a reality show! '*Khayal*' is derived from the Persian word that signifies imagination and is thus characterized by romantic poetry. The origin of this music style is attributed to Amir Khusrow.

It was a journey of discovery. A discovery of the vast talent buried in the far reaches of small towns and cities. I reached out to the best of young classical singers from towns that would be familiar with Urdu: Rampur, Sitapur, Bhopal, Lucknow, Indore and Jaipur. During the auditions I came across several youngsters who had devoted themselves to music and *ghazals* after a solid grounding in classical music. The search itself was an education for me. I am happy to say that several of these young singers have since made a name for themselves in the country, in the world of music. The judges for this programme were Waseem Barelvi, poet par excellence, who surprised me by saying that this was the first time anyone had asked him to be part of a show. His *shayari* at the finale touched the hearts of all in the audience and the participants were indeed fortunate to have the opportunity to listen to him recite his poems. Devaki Pandit, a well-known classical singer, a disciple of Ganasaraswati Kishori Amonkar, and Padmashree Pandit Jitendra Abhisheki and Kavita Krishnamurthy, whose singing and music everybody is familiar with, were the other two judges.

I mention this show in another context, a reference to that sad day when India lost one of its greatest classical singers. It was the beginning of a new year, 9 January 2024. I had just received a call to say the beloved classical singer, Ustad Rashid Khan was no more. It was a day of mourning for the world of Hindustani music. He was known in the classical music fraternity to be the finest *khayal* vocalist of his generation. A Pakistani poet called him 'the living embodiment of the *khayal*'. A celebrated classical singer paid a tribute to him, saying, 'Today music has lost its *khayal*.'

I was in a state of shock. The word sank in, *khayal*, associated with the Ustad. I found I was losing myself in the *khayal* of Rashid Khan Sahib and I exclaimed to myself, 'What a man! Even when he sang the *chhota khayal*, he imbued it with greatness!' He seemed to be submerged in the ripples of his *swar*. When he sang the *bada khayal*, his music would be carried over the waves, a boat overflowing with the emotions of notes, unstoppable, unhindered.

I don't remember when or how I met him, but slowly he won my heart, leaving behind memories that are etched in my mind. Ustad Rashid Khan, of whom Pandit Bhimsen Joshi said that he was 'an assurance for the future of Indian vocal music'. But such words did not have any meaning for him. For him his *gayaki* was his life, his breath. When he played the first note on the *surmandal* and the first notes escaped his throat, one was transported into the world of the *khayal*, another world, where space and time had no relevance. He had no social graces nor believed in them. For me he had a *sufiana* personality, a spiritual, mystic and ascetic way of life. He was a *fakir*, generous, innocent and instinctive. We did not meet often, but the relationship endured the test of time. I had nothing to give him, but he gave me so much, scattering the gems of music around me.

His music transcended all genres. He could not escape the impact of music. It was all around him, the legacy of his family. His uncle, Ustad Inayat Hussain Khan was the founder of the Rampur–Sahaswan *gharana*. Another uncle, Ustad Ghulam Mustafa Khan, was a renowned proponent of the *gharana*. He got his initial training from his maternal grandfather, Ustad Nissar Hussain Khan. It is said that Nissar Hussain Khan was such a strict disciplinarian that he would make his *shishya* practise just one note the whole day. The *guru–shishya* tradition was so strong that the disciple (*shishya*) could not think of disobeying his teacher (*guru*).

From the commencement of my music show, I knew I had to invite him to the finale. I approached him hesitantly, informing him that I would be honoured to have his presence at my show and how much the young singers would benefit from his words of musical wisdom. But I did not have the means to compensate him as was his due. Without any hesitation, he agreed, saying that I should not even think about the financial aspect of the invitation, and he would be really happy to appear on the show.

There was excitement in the studio when the contestants saw Ustad Rashid Khan in their midst. They could not believe that they were to listen to such an eminent *khayal* singer. Kavita Krishnamurthy sang first, followed by Devaki Pandit, but when the Ustad took the stage, he took music to another plane, another height. He infused energy into his singing, mesmerizing the young aspirants and the audience. DD Urdu was impressed that I had been able to persuade the Ustad to be present at this event. It was a milestone of sorts. Though it is not an appropriate comparison, I will still say that Ustad Rashid Khan was no less than a Bollywood superstar. I will be ever grateful to this great man who thought nothing of obliging someone like me without considering the financial loss to himself.

'*Mein khayal hun kisi aur ka/Mujhe sochta koi aur hai*', Saleem Kausar's lines came back to me again as my mind, my *khayal*, took me back to the day of my mother's first *barsi*, death anniversary, in Jaipur. I wanted it to be a memorial to my mother, who loved music and had seen to it that all her children were made to learn one or other of the performing arts. Once again, I approached him, again pleading my inability to match his performance fee. He said that he would come and that I should not give any *khayal* to the fees. He would be accompanied by his *shagird*, disciple Krishna, and a couple of musicians. My excitement knew no bounds. I booked the auditorium at Ravindra Manch, with a capacity of over 800 people. I decided to make it an event to remember for the music fraternity of Jaipur, a city which has a great tradition of music. I invited all the musicians, known and unknown, from the old city, from Ramganj Bazaar, musicians who were great in their own right but had not received any recognition from the city. On several occasions I had included them in my live shows and had got to know them and their families fairly well. They all came, musicians and singers big and small, with their children and their families. There were families of all my music teachers from school and college. These people are good musicians themselves but do not get an opportunity to listen to renowned musicians in India because the programmes are unaffordable for them. Ghulam Ali Khan Sahib too came and I felt that Jaipur had a great memorial not only for my mother but for the whole city. My mother, who lived and appreciated music would have been very pleased with this tribute to her.

I can still imagine and hear Ustad Rashid Khan's music resounding in the city of Jaipur, its echoes flowing into the gullies of the pink city. Today, I find that I am losing myself in the Ustad's *khayal*, wishing I had spent more time with him. It seems strange that you should grieve for someone who was not part of your life. But for me music was our bond, the emotional content of his *gayaki*, different from others of his time who laid greater emphasis on technique.

Music was for his soul, but Rashid Khan Sahib had another interest. He was a great cook. On the rare occasions when I met him, he would invite me to his home for a meal. For someone like me, who did not know the ABC of cooking, his biryani was a miracle. But then cooking too requires a great deal of *riyaaz,* practice, which I am sure the Ustad did daily to perfect the food for the body.

That day I watched his last journey on TV. I was restless since I wanted to be in Budaun, his home town, but I could not make it. His cortège was followed by people from every walk of life and there was not a single dry eye in the crowd. The son of Budaun was being laid to rest.

Later I spoke to his son, Arman, who had been bestowed his father's mantle four years ago, officially becoming his disciple. It is not necessary that a *guru* choose his own son to be his heir; it could be anyone he thinks would completely surrender to music, that being his lifelong dedication. Not every Ustad's child is necessarily going to follow in his father's footsteps; we have a few examples like Amjad Ali Khan's sons, Aman and Ayaan, or Pandit Shivkumar Sharma's son Rahul, Zakir Hussain, Anoushka Shankar, etc. His disciple, Krishna, who always accompanied his *guru* was distraught, saying that he could not see anything beyond his *guru* and now there was nothing left for him to see.

Arman told me a story, which gave me some solace. Since I could not give him his fee at my mother's *barsi,* I commissioned a marble statue of Saraswati to be made by one of the best marble sculptors in

Jaipur and sent it to him. The statue stood in its original packing for several years. It was only a few months ago, when he opened a music institute in Agartala, that the statue was unpacked and installed at the entrance of the institute. Arman said since then his father would pray to the goddess of knowledge and the performing arts every day whenever he was in Agartala. Just goes to show that music has no biases, no discrimination in religion and belief.

As the few moments I spent with Ustad Rashid Khan flit by in memory, I am thankful that I had the good fortune to walk alongside, albeit for fleeting moments, with this man whose voice will remain immortal in the annals of music.

'*Kuchh kaha, kuchh suna, kuhch rah gaya*
Dil ko yoon chhed ke tu kidhar gaya?'

(Something said, something heard, some left unspoken
Where have you gone, after awakening me playfully?)

Gone too soon, Rashid Bhai!

Chapter 23

Uncut Rushes: The Influence of Cinema on My Life

The kind of family background I came from did not encourage children to watch films or listen to film songs on the radio. There was a censorship also in what we were allowed to read. Detective, crime novels and romances were taboo.

Sometimes, during our summer holidays when we visited our uncle and aunt in Jodhpur, we would somehow escape notice and go to the nearby theatre to watch a film. I remember seeing the old *Masoom*, with child stars Honey and Sarosh Irani, and *Zameen ke Taare*, with the two Irani sisters, Daisy and Honey, who mostly played the part of little boys. Honey Irani later married Javed Akhtar and is Zoya and Farhan Akhtar's mother. There was a song in *Masoom*, 'Nani teri morni ko', sung by Ranu Mukherjee, which became a hit. I still remember the lyrics of the song even today, when I am myself a *nani*, a grandmother, and singing it to my granddaughters.

My mother believed that films had a bad influence on young and impressionable minds. When I look back, I recall that the films of our childhood were not 'dangerous', in fact they were somewhat innocent. There was not much violence and if I remember correctly, the police always arrived in a white jeep with *lathis*, after the event, handcuffed the criminals and took them away without any gory battles. Courtroom dramas were very popular as were love stories, mostly about unrequited love. Romance was declared through letters, songs and phone calls. Physical contact was rare and was often censored. I remember how the song *'Jalte hain jiske liye'* sung over the phone and picturized on Sunil Dutt and Nutan in *Sujata* (1959) sent me into ecstasies and still gives me gooseflesh. If only I could be in a similar situation! I would dream of a handsome lover with a sonorous voice singing love songs to me. I remember too, the scene between Pradeep Kumar and Bina Rai. In those days, there used to be a brand of cigarettes called Capstan, which was sold in a red-and-white tin. In this film, the two lovers attached two of these containers with a thin thread and used it as a means of communication. As you know, some sound is carried over this thin thread in whispers. For days, a friend and I would collect these and fashion them into phones like the hero and heroine in the film.

That was the time when many films depicted Muslim culture. The sets, the costumes and the beautiful Urdu dialogues were enough to transport me to a world of romance. The mysterious being within the *burkha,* with only her delicate hands visible, inspired many a *shairi* and *ghazal* from romantic men. How I wished I could have worn a *burkha.* For me it was a beautiful piece of clothing, replete with mystery. Another tradition that fascinated me was the *nikah* ceremony. The bride sitting behind a sheer *purdah* (curtain), and the *maulvi* coming to her to get her acceptance for the contract, was the height of romance for me. I loved the three words, *kabool, kabool, kabool,* with which the contract was sealed.

Many of the films based on Muslim culture depicted *kotha*s, inhabited by courtesans and dancing girls, including the heroine. These films, with the ethereal sets created by the art directors that transported you to a different world, fascinated me. In my imagination I would follow the hero as he walked through narrow gullies and bazaars, with shops on either side selling perfumes, *gajras* flower chains for the hair, *chutilas,* a silk hair braid with tassles, bangles and other fashion accessories. I would climb up the winding staircases, entering a large *baithak,* an entertainment hall, with sheer curtains, bead partitions, *paan,* the betel offering and the notes of the *sarangi.* I was there, lost in a world of music and dance. The heroine would be seated there, greeting her clients with a *naazuk adaab* till the hero, dressed in a sheer Lakhnavi muslin kurta, wrapped in a zardosi shawl, made his appearance, with me following him like a ghost. Stealthy glances would be exchanged, a slight tinkle of the *ghunghroo,* the lamp placed before her as she began to sing, beautiful love songs, directed at her secret lover under the hawk-like eyes of her mother or the madam of the *kotha.*

These films mesmerized you to an extent that you did not wish to leave the ambience of the *kotha*. The music, the costumes, the poetry and above all, the love story gave you sleepless nights.

There were so many of these films, but of course we were not allowed to watch them. We looked forward to the visit of Bachchi Bhabhi, a distant relative who lived just outside Jaipur and would often come over the weekend. She was a film fan and it was with her that we went to watch many of these films despite the reluctance of my mother. Often the thought did cross my mind that I could go to watch a film secretly but could not follow that up since it was just not possible to do so in Jaipur. There were too many eyes watching us and word would get to my mother. The older sisters were our watchdogs too and of course we never had the money for such indulgences. I had a recurring dream in my childhood, a dream that would amuse my readers. You are often asked as a child what you would like to be when you grow up. Fortunately, no one ever asked me that question. My answer would have alarmed them. My dream was to be a dancer at one of those magical *kothas,* which were presented in these films. Of course, we were not aware of the horrific life of a courtesan, the process and the conditions, the bitter truth that forced them into a life of submission. I saw only the dance and the music, the elaborate costumes and the romance of the leading pair. A mother, with her sharp intuition about her children, had already gauged the impact films would have on young minds and tried her best to shield us from that evil. If my mother had even an inkling of my forbidden dream, she would perhaps have buried me behind a brick wall, just as Akbar had done with Anarkali! As it is my heart had melted completely with the lost romance of Salim and Anarkali. For me, that was an example of the perfect love story. I imagined myself boldly singing, '*Pyaar kiya to darna kya/ Pyaar kiya koi chori nahin ki/chhup-chhup ahain bharna kya . . .*'

I am sure most youngsters go through this rebellious period but are kept in check with clapperboards like the one my mother brandished, '*Avesh mein vivek mat khona.*' All my dreams fell in line with her reminders.

Pakeezah (1972) was another film that held me under its spell for a long time, especially the song '*Chalte, chalte yunhi koi mil gaya tha*'. Meena Kumari's delicate raise of the hand, her beautiful, sad eyes, seeking a lover who lived more in her memory than in reality. And the sudden whistle of a train, against the soft moonlight, a steam engine which took her back into a flashback far away from the *kotha* where she was dancing. The sound of the train somehow spelt romance for me too, so much so that I fell in love not only with that scene but indeed with the whole railway department. And God in his wisdom decided that since I could not have the luck of Meena Kumari, with a poetic lover in a train, he placed me in an area, Santa Cruz East in Mumbai, close to the station. That was enough to put an end to my romance with trains. The constant sound of trains and whistles, the rattling of iron wheels on tracks and the ground often shaking under our building, was definitely not conducive to romance.

Apart from Muslim socials, I was enamoured of films which presented heroines who were bound by orthodoxy and could not profess their love. Films with Bengali themes specially portrayed heroines who were shy and coy and were victims of unrequited love. There was the character of the *borda* and the *manjhli didi* and their love story. There was only a suggestion of their attraction for each other in the ordinary acts of life, like playing a game of cards or offering a *paan* or a cup of tea to their secret love. The gentle touch with a deliberate swish of a *dhakai pallu,* the soft Dhaka sari, the knowing looks, unnoticed by the rest of the characters—the romance blossomed secretly but often ended in tragedy, with the heroine marrying a man her parents had chosen. The hero would turn into a Devdas. Somehow these tragic romances always appealed to me. There was always a lot of tears and weeping with my sobs and tears in the background. These stories never had a happy ending.

My imagination led me through many such stories of unfulfilled love. I would cast myself into the characters I had seen on the screen and accompanied by the beautiful songs of those days, I would imagine myself as the tragic heroine. Cinema created an illusion. But sadly, no such hero ever came into my life. I had only the radio and Vividh Bharti to fan my dreams. But I would listen to these songs and write letters which I would post secretly to friends and acquaintances who were patient enough to listen to my tragic tales.

'*Jeevan cinema nahin hai,*' my mother would say. 'Cinema is not real life.' Perhaps her clapperboard came down at the right time and none of us ever thought of crossing the threshold of propriety.

Yes, life was not cinema, but for me, cinema has become life today. I never imagined I would do so many films and that my first film would indeed be close to my dream. *Mandi*, my first film, was based in a *kotha*, and though I did not get to sing on the *sarangi* like Smita Patil or dance like Neena Gupta, I was a part of that milieu. Another irony of my life was that my mother did not allow us to listen to the radio much, but radio became my first step towards an entry into the world of the performing arts. I have done so much on the radio, from Akashvani Jaipur to the BBC in London.

Now that I am part of that world, I can bring down my own clapperboard for the younger generation. Though I do believe that literature is a reflection of life, I can also say that cinema has a great influence on young minds. They can construe this as reality, especially in small towns, where their only exposure to the world is through cinema and now through OTT. But I feel that social media and OTT channels should also be under the purview of censorship. It is the responsibility of cinema and media to provide good entertainment for its audience, but it is as much our responsibility as the parents'.

My film journey began with *Mandi*, but I am grateful to God that I have been given the opportunity to take on diverse roles and age has not withered the infinity and variety of my roles (with apologies to Shakespeare).

Chapter 24

Stars: *Parde Ke Peechhey Kya Hai?*

I started my journey from the small screen to the big screen, small steps to some gigantic ones and now I have also had the experience of working in platforms, such as OTT. I worked in an episode of *Call My Agent*, which I thoroughly enjoyed and my last appearance was in the very popular series titled *Aarya 3,* directed by the brilliant director Ram Madhvani. Our biggest achievement in theatre in our anniversary year is that we were commissioned by ZEE Theatre to record our play Ibsen's *Ghosts,* adapted by me as *Peechha Karti Parchhaiyan* for screening on the OTT platform for ZEE Theatre. There are so many memories with so many special people, directors like Govind Nihalani, with whom I did *Tamas* (1988), *Rukmavati Ki Haveli* for television and the film *Ardh Satya* (1983) with Om Puri and Smita Patil and *Drohkaal* (1994) with Naseeruddin Shah. There was a serial which I cannot forget, *Lifeline,* directed by Vijaya Mehta with leading actor K.K. Raina and Tanvi Azmi, followed by Shyam Benegal's *Yatra* and *Discovery of India.* So many associations and relationships that conjure up images from sepia to black-and-white to colour.

Most of these relationships end the minute the director declares a pack-up, when we have given the last shot, when we leave the location or the set. This was not the case in the films that required the team to live together for several days, at the same location like in Shyam Benegal's films. But this is not true of commercial films. The bonds formed during a shooting end just there. But some relationships live on in the heart, even if your paths seldom cross. Whenever you see them, there is the same warmth, a few words and camaraderie. For me, some of these relationships were for a lifetime, some maturing into family relationships. Every Holi, Diwali, Eid or Christmas, in times of need or in happier times, I remember those people who encouraged me along the way. I am forever grateful to the film industry for these bonds, which have survived over decades. The industry has given me a beautiful family of creative people. There were some of these whom I never met again after the completion of a film, but their advice and comments have taught me a lot in my life. My book would be incomplete if I did not mention these associations. I can happily say that I believe I met only good people, so I am not in a position to run down anyone or even complain. Hangal Sahib, Amitji, Jayaji, Bappi Da, Rekhaji, Raaj Kumar, Ghulam Ali Sahib, Rishi Kapoor, Govind Nihalani, Rashid Sahib, Shyam Benegal, a host of names which would fill up many volumes of a book.

I remember in my schooldays, whenever we went for intercollegiate competitions, with dance, music, debates and dramatics, surprisingly there was always one section which was a diary-writing competition. We did not understand then how important diary writing is. Each page with the written word, is a book in itself. But we never did put down our thoughts and daily activities. Now I find memories are becoming blurred, time is drawing a curtain on them, some have collected dust, some have been crammed in the mind causing a clutter of events and people.

As I said, I did not even realize that my film journey had been so long and eventful. During this journey, I met several actors and actresses and was connected to many either on the small screen or a small role on the large screen. Unknown to me, all these people left a deep impression on me.

Raaj Kumarji

It was in one such film that I met Raaj Kumarji, affectionately known as Jaani in film circles. I was transported to the world of *Pakeezah*. It was as if I was at the start of a journey with the whistle of the train in the background and Jaani was the man whom I had looked at from a distance. Suddenly before me stood the man from the lines of the song, '*Yunhi koi mil gaya thaa/ Sar-e-rah chalte chalte.*' My *rah*, my path, was my entry into commercial films, a small role in a film called

Police Public, directed by Esmayeel Shroff and released in 1990. He was the first actor I interacted with on the big screen. By that time after seeing *Pakeezah*, *Waqt* (1965) and *Laal Patthar* (1971), I had become an ardent fan. I think it was *Pakeezah*, in 1972, that turned me into a romantic. I don't know when and why the director, Esmayeel cast me in the film. Perhaps he had seen me in a play at Prithvi and liked my performance. He cast me in the role of Laxmi, a woman who could not speak but was the only eyewitness to a murder. Raaj Kumarji was the police commissioner. He was investigating a murder committed in the *haveli* of a rich and influential man. There were several well-known film villains cast in the film, including the most famous of them all, Prem Chopra, along with Macmohan. It is not easy to get a role in a commercial film. So, when I got the call, I literally jumped for joy. I had no idea how much I would receive as payment, an issue I hesitate to deal with even now. I did not even consider the fact that as a supporting actress, I was not allowed to take any companion with me—no staff, no hairdresser, no make-up artist. In fact, I wasn't even allowed to bring along a family member. At first, I was a little apprehensive about going alone since I did not know anyone in the world of commercial films. I had gone by myself when working with Shyam Benegal, but that was a different world, where one was comfortable since everyone came solo, and the cast lived together as a family at the location. But in this case, when I heard the line-up of the cast, each better known than the other, and I an unknown entity, I was a little hesitant. The director told me that there were several theatre actors in the cast: Reema Lagu, Naseer, Rakesh Bedi, A.K. Hangal, etc. The moment I heard Hangal Sahib's name, I immediately accepted the film, since Hangal Sahib was like family to me. The film was shot in Mussoorie. It was a cold winter's day, with the hill sides in a pall of mist and a strange mysterious haze. What could one crave for in this weather but a cup of tea! I can have tea at any time, especially hot ginger tea. I would watch the spot boy, once in a while, on the sets, carrying a flask of tea. The appearance and look of the tea were enough to put you off tea and also make you forget all your acting abilities. Despite the craving, one look at the tea made me refuse that essential elixir. I was not aware that Raaj Kumarji was watching this interaction between the flask of tea and me. As I sat there alone in the mist, I watched his personal spot boy arriving with a tray bearing a teapot covered with a tea-cozy with Kashmiri embroidery. Looking at that one could gauge that he had some connection with Kashmir. Most people on the set were scared of him, wary of his sarcastic tongue. He was a superstar. If he was irritated by someone, well that was the end of him. He was known to be eccentric. Often, as I sat sunning myself outside the hotel, I would see Raaj Kumarji sitting at a distance, and when his spot boy poured the steaming hot tea into his cup, my heart filled with envy. I would look longingly at that tray, but not once did his spot boy ever think of offering me a cup of tea. Forget the tea, he would not even cast a glance towards someone as insignificant as I. It is said that the peon of a government servant is more arrogant than the officer himself. This is true of the staff of any star in Bollywood, from his manager to his make-up man and his spot boy or his security. They strut around with an air of self-importance for no apparent reason except that they are part of an actor's personal staff! But my fate took a turn for the better the day Raaj Kumarji himself gestured to me asking me to come to him. And the superstar asked, '*Chai piyogi? Sardi mein chai achhi lagti hai.*' (Would you like some tea? It's good to have tea in winter.) I cast a mischievous glance at the spot boy and readily accepted Raaj Kumarji's offer. It was the beginning of a strange relationship. Sometimes he would ask me to join him for tea. At other times, he would ask the spot boy to carry a cup of tea to me. He was a man of few words. I took to wandering out in the sun, hoping he would notice me, and I would get that much-longed-for cup of tea. Much to my surprise, Raaj Kumarji had made inquiries about me and had got to know a little about this lady whom he shared his *chai* with. One of the things he got to know was that I had come for the shooting all by myself. I will never forget the day I shot my first scene with him. I had the role of the household help in the *haveli* who was the only eyewitness to the murder. Her employers had threatened her and asked her to pretend to be deaf and dumb before the police. Raaj Kumar as the police commissioner was handling the murder case in the *haveli*. All the members of the household, including me, were lined up to be interrogated. As he fired questions at me in his beautiful voice, I was so carried away that I blurted out my dialogue before the climax when I was supposed to talk. The director was in fact very upset with me, but Raaj Kumarji was very sympathetic and glossed over my inadvertent mistake. Of course, I was very happy about the fact that Raaj Kumarji had a lengthy dialogue with several lines to make me blurt out the truth because his voice always held his audience spellbound. And here I was actually facing him, waiting for my cue. I would probably have been speechless and gagged before such a great actor, but the relationship forged over a cup of tea boosted my confidence. He congratulated me on my performance and later that day as I sat sunning myself, a cup of tea was poured by him from the tea-cozy-covered teapot and handed to me by the great man himself! And along with the tea, he gave me an important piece of advice. He said that you are an actor and if you want to continue acting in films, money should not be the only consideration. Keep in mind that never again should you come for a shoot without someone accompanying you. Always bring along someone, either a family member or a security person. This is an unpredictable world, and it is not wise to face it alone. He said, 'Take that decision now, that you will never agree to a shoot without a companion. The film world is a lonely place, and a moment of vulnerability could have serious consequences. An artiste can give his best only when he is emotionally secure. Your status too is enhanced in the eyes of the unit who treat you with more respect. Being alone on the sets can even have an effect on your health, both mental and physical.' At the end of the shoot, as we made the bus journey down to Dehra Dun, in the fog-covered hills, I could only see the mist coming out from the spout of the tea pot. And a vision of a man in white, his feet ensconced in his signature white shoes. *Mera jaani*. His words of wisdom remain with me and to this day I never venture out on a film shoot without my staff. This ensures protection and privacy, and my contract mentions the fact that I will accept a role only if I travel by business class, stay at the same hotels as the main cast and always have at least two of my staff members with me. In Raaj Kumarji's words, a large car and staff members in an artiste's retinue give him stature and earn him respect in the eyes of the film unit.

Who would have thought that this eccentric actor, known to be a man of few words, before whom the film world trembled, would share a cup of tea and advice with an unknown newcomer?

His mask had come off for a brief moment, a moment I will treasure for life.

An Ode to Shyam

19 May 2022. The auditorium resounded with applause on the first view of the trailer, *Mujib: The Making of a Nation*. The Amrit Mahotsav of seventy-five years of Indian independence was being celebrated at the Marché du Film Commercial Branch at the Indian Pavilion of the Cannes Film Festival. After all, the official speeches, appeared the gentle face of the director, Shyam Benegal, sending his video message for this release. Shyam, eighty-eight himself, had achieved another milestone, another biopic after the success of *The Making of a Mahatma* (1996) and *Netaji Subhas Chandra Bose: The Forgotten Hero* (2004).

My thoughts went back to the time, almost forty years ago, when I had met Shyam Benegal for the first time. A friend of mine from college in Jaipur, Meena Pange, had moved to Bombay after marriage. She was married to Girish Ghanekar, an ad film maker, who also worked as first assistant director to Shyam Benegal. Their association went back a generation. Shyam Benegal had joined Girish's father, Govind Bhargava Ghanekar, in the Trio Films having its office in Jyoti Studios at Dadar. Meena, who had seen me on stage in Jaipur, admired my acting abilities and believed that this pioneer of the new wave film movement, Shyam Benegal, was the perfect director for someone like me.

I was not so sure of that. I did not see myself as a commercial movie actress. My sights were set on the theatre. I had not been exposed to much of the performing arts besides the stage. That, though, was an exciting time for Indian cinema. A new parallel movement had started which introduced the Indian audiences to good acting and normal Indian faces. Jaya Bhaduri did films such as *Guddi* (1971), *Anamika* (1973) and *Parichay* (1972) and Smita Patil and Shabana Azmi had established themselves as lead actresses in this new genre. Meena was convinced that I was equal to these actresses in talent. 'Once you face the camera,' she said, 'the rest will be taken care of.' Shyam Benegal had also launched Kulbhushan Kharbanda, Naseeruddin Shah and Om Puri as leading men in his films. Meena said she could introduce me to Shyam. He was casting for his new film, an unusual story, *Mandi* which has an ensemble cast of female characters, mostly from NSD.

I met Shyam Benegal for the first time in his office at Tardeo. As I nervously walked up the stairs, I crossed some actresses with smiling faces, walking down: Anita Kanwar, Soni Razdan and Neena Gupta. Perhaps they had been cast in the film already. My role had a couple more in line, Reema Lagu and Nadira Babbar. I was the third actress asked to audition by Shyam. I gave the audition and was told that they would get back to me later. The role that I was offered was that of a prostitute, the mistress of the *thanedaar,* or police officer, of the village. My first role and that also of a fallen woman who was nine months pregnant and who already had two or three children. The thought came to my mind that if I was going to make a debut in a role like this my journey in this business would take forever. Was this going to be the start of my career or the end? People told me that if he recognises your talent, your career is made and you become part of his repertory. I had dreams of joining the repertory at NSD, but then perhaps Shyam Benegal's repertory was fated for me.

We did not have access to a phone in those days. There was a grocery store across the road and the owner had reluctantly allowed me to give his number as a contact for me in emergencies. But that came with a price—each time I went to answer a call, I felt obliged to buy something from his shop. One day, the shopkeeper called out to me, saying that there was a call for me from Shyam Benegal's office. I leapt down the stairs, my heartbeat matching my steps. Shyam's voice at the other end said just a few words, 'Ila, come to my office tomorrow. You are in the film.' I was speechless. The next day, I went to their office again, a little less apprehensive and nervous than the first time. He explained the role to me and then said, 'Now let us come to the brass tacks.' Not being too proficient in English, I wondered why he was talking of brass, or was it gold. I could not say! I was in a different world. I had got the role so brass or gold was of no consequence especially since I did not understand the meaning. Then his voice pierced my dream world. 'Girl,' he said, 'this is a small-budget film. Since this is your first film, let me be frank and tell you that you will get only Rs 7500.' Who was concerned about money at that time? I said, 'Sir, you decide what you want to pay me!' The word 'negotiation' was not part of our lexicon, neither then nor now!

I cannot describe the elation and enthusiasm that gripped me as over thirty artistes entered the second-class compartment of the train at Victoria Terminal. It was to be a long journey to Hyderabad. Bimal Roy's wife had carried a huge tiffin box since she was also excited that her son, Joy, was going to be the assistant director to Shyam. And her grandson, Aditya Bhattacharya (Babla) was cast in the lead role as Smita Patil's lover. For many of us, the journey had already begun before we set off from VT.

After an overnight train ride, we reached Hyderabad and boarded a bus, which brought us to our destination, the Rock Castle Hotel. It was September and a soft westerly wind caressed us and welcomed us to Hyderabad, the city of Nizams. The hotel was also unique. The rooms were carved out of rocks and it was like living in a cave. I felt as if the romance, the distant, surreal world of films was within reach. The best part was that everyone, from the director to the spot boy, was put up in the same hotel. Our rooms were scattered all over the rock sides. I shared a room with Anita Kanwar. It was a large room facing a square and across from us was Kulbhushan Kharbanda's room. So many memories, too many to be gathered and put together in these scant pages. The location was quite far and all of us used to travel in a bus together, everyone but Shabana and Smita, who were given a car. But they soon abandoned their isolation and joined in the fun of togetherness in the bus. We would sing all the way to the location. Anu Kapur, who came from a family of performers, led the way with *antakshri,* a game where each team takes up the last letter of a song to start a new string. He became such an expert at conducting this that this genre has become his livelihood. I would call him the *antakshri* king!

I cannot ever forget my first shot in this film. It took place inside a tiny tent. It was the scene of a delivery, when I, as the *thanedaar's* mistress, was to deliver his child. The tent was crowded. Since there were no monitors, the director had to watch the actual enactment. Shabana and Smita had told the director that they wanted to see this shot, since they wanted to pull my leg afterwards. I was lying on a bed, with Anu Kapoor as the doctor on call. My baby came out in a flash with a loud scream accompanied by some foul Telugu words, which I realized came from my mouth! This was as real and as close to a baby's delivery as you could have got! The cameraman, Ashok Mehta, captured the shot beautifully and there was applause all around the tent. I had accomplished the impossible—the first scene of my first film in one shot! Shabana and Smita, who had been giggling and stuffing their *dupattas* in their mouth during the shot, also joined spontaneously in the applause.

As for me, the first thing I did was to remove that pillow which Saba, the costume in-charge, had fixed round my middle to depict a pregnant woman and which I had borne through a whole month. Nowadays, a rubber device is used to dress a pregnant woman as was done for Vidya Balan in *Kahani* (2012). Those were days of work and fun. We would play volleyball together, celebrate birthdays of which there were many—Shabana, Smita, Om Puri, Soni, Kulbhushan—it was a month-long celebration of birthdays.

Shabana's birthday was special since her whole family was there—Shaukat Appa, Kaifi Azmi and Javed Bhai. I remember that was the first time I had seen a *dum-ka-bakra*, a whole goat on a spit. I could not stomach that, so kept away, gorging on other Hyderabadi delicacies such as *khubani-ka-meetha* and *double-ka-meetha*. Whenever they had time off, Shabana, Smita and Neena would go to Charminar and shop for Hyderabadi trinkets, such as *rumals*, bangles and, of course, pearls, which Hyderabad is famous for. Vithal Jeweller is known worldwide for his antique pearl jewellery. Shabana would goad me on to buy some pearls for myself. I don't think they knew of my meagre payment of Rs 7500! My mother would often use the saying to warn us not to exceed our limits, '*Kya to nangi pehne, kya nichode, kya odhe, kya bichhaye*,' meaning, a poor woman has nothing to cover herself with, nothing to wash or wear, nor spread on the floor. How appropriate for my situation at the time!

But their persuasion did push me into spending my entire fee and in an attempt at keeping up with the Joneses, I bought a Hyderabadi *satlada,* a seven-string pearl necklace. It would have cost more, but Shabana and Smita told the jeweller that this was my first film so he had to concede by giving me a discount since they were good customers, having spent lakhs at his shop!

The film opened with a premiere at Minerva. A huge poster adorned the front of the theatre. And I was there, a prostitute among many other *randis* from Mandi! A memorable poster. I attended the premiere dressed in a plain, grape-coloured satin sari presented by Arun and around my neck glittered my hard-earned, ivory-and-green *satlada*. The entire payment for my first film hung around my neck, each string resplendent with memories! The poster carried my name in prominent letters: Introducing Anu Kapoor, Harish Patel and Ila Aun. I felt I had arrived.

That was the beginning of a very special relationship with Shyam Benegal. The second assistant director in that film was the late Kalpana Lajmi. She became a very good friend. She herself became a very well-known director and made memorable films such as *Rudaali* (1993), *Daman* (2001), *Chingaari* (2006) and *Ek Pal* (1986), to name just a few. Her mother, Lalita Lajmi, a well-known painter, was the sister of Guru Dutt and Shyam's first cousin. Kalpana called him Shyam Mam, so I too started addressing him as Shyam Mam, 'Mam' being short for 'Mama', mother's brother. Never once did he object to that name.

This was truly a wonderful break for me. I became part of Shyam's repertory, being cast in almost all the films he directed: *Mandi, Susman* (1987), *Antarnaad* (1991), *Welcome to Sajjanpur* (2008), *Well Done Abba* (2009), *Netaji Subhas Chandra Bose: The Forgotten Hero* and *Trikal*. His epic serials like *Discovery of India, Samvidhan* and *Yatra* added a lot to my sense of history and culture. I knew very little about my country before I did *Discovery of India: Bharat Ek Khoj*. Taken from Nehru's amazing book of the same name, which discusses every aspect of India—its 5000-year-old origins, its art and culture, the religion, the literature and languages, its geography and its struggle for independence, every nook and corner had been visited and discussed by Nehru. I took on many roles in this serial. I was Jodha, Akbar's wife, in the episode on Akbar, a role played by Kulbhushan Kharbanda. Little did I imagine that several years later, I would be cast as Akbar's foster mother, Mahamanga, in the film *Jodhaa Akbar* (2008). I feel that this serial should be in every collection of a video library. There were several versions of the Mahabharata, but Shyam's depiction in *Bharat Ek Khoj* stood out because he treated the stories in their dramatic form as plays for the stage. He showed how the Mahabharata has been presented at various stages through drama and traditional folk forms: Dharmvir Bharati's *Andha Yug*, Teejan

Bai's rendering in song and verse. He used folk forms, classical drama, classical music, Marathi drama, the whole gamut of the art traditions of India. He interpreted all the characters in a unique way; Salim Ghouse as Lord Krishna in *Andha Yug* was shown as a cowherd and not as a king, an unimaginable casting! For me, my role as Gandhari in the same episode was perhaps the most memorable role for which I received several accolades, including appreciation from the director himself. I had my moment of glory when the author of *Andha Yug*, Dharamvir Bharati, said that if anyone has ever captured the soul and spirit of Gandhari, it is Ila Arun in this episode. His words gave me gooseflesh and still resound in my subconscious.

Shyam's canvas was vast; Nehru was the author, but Shyam infused it with a life of its own. No book could have provided us with so much information and knowledge as we garnered from working with Shyam. Our motley group was truly a repertory. We were told that we would have to be on standby for any role that came along in the story, small or lead. None of us really cared what role we were offered. We watched in the wings, wonder-struck, as Shyam's genius played out the history of India, putting us in touch with every imaginable form of dance, drama, music and painting. There were many layers in that one serial. Shyam took the writers' plays, but he did not just enact the episode, he created it. The location of an episode decided its language, its set and the performance. The traditions and lifestyle of the village or town were placed in its context—a story set in Mughal times was told in the Kathak style, the episodes from the south were enacted through the medium of Kathakali and Bharatanatyam, and Krishna Leela was placed in the North-East and shown in the Manipuri style.

It was a mammoth task. Govind Nihalani sat with four cameras, with DOP V.K. Murthy. Piyush Jha's aerial shots and Nitish Roy's art direction took the serial to another level. Thirty-five researchers worked on this project, including Satyadev Dubey, Vasant Dev, Shama Zaidi and several well-known littérateurs from different regional languages, as Vanraj Bhatia's music carried us on a vastly varied musical journey, enhancing the visual presentation. Roshan Seth as Nehru and the narrator, the commentary within the narration, spoken by Om Puri—one did not want to miss a word of this enactment.

Even the minute details of a story, the caste and status of a character, their language, customs and way of life appeared before your eyes. To my knowledge, Doordarshan, the official channel, had never before had this level of production. Since it was telecast on this channel, the viewership was enormous. Shyam's monumental dramatization of *The Discovery of India* remains the most ambitious adaptation of Indian history to ever appear on screen. The knowledge that escaped me in college was imbibed in Shyam's classes!

What a difference there was in the productions in those days. Ample research was accumulated before writing the story. The script was vetted thoroughly, and actors had to be ready with their lines. Nowadays, there is very little research, no logical thought process and the script . . . well, the less said, the better.

I do not remember how much we were paid, but the budget was small. I think we were given a salary every month. I am sure it could not have been more than a couple of thousand for each episode. Producers in the present have tried 'negotiation', citing Shyam's remunerations. I tell them, first become Shyam, touch those heights of perfection and then approach me. If Shyam asks me to stand on one foot at the Santa Cruz signal, I will do it, as a mark of my loyalty to him. I will still travel by train, in a second-class compartment if Shyam Babu required me to do so and I would be happy with any role he gives me, unmindful of the financial 'brass tacks'.

Then came *Yatra*, a journey that became my personal journey, from Kanyakumari to Ladakh. This was a unique experience. Several actors and artistes travelled across the length and breadth of India in forty-five days and as the journey progressed, actors from different states joined us, using their traditions of the performing arts. Only Shyam could have had the creative imagination for a magnificent work of these proportions. This was like a discovery of India by train!

I may never have been part of this journey if Shyam had not come to my rescue. My daughter Ishitta was in Class III at the Arya Vidya Mandir and I had no babysitter, so she could not be left behind. I expressed my problem to him and his reaction was immediate. He offered to write a letter to the principal, asking her to allow Ishitta to travel with the unit saying that for a child what could be a better source of learning than this trip? His letter was so impressive that the principal permitted Ishitta to miss class for a month and a half. Thus, she became part of the repertory of Shyam's films. She was given the role of my daughter, with Rajendra Gupta as her father, in an episode on *nautanki*. I had a coupe for myself and her and very often when I was on the sets, she would be watched over by a member of the cast who was free. Usually, it was K.K. Raina, our director now and one of the founders of our forty-year-old theatre group, Surnai. One day, KK felt sleepy while entertaining her. So, he lay down and said, '*Main mar gaya*,' pretending to be dead. But when Ishitta put her hand around his throat to wake him up and he jumped up in fright, Ishitta spontaneously coined these lines, '*Acting ke liye mar jaate hain log. Thoda sa gala dabao, dar jate hain log!*' (People will die to act. But if you squeeze their necks a little, they get scared). When these lines were repeated to Shyam, he burst into laughter and said he would include this in the dialogue for a scene between her and Harish Patel. So not only did Ishitta have a chance to work with a director of Shyam's status, but at the age of seven, she wrote her own two-liner for him too.

Yatra was a true example of togetherness, of bonding and understanding our fellow actors—we travelled together, cooked our meals and washed our clothes, helped each other with our lines and suggestions, and displayed the spirit of *ekta*, a unity in diversity, which was the purpose of *Yatra*. Someone has said that 'travel is the only thing you buy that makes you richer' and how right he was!

Shyam recognized and respected talent. He allowed his actors to improvise and give their own inputs. I was given several opportunities to use my musical and writing talent. His confidence in me provided a platform to use my creative abilities. I became an actor, singer and composer in Shyam's repertory. While shooting a scene, he would suddenly say, 'Ila, you are a singer, why don't you compose a song for this scene?' And somehow, from somewhere, words and music would flow effortlessly into an appropriate composition. While we were shooting for *Susman* in Pochampally, in Telengana, Shyam said, 'Ila, why don't you sing something in this film, perhaps a song related to weaving?' It was a film on the weavers of *ikkat* in Andhra. I sang, '*Charkha Chale . . .*' one of the poems of the poet, Kabir, and I composed the tune and sang it too. It was an impromptu performance, but Rajiv Menon, who was at the camera, was ecstatic. And I sang this without any instrumental accompaniment. When Vanraj Bhatia, the music director, heard it, he decided to retain my composition and said that the only instrument that could be used was the *ektara*, which would not intrude upon my voice and words. The song brought out the loneliness and isolation of my character, a young woman living with an alcoholic husband and depending on her *charkha*, her spinning wheel, for company. This song became a hit, and I was touched when Dhruv, my son-in-law, who was cast in the film as a child actor, asked me to sing that song when he became a successful music director himself. That song had remained in his memory all these years.

I had a small role in *Trikal*, that of a young *kunbi* woman as a helper in the mansion of the Souzasuarez family. Shyam then gave me a great responsibility, that of taking on the role of the lyricist in the film. For me, it was a golden opportunity to discover the real Goa, as I had to travel every day on my free days, to Remo Fernandes's house in Siolim, as he was the singer along with Alisha Chinai. Remo was not very fluent in Hindi, so I had to work on the songs with him. Vanraj Bhatia, the music director, had not arrived in Goa, so I was the virtual tutor to Remo. I would also accompany Saba, the costume designer, on her last-minute forays into the Goan markets looking for accessories and jewellery for the characters. No one could point a finger at me since Shyam himself had given me several mantles to wear!

Shyam is a genius at creating stories around social issues and political tussles. He was commissioned to do a film on soya bean farming in Madhya Pradesh. The documentary was in two parts. The first part featured Neena Gupta and K.K. Raina as a new bride and bridegroom, respectively. The bridegroom did not want any dowry, but since his bride was the daughter of a soya bean farmer, he wanted her to bring the seeds of the soya bean plant as dowry! On their first night together, the traditional *suhaag raat*, the bridegroom asks his bride to explain the seven steps needed in the farming of the plant. Shyam turned to me and said, 'Why don't you compose and sing a *suhaag geet* related to this seven-fold process?' Seven! That magical number, the *satlada*, the seven-stringed necklace that had been the first gift I had indulged in for myself from the proceeds of my first acting assignment with Shyam! My imagination took wing and my necklace took centre stage. In my composition, the bride asks her husband to get her a necklace with seven strings as with each string she incorporates each of the seven steps! That is why I lay so much emphasis on total recall for an actor. One never knows how incidents and things related to your past can be used in your performance. So, it was with my seven strings, put away in a locker since I first wore them but significant enough to still be present in my thoughts!

I worked on another project with Shyam when he approached me to help him with a film he was making on Carmen. I suggested that he should place it within the community of the *kaalbeliyas*, the traditional snake charmers and folk dancers of Rajasthan. He agreed and we did a lot of research on this tribe. I also wrote several songs for this film along with Javed Akhtar. Both of us spent some time with A.R. Rahman, the music director of the film, even recording three songs. But the film *Chamki* did not see the light of day because I think Shyam could not find a suitable actor to play the lead role. It would be a wonderful film if he could revive it, but perhaps that is a thing of the past now.

I learnt a very important lesson while working with Shyam in *Trikal*. I had a small role in the film, but I had to be ready and on the sets, waiting for my entry. Sometimes it would take a whole day of waiting and sometimes my shot would not be taken at all. It is strange how an actor responds to her situation. I did feel that not only was I doing the role of a cook's helper, but I was being sidelined on the sets. While the lead actors dressed in beautiful costumes, I wore the same old sari in my scenes. Soni and Neena would pull my leg and ask me why my shot had not been taken. Provoked by these remarks, one day, as I waited, I must have shown my irritation. After pack-up, Shyam summoned me and said, 'Girl, in this profession you can never get restless and impatient. You will be called for a shot sooner or later. And one more thing, remember, an actor never questions a director on this point. This should be the first and last time that you ever voice this restlessness!' I have taken his advice to heart and have learnt to wait in the wings, no matter how long the wait is!

Whenever I worked with Shyam, I learnt a lot because his fund of knowledge was so vast that he could talk on any subject, from making Gujarati snacks, such as *dhoklas* and *khandvis*, to being a connoisseur of wine and gourmet food, every aspect of politics, history, geography, art and architecture, music and dance; there was no subject he could not discuss at length. He has a finger on the pulse of the socio-political environment of the time. Naturally, his films too dealt with varied subjects. Living in a village with *ikkat* weavers for *Susman* exposed me to the art and also to the difficulties faced by weavers. I understood the value of the co-operative movement which protected the weavers. In *Mandi*, he humanized and demystified the lives of sex workers, bringing women centre stage. The struggle to retain their home in the face of the greed of politicians and realtors was a problem that many in India face. Again, the greed for grabbing land was depicted in *Well Done Abba*, where a huge *baori*, or step-well, disappeared from its location. This was the last film that my mother saw and she identified with it since such incidents have been taking place in small towns where wells and ponds have become redundant and the land occupied by illicit means. I composed a song for this film too, a wedding song titled '*Meri Banno Hoshiyar*' and both Boman and I danced to it in the wedding scene. *Welcome to Sajjanpur*, a satire on politics and society, could be termed a black comedy, but my role in it was made for me and Shyam gave me a lot of leeway to interpret it in my own way. I enjoyed every moment of it and recalling the idiosyncrasies of rural middle-class women, I was able to create a character within the frame prescribed by Shyam. This character caught the imagination of the public and my performance is on top of the list whenever anyone talks about the film and I have my director to thank for it!

When I look around my house, memories of time spent on Shyam's sets are before my eyes, on my walls which bear mementos of my travels either with my husband or with Shyam. When I travelled to Uzbekistan for *Netaji Subhas Chandra Bose: The Forgotten Hero*, my role was short but the schedule was long, so I was able to explore the country. Kulbhushan and I were co-stars, so both of us were free at the same time. We would set off for sightseeing, accompanied by enthusiasts Nira and Pia Benegal, and Atul Tiwari. Since the food was totally unpalatable to us Indians, we were always grateful for anything we could eat. We discovered huge *naans* being baked on the streets, their aroma enticing our taste buds, and we would sit down to devour those freshly baked breads. Wherever we went, we were greeted by Bollywood songs and Indian films on TV. Raj Kapoor was a great favourite, and I was goaded on by my friends to sing and dance to his songs for the benefit of the locals. They would sing along in their own words and often joined me in the dance. On one occasion, we stopped for the bread and I decided to spice it up a bit with some potato which they had. Dancing to the words of '*Joota hai Japani*', I gave the Uzbek cooks a lesson in Indian cooking, each line accompanied by an instruction. *Mera joota hai Japani* (put in the oil), *Yeh patloon Hindustani* (cumin and turmeric), etc. Our meal was delicious, an *aloo-bharta* with the Uzbeki *naans*, with a touch of melody . . . Ah! I have collected porcelain from remote areas—Uzbekistan, Afghanistan, Kazakhstan and different designs of coats from Eastern Europe which I think suit my personality! Each time we returned from our shopping, Shyam would give us the background and history of the article we had purchased! Of course, I wish the paintings and souvenirs on my walls had tongues and not ears so that I could remember all the wisdom garnered from Shyam!

I cannot deny that I was disappointed when he did not include me in the project on *Zubeidaa* (2001). I am from Jodhpur, so I could have contributed a lot since I understand the character, the language and the traditions of that location. I would have loved to have done *Sardari Begum* (1996) too, but the director thought otherwise!

My first brush with the film world also gave me a lot of insight into the psyche of the players on the sets. I watched the manipulation of actresses, the attempt to get close to the director or the cinematographer, the understated steps for upstaging a co-star—and I, as an observer and an actor, realized that there are many untold stories that surround the players in a film unit. Perhaps I too was tempted to join this rat race at some point, but my mother's warning, '*Avesh mein vivek mat khona*,' brought me back to reality and her clapperboard brought the curtain down before the show had even begun! Besides, I was still a small-town girl from Rajasthan, a simple *daal-kachori* among the *rasmalai* of seasoned actresses.

My era is almost over, but I have been enriched by my association with teachers and mentors like Shyam Babu and Alkazi Sahib.

To them, I owe all that I have achieved in my profession and in my life. Many friendships have been forged during my films with Shyam—I count Shabana, Neena, Soni and the late Om Puri among my close friends and know that the common bond of being Shyam's actors will always keep us together.

My relationship has outlived all my assignments with Shyam Benegal, and I sometimes wonder how many of the members of his repertory are in touch with him. I consider myself fortunate that suddenly out of the blue the phone rings and Shyam's voice comes across, 'Ila, how are you? And how is your daughter? What are you doing these days?'

One phone call drew me to his house recently. I had wanted to see him and find out about his health, but knowing that he was not too well, I did not pursue the thought. Till I got a call from Nandita Puri, saying that she would fix a visit with Shyam for me. I was delighted. Shyam Babu makes it a point to attend office whenever he can and that is where I was to meet him. Once again, I climbed the same steps to his office, each step symbolizing each year that I had spent in his company, under his direction.

And there in his room, Shyam Babu gave me the same warm smile that is reserved for his friends and actors. Time stood still and the years overlapped in a maze of thoughts and words. We talked of the past and when I asked him what he missed the most in his retirement from film-making, he said it was the location shooting! As I have mentioned before, Shyam Babu's location shooting was the most delightful part of working with him. In my mind I relived all those occasions, the community living and the close bonds I had formed with each film. Those were moments of joy and hope and in Winnie the Pooh's innocent words, 'We didn't realize we were making memories, we just knew we were having fun!'

The poster of my first film *Mandi*

As Shyam Babu saw me out, I suggested that we take a photograph in front of the poster for *Susman*. Pointing to the poster for *Mandi*, he said, 'Why not this?' My first film with Shyam Benegal! Since 'sometimes memories sneak out of my eyes and roll down my cheeks', I turned my head away and bade farewell to my mentor, carrying with me a short note from him: 'My dear Ila, you were the actress, singer, cook and all-round handy person on all the film productions in which we had the good fortune to work together . . . Those were the days . . . much love and best wishes always, Shyam (19/6/24).'

I walked down the staircase, with the sound of his voice following me, the same voice that had informed me over my grocer's old landline phone saying, 'Girl, come to my office tomorrow. You are in the film.'

Was it forty years ago, or was it just yesterday?

A.K. Hangal

Bandh gali ka aakhri makaan, an inconspicuous dwelling two streets away from me, a lonely home that once was the centre of creative activity, a home that is uninhabited now—I am not talking of Dharamvir Bharati's well-known story by the same name, but the modest dwelling of actor A.K. Hangal: 4th Road, Santa Cruz (East), next to the railway tracks.

My flat, just around the corner, is on the main road. And it was through Hangal Sahib that this became my home, the first flat that actually belonged to Arun and me.

I first met Hangal Sahib in Jaipur when the Indian Peoples' Theatre Association (IPTA) was visiting with its play *Shatranj Ke Mohre*. It was a wonderful play and a great event for all theatre-goers in Jaipur. When I heard that some well-known theatre artistes were coming to Jaipur from Bombay, I could not contain my excitement and arrived at the green room unannounced, carrying a bouquet of flowers. My first sight of A.K. Hangal was his mirror image as he sat in front of the mirror, ready, going through his script. It was a well-known fact that Hangal Sahib never gave up this practice of his. Before the first bell, twenty minutes before the curtain rose, he would be concentrating on his lines, no matter how many shows he had been through. This was the discipline he carried forward in his life too.

There was an instant rapport between us, and I met him several times during his visit. When he heard that I was associated with the theatre in Jaipur, he talked to me about the theatre scene in Bombay and about IPTA. He was keen that I contact him if I ever came to Bombay and he would introduce me to the theatre world.

In 1979, when Arun and I decided to move to Mumbai, Hangal Sahib insisted that wherever we chose to stay, we should make sure that we were close to Prithvi Theatre, a new performing place built by Jennifer and Shashi Kapoor in memory of the stalwart screen idol, Prithviraj Kapoor. The other alternative would be that we stayed close to his home. It so happened that we bought a flat in Santa Cruz East, 7th Road, which was two streets away from Hangal Sahib and a bare 15-minute drive from Prithvi. And so, Paradise Apartment became our home and has been so till today, forty years later. Hangal Sahib became our neighbour, and as time went by, he became a beloved member of our family too.

It was through him that I was first introduced to the theatre world in Bombay through his group IPTA. He would take me to all their meetings, to rehearsals and to performances. He hoped that I would eventually become a member of IPTA. I enjoyed the interaction with IPTA but was conscious that this theatre movement was a leftist group, considered to be the cultural wing of the Communist Party of India. It was started during the Bengal Famine, to protest against the brutal handling of the famine by the British government. The history of IPTA runs parallel to the people's cultural movement in the country and relates to the independence and the anti-fascist movements. IPTA came into existence on 25 May 1943 at the National Conference at the Marwari School in Bombay. It was attended by creative artistes from all over the country. In his presidential address, Professor Hiren Mukherjee gave a call to all those present: 'Come writer and the artist, come actor and the playwright, come all who work by hand or by brain, dedicate yourselves to the task of building a brave new world of freedom and social justice.' IPTA was built on an ideology, a belief in the existence of a just and equal world and was started by members of the Progressive Writers' Association and its first president was none other than Munshi Premchand. IPTA was branded as the vehicle of communist thought and its members were often accused of being anti-national. Hangal Sahib was an activist and a proponent of communist ideology. He was passionate about theatre, specially IPTA.

I did not want to be aligned with any political ideology or cause. For me, all theatre was inspiring and I was longing to explore every aspect of it in Bombay. I told Hangal Sahib this and he understood my dilemma and henceforth did not persuade me to join IPTA. Thus, I did not do any play with them since only members were allowed to be part of the IPTA repertory. I was sometimes a judge for their play competitions, attended several play readings and watched all their performances. He also helped us to find rehearsal space for our plays when we could not afford too much rent.

A few pages on Hangal Sahib are really not sufficient to describe the man, especially by me, who knew him so closely. This was one being who had the demeanour of an old man even in his youth! His voice also had a hint of age and as far as hair was concerned, well there seemed to be no relationship with that human accessory and Hangal Sahib! But he was *shaukeen*, fond of the good life, like the title of a film he acted in, in 1982, directed by Basu Chatterjee. He loved good food and, of course, was known for his sartorial elegance in the film and theatre world. He was always well-dressed and very often would comment sardonically on peoples' casual attitude towards their appearance. He had a critical eye for clothes since he had started his professional life as a tailor in Peshawar.

It became a ritual for Hangal Sahib to come and have dinner with us at least two or three times a year. Though it was an informal affair, he would come not as a neighbour dropping in for a casual meal but dressed to the hilt as if he were coming for a party. When expecting visitors, he was always in his silk *lungi*, a fashion followed by many in the film industry, including Raj Kumar (Jaani). I remember an occasion when Hangal Sahib and my husband Arun and I were going on a book launch together. Hangal Sahib came in a suit, replete with a pocket handkerchief. Arun was in a T-shirt, which for him seemed appropriate enough. But Hangal Sahib gave him one look and asked me quietly, 'Is he going like this?' Arun had to change!

I was not spared either. One day after seeing me performing on the stage for a Filmfare Award Function, he complimented me on the energy I brought to the stage but did add a word of advice, or should I say caution? 'Remember, you are short. Always wear long, flowing dresses. This adds to your height.' The tailor's eye and scrutiny were always present.

Hangal Sahib had two flats on the same floor of the same building. He and his wife lived in one and the other flat was occupied by his only child, Vijay. His living room was small, but his heart was big. And he loved celebrating his birthday. Every year, he would invite about fifteen of his close friends, who would somehow cram themselves into that tiny space. There would be singing and banter and the telling of stories. It was at one such gathering that I discovered his expertise in playing the harmonium. He celebrated his birthday on 15 August, the day India gained independence. This was not his actual birthday since like my mother, his parents also did not know the actual date of his birth. So as a true patriot, who had even been to jail during the freedom struggle, he chose this day as his official birthday. His childlike enthusiasm and excitement as his birthday approached could not but have an impact on those around him. My excitement also escalated as his birthday came closer.

His reclusive wife, a Kashmiri like him, was very seldom seen. But as I stood on my balcony, I used to see her, at 5 p.m. sharp, carrying a bag, on her way to buy vegetables from the nearby bazaar. Dressed in a white sari, hair a dazzling white, she was the embodiment of simplicity and elegance. Each day, Anita, Meena and I would watch her as she walked to the market. Suddenly, one day she stopped coming and Hangal Sahib called me a day later to tell me that she was no more.

Their simple and unassuming life taught me many lessons. He had acted in numerous films, many of which broke box-office records, but his lifestyle always remained simple. And yet in his public persona, he was always perfectly dressed. He believed that we were in the film industry and should always be 'tip-top'. In this field, you could not afford to let your guard down. Everybody wore a mask, an inscrutable barrier to his or her personal life.

Once when I went to see him, Hangal Sahib was surrounded by what looked like postcards with his photograph on them. He was busy signing thousands of these cards. This was an era when there was no social media. The stars' secretaries would send these personally signed photographs to all the fans who sent letters of praise to their favourite actor so that their tribe increased. He said that he received so many birthday greetings from his fans that he felt he must thank them by sending his photograph with a thank-you note. He then told me, 'When you make a name in this industry, never disappoint your fans.' Those words stuck in my mind and today though one does not need to send notes because of social media, whenever I am at an airport or in a public place and fans come to me to take a selfie, I always pose with them no matter how many times I have to stop for these photos. I never tire or get irritated since these are the people who have helped me get where I am today. Without our fans, we are non-existent. Imagine my delight when three generations of one family come and tell me that they have been dancing to my songs. It boosts my morale and confidence and is the elixir that keeps me going.

A.K. Hangal was an amazing storyteller. Stories from his time at the jail, of Partition, theatre anecdotes, tales of his film and television experiences, his communist days—he told these with such eloquence that you listened fascinated, begging for more.

After the passing away of his wife, we became even closer. I told him that whenever he felt like eating hot *rotis*, he should just call Anita or Meena, the soul and spirit of my household, and the meals would be delivered to him, irrespective of whether I was there or not.

In his later years, when he did not have much work and was not keeping good health, I told him I would host his birthday parties. Unfortunately, his daughter-in-law also passed away soon after his wife, so there was no woman to manage his household. He would tell me the number of guests expected and I would order food from the best-known caterer of the film industry, Laakhan. Hangal Sahib had seen every aspect of life, he had gone through the whole gamut— bad days and good days, days of glory and days of neglect, days of felicitations and days of despondency, days of abundance and days of poverty, busy days, days of idleness, days filled with laughter and days of loneliness, and then finally days of poor health.

I must recount one interesting episode in connection with Hangal Sahib. When my daughter Ishitta was getting married, I had planned many functions to celebrate the wedding since I had to return the hospitality and invitations of so many people in the film industry who had invited me for similar functions in all the forty years I had been associated with the film world. There were five or six events, to which various friends and acquaintances from the industry were invited. Hangal Sahib was invited for all the functions, which he happily attended. A few days after the wedding, there was a call from him. Instead of lauding me for my hard work and organizational skills, he said, 'Ila, so many functions are a waste of money. You could have done with less.' I wanted to remind him about his birthday parties, which he celebrated with such enthusiasm and which I had been hosting for so many years! For me, my daughter's wedding was a once-in-a-lifetime event and he had admonished me for making it an elaborate affair! Of course, he believed that the life of an actor is unpredictable, with many ups and downs, and one has to save for any eventuality, especially illness, since actors do not have any insurance either. In the twilight of one's career, when work and money run out, no friend or relation comes to your aid.

And so, it came to pass. His last days were days of misery. Several friends did help him financially. He was old and so was his only son, Vijay, who looked after him to the end. The day came when this brave warrior, actor and crusader admitted defeat and gave up. As he lay on the floor, there were just a few of his friends, IPTA members and people from the nearby *basti* of Golibar, whose cause he championed. There were people of all faiths from Golibar—Hindu, Muslim, Sikh and Christian—to bid farewell to this secular being who would now be a presence only on the screen in his various avatars. But there were no mask-wearing faces from the film industry; those masks now stood removed. As I watched the flames consume his mortal remains, these lines from an Urdu poet came to mind: '*Daba ke kabr mein sab chal diye, na dua na salaam, zara si der mein kya ho gaya zamane ko?*' (They have buried him in his grave without a blessing or a farewell. How has the world changed in a moment?)

I have seen Hangal Sahib in many roles, behind many curtains: a TV screen, the big screen, the stage. I have encountered him in many forms, in many places. Behind these varied curtains was hidden a unique human being who lived many roles. He was a dedicated and principled man, a theatre actor par excellence, a Bollywood actor with a huge fan following, a revolutionary working towards equality in a communistic society, a tailor, and above all, a great patriot.

Today, as I walk on my terrace, beyond the laden trees, I can see that *bandh gali ka aakhri makaan*, the last house in a dead-end lane.

Many thoughts race through my mind, sped on by the clanging of the local train on the tracks near his house, which now lies silent and mysterious.

A.K. Hangal was born in Sialkot, in the Peshawar district of undivided India. To the end of his life, he had a yearning for his *janmabhoomi*, his birthplace. There were barbs on his nationalism when he was invited to the Pakistani Embassy once on 14 August, the Pakistani Independence Day. There were calls to wrest his Padma Shri from him since he was pronounced a traitor. It was as if a man had been denied his place on earth, the place where he was born and has lived for several years. Perhaps now Bombay was his *karmabhoomi*, where he worked and died.

In his last interview, A.K. Hangal had said, 'If you start with a hero's role, that's all you'll remain. You'll never become an actor.' He was truly an actor, a man of many parts and, for me, he was a hero too!

Shabana Azmi

We were celebrating the fortieth anniversary of our theatre group, Surnai, at Prithvi. I had invited a few veterans of the theatre world to inaugurate the festival by lighting a lamp. Shabana Azmi was one of them. As we waited on the patio of Prithvi, ready to light the lamp, with all the other celebrities present, I got a call from Shabana. She said she would not be able to make it since she was stuck in a traffic jam. She apologized. Sulking I said, 'It's okay.' Her voice came over the phone: 'What do you mean by okay? How can I let you down? I am standing outside Prithvi!' I was aghast when she came and gave me a big hug. 'How could I miss this? I wanted to tease you! Are you mad?' This was the phrase she usually flung at me, my mad friend Shabana Azmi.

Shabana, *raat ka pahar*, that time of evening, which is deemed to be the best time of the day or night, the mysterious hour when nature displays its dreamy moments. It is a Farsi word, a mellow sound that conveys sweetness and beauty. And that is how I perceive her, the beloved daughter of Kaifi and Shaukat Azmi, Shabana Azmi.

Our friendship started with *Mandi*. The location was a two-hour drive from the city. She, being a star, had a car at her disposal to take her to the sets. But seeing us lesser actors enjoying ourselves singing in the bus assigned to us, she got out of her car and climbed onto our bus, never to go back again. She is a treasure house of old songs. Our pastime on the bus was playing *antakshari*. She had a song for every letter we stopped at and surpassed all of us in her quick responses. She is also fond of folk songs and perhaps that became a special bond between us. I would sing Rajasthani songs for her and often she would join me. She insisted on learning a song. I have forgotten it by now, but she still remembers it. It was composed by my friend from Jaipur, Himmat Singh, and the words were: '*Mhare Dhaura Kun Ave . . .*' She has learnt the words and tune perfectly and can perhaps sing it better than I can! It is always fun being around her. She has a great sense of humour and loves talking to her friends. Often unknown to them she would subtly pull their leg. Sometimes she is not even aware of her words and is quite surprised when someone remarks on it. When one of us admonished her for that, she would feign innocence and apologize, and we would forget and forgive!

She often called me to her house, which was in Janki Kutir at Juhu. That home still stands, even though she has moved into Sagar Samrat. Janki Kutir was an artiste's home, like mine, very simple, with jute chairs, Gujarati mirrorwork cushions and chosen artefacts. It spoke of the people who inhabited it: the poet Kaifi Azmi and his actress–wife Shaukat Appa, along with their equally talented children, Shabana and Baba. It was as if poetry and *shairi* permeated the atmosphere. It was in the air, in the simple objects that adorned the house, it was there in the gatherings of creative people in that home, the warm hospitality of a welcoming house. There could not have been a better place where one could imbibe the nuances of language and letters. The doors of that home were always open and one was sure to meet some well-known personality in the field of theatre, film and literature. It was here that I was introduced to Mahesh Bhatt by Shabana. And it was here too that I was chosen by Mahesh to sing my first playback song for the film *Ashiana* (1986): '*Jawani Re Mein Kaise Katoon Re*.' The music was given by Jagjit Singh and the lyrics were mine. It was a lively gypsy song and Aarti Gupta enlivened it with her dance.

I was fortunate to have Shabana as my friend. My association with her brought me close to Kaifi Sahib, whom I addressed as Abba, just like she did, and to Shaukat Appa, both of who gave me the love and affection only parents can give. Shabana's relationship with her parents was a source of joy for me. She had a close bond with them and was a great companion to both Abba and Shaukat Appa.

Janki Kutir was the epitome of secularism. Every festival, regardless of its religious association, was celebrated with equal gusto. People of different religious denominations and faiths would sit together to sing and recite poetry and later partake of the feast, which marked every festival.

Shabana and I went on to do several films together with Shyam Benegal: *Antarnaad, Mandi* and *Susman*, as well as several episodes of *Discovery of India* and *Yatra*. She was a part of Shyam's repertory even when she had moved on to commercial roles. Shyam has recounted several anecdotes about Shabana, a couple of which I would like to take the liberty to repeat. When Shabana came for an audition for Shyam's film, *Ankur* (1974), she appeared with plucked eyebrows, definitely unsuitable for her role as a Dalit girl from a poor peasant family. Of course, she did not get the role. Fortunately, since no actress at the time was ready to accept an unglamorous role, she was asked to come again. This time, she came with the 'right' face and made such an impact that she received the National Award for her performance. The other story concerned me. We were both shooting for an episode on Gandhi for *Discovery of India*. I was playing the role of a village woman who worked as a volunteer for the Mahatma. I was supposed to march in a contingent of women and when Shabana saw me, she remarked to Shyam that I had obviously worked hard at my role since my uncoordinated march looked like that of an illiterate woman, with my left arm and leg moving together in awkward steps. Little did she know that I had just not been able to master a simple march moving the opposite arms and legs together! Shyam laughed and told her my plight, which had been mistaken for good acting. During the shoots with Shyam, Shabana and I found we had similar tastes and I remember when shooting with weavers from Andhra for *Susman*, we would go into the village close to our rural locations to look for handloom material, ethnic jewellery and other knick-knacks for gifts. At the end of our shopping, we found to our amazement that we had selected the same designs and patterns.

Shabana's flight into the extraordinary has taken her far from her known frontiers into a world of film and theatre; in fact, all the performing arts. Her personality is such that you cannot but be impressed by her. Not only has she left a stamp on the vast canvas of the national and international cinema scene, but she has also used her voice for several social and political causes. Having spent a considerable time with her, I have seen Shabana in her various avatars. She is reflective not only about her career but also about politics, civil society, gender and religion. I have witnessed Shabana's involvement in social causes. She was an activist, who despite being a celebrity, would stage *dharna*s in support of slum-dwellers and other marginalized groups. She was genuinely concerned about the issues she supported and championed, and did not hesitate to air her views in public. She is passionate about women's position in society and has said, 'In a patriarchal society like ours, women have to fight hard for a seat at the table. Boys are privileged over girls from birth. Equal opportunity and access for both girls and boys must become the norm.'

I had the opportunity to travel to Pakistan with Shabana and Javed Bhai and they made it a memorable visit for me. We were at the same hotel and Shabana and Javed would insist that I accompany them when they went out shopping or visiting their friends. Since Shabana was very close to Faiz Ahmed Faiz's family, his daughters showed us around Lahore. I discovered that we had a similar dressing sense. Once we went shopping for clothes, the beautiful Pakistani *salwaar-kameez*, which was very popular in India at the time. We took at least twelve or thirteen sets into the trial room and bought them all! When we displayed our shopping to each other at the hotel, lo and behold, we had picked exactly the same clothes. Amazed, we both burst out laughing. Shabana said this was an unbelievable coincidence but swore to be careful not to wear the same dresses as me to a venue in India. But one day it so happened that despite all our efforts, we did arrive at Prithvi Theatre dressed in the same clothes! Shabana was sporting enough to genuinely treat it as a cause for amusement rather than complaint.

One more episode in Pakistan stands out in my memory. Shabana and Javed went out shopping for carpets in the Lahore bazaar, taking me along with them. That was the time when they were building their holiday home in Lonavla, a retreat from the hurly-burly of

Mumbai life. The film *Khal Nayak* had done very well at the box office as had the number '*Choli Ke Peechhey*', which I had sung as a duet with Alka Yagnik. With it, I had achieved some fame and popularity not only in India, but its strains had reverberated in Pakistan too. The carpet seller recognized me and asked me whether I intended to buy a carpet too. Now I am very fond of carpets but know that it is very difficult to maintain handmade carpets in the humidity of Mumbai. Besides I had already collected several carpets on my travels, from Uzbekistan, Iran, Turkey, Kashmir and Rajasthan. My mother always told us that *utni hi chadar phailao jitney lambe pair*, meaning, don't live beyond your means. Every time she visited me in Mumbai, after a good meal, she would sit down and with both her hands on the floor, measure the area of my flat. And it always fell short of her expectations for her star daughter. I always had her wise sayings in my subconscious. But finding it difficult to resist the temptation, I also succumbed and bought two carpets. I was just reaching out for the third when I heard Shabana's voice, a perfect reminder of my mother's voice saying, '*Arre,* why are you buying so many carpets? You have a small flat in Mumbai.' Shabana had made a pulp of my reputation and *izzat* in the bazaars of Pakistan! I was close to tears and didn't know where to look. Javed saw my plight and very deftly tried to save the situation by saying, 'Ila has six or seven flats in Mumbai. All these carpets will find a place in one of them.' He then asked the salesman to pack up the third carpet too. Yes, it was a question of my *izzat*, but it is fifteen years since this episode, perhaps more. To this day, those carpets are lying in my Versova flat in their original plastic packing, remnants of my *izzat* pleading to be let out! Shopping sprees with Shabana always ended with me loosening my purse strings, like in the case of the *satlada* necklace from Hyderabad, which still lies forgotten somewhere in my cupboard.

My association with Shabana permeated down to my family members too, especially my mother. It all began with a book. My mother was very fond of reading. Once when visiting me in Mumbai, she was looking for something to read. I handed her the book by Shaukat Appa, *Kaifi Aur Mein,* the story of her life with Kaifi Sahib. The next morning, at tea, she said, 'Ila, Shabana's mother had to struggle a lot in her early life. Living in a commune couldn't have been easy. And yet their love survived all those difficulties.' I asked her how she had finished reading the book so fast since I had given it to her only the previous night. She said that if a book interested her, she could finish it in no time. She had taken just about six hours to finish this book, which had given her an insight into the life and times of people who believed in the socialist idea of India. After reading this book, she expressed a wish to meet Shabana's mother.

Some years later, as I looked at the two of them sitting together on a sofa at Ishitta's wedding, presenting a picture of elegance and grandeur in traditional silk saris, my heart was filled with joy at the thought that my mother's wish had been fulfilled. Shabana and my mother too developed a bond and Shabana visited her several times at our home in Jaipur and the conversation between them would carry on for hours.

When my mother passed away, my two good friends—Shabana Azmi and Jaya Bachchan—came for the *baithak*, condolence prayers, on my brother Piyush's terrace. I can imagine my mother proudly and affectionately saying, '*Dekho*, Jaya and Shabana both came for me.' I looked at Shabana and realized that she could see my pain, just as I had seen the agony in her eyes when I went to Shaukat Appa's funeral. I could see the helplessness and the sense of loss and bereavement, and I knew that here was a friend who could identify with me. I had gone to Abba's funeral too when Shabana, breaking all tradition, had put the symbolic *matti* on his grave, a ritual performed only by men. Her devotion to her parents and the *seva*, or service, she did for them was touching. She has carried on the task her father had taken on to support the women of his village at Mijwan in UP. She is fulfilling her father's dream of empowering the women in the village by training them in the art of *chikankari*, a technique of embroidery from Lucknow and its surrounding areas. Schoolgirls there have been given computers and other educational tools, bringing them on par with schoolgirls in urban areas.

As I look back over the forty years of our friendship, I see an eager, intelligent, young woman, now a woman who has aged gracefully and conducts herself with utmost dignity and maturity. She is and will always be a woman of substance, a woman who believes 'that art should be used as an instrument of social change'.

As I have said before, Shabana loves to tease her friends and pull their legs. If Shabana can pull my leg, professing innocence, I have decided that I can do that too. After seeing *Rocky Aur Rani Ki Prem*

Kahani (2023), I called her up and told her in a despondent voice that she had always been my role model, but it pained me to see her in a kissing scene with Dharmendra, and that I was contemplating finding a new role model. But can I ever do that? Not in this life, nor in the next, or next, or next! Love you, Shabana.

Rekha

As I often repeat, I have never overstepped my limits, my *rekha*, but I did get a chance to work with the Rekha of the film industry. It was in a film called *Jaal* (1986). I had a chance encounter with her once when she stepped out of her car at the gate of Janki Kutir, where she had come to visit Shabana Azmi. Across from the gate is Prithvi Theatre and often after a rehearsal or a performance, we would bump into Shabana. Sometimes we would also accompany her to her house. One day, as I stood talking to Shabana, a car stopped at the gate and out of it emerged Rekha, who joined us. My daughter, Ishitta, four years old at the time, said in her childish voice, '*Retha, Retha, maine apko kal TV par detha!*' (Retha, Retha, I saw you on the television yesterday!)

Rekha burst into laughter and kept asking her to repeat herself at least ten times. She asked her several times, '*Kahan per detha? Phit se bolo.*' Shabana too was amused and could not control her laughter. Finally, she said, 'Retha, stop this. The child will get tired.' This strange conversation was the beginning of my relationship with Rekha. As luck would have it, a few days later, I was called by Umesh Mehra to act in his film *Jaal*. Umesh had also seen two episodes of my TV show, *Showtime,* the ones set in a village and heard me sing too. He had called me himself after seeing the show. He was keen that I act and sing in the film. This film was my introduction to Hindi films as a singer and procured several singing contracts for me. My first song was '*Raina Bawri Bhayi Re*', set to music by Anu Malik. I was cast as the mother of Mandakini, a popular actress at the time. Other than Rekha, the film also had Mithun Chakraborty and Jeetendra. I was new and perhaps this was my first commercial film. But once again I had the same problem. Arun was out at sea, and I had no one to look after Ishitta. Umesh Mehra came up with the suggestion that I should take Ishitta with me since his daughter, around the same age, was also going with them and she would have an *ayah* with them to look after her. Ishitta would also be under her supervision when I was shooting. Jeetendra's daughter, Ekta Kapoor, was also travelling with them, so the children had a good time. Ekta is now one of the most prolific and sought-after directors. So, the next day, I set out, bag on one shoulder, Ishitta holding my other hand, to join the team at Ootacamund, now Udhagamandalam, a beautiful hill station in the Nilgiris.

Ishitta did have a good time. I don't know whether Ekta remembers or not, but Ishitta spent a considerable amount of time in her room, watching television, which was still a novelty. Not all rooms in a hotel had televisions, but Ekta was allowed one and the girls would huddle in one room and watch Doordarshan, the only available channel at the time. All these actors would travel with their tools for entertainment: VCRs, hundreds of cassettes, etc. For Ishitta, it was a bonanza! Since it was the mango season, the stars carried cartons of mangoes with them, which were generously distributed among the unit members. Ishitta got a fair share of those too. This experience did make Ishitta realize that there was a marked difference in the life of star children and the children of strugglers. But Ishitta's spirits soared when one day Rekha, on seeing her on the sets, ran to Ishitta and asked her to repeat the sentence that had caused much laughter and bonding at Janki Kutir. She would not leave before Ishitta had obliged her before the whole unit. From that day, every time Rekha was free, she would lift Ishitta up onto her lap and listen to her baby talk. Rekha was so enamoured of Ishitta that she even offered to babysit her in her hotel room when I was shooting. Rekha had a Lhasa Apso pup, Pishti, who was her constant companion, gifted to her by an admirer.

The shooting was over and we parted company, but the relationship continued.

When I look back over the years, I realize that my admiration for Rekha began while I was still in school. I chanced upon an audio tape of Rekha, conducting yoga classes in two parts. There were no video recordings in those days, but the jacket of the tape had a picture of Rekha, gorgeous in a black yoga suit, in a yoga posture. For several years, I practised yoga following directions given in this tape, mesmerized by Rekha's sonorous, husky voice and soothing music in the background, so much so that in the *Shavasana* posture I was transported to a world of dreams and passed into a deep sleep. I still have that cassette.

What was the secret of this superstar's magic, her beauty, the sparkle when she hit the screen, I could not say. But I was well and truly under her spell.

Sometimes, on one of my lucky days, my phone rings and the sound of the *tanpura* whispers in the background. It is Rekha. She renders one or two new songs she has learnt. Then she asks me how I liked it. I almost vanish into the ground due to guilt or embarrassment. I have been gifted a scale changer by Kalyanji, a Paul harmonium, which is gathering dust, which I have put away in the recesses of my mind and space. Someone has rightly said that when dust covers your musical instruments, it means that your notes and music have also been buried in the sand. You have been alienated from your very being.

Rekha's devotion and pursuit of music and her constant *riyaaz* are perhaps her secret, the sustenance of her fragile but powerful persona, her elusive and youthful beauty. Her disciplined practise of yoga and music is what infuses her with energy and youth. Her fan following is still phenomenal.

I cherish this long and enduring relationship, forged over a chance remark by my daughter and now continuing through our love for music. I am grateful that I have perhaps met the best in the industry, an industry that has taught me a lot about life and people and which still continues to nurture my talent on both the small and the large screen.

Sushmita Sen

It was one of those unbelievably beautiful nights, on an open terrace with a half-moon smiling down on us. I was in Jaipur, shooting for Season 3 of *Aarya*, which is trending on Prime Video. With me was Sushmita Sen, who is the protagonist in the series. This was one of our rare off days together. We were staying at the same hotel, our rooms being across the corridor from each other. We had a few scenes together, so we had a lot to talk about. And somehow, in an informal conversation, we discussed so many incidents and events in our lives that the evening passed by in a flash. There were flashbacks from our lives too. Sushmita and I had worked in a film over eighteen years ago, *Chingaari* (2006), directed by Kalpana Lajmi. I played her foster mother in the film and since then she has always addressed me affectionately as Maa.

Chingaari was shot in a *wada*, a traditional Maharashtrian dwelling, at Wai village in Maharashtra and we were put up in the only resort there. There was Kalpana Lajmi, Mithun Chakraborty, Bhupen Hazarika (the film was based on his novel, *The Prostitute and the Postman*), Sushmita and I. We found a common bond through the armed forces. My brother-in-law and Sushmita's father, both air force officers, were posted together in Guwahati, Assam. There is a unique camaraderie and brotherhood among defence officers and this brought us close and was a comfort zone in our relationship. I was alone. Sushmita had two rooms, one she occupied and the other was for her daughter Renee, who had accompanied her on the shoot and often when I was free, I would spend time with her.

Mithun Da was playing the role of a hypocritical priest, a wolf in sheep's clothing, his priesthood just a cover for his evil ways. His exploitation of women and his complete hold over his devotees had spread fear among the villagers. Sushmita played a village prostitute (Basanti), from whom the priest constantly demanded sexual favours. She was the only one in the village who raised her voice against the misdoings of the priest but could not find any support as no one had the courage to stand with her. Finally, at the end of her tether, Sushmita leads the women of the village in an attack on this despicable man. The scene was a very moving one. Sushmita leads the villagers, wading across the river, with a *dholak* round her neck, which she beats till the end when she kills the priest with a *trishul*, or trident. We both crossed the river together, Sushmita standing tall above me, in a green sari, beating the drum.

There were almost ten takes for this particular scene since there was a huge crowd of actors involved in the shot. Each time, Sushmita, symbolizing Kali, with her long hair hanging loose, came back with the same fire and passion, while the loud, angry beating of the *dholak* shook the landscape like thunder in the sky. Since she was not used to playing this instrument, she had huge blisters on her palms at the end of the final take. Her performance and transformation in the form of Kali still make my hair stand on end.

That day in Jaipur, our conversation brought back many memories. There, under the open sky, a sense of euphoria and nostalgia enveloped us. I remembered how when little Renee would ask her where she came from, Sushmita would draw a heart on a piece of paper and tell her that she was a child born from her heart rather than her stomach. Sushmita had never kept this a secret and had told her that her child was more precious because she had been chosen by her heart. Sushmita told me that she had explained the fact that she was adopted because she knew that in school, Renee would face a lot of awkward questions and comments. She always reminded her daughters that a child chosen by the heart was more loved than a child of the womb.

When Ishitta got married, I wrote a skit about her life and the first person that came to mind to play the role of Ishitta as a little girl was Renee. I called Sushmita and she very readily accepted. Renee had two or three rehearsals with K.K. Raina and on 26 May she came punctually and her performance won the hearts of the audience.

Sushmita smiled and proudly told me that Renee was now twenty-four and had turned into a responsible and mature woman, able to take her own decisions in life. When Renee was ten, Sushmita took the decision to adopt another daughter, Alisah. She also said that she believed that the affection and care she got from her adopted daughters was no less than what her natural children would have given her.

I marvelled at the fact that at the comparatively young age of twenty-four, Sush took the decision to adopt two children and raise them as a single mother. I told her that I found it quite an effort to manage one daughter. It is a huge responsibility to bring up children as it is and to bring them up to be responsible and independent is an even more difficult task.

My mind went back to the time when Sushmita stood on the stage as a participant in the Miss Universe contest, the first Indian to bag that title. In the last round when asked what she believed was the essence of a woman, she had said, 'Just being a woman is a gift of God that all of us must appreciate. The origin of a child is a mother, who is a woman.' In adopting two girls and empowering them to be aware of their 'essence', she has shown the world that she believed in what she had said as she accepted the crown. Very often such declarations are forgotten once the competitor walks off the stage, but in her case, she has followed her beliefs and kept her word.

My husband believes that children from a defence background are very confident and good at communicating. 'Precise, practical and effective,' he says. Sushmita had proved that she is a woman of her word. That night, when I said that I was impressed by the fact that she had followed her conscience, her honest answer was that her decision to adopt was not to prove a point. It was a decision driven by the fact that she genuinely wanted to experience being a mother. A mother is not only the woman who gives birth, but a mother is a being who nurtures and cares for her young. After the shooting schedule was over, she was taking her daughter to Switzerland to admit her in a school. 'Maa, this is the same school where Rajmata Gayatri Devi studied,' she informed me. I thought that these girls had been born lucky, their fate having brought them to the right place. She said, 'I have gone through so many ups and downs, health-wise and with my personal life, but I am grateful to God, who has given me so much.'

In the last schedule of shooting for *Aarya*, Sushmita had taken ill suddenly and had to be rushed to a hospital. She had a 95 per cent blockage in her arteries. But after one and a half months, she was back on the sets with the same commitment and energy, running up and down the stairs, sword fighting and doing her own action scenes, as if nothing had happened. In the second schedule, director Ram Madhvani had an ambulance on standby, but by the grace of God, the schedule wrapped up without any mishap.

In the sequence, she shoots me, not realizing that her gun had a blank cartridge. Unharmed, I pick up my gun and shoot her, not sure if my bullet had met its mark. Her lieutenant Daulat, then fires at me, killing me. As I fell to the floor, Sushmita ran to me and hugged me saying my death scene was excellent and very real. It is very difficult to time the action with the shot and often actors, especially newcomers, fall down dead before the bullet is seen to hit them. We had a good laugh over the various possibilities in this scenario.

As I bade her farewell at the end of the shoot, my eyes fell on her packet of cigarettes. The message on the packet was loud and clear: Cigarette smoking is injurious to health. Because she called me

Maa, like a concerned mother I wanted to tell her that you have just had a second lease of life and you seem to be blessed by God. Why do you indulge in something so harmful? I would have warned my daughter, Ishitta, in the same way, though I know neither of them would heed my advice. But somehow, I didn't have the courage. I just said, 'Take care. You are very precious to all of us. If you love yourself, life and people will love you too.' Those were my parting words, my advice on the tip of my tongue, but not voiced to her.

The moon was waning, the night had advanced. I gave her a hug, a *jaadu ki jhappi*.

Suddenly, she got up and taking a white-and-purple *lehariya* scarf from around her neck, she wrapped it around me saying, 'Till we meet again. This scarf will remind you of me.' I walked away with a lump in my throat.

I know that when people find out I have been shooting with Sushmita, they will be very curious and eager to ask me many questions, since she had been in gossip columns at that time. People are more curious to know about the stars I have worked with rather than about me. They know more about the stars than I do from social media and television and yet they want me to endorse their stories. We spend our precious time wondering about other people's lives. But why should I tell them what is behind Miss Universe's persona and what are the beliefs and secrets she holds in her heart? I also remember reading somewhere, 'Don't sit at a table where they talk about others since when you get up, you are the next topic.'

Vidya Balan

When I was asked to do a film, *Shaadi Ke Side Effects* (2014), I was very excited since I knew both the lead actors, Vidya Balan and Farhan Akhtar.

Vidya came to the industry through ads, some with my brothers, Piyush and Prasoon too, and perhaps some television work, but it was her role in *Parineeta* (2005) that first brought her into the limelight as an actress. I cannot forget how impressed I was when I saw Vidya in *Parineeta*. She was different from the other actresses, who looked like models; she was a mature woman, having the beauty and elegance of the actresses of old times. She brought back the dignity of the original Parineeta, the beautiful Meena Kumari in the 1953 film. In fact, she seemed to represent the heroines of all eras of Hindi films. Her expressive face effortlessly spoke volumes. She looked like a Bengali too. Her eyes, her gestures and her body language were enough to convey her emotions, without the need for words. I was really impressed by her and Saif in the film.

I have done some good films with her: *Sherni* (2021), *Begum Jaan* (2017) and *Shadi Ke Side Effects*. In *Shaadi Ke Side Effects*, I was a house help who was like a mother figure to her, a possessive woman who disapproved of any intrusion in her mistress's life. I got to know her well, and on the sets, I got to see how talented she is and how she transforms herself the moment the camera is on her. In *Begum Jaan*, she was too young to be the madam of a *kotha*. Shabana had done a similar role in *Mandi* and she looked the part, because she was a seasoned actress. She had even put on weight for the role, but for Vidya, it was a great responsibility to take on a role like this at such a young age. I told her that I saw Meena Kumari in her and that she should do *Sahib, Bibi Aur Ghulam* (1962). She would be perfect for the role. She has the emotional strength to express her pain and her desire, the loneliness of a dejected woman. I also told her that she was the right actress to do a biopic of Meena Kumari.

Her choice of films has been amazing. To take on the role in *Dirty Picture* (2011) after *Parineeta* was a bold step. The portrayal of Silk Smita was played so convincingly by Vidya that the audience identified her with it. Her role in *Kahani*, as a spy who pretends to be a pregnant woman, was also an unusual role for a newcomer. She was fantastic in *Sherni* too. She is a natural actress and so was able to take on such a vast range of roles and did not hesitate to accept roles that other actresses would shun. She has done some period films and really surprised me in *Shakuntala Devi* (2012) with her rendition of the title role.

Vidya has a childlike quality that endears her to her co-actors. She also loves to play pranks on the set, which sometimes disturb the shot. On the sets of *Begum Jaan*, she would play pranks on me too. It was hot in Shantiniketan, and the scenes were long. Most of the shots required at least ten people. Scenes like these were difficult to organize and I would get tired because I would be standing for a long time. She was concerned and would always look after me.

But when I had scenes with her, she would crack a joke and make others laugh while she kept a straight face. Once while I was preparing for a serious scene, she asked someone to play the song 'DJ Waley Babu' by Badshah. She knew that if I hear a tune like that, my feet would naturally tap to the music. The shot was ready and she played the song and I could not help moving. The director saw me and asked me to be still, while Vidya stood there serious and ready for her action! Her professionalism keeps me young and on my toes, though her pranks do distract me! She is a good blend of innocence, impishness and seriousness.

I have some beautiful artefacts which she presented me, one of them was a beautiful handcrafted *juda* pin because she had seen me fiddling with my long hair. We would buy a lot of handicrafts at the *melas*, which we visited at Shantiniketan. We enjoyed the shops selling trinkets, saris and handloom material. The saris would be less than half the price of what you get in cities. We loved to listen to the *baul* singers who frequented the *melas* to entertain the villagers. She was always giving me presents. During the shooting of *Sherni*, she presented me with a heavy silver necklace. It was embellished with bells and when the bells rang as I walked, I was reminded of the cows returning home at *godhuli*, the moment of sunset and dusk, which for me had a special significance. When her husband, Siddharth Roy Kapur, came to visit her on location, she took us all out for dinner to a beautiful ethnic place serving delicious Bengali food. Obviously, Siddharth is a very caring husband, and they have a very good rapport in their partnership.

She saw my energy on location and found on Wikipedia that my age had been given as eighty-five! She was very angry that such wrong information was given online and asked all the young actresses to write a protest letter to Wikipedia. I saw her as a devoted daughter when she had invited her mother's friends to her home, if I remember correctly, on the festival of Pongal, when married women get together for a ritual that involves anointing each other with *haldi-kumkum*, turmeric and vermilion, and exchanging gifts.

Interestingly, I discovered an older association with her through her mother-in-law, Salome. My husband, Arun, is a fan of hers ever since he got his first ballroom dance lessons from Salome at the dance classes she ran in Colaba, long before we got married!

Once on a flight together, Vidya asked me whether I was on Instagram. I gave a blank look. That was the time when everyone was sending pictures and promoting themselves through Instagram, but I had never even thought of using it. She said I must get onto Instagram and saying this instantly clicked a photograph of me and posted it online. She explained the whole process to me and showed me some of her reels. Though she is a well-known actress, she makes funny reels to make people laugh, just like my daughter Ishitta. Vidya will always remain part of my film memories.

Nawazuddin Siddiqui

Another actor I admire is Nawazuddin Siddiqui. I have done four films with him: *Manto* (2018), *Ghoomketu* (2020), *Raat Akeli Hai* (2020) and the latest, *Haddi* (2023). He is from NSD and his dedication on the sets is a lesson that actors should learn. He has done mostly intense and serious roles, and I have seen how hard he works to get under the skin of his character. He doesn't talk much, and as soon as he puts on his costume, he is the character he is playing. Thrice I have played a mother figure to his character: a *bua*, aunt, in *Ghoomketu*, who has looked after him since his parents' death. In *Haddi*, I have played his *Guruma*, his mentor, and in *Raat Akeli Hai*, his mother. A journalist commented that Ila Arun reminds her of Nirupa Roy, the quintessential mother of Hindi films, and the *jodi* of Ila and Nawazuddin is the closest to the onscreen mother–son duo of Nirupa Roy and Amitabh Bachchan. To my mind, Nawazuddin is one of those actors whom one must watch on the sets because of what they can teach you. He mesmerizes you and you realize what acting is all about.

Om Puri

An ordinary, but unforgettable face; the simplicity and bluntness of a villager; a deep-throated voice that held you spellbound; and a smiling face—that is how I envisage Om Puri. I met him at NSD for the first time. As I have mentioned before, I had been selected for a short-term course at this prestigious institution. Through the good books of Alkazi Sahib I was able to get a room at the hostel. The hostels for both girls and boys faced each other and were separated only by an iron gate and a small patch of garden, for the sake of propriety. The gate was never shut, even at night since the watchman was 'well looked after' by the students. Om was in the second year, with Naseeruddin Shah and Bansi Kaul. There must have been something in this student that his name was on everyone's lips. Sometimes when we went for our morning walks to Ravindra Bhavan, Om would let out a loud clucking sound like a rooster's morning call. The whole of Mandi House would resonate with this sound which Om Puri declared was his way of exercising his voice. We had a common dining room, so we were always together at the table. He was also from a middle-class background like me and we became friends. One day, Mohan Upreti, the music teacher, called me to the second-year class. He knew that I was a folk singer and asked me to sing something for the class. I sang two songs. Om liked one of the songs so much that he asked me if he could sing it for the impending exams. I was only too happy to let him use it. Thereafter, whenever he met me, he would ask me to help him to perfect the song so that he would do well in his exams. So, we started getting together, teaching and learning the song and sharing many musical moments and time just slipped by. I believe he did do well in the exams, and I flattered myself that I had contributed towards his success.

My course was over and after six months I returned to Jaipur. Later, after my marriage when I moved to Bombay, Om Puri had already established himself in parallel cinema with memorable films such as *Ankur* (1974), *Aakrosh* (1980) and *Chakra* (1981). But it was when we met on the sets of *Mandi* that we became close friends. Om would regale the cast and crew with stories of our singing lessons, and he would always give me the credit for his doing well at the exams. This inevitably ended with all of us singing the song.

And so, our association grew with the films we did together—*Susman, Yatra, Antarnaad* and *Ardh Satya*—and our friendship grew deeper. We started visiting each other at home. But I had the greatest time when we did *West Is West* (2010). He was perhaps one of the first Indian actors to have made a name for himself in overseas productions. I realized that to be a successful actor in foreign films, it is not necessary to be proficient in English. His histrionic skills, his common face, his deep voice and his Indianness helped him to rise to heights in foreign films. He had won so many national and international awards that he said there was no place for them in his home. He had come from a village and carried the simplicity of his origins, and for me, he brought back memories of my childhood and adolescence in Purohitji-Ka-Bagh. I remember there were several trees of sweet guavas in the gardens of my home, and Om Puri was a sweet guava in my imagination, attracting squirrels to nibble at his face since every female actor who co-starred with him developed a soft spot for him. His sweetness drew everyone towards him. His wife Nandita related a story that still brings a smile to my face. When they had decided to get married, he told her that their child would address all his co-actresses as *mausi*, a term for one's mother's sister, and not *bua*, a term for the father's sister since he could then take liberties with his so-called sisters-in-law which he couldn't with someone who was addressed as *bua*, his sister! His relationship with a *bua* would have to be clean and above board! Nandita always joked about the fact that she was a little apprehensive when meeting Om's lady friends. I remember once after their son Ishaan was born, both Neena Gupta and I went to visit them. Nandita, looking at the two of us told Ishaan that his *buas* had come to visit him. Om, his face wan, told him, 'No, *beta*. This is Neena *mausi* and Ila will be your only *bua*. Remember that!' Neena heaved a sigh of relief, but I was happy since by now I was fed up of being a *mausi* to the children of my four sisters! This was a special relationship since I always wanted to be addressed as *bua*. So, to this day I remain Ishaan's sole *bua*.

One day, on the festival of Raksha Bandhan, I got a call from Om asking me whether I was coming to tie a *rakhi* on my nephew's wrist. I was honoured and arrived with *rakhis* and that day not only did I tie a *rakhi* on Om's wrist, but my daughter Ishitta also came with me to tie a *rakhi* for Ishaan. And this bond of *rakhi* was the thread that bound us together for life.

After the success of *East Is East*, it was decided to make a sequel to that. When they were casting for *West Is West*, the producer, Leslee Udwin, called me for an audition to Sea Rock Hotel in Bandra. If I am not mistaken, this film followed *Jodhaa Akbar*, in which I had a significant role. Leslee then explained my role to me saying that I was to play Om Puri's first wife, whom he had left behind in his village in Pakistan when he left for England where he married an Englishwoman. The director asked me whether I knew Punjabi. I replied nonchalantly that even though I did not know the language, as an actor I would take up this challenge. When I received the script, I persuaded an old friend, who was from Multan before Partition, Devendra Malhotra to teach me how to speak Punjabi. I would call him on the landline and spend a lot of time perfecting the accent. The scene depicted the return of Om and his family to Pakistan and the two wives meet for the first time. Neither of the wives knew the other's language, so they could not communicate with each other. The scene between the two wives, one who had lost him and the other who despite living with him could not claim him fully, in sign language, gave the audience gooseflesh. When I gave the audition, Leslee had tears in her eyes. She told me that Om Puri had told her that Ila is a good actress, but she is not a Punjabi and will not be able to speak the language. I boxed Om on his back and asked him why he had said something that could have cost me my role. He said that he was indeed amazed at my having mastered the language. The Punjabi spoken in Pakistan is a mix of Multani and Punjabi, quite different from the Punjabi spoken in India. Om said my language was better than his. From that time, wherever we travelled for the promotion of the film or for film festivals, to Toronto, England and Abu Dhabi, Om always mentioned how I had mastered an alien language for my role. He also recounted why I was his son's *bua*. Then he would tell the audience how it was because of Ila's training for a Rajasthani folk song which made him score good marks at the NSD. He would then ask me to sing two lines from the song and he would continue to sing the entire song. I felt this song also became a bond for us like our *rakhi*. When we were leaving Abu Dhabi, after the film festival, it was Raksha Bandhan again. I bought a friendship band at the airport and tied it on both Om and Ishaan. Om gave me money, which a brother traditionally gifts his sister, in foreign currency.

When we spent a long time together shooting for *Yatra*, on a train, Om would invite a few close friends to his compartment which he called his *ghar,* or home. There from under his bunk he would draw out, almost like a magician, all kinds of goodies which we would all feast on. His coupe became a home from home, not only for him, but for all of us co-actors too.

But his time among us was very short. On 6 January 2017, he passed away at the age of sixty-six, leaving several half-finished films. That day, I lost not just a friend but a *rakhi* brother too. I wait for a phone call asking me to sing our favourite song. Many evenings when he was in a good mood, I would get a phone call from him, regardless of what time of day or night it was and there would be the same request, 'Ila, sing that song for me. *Tanak chadiyali kanchli ne kankh mein le gayo.*' Saying that he would put me on speakerphone and make the whole world listen to my song. But there is no phone call, no demand for the song that had brought us close together. When he put me on speakerphone, I often wondered who could be listening to my song. But today, I wait for that call and his deep, sonorous voice saying, 'Ila, sing that song.' I still have that *rumal*, or hanky, that he wove during the shooting of *Susman*. Om preferred to stay in the village among the weavers to learn how to weave. He made one for Shabana, one for Neena, one for Shyam and one he gave me. I was surprised and moved when a few days ago, his wife Nandita gave me a scarf woven by the same weavers' company called Ramulu! Memories are made of this.

I miss you, Om.

Rishi Kapoor

Perhaps the most famous and powerful family in Indian film industry is the Kapoors. Prithviraj Kapoor can be called the founder of Hindi cinema. Four generations of Kapoors have graced the silver screen so far and I was lucky to have met Prithvirajji, Rajji and Rishiji.

I met the eldest of the Kapoor clan, Prithvirajji at Sisodia Rani Ka Bagh in Jaipur when he came there for a shoot. Pinchoo Kapoor, who had directed me in several plays and ran a theatre group called Abhisarika, was a distant relative of the Kapoors. He took me to meet Prithvirajji. Pinchoo told him that I sing very well, so he asked me to sing for him. I sang a Punjabi song—'*Maiyyan Mein Laung Gavan Ayyan*'—in two voices: male and female. Prithvirajji laughed and asked me to repeat it again and again because he found that most amusing. I will always remember that day at Sisodia Rani Ka Bagh.

One day I got a call from Tahir Hussain Sahib, Aamir Khan's father. He had also seen me on *Showtime* and contacted me since he wanted me to sing a song for a film he was making, *Hamara Khandaan* (1988). I had never sung a solo for a film so far, so I was excited about the prospect but also nervous. It was to be directed by Anwar Pasha and the cast had Rishi Kapoor and Tabu's sister Farah Khan in it. So far, I had not taken my singing seriously and sang whenever I was asked to, without going out of the way to promote myself as a singer. But here I was, being offered a number as a playback singer, something I had not even thought of in my wildest dreams. Something was changing. Somehow Bombay was finally listening to my songs and appreciating me. When I was selected, I went nervously for a sitting at Laxmikantji's house. I passed every test they asked me to take. It was a Sufi song titled '*Mere Maalik Mere Maula*'. The director wanted me as did the producer and I think I had impressed Laxmikantji too. Those days, as I have mentioned earlier, recordings used to be very different. Even the hero and heroine sometimes dropped in to listen to the song, and very often, a photographer was lingering outside too. The recording was to be done at Mehboob Studios. Rishiji also came for the recording to hear me sing and I couldn't believe that members of the press were there too. There were several film magazines who sent their photographers and before you knew it, your photograph at the recording studio would appear in some magazine or the other like *Box Office*. For me, it was a new experience and I was still in a daze. I was thrilled when I was presented a bouquet and was asked to be photographed with Rishiji. He had sat in the studio and listened to my song a couple of times and when we were leaving the studio, he congratulated me and told me that he loved the way I sang.

Being face to face with a scion of the Kapoor family was a memorable moment for me. I reminded him that I had met him once before at Jaipur at Rambagh Palace when he had come for the shooting of *Mera Naam Joker* (1970). With so many stars arriving there for the shoot, Jaipur was in a festive mood. I was one of the lucky ones who could go into Rambagh Palace Hotel because of my director. I told him I had been introduced to him by Pinchoo Kapoor, who had directed me in several plays in Jaipur and who was a distant relative of the Kapoors. I told him I had been very keen to meet Raj Kapoor's son. He laughed and that put me at ease. Pinchooji had introduced me with pride, saying I was Ila Pandey, who has acted in several plays with him and is a very good actress. And he said, 'This is my Chintoo Baba.' Obviously, Rishiji was not happy with this introduction, but he was known as Chintoo in the industry. He was very happy to be doing a film with his father. He looked very good, a chubby red-cheeked youngster, roly-poly, in a school dress. He said hello and then went off with his friends. I also told him that I had an autograph book his father had signed, writing, 'Choose your love and love your choice.' I still have that autograph book with me. When I saw *Mera Naam Joker*, I loved Rishiji's portrayal of the young Raj Kapoor in the film. I saw his *Saagar* (1985) and *Bobby* (1973). Later when I moved to Mumbai, I passed through tiny pathways to the road that led me to Bollywood. And here I was singing a solo song in a film starring Chintooji! Tahir Sahib told him that I was very nervous while singing. All those at the recording were surprised and asked me why I had been scared since I sang very well. Someone suggested that since I was an actress and had sung the song, why not let Ila do the role of the Sufi singer and picturize her song on her? Chintoo also agreed. Tahir Sahib was convinced and asked me to come to his office the next day. He said that he also felt the song would be more powerful if it was picturized on me. A Sufi song sung in my free-spirited style would be difficult for any singer to lip-sync to. So, it was decided and I was cast as the singer singing my own song. This was filmed in Yousmarg, Kashmir, which translated means the 'meadow of Jesus', since Jesus was supposed to have visited this area. It was supposed to be a four-day shoot, but it rained every day and the shooting stretched for ten days. Since we could not shoot because of the slush left over by the rain, we had time to spend with each other. I was lucky to get to meet Chintooji's family as well as Aamir Khan's family. Aamir was not in films at the time but had come to Kashmir with his family to see his father's shooting. Aamir and Chintoo lived in a houseboat on Dal Lake, while we were put up at a hotel on Dal Lake. A large portion of the song was shot at

Yousmarg. In the scene, Farah and Chintoo watch me, a Sufi singer, sitting atop the straw roof of her hut. The last portion of the song was shot at Charar-i-Sharief, a famous *dargah*, shrine or tomb, where it is believed that if you tie a piece of string and wish for something, your wish will be fulfilled. The young lovers had very little hope of a union since Farah was the daughter of the caretaker in Chintoo's home and there was a vast gap in the status of the two families. But there was still hope in their hearts and they promised that they would come back and untie the knot when they got married. I also tied a knot during my stay there. I can't remember what my *mannat*, or wish, was and whether it was fulfilled, but sadly I could not go back to untie that knot because soon after militancy started in Kashmir and terrorists were holed up in this *dargah*. There was a bomb blast causing extensive damage to the *dargah,* which had to be shut down for a long time.

As usual, memories are good and bad, and the tragedy of Kashmir, my beloved Kashmir, would haunt me for a long time. So started my association with Chintooji. Whenever we met, there would always be talk of NSD and Rajasthani songs. We often met on our walks and his greeting was always: '*Kaisi hain, Ilaji?*' (How are you, Ilaji?) and perhaps a few words would be exchanged, except at the gym, where he would give me a warm smile while lifting weights!

It so happened that after '*Choli*', in 1994, I was invited to join a world tour with several famous actors. In those days, these tours were grand and glamorous. Chintoo was part of the group of actors. We toured Canada, the US and Dubai. The stars who had hit films were included as well as singers with hit songs. Overseas Indian were crazy about Bollywood film stars. Tickets I believe were sold in black for these shows. I had been asked especially by the overseas sponsors after '*Choli*'. I had the opportunity to spend some more time with Chintoo and Neetu, Akshay Kumar, Shah Rukh, Saif, Juhi, Raveena and Ashwini Bhave. There used to be a caravan of seventy or more travelling together for a month and a half. I got to know Rishiji at close quarters. All of them would encourage me when I went onstage.

Chintooji loved good food, like the rest of his family. Many of the Indian families entertained us mainly because of Chintoo, who was one of the most popular stars in the group. But he did not like to be under constant public glare and would sometimes get irritated. It so happened that years later I met him at the Gold Gym. Everyone was in awe of him, and he did not talk much to anyone. What they were surprised about was that no matter what he was doing, he would aways give me a smile as a greeting. Sometimes he would say a few words, asking me about my brothers, who he was very fond of. The film industry is a family and often we come across each other during festivals. I met him at the Bangalore Literature Festival, where his book *Khullam Khulla: Rishi Kapoor Uncensored* was being released. When I went up to get him to sign the book, he asked me why I had bought the book. He said that he was going to gift a copy to each of his well-wishers who were there. I told him, I had to buy it. 'If I ever write a book, everyone would want a free copy, so there would be no sale. So, I do not accept books as gifts from authors.' He laughed and said everyone would buy my book, saying he would too. But I am sad that if this book gets published, he will not be there to buy a copy. The session on his book was very interesting. Many stars are not good at communicating with the public, but he was very knowledgeable and spoke very well. It was sad that cancer got the better of him. I sent him many messages while he was at the hospital in the US. The last time I met him was at the Bachchans' Diwali party. He looked well and did not look as if he was battling cancer. I ran towards him and gave him a hug, telling him that he looked well. After that we heard he was in and out of the hospital. During lockdown, he was seen banging a thali as desired by Modiji. I remember that was 22 March. I saw him once again at his sister Ritu's funeral. On 30 April 2020, he was gone. A day earlier, we had heard of the passing away of another brilliant actor, Irrfan Khan. We lost many great actors during lockdown. There was a pall of grief and a strange silence in the film fraternity when Chintoo left us. A man who loved parties and people, full of life and laughter, left us in the silence of the lockdown, quietly. He walked away from life, his family looking on, his fans and friends unable to say their goodbyes, because of a deadly disease that imprisoned us all. I have not deleted his number and still feel I can call him.

My bond with him was from the heart. Now all the connections, on the phone, the SMS, seem to have snapped. Since we had talked about books that day in Bengaluru, I would like to pay him a tribute in this book remembering the song from *Mera Naam Joker*.

'Kal khel mein hum ho naho /gardish mein tare rahenge sada/ jee chahe jab hamko aawaz do/ hum hain wahin/ hum the jahan.'

(Whether I am there or not/the stars will always shine through the haze/

Call out to me whenever you wish/ I will always be in the space I was in.)

Long Live Amitji

Amitabh Bachchan (Amitji)—who am I to write anything about him? He is the superstar of the industry, its Don. Whenever I come face to face with him, I am left speechless, choked, and when I think of him, I join the millions of fans who hold him in adulation. I dream about his beautiful, sonorous voice and long to listen to the timbre of a tenor. When I speak of my film journey, there are so many people who have influenced me, some have inspired me—Amitabh Bachchan is one who stands out in my memory and in my story.

Khuda gavah hai ki (As God is my witness) I am a BIG fan of BIG B of the Big screen.

I met Amitji for the first time at music composer Kalyanjibhai's place. Kalyanji was a remarkable human being. If he took to a person, he made sure that the bond lasted forever. We had just moved to Bombay and were living in a flat on Forjett Street, not far from Kalyanji's house on Peddar Road. Kalyanji called me up one night. I was always nervous when there was a call from him. He was an insomniac and hardly slept at night and expected his friends to share his nocturnal habits. When I answered the phone, he asked me what I was doing. I thought that was a strange question since it was late at night. Then he proceeded to invite me home. I was on the verge of making an excuse when he stopped me in my tracks with his next sentence. 'Amitji and Jaya are also coming.' My heart skipped a beat. Sleep was thrown out of the window. There was no stopping me then.

Amitabh, the legend! I was to meet him in an intimate circle of friends. In my college days, whenever I stole out of the house to see a film secretly, it was mostly films with Amitabh Bachchan as the hero, my hero. I think that was the time when he had shot to fame with *Zanjeer* (1973) and was acting in *Don* (1978). Before you could say Jack Robinson, Arun and I were at Kalyanji's home. Amitji and Jayaji were already there along with Chandra Barot and the actress, Shammiji. We had a simple but delicious Gujarati meal and then the party really began. Kalyanji always seemed to have one hand on the harmonium, perpetually ready for the singer and the song. Even his conversations were interspersed with a few notes on the harmonium, his fingers poised for music. During the conversation, he mentioned to Amitji that I was a singer and well known for Rajasthani folk songs. Amitji looked at me and asked, 'Do you know the song *"Chirmi"*?' I think he had heard that song sung by folk singers in Jaisalmer when he was shooting for *Reshma Aur Shera* (1971). I was a little nervous, but I was not going to miss this opportunity. I sang *'Chirmi'* and in my enthusiasm added a few more songs! Kalyanji then asked Amitji to sing some UP folk songs, which he promptly sang. Amitji is rooted in the soil of UP and very close to the language, poetry and music of that state. I think at that time they were looking to include a folk song in *Don* and that is why they were listening to several folk songs. And they hit upon that song which made waves amongst the audiences, *'Khaike Paan Banaras Wala'* sung by Amitji himself in his inimitable way, bringing forth the fragrance of the very streets of Benaras, now Varanasi, and accentuating Amitji's bond with UP. It sent the crowds in the cinema halls into ecstasy and became an all-time favourite. My meeting with Amitji and Jayaji and the conversation between the two gentlemen Kalyanjibhai and Amitji was really something special for me, a few hours of pure joy.

Sleep eluded me for several days after that evening. In my mind, I repeated a question to Kalyanjibhai: 'When will you call me again for an evening like this?' But the link to my coming close to the Bachchan family was really Jayaji. After a few months onshore in Mumbai, when Arun set sail again, I joined him and we spent eight months in London. I could not sit still, so I got a job as a freelance contributor with the BBC. There I met Himanshu Bhaduri, who was managing the Hindi programmes. I did a lot of work with him, in many fields: sports, news, culture, health and education. The English scripts had to be translated into Hindi and then broadcast on a microphone to the Hindi-speaking population of the UK. Himanshuda liked my style and work and as I left for Mumbai, he told me that I must visit his niece there. When he told me his niece's name, I was stunned. It was Jaya Bhaduri. Himanshuda had casually mentioned his niece, one of the most loved actresses of the time without dwelling on her fame. How could I forget *Guddi, Mili* (1975), *Abhimaan* (1973) and *Zanjeer*. In fact, later, the cover and title of *Chhappan Chhuri* as well as my look were inspired by Jayaji's role in *Zanjeer*. No matter how much fame and success you receive, for your family you are just a niece like Jayaji was for Himanshuda! Jaya and Amitabh were married by this time, but this information was also conveyed to me without any emphasis. He in fact talked very affectionately about his brother, Jayaji's father. He gave me their number and said I should see them, as they are very nice people and would definitely be happy to meet me. I did contact Jayaji on my return to Mumbai and she even invited me to their house Prateeksha, for a cup of tea. While sipping my tea, my eyes were wandering, searching for Amitji. Jayaji seemed to have gauged that and said that Amit was mostly out on outdoor locations. I was really embarrassed. After this visit, Jayaji would invite us to some of their parties at home, which ensured that I would meet Amitji sometimes.

Because of my close relationship with Kalyanji, I would catch the occasional glimpse of Amitji from afar. My respect and attraction for Amitji, almost like hypnosis, stemmed from the fact that despite having lived away from his home town of Allahabad (now Prayagraj), despite his popularity, his association with the rich and famous and his education in an English-medium school, he still retained a great love for UP. He was knowledgeable about its culture, its music, its poetry and folklore and was steeped in the language and soil of Uttar Pradesh, the fragrance of Allahabad. The city of Mumbai, this *mahanagari*, changes people who flock to it. But this *Mahanayak*, this superstar, has still retained the essence of Allahabad.

My maternal grandparents were from Allahabad and my mother also carried the ambience of that city into her matrimonial home.

Our home was a place where literature and language thrived. With their morning cup of *chai,* my parents would discuss writers and poets. My father would spout the poetry of Harivansh Rai Bachchan, Amitji's father, one of the leading littérateurs of the time. Hindi poems are often sung and my father would sing a few lines from it. My mother, who was a voracious reader, had read almost all his works and had imbibed the very spirit of Harivansh Raiji. As a result, we, the children, were also influenced by this love for the written word.

I am touched and impressed by Amitji's respect for his parents, his dedication to them and the reverence with which he talks about them. I am reminded of my parents when I hear him speak, using the accent and idioms of UP, especially words like *biyah,* or wedding, and the expression *ainyee*, which is an exclamation used by people from UP. I feel my past has been rekindled and brought before my eyes.

Since then, I have seen Amitji at close quarters on many occasions. My first encounter with him as an artiste was in *Devaa* (1987), where I had the privilege of actually sharing screen space with him.

One day I got a phone call from Subhash Ghai, one of the leading directors of Bollywood who had made many blockbusters. Ghai called me to sing a song for *Devaa*, starring Amitabh Bachchan as the dacoit Devaa. I was very excited, since like most women at the time, I was a devoted fan of Amitabh. I got to Mehboob Studios, where the song was to be recorded. It was like entering a world of dreams. It was the place where the epic film *Mother India* had been shot. Then came *Amar* (1954), *Kaagaz Ke Phool* (1959), *Hum Dono* (1961) and *Guide* (1965). For me, it was hallowed ground since the footsteps and voices of heroines and heroes of my childhood still resounded there for me.

As I entered, I saw the music directors, Laxmikantji and Pyarelalji. This was the beginning of my life in Bollywood. I was never given a complete song for a long time. I sang a part of the song and always had either Alka Yagnik or Kavita Krishnamurthy pick it up and complete the number. In this case too, I sang the opening lines of the song, as a voice from the village and it was continued by the heroine, in the voice of a known singer, Alka Yagnik. Despite my nervousness or perhaps because of it, the song was recorded in two takes. In those days, the ambience and mood of the film were created through the medium of the song. The first recording was attended by a multitude of people—the director, the music director, the lyricist and sometimes even the lead actors. Photographers would click photos and these would be used as publicity for trade magazines such as *Box-Office* to let producers and financiers know that a film was going on the floors. To my surprise, my husky, slightly raucous voice appealed to all those who heard the song. I suppose it was a very different voice than what was generally accepted for playback singers. I got several compliments, but sad to say even at that time, I did not take myself seriously. I left feeling pleased with myself and was in seventh heaven. A few days later, Subhash Ghai called me again and dropped a bombshell. The title song that I had recorded was going to be the *mahurat* shot of the film. It would be used for the publicity of the forthcoming film. The heroine had still not been finalized, so the song was to be picturized on me. I was in a state of shock and barely heard that he was asking me to report for this shot four days later. 'We have decided that the song will be sung at an *adda,* where the dacoit Devaa, played by Amitabh Bachchan in the lead role, goes for his entertainment. It will be picturized on you.' Arun, my moral support on such occasions, was sailing, but fortunately my good friend from Jaipur, Himmat Singh, was visiting, so I took him along for the shoot.

The atmosphere at Filmalaya was magical. And Pandhari Dada, the legendary make-up artist of Bollywood, performed a miracle with my make-up by giving me a dusky complexion, haunting eyes and accessories that transformed a simple small-town girl into a seductress. Confident behind my look of a gypsy dancer, I walked out for the *mahurat* shot.

But as I came to the set and saw Amitji in his formidable dacoit costume, my knees started shaking. I was actually going to be in the same shot as Amitabh! As I walked in for the take, I was in for a shock. The words, '*Hua pyaar magar, bhoole se agar ladd jaye nazar to kya kijiye*', suggestive and bold, were directed at Devaa and I had to sing them! I was a gypsy dancer trying to seduce Devaa. The renowned choreographer Saroj Khan was the dance director. She asked me to dance to the song, showing me gestures and moves that were too bold for my middle-class morality. I was a folk dancer and not used to the *latka-jhatkas* that Saroj Khan introduced into her dances.

My mother's clapperboard descended with a thud. I became nervous at the idea of performing such a sensuous number and voiced my apprehensions. I could sense that Sarojji was not too pleased with my stance. I excused myself saying that I was not comfortable with those moves, though it took a lot of courage on my part since I was a newcomer, acting with big names and being directed by the likes of Subhash Ghai and Saroj Khan. But they needed a sensual dance, which I was not comfortable with. When I look back on that day, I still cannot believe that the two directors, Subhash Ghai and Saroj Khan, allowed a young newcomer to follow her conscience and change the dance for me. Saroj Khan choreographed the song in such a way that I sang it seated, while two young girls danced on either side. Once the music for the song started, there was no stopping me. Completely oblivious of all the stars around me, I sang with an abandon that fascinated the listeners. Saroj Khan did not have to give me any instructions. My spirits soared when I saw Amitji's gesture conveying his appreciation as I sang.

The mahurat shot was over and the press flocked to meet Amitabh Bachchan. As I sat in the green room removing my make-up, I could not believe that I had lived through such an unbelievable moment. Was it real or had I just imagined it all? I waited eagerly for the shooting of the film. Ashok Mehta, whom I knew from my *Mandi* days, was the cinematographer. He called me from the editing room complimenting me on my singing. Later, he called again and gave me a sneak preview of the shot. I was thrilled. It was indeed a beautiful shot. And Ashok used his creativity in another shot. Devaa, sitting in a railway compartment, looks out and remembers the song and sees my face juxtaposed against the bars of the window. I don't know how Ashok managed such a remarkable technical feat in those days. My face emerges from the shimmering moon onto the compartment window. I cannot imagine how Ashok made me look beautiful too!

But like a beautiful dream, this too dimmed into the past. As I waited restlessly for the shooting of the film, there were rumours in the newspapers that the film had been abandoned due to some misunderstanding between the people involved. Subhash Ghai got involved in other projects. There was no shortage of work for Amitji. As for me, before my flight of fancy had even taken off, it crashed like a helicopter, shattering to pieces on the ground. I accepted my fate stoically, hoping for another chance to work with this charismatic actor.

Once Kalyanji called me for the premiere of *Khuda Gawah* (1992), starring Amitabh Bachchan and Sridevi. I loved the film. As I watched the film, memories of Devaa came back to me since his look was similar to his look in *Devaa*. I wanted to reconnect with him and greet him with a *pranam*, a greeting, but missed the chance since he was surrounded by security guards. But as I was driving back to my home at Santa Cruz, my daughter noticed his vanity van ahead of us. I asked my driver to follow his van so much so that we overshot our turn. I was determined to see him and I am ashamed to say that I actually called out to him when I saw him getting out of his van, like a young teenage fan. But again, the ring of people around him— security, photographers and fans—prevented me from reaching him and to my great disappointment, he disappeared into the hotel while I returned home, crestfallen, waiting for my next chance.

The chance did present itself, though not in the form of a film. HMV had commissioned me for an album of folk songs that became famous as *Chhappan Chhuri,* which had eight numbers written and composed by me, including 'Resham Ka Rumal' and 'Assi Kali Ka Lehnga', which to this day remain popular during performances and wedding celebrations. Joy Roy, son of the well-known director Bimal Roy, was the co-ordinator for this album for HMV. There was no social media in those days, and I certainly did not have the means for a media launch or promotion. Joy and I both decided that the album should be released by Amitji, who was at the top of his career at the time. This would be good publicity for the album too. We talked to his secretary, Shekhar, and arrived at his residence Prateeksha at Juhu. Known for his punctuality and impeccable manners, Amitji was waiting for us in his living room. We presented our request to him and waited with bated breath for his answer. Very graciously he said that he was very busy at that time, but he would be delighted to release this album. He thought a while and then said, 'Why don't you come to Filmalaya, where I am shooting for the film *Indrajeet* (1991)? I will release the album on the sets in between shots.' I was touched by his answer. I knew of his interest in folk music and that he himself had a vast repertoire of Avadhi songs. We were treated to some of these in his later films. The next day, we went to the sets of *Indrajeet,* carrying our colourful publicity poster, designed by Prasoon Pandey and Sonal Dabral accompanied by our photographer. True to his word, there, in his costume as a police officer, Amitji released my album. I like to believe that this was an auspicious beginning for me. The much sought-after superstar released my album and I am convinced that it was his Midas touch that helped *Chhappan Chhuri* reach the top as the most popular of all my albums. Today, after so many years, I run into students at schools, travellers at airports, in India and abroad, who come and tell me that they have danced to my songs from this album. Some say they have received awards at competitions when they dance to '*Resham Ka Rumal*'. In fact, seeing how popular the first song is, I wonder why I did not name the album *Resham Ka Rumal* rather than *Chhappan Chhuri*! But all eight songs were super-duper hits.

As time went by, our relationship with the Bachchan household continued through other members of the family, my brothers, Piyush and Prasoon. We shared many moments with them, especially during Holi and Diwali. After the Holi celebrations in our home in Jaipur, I felt that Amitabh and Jaya's Holi get-together had the same warmth and festivity that I missed on leaving my home. The *gujiyas* (sweets) served at their house too compared favourably with those that my mother made and distributed at Holi.

One incident that I remember with great regret is concerning a harmonium. When I wrote the title song of the film *Pighalta Aasman* (1985), with Kalyanjibhai's music, he presented me with a scale-changer harmonium from Paul company, one of the best at that time. Kalyanjibhai had ordered two and gave me one in appreciation for my song, telling me I should do my *riyaaz* with this. But after a week, to my surprise, he called me and politely asked me to return the harmonium because somebody very close to him wanted it. I was taken aback and bluntly refused to give it back. Later I came to know that this person was Amitji. If only Kalyanjibhai had told me so at the time, I would personally have gone and delivered it to Amitji unmindful of the fact that my *riyaaz* would have suffered.

Amitji has been a keen supporter of my theatre group too. He is a theatre buff and whenever we did a new play, he would always bless me and my actors. Once he graced our play with his presence at Prithvi. The play was *Namaste, Jai Shri Krishna,* which I had adapted from Tom Dudzick's play *Greetings* in the Avadhi language, a language Amitji loves and can speak fluently. His presence filled the theatre and encouraged the actors to give their best. His coming backstage to meet the actors and his appreciation of our performance was the icing on the cake—an evening they will never forget.

I could go on and on about Amitji. My dream of acting in a film with him in a good role had still not been realized. Then one day there was a call from Yashraj Studios. They were starting a new film, a huge project with Amitabh Bachchan and Aamir Khan. Viktor, the director, read the role out to me, but I was not listening to him. I had my fingers crossed and prayed to all the gods I could think of. I am sure I said yes, even before he had finished! My heart did a somersault as I prayed to God that this opportunity should not pass me by this time. I did get the role. Amitji was playing the part of the captain of a pirate ship, and I was to be his assistant and housekeeper. It was a small role, but just sharing screen space with the superstar and enacting a song sequence with him, wasn't this the realization of my dream?

The film was *Thugs of Hindostan.* I was very nervous the first day on the sets, and Amitji, sensitive to my apprehension, actually said, 'Why are you afraid? You have been in a film with me before this.' That he actually remembered the aborted film *Devaa,* eased my fears and gave me some confidence to act alongside this phenomenal actor, the superstar and heartthrob of India.

On the sets I saw Amitji in his costume designed by famous costume designers Rushi and Monshree. His cloak was said to weigh a hundred kilos! The make-up was very difficult, involving prosthetics and special effects. A prosthetic specialist, Domini, was called from the US to work on Amitji's face and she did a magnificent job of transforming his personality.

My make-up too was amazing. My costume included a turban, which I had on throughout the film. Amitji too sported a *pugree,* a light turban, and he and I shared the costume assistant who was an expert at tying *pugrees.* I must say I was as curious as a child, drawing out little nuggets of information about Amitabh from this gentleman. Like most people who have worked with him, this gentleman also spoke of his dedication, his involvement in his role and impeccable manners.

We were shooting on a small island off the shores of Thailand called Poda Nui. We would get up at 4 a.m. and set off for the location in the cold, a journey that took an hour and a half. Then the tedious sitting for the make-up, which sometimes took about two and a half to three hours! It was not an easy shoot. The last part of the path to the location was very cumbersome. It was a steep climb, and one had to cross a river. The costumes were so heavy that going up a steep hill dressed like that was hazardous to say the least. Two palanquins were provided for us, one for Amitabh and the other for me. I think the second palanquin was for Aamir, but he refused to be carried and insisted on walking up. So, in deference to my age, I was assigned that palanquin.

I discovered Amitabh's addiction to electronics on this shoot. His spot boy carried twenty-two mobiles, each with its distinct ring. Amitji explained the reason for this. He was a firm believer in the role of social media in his profession. Amitji never socializes on his sets. He prefers to retire to his room and spend his time either reading or communicating on social media. He carries a whole lot of books on his shoots, including his father's literary works, and he doesn't need any company since he is busy sending messages to his fans on social media like an eager child. I found out about this when after much persuasion, Viktor and I were granted permission to visit him in his room. The room was flooded with electronic gadgets—cameras, music, a desktop and other unidentifiable paraphernalia. It was he who taught me how to send messages in Hindi.

But the most endearing facet was when I would see him, sprawled on four chairs, chin down, sunning himself. He would say he was taking in vitamin D! If I was lucky, his spot boy would once in a while draw up my chair next to him and I would be offered several brands of biscuits. His second spot boy carries about fifty types of biscuit tins out of which at regular intervals, he pulls out some of these and offers them to Amitji on a plate carried for the purpose! These biscuit tins fascinated me and one day out of curiosity I asked Amitji why he had so many biscuits following him. He said that after the accident on the sets of *Coolie* (1983), he was advised to eat small quantities at short intervals and he thought the most convenient would be a biscuit! Since then, I have also started enjoying biscuits, especially with my tea!

My journey in films has so many memories of time spent with the Bachchans and the love and respect they gave to our family. How can I write just a chapter, when I could perhaps write a whole book?

We are connected on WhatsApp messages; his replies to my messages are very brief, just *shubh kamnaayein* or *sneh*, or *abhaar* and my message is always, 'Take care, you are very precious to us.'

Long live Amitji!

If we stop to examine the dazzling curtain that is drawn over each life, each performance and each individual and have the courage to pull it aside, perhaps we will come upon the secret that lies behind that curtain, *parde ke peechhey kya hai?*

Chapter 25

Property: *Well Done Abba!*

I have done many films with Shyam Benegal: *Mandi*, *Trikal* and *Welcome to Sajjanpur*, but one film, *Well Done Abba*, seemed to reflect my struggle in life—to own a piece of land which I could call my own. This was one of Shyam Benegal's less-watched films. Very often it happens that good films lose out since they do not have a good release. This was often the case with Shyam's films. He received international recognition, but his films did not reach the common man for whom they were meant. *Well Done Abba* was a satire about a man who puts his entire life's savings into buying a plot of land with a *baori*, or a step-well. But when he goes to claim it, the land which is marked on a document had disappeared and there was no sign of his plot or the *baori*. According to the map, there is a different plot of land in its place. The story is about this man's dogged fight through fair means and foul to regain his lost property.

When I signed the film, I did not pay much heed to the story. But when Shyam got all the cast together to tell them the story about land scams in India, I could not help but laugh. Shyam talked about how everyone from builders to politicians and the municipal corporation is involved in the scam, cheating the common man of his money, his land and his dreams. Shyam looked at me quizzically and said that my reaction convinced him that the film would be a success, a good comedy. He said, 'You laughed even before I started the story.' I said, 'No, sir, I am laughing at the tragedy in my life.' 'Why?' he asked, curious. 'Have you experienced something similar in your life?' I told him that I had gone through this fraud not once but several times in my life. In many cases, whenever I bought a plot of land, for which

I had all the relevant documents, and went to survey my property, that particular plot had disappeared just like in this story. It had been converted into a settlement for labour, a *mazdoor* camp or the number of the plot had been changed. It is said that *zar* (land), *zameer* (integrity) and *joru* (wife) must be handled with care. I could vouch for my honesty and the responsibility of the last rested with my husband, Arun.

But let me come to the first, *zar*, land. I bought my first piece of land from my parents. My father was the general manager in the Central Bank of India. But before that he had been a registrar in a cooperative bank. By God's grace or otherwise, he was blessed with several offspring, of whom seven were daughters. Like most parents, he would invest in plots whenever he could find something within his means on his limited resources. Having served in a co-operative bank, he had some knowledge of small investments. He bought land in various cities in Rajasthan, Sambhar, Mount Abu, Jodhpur and Jaipur as investments for his daughters' education and weddings. When I got married, my mother mentioned that they had a piece of land in the posh locality of Civil Lines in Jaipur, an area inhabited by the elite of the city. They wanted to sell this plot and asked if I would be interested. The going price at the time was Rs 18,000. My parents thought that my husband being in the merchant navy could afford that kind of money and this would be our first step towards investing for our future and the land would prosper within the family. I wrote to Arun, who was sailing at the time, and he promptly sent the money. Now the land was in my name. I was perhaps the first one in the family to own a piece of land in my home town in a locality that had the mansions of the rich and famous. I was on cloud nine. Time passed and people warned us that land should never be left without a demarcation. More money was sent, and we enclosed it with a wall for safety. Satisfied with my acquisition, I left to join Arun onboard his ship. A few years later, when we came ashore, Arun expressed his desire to see this piece of land and we arrived at the site. Our advent seemed to have caused a commotion. Suddenly, there was a loud clanging of bells. We thought perhaps there was a temple built in the area in the four years since we had been gone. But we were stunned to learn the truth. In these four years, the government had changed. And each time a new party takes over, they bring with them their own vote banks. Sometimes it is caste-based, or class or the religious card that is touted for votes. The victorious political party had romped through the elections by selling dreams to the labour class, the *mazdoors*. Promptly a *mazdoor nagar* had come up on this land with homes for labourers. So many people are involved in these illegal land dealings that it is impossible to unravel the truth and extricate your own property. Politicians, builders and other departments are hand in glove. The bells seemed to be a signal for a mob to gather. Several people armed with lathis appeared from nowhere and menacingly asked us which land we were talking of, and who claimed to be the owner. They warned us that even a step further would spell danger for us. I was in a state of shock. Arun, not used to this kind of hooliganism, decided that retreat was the best option. It was a cold winter's day. We came home, breathed a sigh of relief and drank a hot cup of tea to get our wits about us.

A new chief minister had just taken over. He was a friend of my father's and on his suggestion, we went to meet him. Our spirits soared, and our morale went up. He assured us that this was pure hooliganism, and his government was in the process of making a blueprint to counter this injustice. He said that they would use bulldozers to demolish all the structures and the grounds would be cleared overnight. A lot of influential people owned plots there so our plot would also be saved. We felt reassured. But days and weeks went by and there were no bulldozers, no demolitions and my piece of land could not be rescued from the clutches of the illegal occupiers. Governments came and went, but these were like ripples in the sand around the land of the rich and famous. No progress was made, and our chief minister soon left Rajasthan to take over as the vice president of India! I was so disillusioned by this that my heart distanced itself from this plot of land and I was determined to assign this to my overburdened memory. As it is I have paranoia when it comes to legal matters. Courts, lawyers and government offices frighten me. An artiste can weave several warps and woofs of pageantry and tales but does not want to get entangled in the mesh of the threads of legality.

I wanted to obliterate the memory of this plot of land, to forget that I ever owned a piece of property in the posh precincts of Ajmer Road, in the midst of the rich and influential. The word Ila, my name, means the earth. Imagine, a woman whose name envelops the world, the earth, had her land, the ground beneath her feet pulled out from under her. There is a saying in Rajasthani that the heart shudders even if a tiny piece of our land is given away. But in truth, I was not destined to possess a piece of land and yet in my subconscious, I must have had the hope that there must be some little corner of the earth that was looking for me! And the opportunity presented itself once again. A little distance away from Mumbai, in the hills of Karjat, a developer called Date was advertising the sale of land on which one could build a row house—a quiet, cool haven, far from the madding crowd. It was as if this advertisement was beckoning me. Plots were being developed and the ads said that you could build your own house, the dream house you had always envisaged. Many other artistes and members of the creative community, who found the confined spaces of their tiny matchbox-like flats in Mumbai claustrophobic and wanted to see the vast sky and stars, were persuaded to buy plots in that area. Prominent among them were art director Nitish Roy and the actor Amrish Puri's nephew. They needed breathing space where they imagined they would work better. There was one more attraction. The land was cheap, and Arun and I were coaxed into buying a plot there. I felt that finally my dream was being realized. The foundation of the house of my dreams was already laid. But before that dream was fulfilled, the house came down to earth with a crash and was shattered to pieces. We discovered that the plan to divide the plots had not been passed by the authorities. Somehow, we had the land registered, but so many alarming rumours reached us about this project and being so far in Mumbai, we could never hope to get down to the truth. Nitish Roy was so worried by these rumours that he sold off his land and decided to go to Hyderabad. I was also contemplating this course of action, but some of my well-wishers advised me that land does not give back dividends immediately. Now that the plot had been registered, it was safe. It should be left in the hands of God, supervised and checked once in a while by us.

It is rightly said that there is a big difference between Brahmins and traders. Brahmins are supposed to concentrate on acquiring knowledge, to be satisfied with two square meals a day and generally leading a simple life. Landowners and traders are a different breed. I should have foreseen that land bought by a Brahmin is seldom fruitful. We just did not accept the writing on the wall. We held on to this piece of land, imagining that like many other actors and actresses, one day we would also have a farmhouse, where I could escape to write scripts in isolation, have music 'sittings' or have rehearsals for plays. Carrying this pot of dreams on my head, I lived in an unreal world, a world of hope and imagination.

Because of the distance, we seldom visited the place. Arun was sailing frequently, and for me, it was a gargantuan task to make it on my own. We satisfied ourselves by inquiring about the place from Amrish Puri's nephew. But there were occasional rumblings in the mind about the condition and status of the place and whether it was still intact or was there a *mandir* or a *mazdoor nagar* on it? Or was it possible that the plot existed only on paper?

Days went by. *Khal Nayak* was released and the song that I had sung with Alka Yagnik, '*Choli Ke Peechhey*', was a huge success. And with it my popularity and my financial status got a huge boost. I was busy most days of the month. I travelled abroad at least for five or six shows every month. I had finally reached a stage when I was filing my own income tax returns! That is when I came in contact with the community called CAs! Director Rajkumar Santoshi, who was a good friend and who had directed box-office successes like *Ghayal* (1990) and *Ghatak* (1996), suggested the name of a CA who handled several film accounts. I protested that I was not big enough a star to need someone 'filmy'. Rajkumar assured me that this gentleman would look after my needs as a family member.

I cannot disclose his name, but let's refer to him as Salil Fakri. This man is a big name in film circles. As for me, I had made a name, but my persona was small in my estimate. An artiste's life is short-lived, as a Hindi saying goes, 'Four days of moonlight, then the long, dark night.' Salil Fakri insisted that for him all his clients were equal and he treated them all alike. He said I should have faith in him. He would designate an accountant from his firm to handle my account, but he would file my returns himself. I was as important to him as any of his superstar clients. I thought here was a good man and with this trust, a new relationship was established. My trust in him stemmed from the knowledge that many of my friends in the industry were his clients: Bappi Lahiri, Madhuri Dixit, several well-known painters, Sunny Deol's production house, etc. My own status in the industry would be enhanced by my association with a trustworthy and respected CA.

Then one day this gentleman made a suggestion that awakened my latent dreams. Salil told me that he had just bought a piece of land a little beyond Malad, on the way to Madh Island where he was building a house for himself. He said that since I was making money with shows after 'Choli Ke Peechhey', he could with his contacts get me a plot of land too.

I remember it was a Sunday. Accompanied by Arun and some close friends and Salil's family, I arrived at the spot. Salil's wife served us hot tea and sandwiches which she had brought with her. We sat down on durries spread under a huge banyan tree. I think that was the day of the *mahurat,* the ground-breaking ceremony, for Salil's plot of land and we picnicked under the shade of palm trees. Salil introduced us to a gentleman, known only as 'Masterji' by the village since he was a teacher and had taught many of the children in the village, thus gaining the trust of the villagers. As a result, he became the agent for their land. When the villagers needed money, they would sell their land to Masterji at very low rates and Masterji, using Salil's film contacts, would sell this land to rich film stars. I don't know what kind of a plan Masterji enticed the farmers with, but he had several acres of land in his ledger. Salil must have convinced Masterji to sell him the land at low rates since he was getting him several buyers.

After the Jaipur land fiasco, I had sworn never to nurture the dream of owning property. But Salil said that a person should think positively. Masterji, perhaps reading the uncertain look on my face said that I should not worry and that he would find me a small plot near Salil's land. If I was happy with it, I could buy it. I thought that after two bitter experiences in possessing my piece of land, could there actually be a piece of land that would justify my parents' choice of my name—Ila, earth? It was a laughable fact that a woman called

Ila did not possess an inch of land! Could this land, in Malwani, close to Madh Island actually be mine? I was so happy at the prospect that I felt like dancing, Ila dancing with *ghunghroos* on her feet! I danced tirelessly at several shows, like Meerabai, with bells on her toes! Once again, I started dreaming of having a place in Mumbai. I thought that as Mumbai was my workplace, my *karmabhoomi*, I could be close to it, a better prospect than Jaipur. I was also happy about the fact that many well-known people from the film fraternity, like Subhash Ghai, had their bungalows close by. The Raheja group of builders had constructed some flats there too, which housed many a rising and waning star of the film industry. Development of that area was in full swing so the land would only go up. The goal of owning a plot in the vicinity of stars and under a starry sky was only a step away.

Now I ponder over the fact that if the CA could have built his house on that land, why is it that I have not been able to do so in the thirty years since I acquired the plot? There are several reasons behind this, some unfortunate and some inevitable. If I wished I could have built a small theatre like Prithvi. Since Kunal Kapoor does not give out dates easily at Prithvi Theatre, I would have the run of the place, performing as I wished. Perhaps I could have theatre workshops for children, a rehearsal space maybe? But when I was shown this piece of land by my CA, I went to verify the map at the municipal office and was in for a shock. This large piece of land had an FSI, floor space index, of only 0.5 which could be used for building. I did not understand the connotations of that. The explanation was that this L-shaped piece of land had been consolidated by joining several *khasras* of small pieces of land. What was a *khasra*? I recalled that in my childhood I had heard this word. The rash that came after a bout of high fever was termed *khasra,* which in English is measles. This word, related to land had a different meaning altogether, a meaning which I was not familiar with. Salil was aware of this problem, but he did not mention this to me. His plot was clean and on the basis of this he had even taken a subsidy to start computer classes for the village youth, a plan that he never intended to implement. The subsidy was used to subsidize his own massive bungalow!

As I was contemplating which corner of the land I could build my bungalow on, another notice was sent to me. Masterji said he would have to give the villagers access to their land behind my plot by taking part of my land for a road. For that he would have to take a piece of land from my plot by breaking down a portion of the boundary wall. He pacified me by saying that Salil would also lose a portion of his land. If we did not allow that access, the villagers would be up in arms. Now I am a real coward when it comes to confrontation with all things legal. I decided that silence was the best part of valour, since any shouting and fighting would be detrimental to my voice, and I may never be able to sing again! So it came to pass that a path was created through my property, but alas, not an inch of space was acquired from Salil's land. His wall too remained intact. I could not keep quiet now. I confronted Masterji, quarrelling over this injustice. Without being ruffled or angry, Masterji calmly told me that I was not to worry; he would compensate me with an equivalent piece of land from the other side. I cannot still comprehend what the settlement was he claimed to have made, but I only know that that so-called extra piece of land came under the category of agricultural land. I was slowly coming to the conclusion that my dream would never be fulfilled. The only solution was that I should do what farmers do—grow vegetables on that land and set out to sell them in a basket carried over my head. I had visions of sitting at Sanganeri gate in Jaipur with my vegetables laid out on the platform or wheeling a cart full of vegetables selling them to housewives. People are very conscious of organic farming these days and go in for exotic vegetables such as kale and various types of lettuce.

Twenty-five years have passed, or maybe more. I have put in my entire earnings from all my recordings and shows into this venture. The dream of owning my piece of land was as close to my heart as a *choli* is. Many a time, it crossed my mind that like the Maharajas and Maharanis of the past, who built canopies as memorials to themselves, I should also do so on my barren plot of land. We used to see many such memorials outside Amber Fort when we went for picnics in that area as children. This was a unique idea since I do not know of any celebrities from the film world who would be remembered in this way. I would have my own burial ground which no one could claim to have. If that failed, I was ready to form a trust, like the

Birla family has, and build a temple over it. Why should I not take advantage of my Brahmin origins? I would transport marble statues of Ram or Krishna, Ganesh or perhaps my family deity, Vindhyachal Devi, and install them in this temple. There would be hymns sung, prayers and rituals performed in the mornings and evenings, with devotees making offerings of sweets and money. This would be my pension in old age. After all an artiste's mind is allowed to wander in the pastures of dreams! Thus, I kept the dream of my Malwani home locked up in the safe recesses of my heart. I sometimes feel that perhaps I should will this land to my two granddaughters. It could perhaps fund their education. Whatever transpires, this land shall not be lost in vain. Even if my dream does not materialize, my dream for my granddaughters' will be fulfilled.

My readers must be wondering about the oft-repeated word, property, land, *zameen*. But once again, I regret to say, for myself and for you, reader, that this was not the end of our 'land story'. There was more to come.

In the middle of all this, Arun got taken in for another land episode, a deal he did not even discuss with me, his dream garden. A builder named Parasrampuria was advertising to sell a huge piece of land. The headlines said: 'Now you can be the owner of your own mango orchards.' The plan sounded enticing. One had to pay a sum of money and the orchard would be yours. The builder would take care of it and when the crop was harvested you would get the fruit in Mumbai. They assured us that when you sell the land, you would get the going price for it. For Arun, it felt like a win-win situation. The proximity to Mumbai clinched the deal and once again—we were victims of daylight robbery! As for me, I was already on the path to owning a mango orchard. I recalled the days at Purohitji-Ka-Bagh, our childhood home, full of fruit trees, which we would climb to pluck off guavas, *jamuns* and mangoes. Now we would actually have an orchard, not the one by proxy in a rented house in Jaipur. I would have several varieties of mango: the king of mangos, the Alphonso, kesar, Ratnagiri. My mother always harked back to the taste of the *dasseri* mangoes in her native Allahabad. I would show her the taste of real mangoes, the brilliance of the *hapus* or Alphonso. I thought of the mangoes sent by stars from their farmhouses, with fancy chits stuck on them, and I imagined my mango parcels being dispatched with my name on them to my friends and some producers. They would get the mangoes and I some work! I could see peacocks dancing in my garden, squirrels and parrots and *koels* cavorting on trees and branches and like the *maalin* of Purohitji-Ka-Bagh, I would be chasing monkeys. Suddenly, there was a crash, and I was on the floor, clutching my dreams in my arms. So, another fall, one more dream shattered! We got the news that there had been a raid on the builder's office, and it had been sealed! The Parasrampurias fled, taking with them my mango orchard.

That is when I realized that my relationship with land, the earth, was limited only to my name, Ila. This would not become a reality. I swore that I would never again allow this dream to cross the threshold of my eyes. How true was the lament of Bahadur Shah Zaffar, the exiled poet–king of Delhi, the last emperor of a great dynasty, 'How unfortunate is Zaffar/ That even two yards of earth did not fall to his lot/ For his burial.'

But I am not one to accept defeat. Just like the owner of the step-well in Shyam Benegal's *Well Done Abba*, I am determined and confident that 'this land is my land', and one day, it will indeed be mine. And I shall bequeath this piece of land to my only child, my daughter. And I can hear her say with pride, 'Well done, Amma,' not Abba, with perhaps a pat on my back!

Chapter 26

Paradise 3: *Kiska Yeh Jahan Hai?*

Friendship is like a book. It takes a few seconds to burn but it takes years to write.

Some relationships are difficult to define. One such is K.K. Raina, who first came to Paradise as a theatre actor. If Arun is the foundation of Paradise, KK is one of its strongest pillars. He has become a part of the family, and we spend a lot of time together. I am sure most people wonder about this friendship. Their eyes pop when they see a married woman with a single male and the same male all the time. I can imagine them gossiping behind my back. I remember the lines from *Amar Prem* (1972), '*Kuchh to log kahenge, Logon ka kaam hai kehna/ chodo bekar ki baton mein/ kahin beet na jayein raina*'. (People will talk,/it is their business to talk/let us ignore this inane gossip/lest our lives are wasted in this futile conversation.) And so Rainaji became a member of our family.

Arun was always out, and I was a little apprehensive in accepting people into my house unless I was sure of their intentions, which of course are difficult to gauge. Among my close women friends there is Anjulaji, Shilpa and Avni. My male friends are Binny, Razdan who is no more and of course, KK. We have been not only friends but also colleagues since we are in the same profession. He is the backbone of all my recordings, my live shows and of course the transcriber and critic of all my plays and writing. He took on the task of managing all my affairs when Arun was away. I count him as my best friend, but I am not sure he reciprocates the feeling. He would say that his best friends are his books! His full name is Krishna Kumar, KK for short, but I tease him and say that the KK stands for *kitabi keeda*, bookworm! I believe the real definition of *kitabi keeda* is white ants. They devour books and paper, but they have nothing to do with the content of the book. They don't understand it and yet they lick the paper clean. KK doesn't lick his books, he devours them! He sleeps, eats and lives books. There is a word for someone who sleeps with books—librocubicularist. He is not concerned that he has no land or bed or *razai*, blanket, as long as he has his books!

KK has been more like a mother to Ishitta than I have. She calls him her 'boobless mother' while I am the useless mother. For my granddaughters, he is Jhumku. From their birth to the present, KK has played the role of the Kabuliwala for them. He reads the stories of the Ramayana and the Mahabharata to them along with the story of Kabuliwala. He would also dress up in the clothes of the character, carrying pistachios, almonds and currants. Krishna Kumar has lived up to his name. An intelligent man, an excellent actor and a great director, he has never compromised on anything he has taken up. He is scrupulously honest, both intellectually and in his dealings with colleagues and friends. A calm and sensitive man, he lives life by his principles. A man apart, he does not have an envious or mean bone in his body.

This relationship started at the Prithvi when I went to see a play *Ek Ruka Hua Faisla*. I was so impressed by his performance that I went backstage and asked him to join me in my theatre activity. He was kind enough to agree. As a result, I got to know all his colleagues and classmates from NSD, all of whom were accomplished artistes and a few of them—Vijay Kashyap, Virendra Razdan and K.K. Raina—became the pillars of our new theatre group, Surnai. Another Kashmiri, Lateef Binny, also joined the group and KK, Razdan and Binny took a room together at Malad. Being Kashmiris, they were comfortable together. From Malad they moved to Juhu. Every eleven months their lease expired and they had to start searching for new accommodation. Finally, changing one home after another, they landed up close to us, in Prabhat Colony. Since they were closer, their visits became more frequent. PGs in Mumbai get nothing but a room, so every time they felt a craving for Kashmiri food they would come across with their ingredients and cook *yakhni, korma* and *rajma, dum aloo* and *paneer*, the staple Kashmiri food. It is said that language and food make friendships even stronger, and the people who give you their food, give you their heart. Binny spent more time with Ishitta rather than in the kitchen. I don't know what strange games they played that they ended up breaking all of Ishitta's hair bands!

Gradually friendship changed into stronger bonds, so when I used to tie a *rakhi* for Piyush, two more brothers were added to the list: Binny and our tailor Shekhar from Jodhpur, who was my tailor and designer for many years in Mumbai. All of these friends have progressed in life and now have families and homes of their own, but I am happy to say that Paradise was home for them and will remain so forever.

These were people close to my heart and my home was opened up for them for another reason. In the 1990s, when militancy started in Kashmir and people lost their homes, the sting of it was like a splinter in their throat. Their lives were shattered, their roots snatched from them and there was a financial earthquake in their lives. Till now, despite their exodus from Kashmir, they stayed connected to their roots in the Valley by visiting on holidays. But when terrorism took hold of Kashmir, their relatives and friends were forced to live as tenants in the houses of Dogras in Jammu. Those who had no money, moved to tents in refugee shelters. People used to living in icy-cold valleys were left to languish in the scorching heat of the plains. Today, when I see people protesting and lamenting about refugees living in Syria, Ukraine and Gaza, I am saddened by the fact that not a voice is raised, not a word of sympathy is uttered about their own countrymen whose homes were destroyed and who were uprooted and live as refugees in their own country. They had to struggle with the summer heat, their camps were infested with scorpions and snakes. They lived in crowded accommodations with very little breathing space. And yet, no one raised their voices. The press also chose to remain silent. The entire film industry remained a mute spectator. Political parties turned a blind eye to their suffering. People were hesitant to rent out their houses to them. They tolerated this humiliation because they had no choice and no voice.

I have seen all this at close quarters. Friendship is tried and tested in moments of sorrow, but I had nothing to give them except consolation and a place in my home. We would all sit together and share our sorrows here in this house. Whatever happened in Kashmir, affected not only the Hindus but also had a significant impact on Muslims and their businesses. I had visited Binny's house in Kashmir—his family were farmers and owned huge farms—and I was touched by the hospitality and affection I received from them. Gradually, in order to save his life, he also left his fields and business behind in Kashmir.

The tragedy of Kashmir brought KK's family and ours very close to each other. I had bought a small flat in Versova with my earnings and I invited them to stay in this apartment. The whole family—KK, his mother, whom we fondly called Bhinji, his father, his sister and brother—spent a long time in this apartment. KK is not only our friend but the friend of the entire family. Whenever we celebrate any festival in our family, when someone is sick or there is some unpleasant news, KK is found standing with the family like a rock. When my mother came from Jaipur, the first thing she would ask was, 'Where is KK? Tell him to visit me and to bring along some books and some *kadam ka saag*!' Binny, our Muslim friend, always treated my mother to a vegetarian *thali* at the Hare Krishna Temple restaurant, Govinda, on Janamashtmi, a treat she remembered till the very end of her life.

Time heals all wounds, but the scars are still fresh in their hearts and minds. Razdan did well and earned from his role as Vidur in the Mahabharata and bought his first house at Nalasopara and then shifted to a house in Vasai. KK also first invested in Nalasopara and later in Malad, which is his home now. Binny also bought a house in Andheri, where he lives with his wife and daughter. They are all well settled, though Razdan's passing away so many years ago still hurts. I can proudly proclaim that Paradise saw the beginning of all their careers and the moral support that all of us received from each other gave us the courage to find our place in life.

All these events happened around Paradise or flourished within its boundary walls. Paradise has seen many events: marriages, divorce, birth of grandchildren, sister's grandchildren, demise of dear ones, especially missed is my brother-in-law, Ajay Awasthi. My nephew Abhijit, Umaji's son, spent a few months before he got a job here. Now he runs his own, successful ad company, Sideways. Another nephew, Nihar, Ramaji's son, spent some time with us looking for a job here. There were so many additions to the family in the forty years that we have been here, additions that have brought in changes in the mindset of the older generation. When my sisters got married over fifty years ago, they all married Kanyakubja Brahmins and so did I. My mother, though modern in certain aspects, was adamant about marrying within the community. But when my brothers married outside the caste, Piyush a Maharashtrian, Nita, and Prasoon a Punjabi, Gayatri, she decided that she had to change with the times for the sake of her sons and accepted them all with open arms. Nita, after being in advertising for several years, has studied to become a vet. Gayatri is a graphic designer from NID and has taken to gardening in a big way, supplying plants for my tiny balcony.

From Indrangan in Jaipur to Paradise, we had created our own Pandey Republic in Mumbai. Hindu, Muslim, Christian and now my converted Buddhist daughter; many religions were amalgamated into the fold. Spouses from different regions—Maharashtra, Gujarat, Tamil Nadu, Karnataka, Bengal, the US—brought their own customs and traditions—different regions and different religions. We are still waiting for a Sikh and a Parsi addition to the family. Perhaps the next generation will oblige us!

Paradise was a 'pee stop', a *sulabh shauchalya*, for people crossing to go from the north to south Mumbai It was a tea stop for those catching flights and even trains from the Lokmanya Tilak Terminus. Friends and relatives and the relatives of friends came for a nap in between meetings or rehearsals. Once Piyush and Ranjan Kapur dropped in for a breakfast of *parathas* between a cremation and a meeting, a visit that would have horrified my Kanyakubja relatives since you couldn't even enter your own home without first cleansing yourself after a death ritual. The Santa Cruz market nearby and the Hasnabad Lane provided the venue for all the needs for weddings, so whenever a wedding was in the offing, Meena and the girls of the family would bring the material and sew and decorate and pack all this paraphernalia. Of course, the costumes and props for our plays also found space here, amidst all the inhabitants.

There are many stories, but a very important part of this house, the guardian angels of Paradise, have been Anita and Meena. Every home in Mumbai and elsewhere in India has helpers who work to make our lives better, despite hours of work and hardships. They leave everything behind—their villages, homes and relatives—and come from far-flung villages to make a life for themselves. There are countless stories related to their lives, and the many compulsions which have forced them to uproot themselves at a young age to support their families. When they come, they accept your house as their own and spend their working years in making life easy for you. We fail to recognize their contribution and very often treat them unfairly. There are stories of how young girls are taken advantage of by male servants and sometimes even by the *sahibs*.

Two girls came into my life: Anita and Meena. Meena has been with us for forty years now. She used to come to our house with her mother Lakshmibai, who was our cleaning woman. When and how Lakshmibai got the name Parveen Babi, I don't know. But Ishitta called her Babi instead of Bai, so I said if she was Babi, then might as well add the name Parveen for her and so she remained Parveen Babi for the household. When she came to work, she was accompanied by an eight-year-old girl, her daughter, Meena, who would come after her class at Poddar School. She was intelligent and well-mannered and a very active and alert child. She was also an artist, and excellent in arts and crafts, and loved decorating the house with *rangoli* and flowers. She was a little older than Ishitta and enjoyed playing with her dolls and toys while her mother worked. She wanted to study further after school and enrolled for a certificate course at Chetna College. She was always trying to upgrade herself and we encouraged her as much as we could. She appeared for her BA in commerce, perhaps thinking of this degree for a future job, though she had no interest in the subject. She attempted the exam a couple of times but was unsuccessful. She was so disheartened that she decided that a degree was of no value.

Her mother asked if she could stay with us and help Anita in household work. I was happy to have a second hand to do odd jobs. So, she came and started living with us and turned out to be a real asset. She soon became the pivot of all the activities in the house. Not a leaf in the house stirs without her knowledge. Starting with sewing, embroidery, weaving, making new things from *jugaad*, typing, cooking, she had ideas which took her ahead of everyone else. And during the forty years of Surnai's journey, Meena not only handled the backstage, the costumes and property for at least thirty years of her life, but also contributed to helping with the props, sets and costumes. Well-known designers cannot compete with Meena's imaginative power. There is no comparison to her expertise in arrangement and organization. Our backstage artistes admire her talent. She is indispensable to me, handling my correspondence, my emails and all the properties and costumes for our shows.

Several girls and boys who came as backstage help failed to live up to our Meena. Ultimately, everyone depended on her. Most of them came as backstage help, but always aspired to come up frontstage! No one takes backstage work seriously, but it is a huge responsibility and discipline and could help you to reach the level of a director. Because of Meena's efficiency, we never had to hire a trained, experienced person from outside. In fact, we joke with her saying she can open her own workshop on backstage management.

Her family had seen days of poverty, a family of two brothers and one sister, in which all three children were talented. One brother, Kalu, used to play the drum very well and the other brother was running a catering business. Kalu later got a job in Fab India, through our niece, Swati's friend. If Kalu were alive today, he would have been on a managerial post. But unfortunately, he died in an accident at a young age.

Meena is an introvert and even after forty years I have not managed to get an insight into her innermost feelings. She does not open up and allow anyone to invade her privacy. Something prevented her from getting married and then the death of her parents deprived her of a home she could retreat to once in a while.

When Ishitta's children were born, Meena became a godmother to them. The love and affection they give her is heart-warming, far more than what I get from them. So, blood relatives and 'blood aunts' are not always the favourites. Children can differentiate between the ones who really care and those who just fake it! Meena is a living example of that.

Anita had been with us for some time before Meena joined us. If Meena raised Ishitta's children, Anita raised Ishitta. She took over all the responsibilities of a mother and guarded her with her life. She kept a watch on all her movements and knew where she was going and when she would be back. Anita arrived at our door on her own, an amazing girl of almost twenty years. She was very intelligent and had knowledge of the whole world without much formal education. She had the desire to move forward. Although she had studied only up to Class VIII, her general knowledge was that of a highly educated person. She wanted to keep up with the news and wanted to know about the state of the world. She was always questioning whatever was happening around her: 'Why? *Kyun*?' Sometimes there were no answers to her queries. One day I saw that she was writing a letter very seriously. When I asked her who to, she said, 'Rajiv Gandhi.' He was our prime minister at the time and this young girl was actually penning a letter to him! The content of the letter is paraphrased here. 'Mr Prime Minister, you talk about removing the slums of Bombay, have you ever wondered where these slums come from? These are those poor, hungry and illiterate people from villages who have come to Bombay under compulsion in search of work to make ends meet, their fields have been snatched away from them, along with their livelihood. Have you ever thought about their hunger and unemployment? They are also citizens of India.' She posted this letter and the interesting thing is that she got a reply from Rajiv Gandhi's office! Shabana was so impressed that she quoted Anita's letter in some of the protests that she led in support of slum-dwellers in the 1980s.

Today I am happy that she is settled with a good husband and has a daughter who is a chess champion at the high-school level. Enterprising as ever, Anita has her own start-up, which she opened during Covid and sells *chivda* and other savouries from her home.

There were many marriage proposals for Meena. But they were not able to match the environment in which she has been living for forty years, or her abilities and sensibilities. Once girls have seen a better standard of life in cities, and are educated, their outlook changes and they cannot go back to where they have come from. Meena had grown up in a liberal environment, how could she go back to live in a narrow, restricted world again? She chose the life of a single girl and served her parents till the end of their lives, both financially and emotionally.

Thousands of stories were born in Paradise. But with time, not only are we getting older, the walls of our house are also ageing. The streets outside the house too are changing. While the government claims that they are planting more trees, a few years ago the 100-year-old bottle rain trees, which was one of our reasons for buying this house, were mercilessly cut down and a new building started growing in place of the trees. Not one person from any of the buildings went down to protest this illegal act including me. I am ashamed of my apathy and wonder why I did not, like Gaura Devi of the Chipko movement, step out to hug a tree and prevent its death? I have suffered the consequences. The sun that drifted on to my balcony every morning and to which I would offer my daily *surya namaskar*, has been swallowed by the same building. We buy a house, carefully selecting the location, the direction it faces, how much light each room will get, and before we know it, all the promises that the builder has lured us with are reversed. The builder is aware of the plans in advance but chooses to fool us into buying his property. How do we get trapped in the whirlpool of his promises? Now so many buildings have come up nearby that the distance between houses has reduced. Even the journeys on foot have been snatched away from us due to the heavy traffic on the roads. The footsteps that I had got used to, of people I knew and which gave me a feeling of safety and security, are heard no more. The noise and smoke of vehicles is poisoning the air, sometimes destroying our senses. Where do so many people come from and where do they go?

Many people ask me why I don't move into a bigger flat, a tower perhaps. I have two flats in a tower in Goregaon East. My niece Swati, whom I have mentioned before, came to visit me recently and she asked me the same question: why do I not shift into a bigger flat? My answer to her was that my world is this flat, my heaven, my creative space. I reminded her that my mother, her *nani*, had always said live within your means. I live in Paradise and have no intention to move into a Fool's Paradise! It is true, I didn't have the heart to shift into those flats, because the story of my life is etched in every brick and stone in Paradise. I visited a friend in a tower recently and felt I was dwarfed by the enormity of the buildings around me. Why would I live in a building that reduces my personality to a zero, where my clothes and my car would be noticed, where friendships would be weighed on the scale of status? There is no pleasure living in a place where you have to dress up, paint your face and colour your lips just to go vegetable shopping! My mind does not allow me to take this step. None of the new flats that I have bought in the last forty years can give me the kind of peace that this house has given me. Even though the sunlight has diminished beyond the walls, the light of memories still remains in this house. My daughter's childhood was spent within these walls. Little Ishitta learned to take her first baby steps on the floor of this apartment.

This house has witnessed so many ups and downs, and now we have heard that this building is going for redevelopment. That means our house has become old, but can something become old even at forty? For me, it is still young and beautiful. When I look at Paradise, I remember those four lines written in awe of the beauty of Kashmir by poet Amir Khusrow, 'If there be a heaven on this earth it is here, it is here, it is here.'

Let us remember this Paradise: 'Where love resides, memories are created, friends always belong and laughter never ends!'

I shudder at the mere thought that Paradise is about to go into redevelopment, and I imagine myself sitting on the debris of memories, sobbing. Will my Paradise be lost?

Chapter 27

Hats Off: Awards and Rewards

Come 24 January and I am on tenterhooks. Restless and sleepless, my eyes wander to my phone. Will there be a call, a message from the Ministry of Home Affairs, informing me that I have been conferred a Padma Award, to be announced on Republic Day? And yet why do I even think of something that is impossible and can never happen, something that I probably don't even want? Then why do I nurture this thought? The seed of hope was sown in my mind by our late Vice President Shri Bhairon Singh Shekhawat, who was from Rajasthan and had been chief minister of the state for several terms and then became the Vice-President of India. Often, he had mentioned to me and sometimes in public too, that Ila has done so much for Rajasthani culture not only at home but all over the world that she can truly be called an ambassador for Rajasthan. He said that I had brought the youth of India back to their roots by making them dance to the tune of traditional folk songs, presented in a modern context. 'For several years, every school, every function, every wedding had people dancing to her traditional songs.'

But long before Bhairon Singhji gave me that status, I had already unofficially decided that I was going to take Rajasthani music to all parts of the world. The perfect opportunity presented itself when I was going to join Arun for the first time on the ship anchored at Baltimore. As it is I was very nervous, not knowing anything about a sea voyage and apprehensive about stepping onto a foreign country for the first time. Jaipur was a small town at the time and even the trip to the airport at Sanganer seemed like a voyage! My parents came to drop me, a farewell to a VIP, with garlands and flowers.

337

At the time I felt I was going not to meet my husband but as an ambassador for India. I had great dreams of spreading the culture of my country, little realizing that most of my time was going to be spent at sea! For me, it was like going for an Indian festival or a Miss India contest. The amount of preparation that went into making this idea a reality took a long time. I ordered a sari for the trip, I, who was most uncomfortable in that attire. I had it embroidered in the Gujarati stitch Ahir, with designs of animals and birds done in chain and herringbone stitch, practised by women during the lean farming season. Every colour you could think of was on that sari—mauve, green, blue, orange—enhanced by a Kutchi mirror-work blouse. I wore a huge red bindi. On my shoulder, besides all the other bags I was carrying, hung a *dholak*. What was I thinking: a young second engineer's wife, going to join him officially in another country, looking like a *nautanki* artiste! With all this baggage, I boarded the aircraft to Mumbai from where I was to take an international flight. The moment I sat in the aircraft, the magnitude of the moment struck me. I was going to leave India for the first time, leaving my parents behind, changing flights twice before I got to Baltimore, getting on a ship and sailing off with a man I had just about got to know. And the flood of tears started, sobbing as if my heart would break. I wiped my tears with the end of the brand-new mauve sari! I don't think I cried as much even when I left my home at the *bidai*, the send-off to my marital home, as I did at that parting. A foreign couple on the flight was watching me. They were obviously frequent visitors to Jaipur and familiar with Indian traditions. My father asked them to look after me. Between Jaipur and Mumbai, I sobbed so much that this couple asked me why I was so upset. When girls go to meet their husbands, they are generally happy. Had I been forced to marry this man? Is he a total stranger? I told them I was happy, but I was a very emotional person, and tears came easily to me. We started chatting, and as we were landing at Boston, the stop before Baltimore, and their destination, they asked me if I had money. I told them I had traveller's cheques, which my father, being a banker, had thought it wise to give me. The gentleman said that Boston is a long wait, and I would need some cash for a cup of coffee and something to eat. He drew out eleven dollars. I was most embarrassed and kept telling them that I would return the money as soon we reached Baltimore since my husband would be there to receive me. On my insistence they gave me their address and said they come to Jaipur often for their jewellery business and would collect the money there. When we reached Boston, I went through immigration and was horrified to see the customs examining my *dholak* by banging on it. They didn't know what it was and spent so much time inspecting it, rolling it around and beating on it, that I was sure it would break or become dissonant. They even put it through a scanner before letting it go. So, armed with my ambassadorial paraphernalia and my eleven dollars I went into a café to get some food. There was a huge menu, but of course, it went over my head! I was travelling on TWA, which did not serve Indian food. I had not been exposed to Western dishes till then and was looking for a bit of spice in my food. Hesitatingly, I asked them if they had anything vegetarian. They said yes, mashed potatoes and corn with a dash of tabasco. I settled for the only vegetarian dish they had. But when it was brought before me, it was the best dish I had ever had! Since then, I have looked for that dish on my subsequent journeys abroad, but sadly, they have never heard of it. That aroma still haunts me in my culinary pursuit, though now I am familiar with global cuisine. It was great to see Arun waiting for me at Baltimore. I was so excited and wanted to give him each detail of my first journey out of India. The first thing he did was to call up that generous couple on the number they had given me and made arrangements to return the money. So, there I was in the United States of America, the 'unappointed', unacknowledged, self-proclaimed cultural ambassador of Rajasthan! But I felt I had carried a huge burden for this title and as often before, I remembered my guru, Raghunathji!

And that was my intention even as a teenager when I went for youth festivals and danced with folk dancers from all over India on Republic Day, the response from the audience and my peers was my reward. Or was it possible that I was made aware of the honours conferred on Republic Day even then, as I danced down Rajpath, in front of thousands of people, past the President and other dignitaries? Folk music is in my DNA. Nothing gives me more pleasure than spending time with folk singers and dancers. I have truly given them as much stage time as I have for myself in several of my programmes. They have been cultural secretaries to my ambassadorial presentations.

Another occasion for which I would be considered an ambassador for India in the realm of folk music was when I was invited to the prestigious Smithsonian Institute in Washington DC in 1999. This was part of their celebration of Rajasthan Week, which was jointly sponsored by the Smithsonian Institute, the Embassy of India and Air India. I was invited to give a lecture-cum-performance on traditional Rajasthani folk dances and music with four folk artistes, which is retained in their archives.

I get several phone calls after the award announcements, lamenting the fact that I was not on the list, thus provoking me to vent my disappointment in private. I was told that this year's list comprised five Padma Vibhushans, seventeen Padma Bhushans and 110 Padma Shri awards! Once when I congratulated Anup Jalota on his Padma Shri, he said that I should have got one and went on to say that I would get it the following year. When people put such thoughts in your mind, without realizing it, you start having misconceptions and hopes about yourself, which would never have surfaced otherwise. Where do I stand amongst the vast talent of India? I consider myself just a cog in the wheel of the music fraternity of India, the wheel of the bullock-cart I started my journey on. I told Anupji that everyone tells me that I should have been an awardee, but how can I get one? He said someone will have to nominate you. 'Maybe I could do it since a Padma Shri awardee has the privilege of nominating,' he offered. But his next sentence shattered the tiny bit of hope that I had. He explained, 'You have to do a lot of lobbying too. Either your state nominates you and for that you have to meet the CM or an MLA or MP. You have to keep good relations with the officials of the state.' I laughed and said, 'I have no time for my own work, how do I take time out to socialize with the bureaucracy, become a courtier in their *darbar*? Only for the Padma Shri? And what after that, will I still have to kowtow to them?' He smiled a wry smile as if conveying that there was no hope for me. 'Lobbying is necessary,' he said. At that time, I said that an award is hardly an award if you have to lobby for it and ask for it shamelessly. One should get an award for one's work and reputation. If I do lobby, will I be able to face my image in a mirror? My photographs would be on the pages of newspapers, but would I see the real me? I remembered these words, '*Aina dekhane wale/dekha toone/ Aina dekh raha hai tujhe hairan hoke.*' (You who glance at yourself in a mirror/do you not see that the mirror looks back at you,/bewildered?)

That would not be my real face. But still listening to people, I must confess, a hidden desire did well up in my mind, the aspiration for a Padma Shri. I wanted to get the Padma Shri for a very personal reason—my mother's sari. My mother had once gifted me a very heavy gold Kanjeevaram sari, saying, 'You are gaining in popularity and fame. One day I know you will get a prestigious award like the Padma Shri. I want you to wear this sari on that occasion, though I know you don't like to wear saris, something that I have always regretted. You have sung so many folk songs, you act and you have worked with great directors like Shyam Benegal. You have given so much to charity by performing for NGOs, helping the hearing impaired, the blind, those afflicted with leprosy and cancer, you will definitely get the Padma Shri. And when you do, don't forget me.' She left this world with this dream unfulfilled, her eyes full of hope for me, finally closed without seeing me in this sari, which I believe she had hidden away from all the others in the family who might have coveted it!

My belief was the same then as it is now. An award sought after, manipulated, is not an award. You can fool the world, but you cannot fool yourself. I have been running a theatre group for forty years, without any support from the government. We perform throughout the year in different parts of the country, getting rave reviews and extensive press coverage and accolades from the audience. We have a repertoire of twenty-six plays, which we have performed, ten adaptations and four original plays by me. Surely those who are the selectors are getting some information about this, some whispers. Are the selectors unaware of what is happening around them in the world of the performing arts? A committee is formed for this purpose and their job is to look for the best. But they don't seem to know how and where to look for artistes and I don't know how to lobby.

The Filmfare Awards also have a lobby. That is why Aamir Khan has stopped attending any of these award functions. Even if he has received an award, obviously without lobbying, he has never gone to receive it. This was because, in this line, awards are the result of your lobbying and knowing the right people. I have heard that some awards are actually bought. Rishi Kapoor had mentioned in the release of his book *Khullam Khulla: Rishi Kapoor Uncensored* that when he was young and naïve, his award for *Bobby* had been lobbied for! I was on the jury of the *Screen* Awards and know how many calls I would get recommending contenders for the awards.

The Oscars too depend on fierce lobbying. That is why Ashutosh Gowarikar's *Lagaan* (2001) never made it to the awards. My mother used to recite Kabir's *doha*: '*Bin maange moti milen, maange milen na bheek.*' (Pearls are given to you unasked, but if you ask, you don't even get alms.) These days you get something only when you ask for it. I sometimes feel that the financial status of a beggar is better than ours! But I guess I cannot complain. After several years, I was thrilled to get a certificate of participation for the Grammy award, after the success of *Slumdog Millionaire* and Rahman Sahib's award for music and the song '*Ringa Ringa*' sung by Alka and me. This is the highest international award for music. Before this, the song '*Choli Ke Peechhey*' had already received the Filmfare Award and my original song '*Nigodi*', got the Channel V award for best song. I had been nominated for 'Best Supporting Actress' in *Jodhaa Akbar* and *Welcome to Sajjanpur*.

At the Toronto Film Festival and the film festival in Abu Dhabi, I was nominated Best Supporting Actress for *West Is West*, without lobbying, which made me very happy. To top it all, there can't be a bigger award than the King's Order of Merit-Knight 1st Class from the King of Norway, on par with the British OBE, for my contribution in making Henrik Ibsen famous in India. I also received the Best Actress award for the children's film *Gauru* (2018), directed by Ramkishan Choyal for the Children's Film Society at the Shanghai Film Festival.

Besides the King of Norway, I have been honoured by two scions of the royal houses of Rajasthan. The Maharaja of Jaipur honoured me with the Maharaja Bishen Singh Award for my contribution to the preservation of the folk culture of Rajasthan and as I write this book and mention my association with Jodhpur and Mehrangarh,

I have just got the news that my name has been finalized for the Marwar Ratna Award, the Maharaja Vijay Singhji Award, for 'your outstanding achievement in Rajasthani folk music' presented by His Highness Maharaja Gajsinghji of Jodhpur on the Foundation Day of the state of Jodhpur. What a coincidence that the award ceremony will take place in the courtyard of the Mehrangarh Museum, from where I started the story of my origins in Chapter 1!

Do the other awards matter?

As far as the Padma Awards go, what amused me was one of the notifications for the awardees: 'The award does not amount to a title and cannot be used as a suffix or prefix to the awardee's name on letterheads, invitation cards, posters, books etc. In the case of any misuse, the awardee will forfeit the award.' When I looked at that, I gave full marks to parents who had anticipated that the world of awards would be messy, so circumventing that mess, they gave their children names that would ensure that they did not need any awards. Our friend and colleague, actor-writer-director, was named Bharat Ratna by his father. Now whether he gets an award or not, for his parents and friends, he will always live with that title, a title an awardee will never be allowed to use! There are three boys in the family: Bharat Ratna, Bharat Bhushan and Padma Bhushan! I met a girl in Bhopal, the wife of an NSD alumni, S.B. Josalkar working in the Goa Akademi, who was called Padma Shri. In the south, children are conferred the title of Padma Shri the moment they are born, since that is a common name for girls. The government can give an order that you cannot put the title of Padma Shri before your name for common use, but if the parents have already bestowed that honour on you, well you are on your way! Perhaps this award given by your parents is the best award, and that which is won through lobbying and manipulation is a lie. And I hate lies.

My son-in-law, Dhruv is really concerned. 'You deserve it,' he says. 'This time we will submit your name as soon as the list opens up.' I was touched and thought if my children think so, then I have already got my award and reward. I just heard that now you can nominate yourself, online! I find this ridiculous. Nominate yourself? If I stoop to that, how will I ever be able to look at myself in the mirror when I go to bed at night?

When I am greeted by people at airports and public places, who say they have won prizes in dance and music competitions, for my songs, and that grandmothers, mothers and daughters and often sons, have danced to my music, my joy knows no bounds and I know I have got my Padma Shri. Without lobbying for it! As Tom Cruise has said about awards, 'But my journey is not towards that. If it happens, it will be a blast. If it doesn't, it's still been a blast.'

It has been a long and eventful journey with my contribution in many fields as actor, lyricist, composer, costume designer, and of course, singer. And the journey still goes on.

Epilogue: IA vs AI

I had a nightmare. There was a knock on the door of my wisdom.

Knock! Knock!

IA: Who are you?

AI: AI.

IA: So what? I am IA, Ila Arun! Your full name?

AI: Artificial Intelligence. I want to help you.

IA: Oh no! Get lost. I know you are going to devour me.

AI: (laughs) Don't heed these rumours. I can help you, enhance your voice, make you ageless. Your voice will be heard for eternity.

IA: Rubbish. Let me sleep. Don't talk of eternity. We are struggling to exist in the present. You are killing all the artistes, singers and musicians. I hate you.

AI: Let me in. I will tell you about the many advantages. Let me come in or I will keep knocking at the door of your wisdom.

IA: I am afraid of technology. Of what you can do to me. You are my nightmare, and you could destroy my very soul, my writing, my singing, my acting!

AI: Ah, that is what I am trying to tell you. I can enhance your writing by providing the supportive tools so that you concentrate on the content!

IA: (laughs) I need no supportive tools. I still use pen and paper!

AI: (Speechless)

IA: And I write in Hindi!

AI: That's it! AI has the ability to read text in different languages. I can help you by providing you with text-to-speech and speech-to-text in thousands of languages.

IA: No! Then I can finally stop using AB and switch to AI? Then what will Anjulaji do?

AI: Use AI to translate Bantu, Chenoua, Esan, Inupiaq or even Chinese into English!

IA: And what about my music? I think I was better off in Rajasthan, singing for myself. But I got tempted by this music industry and came to Mumbai, thinking I could also make an album. I was fascinated by the music industry, which is constantly growing and evolving. I have seen vinyl records, spool tapes, cassettes, CDs and then digital music. But now I foresee an end to all this. You are killing artistes. I must confess I have also been tempted by technology for a second. Sometimes during a recording, my keyboard player would play around with certain samples of musical instruments, the flute, violin, *tabla* and *dhol*. He proudly told me this keyboard was from Yamaha in Japan and could produce the sounds of almost any instrument. The thought flashed through my mind that I could now travel only with a Yamaha keyboard and save on the cost of musicians. How selfish I was! But I have a conscience, which you don't have. I had seen the disappearance of musicians at recordings. In place of the hundred musicians in the past, now there is only one keyboard player. Even the music directors are missing. All these musicians were rendered jobless by this one intruder. Gradually some of them died, some took to drinking. Now you are going to attack us, by using voice manipulation in a variety of ways, timbre modification, pitch correction and vocal synthesizers. I accept pitch correction; you will be helping me since as I grow older, I am losing my breath and tech can help me.

AI: There you are . . . I can make you ageless and immortal!

IA: Yes, I will become immortal while I am still alive, because you would have cloned me. But you have ulterior motives. You will make a virtual singer out of me. You can copy various pitches, breathing, pauses and create a synthetic singer.

AI: As I said, it will be useful to you especially since you have a unique pitch others find difficult to match!

IA: This is good for the composers and producers but what about the singers? And me? What about all my *Oohs* and *Aahs* and *Orayys?*

AI: Sorry! Those will be difficult even for AI. Maybe we can produce a virtual Raghunath to put those in. Do you have a photograph of him?

IA: (screams) Remember, man has created you, you cannot create a man. You must have parents who created you.

AI: I have a father, John McCarthy.

IA: And your mother?

AI: I am born of the mind and not of the womb. One parent is enough for me.

IA: Virtual humans! That means Nita Ambani can become Ila Arun, though I doubt if she will want to, but can Ila Arun become Nita Ambani? No, because she doesn't have the resources. So as always, the winner takes all and as always, the winner is wealth and now AI!

AI: No! No! I will never use my intelligence to make you Nita Ambani! I am going to her next. I want two clients rather than one!

IA: I am an actor and I live on hope. I console myself by believing that while AI may have its merits, it will never be able to replace the unmatched spirit of human performance. I am convinced that you will never be able to create the emotional depth, creativity, the genuine interaction that actors bring to their craft. It is the human touch that makes even an ordinary actor truly extraordinary. You may kill us, but you cannot destroy our spirit! Don't forget that Hollywood writers and actors have won their case against AI and the producers who exploit them. Could AI have lasted 148 days without work? You would have become lazy and useless!

AI: That is why I am asking you to let me in so that I can have eye contact with you. The only thing that you actors understand! You must know ki AI *ke peechhey kya hai*!

IA: AI *ke peechey IA bhag rahi hai*! So, using a line from my song, I say, 'Door hat ja re hat ja chora door hat ja/ doongi mein aisa jhatka/ door hat ja re hat ja!' (IA is chasing AI. So you had better run, boy, run/ I'll give you such a push that will throw you further than you can imagine!)

And AI was swallowed up by the earth! I woke up from this AI nightmare, praying that my mind would never be manipulated by it again!

Words: English-Vinglish

People have often asked me why I have not written a book on my life. There is a line in my play, *Hardit Kaur Gill*, an adaptation of Ibsen's *Hedda Gabler*, '*Man mein toh puttar, mai roz kitaab likhtee hoon, par likhna itna aasan thodi na hai.*' (I create a book every day in my mind, but actually writing one is not that easy.) I am an observer, I connect with people, conjure up myriad words, string sentences in my mind, every day. But I never got down to writing my own story.

Until now.

I have been clear about one thing from the beginning. Whenever I write my story, it has to be written in my words, straight from the heart. I write in my mother tongue, Hindi.

But the sad reality of today's social media-obsessed world is that people have lost interest in reading. Readership is dwindling and Hindi readership in particular has fallen. I was eager to reach a wider base of my fans and colleagues, but I also wanted to talk to the younger generation, especially my grandchildren. After the launch of my brother Piyush and my sister Tripti's books, Milee Ashwarya from Penguin Random House India asked me when I was going to write a book for them. That is when I took the decision to write in English.

Here's a confession: While I am comfortable in English, its punishing rules of grammar and usage of articles often play tricks on me. I decided to tell my story through someone who would understand but not alter my voice, who would embellish but not magnify my authenticity and who would represent my truest self. I looked no further than Anjula Bedi, who I respectfully call Anjulaji.

Anjulaji has been my role model right from my college days. She grew up in Jaipur and went to college with my older sisters. She then taught English literature and drama in Kanoria Mahila

Mahavidyalaya. and we acted in a couple of plays in Jaipur. After marriage, we both moved to Mumbai almost at the same time and when I asked her to join me in my theatre activities, she agreed.

A founder member of Surnai Theatre and Folk Art Foundation, Anjulaji is the backbone of our group. She has acted in many of our plays. She is a friend of the family, with deep connections with all my family members: my mother, daughter and granddaughters.

Anjulaji can read my mind, in English, the nuances of my expressions and the pauses within. She has been a witness to my journey thus far: my struggles, my triumphs, the small joys, the big wins and what I have become today. I have a deep connection and sense of comfort with her that I feel with very few people.

The process was simple: I wrote my story in my own words, narrated it to her and like a skilled jeweller, she polished my speech and crafted my narrative, one word at a time.

I want to share my story with the world, Ila Arun in her own voice—raw, earthy and playful. *Pardey Ke Peechhey Kya Hai*? The story of Ila Arun as told to Anjula Bedi.

Acknowledgements: Curtain Call

I dread the time of the curtain call. At the end of the play, after having spouted lines and lines of dialogue, I am called upon to give thanks and to introduce my cast. And my mind goes blank! I fumble for words, forget to acknowledge my supporters; in fact, I cannot even remember the names of my cast with whom I have spent several months rehearsing! Today, as this book leaves my hands, I am like an empty vessel, a vessel that makes no noise, so I don't know how many I will remember and how many I will forget! Here, I would like to apply the words of Khalil Gibran, 'Forgetfulness is a form of freedom' and so the *banjaran* in me will try to remember whatever I can and before anyone has the time to sulk, I will be too far away to hear those words! So here I go.

Milee Ashwarya, the publisher of PRHI, who motivated me and had faith in my writing.

Satya Saran, who initiated my meeting with Penguin.

Anjula Bedi, who interpreted my story in English, and K.K. Raina, who read the manuscript again and again and kept us on the right track.

But the book would not have gone ahead at such high speed without the support of my nephew, Abhijit Avasthi, founder of Sideways; our friend and adviser, Murali Neelakantan, who for the first time in my life made me scrutinize contracts and legal documents; and my close friend Tarun Katial, founder and CEO, COTO.

My husband, Arun, who, despite not knowing what I was writing, gave me the space to think and to stack every nook and corner of the house with discarded manuscripts.

Meenakshi Surti, my backstage worker, who has spent days and nights keying in and cutting and pasting all my chapters, at all times, keeping several tabs open for me!

351

And my silent supporters, my nieces, Disha Mishra and Shruti Bajpai Trivedi. The cover photograph for the book was shot at the Royal Opera House in Mumbai. And while I waited, I gathered a bit of the history of the theatre. It was a fascinating tale—and somehow, I felt a close connection to the theatre and its history. I was told that Prithviraj Kapoor, one of the pioneers of the Indian theatre movement, had himself performed some of his best-known plays—*Batwara, Paisa* and *Deewar*—at the Royal Opera House on the same stage where I was being photographed; the velvet curtain from behind which I was peeping, had parted for him too! After the curtain call, he would stand at the entrance with a sheet, collecting donations! For me life had come full circle—Surnai was born on the floor of Prithvi Theatre, took its first step at the National Centre for the Performing Arts (NCPA) and today, it was curtain call for my book from behind the velvet curtain of the Royal Opera House.

Our last days of writing and editing were at my brother Prasoon and his wife Gayatri's beautiful, rustic home, Fursatganj at Alibagh. Surrounded by hills and fields, what better setting for a book like this? In the middle of tea, breakfast, beer, lunch, another drink, dinner and gossip, the book has taken its final shape, Now I have several tables to sit at, besides my own dining table. Perhaps this is the beginning of my second book . . .

Before the curtain comes down, there are several others who though not directly concerned with the book, need to be acknowledged for their interest and support in our journey. The late Ramakrishna Bajaj, who was our greatest supporter when our theatre group was born, and now his son Niraj, who has readily come to our aid at very short notice in our *natakon ka safar*. Ramesh and Kumar Taurani of Tips, who have helped us tide over many financial obstacles over the years. Amrapali Jewels, whose showcases have been accessible to me on several occasions for my plays or live shows, including the cover picture.

For better or for worse, the curtain comes down on my life story!

Scan QR code to access the
Penguin Random House India website